Donald McRae was born in South Africa in 1961. He worked as a teacher in Soweto for two years before moving to London in 1984. He writes for the *Guardian*, and has won numerous awards for his journalism. He is also the author of eight books. *Dark Trade: Lost in Boxing* and *In Black & White* both won the William Hill Sports Book of the Year prize, while *Winter Colours: Changing Seasons in World Rugby* was shortlisted for the award. All three of his sports books have been re-issued in 2014 with new material.

Also re-issued in 2014 are *Every Second Counts*, the story of Christiaan Barnard and the race to transplant the first human heart, and *The Old Devil*, the biography of American lawyer Clarence Darrow. His family memoir of growing up in apartheid South Africa, *Under Our Skin*, is also available from Simon & Schuster.

Donald McRae lives with his family just outside London. He is currently working on his next book, about the boxer Emile Griffith, which will be published in 2015.

IN
BLACK & WHITE

The Untold Story of
JOE LOUIS AND JESSE OWENS

DONALD McRAE

**SIMON &
SCHUSTER**

London · New York · Sydney · Toronto · New Delhi

A CBS COMPANY

First published in Great Britain by Scribner, 2002
This paperback edition published by Simon & Schuster UK Ltd, 2014

A CBS COMPANY

1 3 5 7 9 10 8 6 4 2

Simon & Schuster UK Ltd
1st Floor
222 Gray's Inn Road
London WC1X 8HB

www.simonandschuster.co.uk

Simon & Schuster Australia, Sydney
Simon & Schuster India, New Delhi

A CIP catalogue record for this book
is available from the British Library

ISBN: 978-1-47113-533-0
Ebook ISBN: 978-1-47113-472-2

Typeset in the UK by M Rules
Printed and bound by CPI Group (UK) Ltd, Croydon, CR0 4YY

PICTURE CREDITS

Pictures 1-2, 7, 23, 27, 38: courtesy of Ohio State University Photo Archives;
pictures 3, 5, 8, 10-11, 13, 15-16, 33, 39-42: Corbis; pictures 4, 6, 12, 17-18, 22,
24, 30, 35-6, 43-4: Popperfoto; pictures 9, 19-21, 28-9, 32, 34, 37, 45: Getty
Images; picture 31: courtesy of Pugshots; pictures 25-6: Associated Press.

For Alison

Contents

Prologue

Snapshots

Chicago, 11 July 2000

Ruth Owens gazed at the photograph in her small study. She sat quietly on the old rocking chair, her hands resting in her lap, as she held the black-and-white snapshot – an image of Jesse Owens and Joe Louis relaxing together on a sunlit wall in 1935. As they stared back at her, their contrasting expressions frozen in the dark frame, Ruth's face suddenly brightened at the sight of her young husband and his friend in their dazzling new suits.

'Oh my,' she said. 'I sure am glad I dressed up now . . .'

Ruth wore a red trouser-suit and silver shoes. She had brushed back her hair, touched up her lipstick and slipped on a thin gold necklace. Ruth was eighty-five years old. Jesse and Joe, in the quivering snapshot, were both only twenty-one. They were already famous. Jesse Owens was the world's greatest runner and jumper. Joe Louis was the deadliest fighter on the planet. They were about to create some of the most celebrated moments in sporting history.

In August 1936, in front of Hitler and an imposing phalanx of Nazi commanders, Jesse Owens won an unprecedented four gold medals at the Olympic Stadium in Berlin. His athletic brilliance was rivalled only by the ideological resonance of a young black man like him, descended from sharecroppers and slaves, denting the myth of Aryan supremacy. Joe Louis's two fights against Max Schmeling in New York, in the summers of 1936 and 1938, were as politically-loaded and dramatic. His crushing defeat of the German boxer in their second encounter provided the momentum for a peerless twelve-year reign as the heavyweight champion of the world.

Ruth sighed as her bony fingers traced the outline of Jesse's face. She then tapped Joe on the shoulder as if to say hello to his old pal. 'Look at them,' Ruth said, 'they already got that shine about them. You can just tell they're going places.'

Jesse's face was split open by his familiar smile. Joe, his lips parted slightly, had dropped his usual deadpan mask and seemed mildly amused.

They lived in strange and bleak times. America was divided into two separate and unequal worlds. 'Negroes' were barred from white schools, hotels, restaurants, parks and beaches. They sat in the 'coloured' carriages of trains and the back seats of buses. It was the same in sport. No Negro had ever been allowed to play major league baseball. Another twelve years would pass before their disciple and friend, Jackie Robinson, could make his momentous debut for the Brooklyn Dodgers in 1947. Other professional sports were also sealed tight and white. The ban against black players in American football would stretch to 1946; and in basketball to 1950.

Boxing was a curious exception. Black men, under restricted circumstances, were allowed to fight white men. Yet twenty years had passed since the reviled Jack Johnson had lost his world heavyweight title. He had been the first Negro to hold the championship and, since his fall in 1915, no black man had even been allowed to lodge a challenge for the heavyweight crown.

The track was similarly confined. The American Olympic team in 1928 was exclusively white. In 1932, at the Los Angeles

Olympics, only four black athletes were picked for the home track team. Even the most successful of that quartet, Eddie Tolan, who won gold in both the 100m and 200m, remained an invisible man in white America.

Jesse Owens and Joe Louis changed everything. In 1935 they became the first black stars in American sport, busting open the country in a way not even performers like Paul Robeson and Bill 'Bojangles' Robinson, or Louis Armstrong and Duke Ellington could rival. Jesse and Joe tried not to think too much about the terrible burden of their breakthrough, for sometimes it felt as if they carried the weight of an entire race of people on their shoulders.

'Jesse was not an angry or a bitter man,' Ruth said. 'Neither was Joe. They didn't hate anyone. They just wanted to make something of themselves. They were real proud. They might seem quiet if you put 'em next to any of these modern fellers you got today – but quietness don't diminish pride.

'I switch on my television now and whenever a game comes on I see black fellers in starring roles. Black men look like they rule sport in this country now. It's the only area where they are right on top. It was nothing like that in the 1930s. America was white and that was that. I can't say it bothered me much. Like everyone, I just knew it didn't do you no good to dream of making it to the big time. It was impossible. And then, y'know, along came Jesse and along came Joe . . .'

I travelled to Chicago in the summer of 2000 with the story of a race echoing through my head. Six months earlier I had discovered it by chance. On 4 July 1938, only two weeks after destroying Max Schmeling, Joe Louis had raced against Jesse Owens. An image of the poker-faced and flat-footed world heavyweight champion running against the flying and smiling 'Fastest Man On Earth' fascinated and bewildered me. Why were they racing against each other in such an unequal contest?

What had driven them to such burlesque – especially so soon after they had supposedly conquered the world?

I remembered the famous photograph of Owens breasting a ribbon of tape as he won the 200m final, and his third gold medal, in Berlin. His nearest grimacing rival, five metres adrift, looked trapped in agony. Owens, however, offered a study of grace and beauty. I had also seen Louis's one-round demolition of Schmeling again and again. It was a reminder that boxing had once mattered to tens of millions of people.

I began to piece together my limited knowledge of Owens's post-Olympic career. I knew that, sometime after Berlin, he had ended up running against horses, motorbikes and, as I had just learned, Joe Louis. But what had happened to Jesse Owens to take him down that shadowy road? And who could have persuaded the famously stoical Louis to confront Owens in a circus sideshow?

I found a brief report of their race in a sixty-two-year-old edition of the *Chicago Defender*. The bare details were enough to floor me.

Jesse and Joe had been born within eight months of each other in Alabama. They were the grandsons of slaves and the sons of sharecroppers. They both stammered. Their families moved north in the 1920s, and then they discovered themselves in sport – Jesse as a runner on the sidewalks of Cleveland and Joe as a fighter in a Detroit gym. They soon realised how much they also loved pretty girls and swanky clothes.

There were stark differences. Joe never smiled in public; Jesse rarely stopped grinning. Jesse looked as if he had found paradise as he ran 'smooth as the west wind', and for free, on the amateur track; Joe marched silently into the obscenely-moneyed and gangster-ridden world of professional boxing. Joe was surrounded by an all-black entourage; Jesse's mentors and coaches were white. Jesse had made it to college; Joe was dismissed as a virtual illiterate. Joe said little in public; Jesse loved the idea of becoming a motivational speaker. And, of course, Joe was a ferocious puncher while Jesse was a serene runner and jumper.

Within months of meeting each other in the mid-1930s they became heroic figures – and the first black men to scale that American summit of adulation. They faced triumph and despair within an extraordinary twenty-two-month period. The thrill and significance of Owens's four gold medals were soon tarnished, while Louis's encounters with Schmeling were brutal exercises in humiliating defeat and exhilarating victory. They were revered for their patriotism in World War II and yet, in the more militant 1960s, they were derided as 'Uncle Toms'. Jesse and Joe, who had been friends for forty-five years, both died at the age of sixty-six.

Apart from also running against trains and dogs and baseball players for money, Owens had been a bankrupt dry-cleaner, a sacked suit-salesman, a slick public speaker and an admired government representative around the world. He had been hounded by the IRS and followed by the FBI. Owens had been forced down this path of confusion only a week after he won his last gold medal in Berlin. His refusal to continue a post-Olympic barnstorming tour across Europe, and his interest in the commercial opportunities emerging in the wake of Berlin, resulted in him being banned for life as 'a professional' by vengeful American athletics administrators.

'They took away his career,' his daughter Marlene Owens Rankin told me in Chicago. 'They took away his life. Today it would be the same as some administrator telling Tiger Woods his career is over. Can you imagine how Tiger Woods would have felt, and how the rest of the world would have reacted, if he had been told at the age of twenty-two that he could never again participate in serious competition? It seems ridiculous now when you consider the multi-million deals that await any athlete who wins the Olympic 100m gold. But America was very different in 1936. On the one hand Jesse was being touted as this legend who had beaten Hitler. Yet he was continually reminded that he was not so special. He was still black.'

Unlike Owens, Louis had been forced to fight on for years after he should have retired. He held the world title between 1937 and 1949 and made twenty-five successful championship defences. It is a record which will almost certainly never be broken, and yet he ended up destitute. Hunted by the IRS, Joe Louis was reduced to wrestling, pretending to be a lion-tamer in a circus and working the TV game-show circuit. His debt was in the millions as he slid helplessly into drug addiction and a psychiatric institution.

At the same time, Louis's name was invoked by black leaders from Martin Luther King to Malcolm X. There is no more chilling or heartbreaking tribute to the impact of Louis on America than the anecdote related by King in 1964. Recalling the day when a young black American on Death Row was gassed, King told how the condemned man fell to his knees and cried: 'Save me Joe Louis, save me Joe Louis, save me Joe Louis . . .'

Their entwined legacy has a long way to run yet. Carl Lewis equalled Owens's medal haul at the 1984 Games in Los Angeles without evoking a similar resonance. Lewis had an expansive and lucrative career. He did not have to race horses. He did not have to run against Mike Tyson. He did not have to move into the laundry business or work in a suit store. Instead, Lewis became a different kind of salesman. He made commercials for fast cars and rubber tyres. He marketed himself relentlessly. Lewis became impossibly rich – and unpopular. In *Newsweek*, in 1984, he was described as 'a master self-promoter . . . a fabled loner with a whining attitude'. That damning assessment concluded that 'mere records do not make legends'. Lewis's LA achievements, after all, lacked the historical context of Berlin in 1936.

That same legacy made Joe Louis the most significant American sportsman of the last century. Only Muhammad Ali can claim to have had as profound an impact. Ali flowered and then flamed at the height of the Civil Rights movement. Louis cut a more solitary figure as he stoically punched his way to glory in an overwhelmingly white world in the 1930s and 1940s. The political changes Joe Louis instilled into American life were breathtaking.

In Chicago, Ruth Owens told me her memories of Joe and, especially, of Jesse. I then spoke to Joe's son, the equally impressive Joe Louis Barrow Jr, who also knew Jesse from his years in Chicago. 'Jesse and my father,' Joe Jr said, 'were pioneers. They challenged and changed America's conscience. Out of the terrible adversity and suffering of Jesse and Joe came real beauty and courage. And at least they were not alone. They had each other. They were great friends.'

This book is largely about that friendship. And so, from my starting point in Chicago, I tracked them to Cleveland and Columbus and Detroit and Ann Arbor, and moved through New York, Washington DC and Los Angeles, via Berlin and Havana, before ending up with them in the desert in Phoenix and Las Vegas. In each city there were new voices and old memories. Some of those I spoke to have since died – like Ruth Owens and Eddie Futch, Joe's friend and sparring partner in Detroit who became boxing's most legendary trainer. Others, from Earl 'Wimpy' Potts, one of Jesse's neighbours in Columbus, Ohio, to Amber Young, a foster-daughter of Joe and Martha Louis, were relatively unknown. Yet they told me stories of such sweet illumination that I left them with the certainty that I knew just a little more about Jesse and Joe.

The same principle applied when I undertook the more ghostly task of hearing the voices of those who had died before I could meet them. I had the precious opportunity to use a small pile of tapes, loaned to me by the good and the generous, of private interviews with their departed friends and rivals – from

Eulace Peacock, Dave Albritton and Marty Glickman to Freddie
Guinyard, Rocky Marciano and Billy Conn.

Although both Jesse Owens and Joe Louis have been dead for
over twenty years, this book attempts a journey of discovery. I
came to write it with a fierce longing to know what lay behind
Jesse's smile when he was reduced to racing horses or dogs. I
tried to find out what Joe felt, beneath the deadpan stare, after
another draining world championship fight saw him hailed by
millions as the saviour of his race. How deep was the emotional
cost, to both men, of facing personal trauma and glory with the
same public demeanour? Did they still smile or stay deadpan
when some of those who followed, like Muhammad Ali or
Tommie Smith, rejected them and their old-fashioned ways?
Which great sporting figure today would survive such a shifting
reality?

As the wondering gave way to the writing, and my admiration
or affection for Jesse and Joe rose anew with each page, so I
came to know them. Uncovering so much new and revealing
material about their friendship and shared fate, it felt to me as if
they were alive again. Whether clamping on my earphones as I
listened to them talk on old tapes, or watching them laughing
and moving a few feet away from me on a small television screen
on my desk, their voices echoed through the room in which this
book was written. I listened closely to them as I wrote, in the
hope that those voices would also fill the pages which follow.
When I neared the end, and as my own time with them drifted
away, I realised how much I was going to miss them. It was then
that I felt happiest with this book. I knew that this story, once
more, had become their own. It belongs again to Jesse and to Joe.

PART ONE

Dark Stars
(1935–38)

Chapter One

The Race

Jesse Owens woke early that Monday morning, on Independence Day. He knew at once that it had come back to claim him. The same sense of dread had followed him from Berlin to Cleveland and, gathering in force, found him in places as faraway as Albuquerque and Havana. It returned at night, sweeping over him as he slept the empty sleep of an exhausted man in the backroom of a black boarding-house on the south side of Chicago.

He was just twenty-four, and still the fastest man in the world, but Jesse was already worn out. It no longer mattered that he had not run a real race for nearly two years. He was sick of running. The dread caught him when least expected; he had not anticipated feeling like this when the streets hummed in celebration of his great and unshakable friend, Joe Louis. Yet, that afternoon, Jesse would face Joe in a stunt that now seemed as desolate as it was strange.

On his way back from the rickety ballpark the night before, his mood light and airy, Jesse had walked with some of the American Giants, a Negro baseball team from Chicago. Their voices boomed with wonder as they relived the last terrible seconds when, facing each other in a New York ring two weeks previously, Joe Louis and Max Schmeling had waited for the bell. Inside cramped and hushed houses across America, people had gathered anxiously around their box radios. It was as if their own fate would be decided by a struggle between Louis, their cherished Brown Bomber, and Schmeling, the German fighter supported by Hitler and every white cracker in America.

Never before, Jesse said, had so many black voices been as silent as they were in that moment. The only sound was the low-pitched commentary of Clem McCarthy. He described the two fighters moving towards each other under the hot lights of Yankee Stadium, just across the river from Harlem. They were all in the ring then, with Joe, as the bell rang.

Two minutes later, they erupted. In Chicago, just as in Harlem, people ran from their homes. They ran into the black summer night. They took to the streets, howling *'Ah told ya so! Ah told ya so!'* as if they had never doubted that Schmeling would be shattered by King Joe. Some of the men and women who poured down South Parkway pasted the phrase on themselves. *'Ah told ya so!'* was printed in large black letters on sheets of watermelon-pink paper which, with little strips of tape, they stuck to their shirts and dresses. The words danced in front of them as they ran, still screaming at anyone they saw: *'Ah told ya so! Ah told ya so!'*

They were joined by ramshackle bands who beat out a delirious noise on wash tubs and steel trashcans as they swung up Indiana Avenue and across 43rd Street. Car horns blared in time with the marching players. Tiny girls bobbed on the sidewalks as older boys emptied bottles in a gulp – *'Do it for Joe!'* they yelped – before smashing the coloured glass in front of the watching policemen.

Harlem had shimmied in similar ecstasy, especially at those

haunts where Jesse and Joe hung out – the Cotton Club, the Memo Club and Small's Paradise, where the girls were lovely and the gangsters were deadly. On the streets, 100,000 black men and women rushed up and down Lenox and Seventh Avenues. One of them, forty-year-old Jacob Enlow, bawled out a single name – '*Joe Louis! Joe Louis! Joe Louis!*' – until he dropped dead on the street. The rest raved on until a pale dawn took the edge off their historic partying.

Jesse was at his happiest when he thought about everything he and Joe had achieved over the last three years. Ever since the summer of 1935, when they became the two most famous Negroes in America, the most renowned black men in the world, Jesse and Joe had been more than just friends. They were a team, two brothers from Alabama, the perfect match of a blistering runner and an ice-cold fighter.

Jesse pulled out the newspapers he'd shoved into his suitcase. No matter how hard he tried, he rarely got round to reading much. Jesse kept on collecting papers though, sometimes tearing out clippings for the scrapbooks he and Ruth had started before they were even married. Lately, as the piles of cuttings grew and the newest scrapbooks remained untouched, he had begun to limit his quick scour to material he might use in his speeches. Having conquered his childhood stammer, he was becoming increasingly accustomed to talking through a microphone to the crowds who turned out to watch his exhibition races. Jesse always spoke in rousing terms, mostly about the four gold medals he had won in the 1936 Berlin Olympics or the way in which Joe Louis inspired every Negro in America. Jesse liked to pepper his chat with uplifting quotes, but it wasn't easy finding encouraging copy in the white newspapers.

Even though the papers were full of Joe Louis, their reports were often twisted. The latest edition of the black weekly, the *Pittsburgh Courier*, had pieced together the views of the country's leading sportswriters to offer an overview of Joe's impact on white America. Jesse did not always recognise his friend in print. Joe Louis could fight better than anyone on the planet but, no matter how hard he hit a man between the ropes, he was the softest guy you'd ever meet. The press turned him into something different.

Jesse began to underline some sentences. For Dan Parker, of the *New York Daily Mirror*, 'Louis has finally come into his estate as a great world's champion. If anyone doubts his greatness after his masterful job last night, he's plain plumb prejudiced.' Yet Henry McLemore, the *United Press* columnist, was appalled by the sight of 'this ruthless, unmerciful killer'. Louis had become 'a jungle man, as completely primitive as any savage, out to destroy a thing he hates'.

O.B. Keeler's report in the *Atlanta Journal* turned into a lament. 'Joe Louis is the heavyweight champion of the world and, so far as this correspondent can see, there is nothing to be done about it. Our fastest runners are coloured boys, and our longest jumpers and our highest jumpers.' In the *Chicago Daily News*, Hugh S. Johnson tried to answer Keeler. 'It is nothing for us to weep about and seek white hopes. These black boys are Americans – a whole lot more distinctly so than more recently arrived citizens of, say, the Schmeling type. There should be just as much pride in their progress and prowess under our system as in the triumph of any other American. For all their misfortunes and shortcomings they are our people – Negroes, yes, but *our* Negroes.'

Even if his last competitive race had been on 15 August 1936, when he completed the third leg of a meaningless relay for an American team in London, Jesse had not forgotten what it felt like to be a champion. He was only twenty-two when American officials banned him, a day after that London race. Jesse was branded a 'professional' – which, on the track, was a word even more damning than 'nigger'. Sometimes he thought his heart would crack if he considered the full and bitter truth. He would never run or jump in competition again.

In the first week of August 1936, Jesse Owens had dominated the Nazi Olympics in a way they said would never be matched. Each day had begun with Hitler's gleaming entourage of Mercedes convertibles sweeping through Berlin. Ecstatic Germans raised their right arms and shouted, '*Heil Hitler*!' Thomas Wolfe, a young American reporter, wrote that 'something like a wind across a field of grass was shaken through that crowd'.

Inside the massive stadium, surrounded by black and red swastikas fluttering against a leaden sky, Hitler, Goebbels, Göring, Himmler and a hundred thousand more Germans stared down from a towering height at the Olympic star – a young Negro who came from the cotton-fields of Alabama.

Hitler wanted the Games to showcase Aryan superiority. In America, Jesse's talent was also described in racial terms. The US team's sprint coach, Dean Cromwell, believed that 'the Negro athlete excels because he is closer to the primitive than the white athlete. It was not so long ago that his ability to sprint and jump was a life-and-death matter to him in the jungle. His muscles are pliable and his easy-going disposition is a valuable aid to the mental and physical relaxation that a runner and jumper must have.'

Jesse Owens won gold in the 100m, the 200m, the long jump and the 4×100m relay. Sitting in the American Ambassador's box, Wolfe whooped with delight. His excitement supposedly outraged Hitler. The writer's own attitude was more revealing: 'Owens was black as tar, but what the hell. It was our team and I thought he was wonderful. I was proud of him so I yelled.'

Nine days later, Jesse Owens was ruined as an athlete. Dan Ferris, the Secretary of the American Athletic Union (AAU), sneered his confirmation in Berlin: '*Owens is finished.*' Jesse had been locked in struggle ever since. In January 1938, he had again approached the AAU, convinced they would relent and lift his ban. He was wrong. They insisted he was a professional – and yet he was broke.

In order to survive, Jesse accepted a job as a cloakroom attendant – on a wage of $30 a month. The four-times Olympic champion was responsible for cleaning the cloakroom at a public pool in Cleveland. He relied then on a saying he thought was almost profound: 'while a man needs only three muscles to smile, it takes twenty-six muscles to frown'. Jesse smiled. He told his jokes. He tried to be the best cloakroom attendant they had ever seen – just as he would try to be the best exhibition runner, nightclub entertainer, political speechmaker and basketball manager.

In June 1938 he became a playground supervisor for the Department of Recreation in Cleveland. The pay was a little better and the job title a little snazzier. But keeping an eye on the swings and slides, even for $1,100 a year, was not quite what he'd had in mind when the offers first poured in from Berlin.

Most nights, after work, he jumped into his car and headed for another game or a show. Jesse ran against greyhounds and horses, with names like Sweet Harmony and Heartbreaker, in Akron and Alliance. He'd also been one of the prime attractions at the first game of major league baseball to be played at night in New York. On 15 June he drove from Cleveland to Brooklyn, and made it just in time to pick up a newspaper before he reached Ebberts Field late that afternoon. One of the clippings still lay in his suitcase, waiting to be stuck to the pages of a scrapbook. The words touched something inside him. Previewing the groundbreaking night clash, the *New York Post* argued that the Brooklyn Dodgers and the Cincinnati Reds would be upstaged by one man.

'They will see a graceful, superbly-built Negro running and jumping in the gathering darkness. They may not recognise him immediately, but every ball player will know him as soon as they hear his name. For that will be Jesse Owens, two short years ago an international athletics celebrity, making $100 for the night. And it isn't every night, every week or every month that Owens picks up an extra hundred. By all odds the most famous athlete on the field, Owens will also be the least fortunate. He attained a degree of proficiency in his sport far above the reach of any Dodger or Red in baseball when he won four gold medals at the Olympic Games . . . tonight Owens will be on display for half an hour. He will give handicaps to ball players in a 100-yard dash. He will skip over a flight of low hurdles and try to beat ball players who are running 120 yards on the flat. He will give an exhibition of broad jumping. The holder of six world records will be one of the trained seals rounding out the show. It's a terrific come-down, but it's a living.'

Three weeks on, in Chicago, Jesse would put on another show with Joe Louis. There would be a swell crowd, the place would be jumping. Most would be there to see Joe, but he and Jesse would do it together. The promoters had tagged it *The Fastest Man in the World vs the Heavyweight Champion of the World!*

This kind of life would not last for ever. A couple of strangers had turned up a few months before and promised Jesse a fresh start. They were taking him to the cleaners. He felt the old tug of excitement as he imagined telling Joe the news. Joe would grin when he heard that Jesse was moving into the laundry business. This side of Jesse Owens, Joe Louis was the sharpest dresser around. His dozens of suits, full of checks, stripes and plaid, were cut especially for him by Billy Taub in New York. He dazzled when he strolled along in those 'swagger-style' suits while wearing green socks and two-tone shoes. Joe even stuck notes on his mirror, reminding him when and where he had last worn a particular outfit.

The cleaning game was right up their street. Jesse already had the address of his first store, the name and the logo. On Cedar

Avenue in east Cleveland, the Jesse Owens Dry Cleaning Company would offer *A 7-Hour Service by the World's Fastest Man!* How could he lose?

Joe Louis headed for the ballpark, and his race against Jesse Owens, in high style. He wore a wide-brimmed cream trilby, trimmed in black, an emerald green jacket with a gold silk handkerchief peeking from the breast pocket, a crisp white shirt, dark green riding breeches and camel-coloured boots. The champ had spent the morning at Washington Park, on the far side of south Chicago, with his favourite horses, MacDonald's Choice and Bing Crosby.

It was his first chance to ride them since they'd returned from the inaugural Negro Horse Show. His black managers John Roxborough and Julian Black had, as usual, done an immaculate job, hosting the show of sixteen horses at the Utica Riding and Hunt Club, a suburban livery stable with a large outdoor parade ring thirty miles from Detroit. On 26 June, four days after he had put Max Schmeling into hospital, Joe competed in the Owner Ridden Class and picked up a third place. Even that yellow rosette, on MacDonald's Choice, gave Joe a bang – but it was nothing like watching Bing Crosby. He was some horse, worth every cent of the $1,500 Joe had paid for him. Joe let one of the experts ride Bing at Utica, just to see what he could do. He won two first places. Joe thought it would be a blast to tell the real Bing Crosby, when they finally made that golf date the Hollywood crooner kept planning, about his victorious namesake.

That morning in Washington Park, however, he'd thought more about Jesse than Bing. Joe had about the same chance of outrunning the fastest man as Jesse had of staying on his feet in the ring with the world heavyweight champion. It was a joke, a cheap $50 stunt. Joe didn't need the money. He'd made $350,000 for two minutes and four seconds of work against Schmeling.

In 1936, while Joe recovered from the excruciating pain of losing to Schmeling the first time round, Jesse paid the Germans back big time. He hurt them when they were still crowing about Schmeling and the way he had clobbered '*der Neger*'. When Jesse came back from Berlin, there was wild talk of movies and prime-time radio shows. Joe's pal, Bojangles Robinson, the tap-dancing ace who had been the first Negro to crack Hollywood, stepped in to help Jesse. There was nothing Bojangles didn't know about the entertainment industry, whether stomping through a season at the Savoy or starring alongside little Shirley Temple in her latest curly-haired smash. Yet one offer after another faded away. In the end Bojangles got Jesse a deal to lead an orchestra – but Jesse was a runner and a jumper rather than a singer and dancer. It soon went wrong.

Jesse ran against his first horse in Cuba in December 1936. Bojangles's manager, Marty Forkins, had taken over Jesse's affairs. Marty thought Jesse should run for cash against anything that moved fast – whether a horse or a dog, a train or a motorbike. Jesse beat the horse, but there wasn't much pleasure in it.

Joe hated seeing Jesse out on the exhibition circuit. He was a beautiful runner, and a real smiler. Their friends laughed whenever they saw the two of them together. Jesse would be grinning and Joe would be deadpan. They had their reasons.

Joe Louis, the Brown Bomber, struck fear into fighters. Some of his bouts were decided before the first bell. When they saw his unsmiling face, where the black eyes were still and the mouth seemed forever sealed, they knew what he would do to them. The Bomber nailed everyone in the end.

Roxborough and Black had taught Joe well. He understood that if you were a young nigger paid to knock out white men you did not walk around with a big grin spread across your smacker. Folks would think you were taking pleasure in hurting a white fellow. It was safer to keep deadpan.

They called Joe a robot, assuming he was devoid of human

emotion. But he knew what it meant to be afraid. On 4 July 1934, exactly four years earlier, Joe had made his pro debut in Chicago. In a dingy dressing-room at the Bacon Casino on the South Side, his black trainer Jack Blackburn spoke softly as he covered Joe's trembling hands in white gauze: 'Chappie, it's mighty hard for a coloured boy to win decisions. The dice's loaded against you. You gotta knock 'em out and keep knockin' 'em out to get anywheres. Don't you ever forget that.'

Joe walked through the smoky arena and ducked between the ropes. He looked across the ring at Jack Kracken, an experienced club fighter. Joe could taste his own fear, but he moved to the centre of the ring to fight. Joe knocked out Kracken in the first round. He was on his way, having made $59 for the night.

Art Sykes, his eighth opponent, was one of the few who refused to surrender early. 'I hit him a hundred times,' Joe said, 'but couldn't keep him down. I didn't want to hit him no more. When he went to the floor in the eighth and got the count, I was glad it was over. But when I left the doctors were still with him in the dressing-room. I called the hospital all night to find how he was doing.'

Sykes survived, but he never fought again. 'They come in there to give it to me,' Joe explained. 'I have to give it back. I can't say it's a sorry feeling, but I don't like to do it.'

Beneath his mask he sometimes felt just as jumpy as he'd been in Black Bottom, that east Detroit ghetto where he first learned that life could be mean and cruel. Joe was thirteen when he arrived from Alabama. His southern stutter made him sound like a dumb country nigger to every Black Bottom kid who mocked him.

Joe had not forgotten how his tongue would trip over certain words. His face twitched with the effort of forcing a word from his mouth as small boys laughed at him. Boxing was different. In the ring his breathtakingly quick hands spoke their own fluent language. And whether his opponents spoke English or Italian, German or Spanish, every single one understood the meaning of his punches. Joe Louis had discovered a universal eloquence in boxing. He fought with a bright and lucid clarity.

They called him Poker-Face and Deadpan Joe. His shyness complemented that expressionless look and made it easy for him to follow the advice of Roxy and Black. Insisting that his toughest fight would be out in public, his managers instructed him to appear quiet and dignified. 'And for God's sake,' Roxy pleaded at the very start, 'after you beat a white opponent, don't ever smile!'

'That's what Jack Johnson did,' Black added.

Before Joe won the world heavyweight title in Chicago in the summer of 1937, there had been only one Negro champion in history – Jack Johnson. His reign from 1908 to 1915 made him America's most hated man. Joe had heard all the stories about 'Papa Jack'. They had been drummed into him as a warning.

When he used to change for his sparring-sessions, Smiling Jack would stuff a ream of bandages down his tight trunks to make himself appear hugely endowed to startled spectators. The former heavyweight king, John L. Sullivan, thundered that 'the size of a nigger's penis is not to be discussed in public'.

On 4 July 1910, on another kind of Independence Day, Johnson had destroyed the Great White Hope, Jim Jeffries, with such contemptuous mastery that race riots spread across the country. Thirteen black people, from Macon to Philadelphia, were killed by white gangs. Two days later, in an editorial entitled 'A Word to the Black Man', the *Los Angeles Daily Times* warned Johnson and his followers:

'The white man's mental supremacy is fully established and for the present cannot be taken from him. His superiority does not rest on any huge bulk of muscle, but on brain development that has weighed worlds and charmed the most subtle secrets from the heart of nature. Do not point your nose too high. Do not swell your chest too much. Do not boast too loudly. Let not your ambition be inordinate or take a wrong direction. Remember, you have done nothing at all. You are the same member of society you were last week. You are on no higher a plane, deserve no new consideration, and you will get none.'

'Papa Jack' was notorious for appearing in public with white prostitutes. And then, soon after he became world champion, he married a young 'milky-skinned' Chicago woman called Lucille Cameron. When she denied angrily that she had been abducted, the ominously-named Frank Force declared in the *Police Gazette* that Johnson 'is the vilest, most despicable creature that lives. In all sporting history there never was a human being who so thoroughly deserved the sneers and jeers of his fellow creatures. He has disgusted the American public by flaunting in their faces an alliance as bold as it is offensive.'

In Congress, Georgia's Republican representative Seaborn A. Roddenberry broke down in tears. He insisted that racial war would ensue if the government failed to prevent 'sombre-hued, black-skinned, thick-lipped, bull-necked, brutal-hearted Africans' from corrupting white women. To feverish applause from a packed house, Roddenberry concluded that Johnson's marriage 'is repulsive and averse to every sentiment of pure American spirit. It is abhorrent and repugnant to the very principles of a pure Saxon government. It is subversive to social peace. It is destructive of moral supremacy, and ultimately this slavery of white women to black beasts will bring this nation to a conflict as fatal and as bloody as ever reddened the soil of Virginia or crimsoned the mountain paths of Pennsylvania.'

The champion was forced into exile. After losing his title in dubious circumstances to Jess Willard in Havana, Cuba, in 1915, Johnson was imprisoned on his return to America for contravening the Mann Act which forbade the 'interstate or foreign transportation of women for the purpose of prostitution or debauchery'. Willard declared that he would never again fight a Negro. Grantland Rice, the famed sportswriter, celebrated the new champion's stance in purple prose: 'The Big Shadow over the fight game has been lifted at last. When Jess Willard wrested the chaplet of apple blossoms from the sable brow of Jack Johnson, he did something more than restore the heavyweight championship to the Caucasian caravanserie. For beyond this, he swept away the big barrier which had clogged the game's popularity for five years.'

At the Horse Show in Utica, Roxy and Black had shown Joe a newspaper article Johnson had supposedly written. After four long years in which Johnson had constantly undermined Joe, supporting his white opponents with poisoned zeal, the former champion recanted. In the *Pittsburgh Courier* on 25 June, three days after the destruction of Schmeling, Johnson said, 'I am forced to reverse my opinion about Joe Louis.' He now argued that 'no man could face Joe and live'.

Every hardship on Joe's way to the title seemed to have something to do with Johnson – and the need to appear his direct opposite. Joe had to be a fighter who never raised his arms or smiled triumphantly, a man who was meant to be without desire. It was lucky for Joe that he'd learned the art of discretion almost as soon as the girls started chasing him.

Jesse understood. They each had a beautiful black wife. Within a few months of each other, in 1935, Jesse married his childhood sweetheart Ruth Solomons and Joe the gorgeous Marva Trotter. Amid all the hard work on the road they hit the town together, discreetly, and had their fun. Joe's managers were still keen that he should describe a simpler picture of married life. In February 1938, they arranged for an article to be printed under his name in *Liberty*. They called it 'Why Married Men Become Champions'.

'My wife answered the telephone,' Joe's feature began.

'"Honey," she said, returning to the den where she had been playing the piano, "your friend Jesse Owens just arrived in town with a basketball team. Invite him out to dinner. Get up a stag party for him tonight." Would I invite Jesse Owens out? Let me at that telephone! Soon the party was all arranged and we gathered in my apartment to show a great champion and a grand fellow a good time . . . And I thought how swell it was being married and owning my own home where I could entertain friends. Now suppose I was a bachelor and wanted to show a friend like Jesse Owens he was welcome in Chicago. I'd probably have taken him to some public place for dinner and some scandalmonger would say: "Look, Joe Louis is stepping out." That would fire a chain of rumours, and before long people would have me doing things unbecoming to a world heavyweight champion.'

Joe revealed how he and Jesse stayed in peak shape. 'Jesse said to me, "Joe, I can't understand Gene Tunney at all. He says Max Schmeling will knock you out again because he says you haven't kept yourself in the best condition. Now I've been around with you a lot and the only dissipation you ever did was to eat an extra dish of ice-cream."'

He couldn't quite remember when he and Jesse started throwing around words like 'dissipation', whatever the hell that meant, but Joe pressed on to claim that married men made the best athletes. Jesse explained the reason. 'Joe, the best thing I ever did was get married. When a man is married to the right girl and happy with his home, why he doesn't think about gallivanting around. So when he has a job to do – like breaking a record – he doesn't mess around with it. He breaks the record.'

Liberty were less interested in the fact that no matter how fast Jesse Owens ran these days he was lost to sport. Instead of racing against the best sprinters in the world, Jesse would line up that afternoon against Joe Louis. The only record they might make would be the yawning distance separating two champions when the winner hit the tape. Joe winced at the thought of the looming embarrassment.

The two men sat on a hard wooden bench in the front row of American Giants Park. Jesse had pulled on a crimson vest and white shorts. Joe, despite having removed his green jacket beneath the hot sun, still wore his riding kit. The fighter ate his second ice-cream of the afternoon. Joe, like Jesse, was twenty-four years old. He seemed oblivious to the fact that almost 7,000 pairs of eyes focused on him.

'Feelin' confident, champ?' Jesse joked as the heavyweight brought the mound of melting strawberry to his mouth.

Joe looked up in surprise, before suddenly remembering that they were only ten minutes away from the race. 'Well,' he drawled, 'one more o' these babies ain't gonna make no difference . . .'

Pink ice-cream trickled down the sides of the cone. Joe sucked in a blob from the top before he cleaned up the cone with his tongue. Joe's friend, Mack Jones, burst out laughing. 'My money's still on you, Joe,' Mack yelled as he clapped the champion on the back.

On Saturday night, while Joe had hit the Savoy on South Parkway to watch the Chicago girls rip through the hot new dance they called the 'Joe Louis Victory Shuffle', Jesse had strutted through four less glamorous charmers. In a broad jump display he leapt 24 feet and 8 inches. It was more than two feet down on his world record but he had been jumping alone and had little incentive to stretch himself. He then ran against John Lewis, the former Wayne University star. While Lewis ran a flat hundred, Jesse had to clear eight low hurdles over the same distance. It was tight, but Lewis won by a yard in a time of 10.1 seconds. Jesse then beat five local softball aces over 120 yards after he had given each a ten-yard start. And then, for his last dash, he took on Milton Byers who played for Joe's travelling softball team, the Brown Bombers.

Joe knew how fast Milton could run but even a five-yard start was not enough to save him over a hundred. Jesse was two yards ahead at the end. They announced his time at nine seconds flat. Jesse had run well; but it hadn't been that quick. He called over Eddie Tolan, the 1932 Olympic champion in both the 100m and 200m. Tolan, roped in to act as an 'official judge', insisted that they measure out the length of the track. He stood over the guys holding the measuring tape to ensure they got it right. They did this time. The track was five yards short. Yet, as far as Joe was concerned, nine seconds flat for 95 yards was still pretty speedy.

Jesse had already moved on to his next scheme. 'Hey Joe,' he quipped, 'ain't that some logo I got? *A 7-Hour Service by the World's Fastest Man!*'

'Sounds a winner to me,' Joe winked as he popped the cone into his mouth and swallowed the last of his ice-cream.

The race was scheduled for three o'clock. Joe had spent the first hour at the ballpark signing his name and acknowledging every flush-faced fan with deadpan courtesy. He didn't mind. An adoring crowd at a Negro League double-header was nothing compared to the crush that usually engulfed him as people rushed to him as if he was some kind of saviour. At least these folk allowed him to eat a couple of ice-creams and talk to his buddy.

'How the Alabama boys do yesterday?' Joe asked as they watched the last Birmingham Baron batter walk slowly back to the dug-out at the end of a 12–2 hammering by the local American Giants. He knew Jesse had sprinted through yet another exhibition in the midst of a Sunday afternoon double-header between the two teams.

'They lost both,' Jesse said.

Joe had been born to sharecroppers at the foot of the Buckalew Mountains in Alabama. Jesse came from Oakville, a tiny sharecropping community ten miles from the nearest town of Decatur in northern Alabama. 'We better put on a better show than Birmingham,' Jesse said.

'Yeah,' Joe grunted.

'You gonna run in *that*?' Mack asked, gesturing towards Joe's dressage outfit.

'Sure,' Joe said. 'A vest and shorts ain't gonna make me any faster.'

They pressed their way through the crowd until they reached the edge of the field. The spectators clapped rhythmically as a tinny microphone introduced 'the two most famous Negroes in America'. Jesse and Joe looked at each other and almost smiled. It was race time.

'You ready?' Jesse asked as they walked towards the make-shift starting line.

Joe nodded, and then asked his own question: 'You still want to do it this way?'

'It's what they want,' Jesse said.

'OK,' Joe shrugged. 'Let's give 'em what they want.'

The Olympic champion was five feet ten inches tall and weighed a lean 165 pounds. His legs were powerful, bursting with all the muscled spring and strength which enabled him to jump further and run faster than any man alive. Joe, meanwhile, had the body to match his title. The heavyweight champion of the world was six feet one and weighed 205 pounds. His neck, shoulders and back looked massive, his chest and stomach a brown wall of muscle beneath his white shirt. He had no need to run. He could just stand and punch. Joe liked moving forward steadily, with the sticky resin of the ring floor making him believe it was impossible he would ever fall.

Jesse skipped down the oval turf with a typically light step. It no longer mattered if he raced against a dog or the heavyweight champion of the world. Jesse was always ready for the track.

They lined up alongside each other. In the deepening silence, Jesse arched his back and readied himself for an explosive start.

A half-crouching Joe looked like a weary boxer waiting for the last round bell.

At the sound of the starter's gun, Jesse leaped forward with a jerk. After a few long strides he tripped over his tangled feet. It was a clumsy fall, a hammy piece of acting even to the screamers high up in the cheap seats. Jesse Owens was down, as helpless as any man struck low by the Brown Bomber.

Joe ran his hardest, his legs thundering down the channel in a way they never did on one of his dawn runs. He was halfway to the tape by the time Jesse picked himself up. The gap was too wide. Jesse could not catch the champ. He crossed the line close behind Joe. The crowd rocked with delight. The World's Fastest Man had stuck to his new script.

Jesse stretched out his hand as Joe turned towards him. The fighter pulled him in close, as if consoling an opponent in defeat. They held each other for a moment, their heads bowed. Jesse spoke softly. 'You ran real well, champ.'

'Yeah,' Joe said, his face empty and still.

They broke apart. Joe kept his head down as they walked back towards the cheering crowd. Jesse lifted his right hand and, beneath a clear blue sky, smiled his most brilliant smile. They had made it. They had both risen and fallen and risen again. They were icons who had come a long and dizzying way from the summer of '35 when, as a couple of twenty-one-year-old Negro kids, they had set out together on the greatest journey in sporting history . . .

Chapter Two

Track Time

Detroit–New York, 14 May 1935

Late at night, in the swaying carriage, Joe Louis stared into the sudden darkness. When they snuffed out the small gas lamp above his head, even his reflection had disappeared from the nearest window. No one could see his face any more. Joe liked it that way. The familiar voices rolled on, their whispering sounding more urgent the faster the train sped towards New York. They talked of everything he would need to endure. Joe had to be ready. He would be tested like never before. A single mistake would not only ruin him: it could set his people back twenty years.

They had left Detroit at 5.25 that Tuesday afternoon and, after six hours of hard talk, he lost himself in the lonely rhythm of the train. Deadpan Joe was still called a nigger across America. It didn't matter. He had turned twenty-one the day before, and was bursting with desire. The journey would last fifteen hours and ten minutes but, at the end of it, he'd walk through Harlem for the first time. Joe wished he was already there, in Small's Paradise or the Memo Club, eying those easy New York girls, those smooth honeys with the long legs and the glistening lips.

He would not be distracted for long. Serious work loomed over everything. Six weeks from that exact night, on 25 June 1935, Joe would confront a pale giant in the Bronx. Primo Carnera, the 'Man Mountain' and heavyweight champion of the world less than a year before, would dwarf him. At his birth just outside Venice in 1906, little Primo had supposedly weighed twenty-two pounds. He had grown steadily ever since. The six foot seven inch, 264 pound Carnera had a reach of eighty-two inches – longer than any champion in history. He had feet like small canoes and hands as big as paddles. Early in 1933, in a championship eliminator, his fists had killed Ernie Schaaf, a boxer from Boston.

With his outstretched arms and stiff walk, and a hideous smile that pulled his lips high above yellow teeth to reveal the discoloured flesh of his protruding gums, Carnera was a ringer for Frankenstein. The men around Joe Louis, however, were smart. Jack Blackburn, his trainer, reassured him that Carnera was just a lumbering hulk. He had been discovered in Paris in 1928 while working as a circus strongman who performed 'legendary feats of strength'. The most popular of these stunts saw the Italian use his bare hands to stop two cars driving in opposite directions. He grabbed the thick ropes tied to each vehicle and, even as their engines roared, the cars remained motionless.

'That don't make him a fighter, Chappie,' Blackburn told Joe, using the name he gave to everyone he liked. 'Carnera got brute size, but he can't fight. You can cut him down, jus' like some big old tree. You hit him to the body, then you go to the head. If you do that, Chappie, you got him.'

'OK, Chappie,' Joe had replied cheerfully. He always called Blackburn by the trainer's own favourite greeting. Joe knew Chappie Blackburn was never wrong. Besides, a week earlier, on 7 May, Joe had knocked out Gene Stanton in Kalamazoo, a town halfway between Detroit and Chicago. It was his twenty-second straight victory – and eighteenth KO – in the eleven months he had been hitting men for a living. 'Da Preem', as they tagged Carnera in New York, could not scare him. Joe's skin only prickled when he thought of the murderous mob surrounding the Italian. They were led by Oweny 'The Killer' Madden. They came from the underworld.

Joe opened his eyes at the forlorn whistle of the train as they entered a tunnel. It was just after midnight. They were moving into treacherous territory. Joe felt a surge of emotion. It would be all right. It would be okay. Apart from Chappie and his two managers, John Roxborough and Julian Black, he was accompanied by Bill Bottoms, his cook, and Freddie Guinyard, his oldest friend from Detroit. They made up one of the few black entourages in boxing. Together, the six of them carried a dream: that Joe Louis would become the first black man in twenty years to fight for the world heavyweight title.

Roxy and Mr Black, two short and chubby middle-aged men, were deceptively cuddly. Each had a round fleshy face. The difference was seen in the eyes. Roxy's were twinklers. Mr Black's were chillier. Joe had met the twinkler first, in Detroit, where Roxy ran the numbers racket. He was a cultured hustler, the son of a New Orleans lawyer and the younger brother of Charles Roxborough, the first black member of Michigan's state legislature.

Julian Black gave Roxy the financial clout and gangland muscle to protect his young fighter. Joe shuddered when he first heard that his co-manager was a qualified embalmer. Mr Black had since moved on to a livelier vocation which saw him control the numbers on Chicago's South Side as well as a speakeasy called Elite Number 2 – Chappie Blackburn's chosen drinking den.

At fifty-two, Blackburn was still wiry despite the ravages of drink and creeping arthritis. He had the unblinking face of a man who'd stare down 'The Killer' without a shiver of hesitation. Below his copper-coloured head, an ugly scar ran across his left cheek. It stretched from his ear to the corner of his mouth. Blackburn had been slashed in a bar-room brawl. Although they never spoke about it, Joe knew that Chappie had been in prison for four years after a bloody night in Philadelphia when, 'berserk with drink', he killed a man. It was there, behind the stone walls of a jailhouse, that he began to teach men how to fight.

Before his imprisonment in 1909 Blackburn had fought hundreds of battles between the ropes. He counted his losses on one gnarled hand. Blackburn had laughed when Roxborough and Black approached him in Chicago. They wanted him to train their Negro amateur, Joe Louis, towards a crack at the championship. It was the stupidest idea Blackburn had heard in years. 'That ain't gonna happen,' he said, referring as much to his wasting time on a nigger-kid as the miracle of another black man being given a chance to prove himself the best fighter in the world.

Blackburn said damned Jack Johnson had ended everything for black heavyweights. So far he had been proved right. No black fighter had been allowed to challenge for the championship since 1915. Blackburn took particular pleasure in retelling Joe the story of the day he had sparred with Johnson. He had gone after the big man with blurring fists and fast feet, and bloodied Johnson's nose. Johnson never forgave him. Blackburn, in turn, took every opportunity to deride boxing's lone black champion.

He had been inclined to do the same when Roxborough and Black pressed him to train Louis. Blackburn's scornful refusal turned to amusement when he heard that they would advance him a month's wages – at $35 a week. 'This'll be the best job I ever had,' he cackled. 'Usually got to whip my man to get my pay. But I gotta tell you one thing: you ain't ever gonna make a success of this kid. He ain't ever gonna make no money worth shaking your finger at. He's a nigger.'

Blackburn was as blunt when he went to work on Joe in a

run-down Chicago gym in June 1934: 'Y'know, boy, the heavy-weight division for a Negro is hardly likely. The white man ain't too keen on it. You really gotta be something to get anywhere. If you ain't gonna be another Jack Johnson, you got some hope. White man hasn't forgotten that fool nigger with his white women, acting like he owned the world. You gotta listen to everything I tell you. You gotta jump when I say jump, sleep when I say sleep. Other than that, you wastin' my time.'

Joe was raw, but Blackburn only needed to say something once for the kid to get it. He listened rather than talked, worked rather than boasted. If he kept at it, Chappie thought, he could be some fighter. After his winning debut at the Bacon Casino in Chicago, Louis boxed seven nights later at the same venue. On 11 July 1934, fifty-six-year-old Jack Johnson turned up in a crowd of 1,800 to watch Louis knock out Willie Davis, a pasty veteran in the third. Johnson's presence at ringside was noted by newspapers in Chicago, Detroit and New York. They paid even more attention to the promise of the twenty-year-old fighter they described as 'poker-faced'. Joe was more inter-ested in the fact that he made $62 – a rise of $3 from his first purse.

His fifteenth bout, against Lee Ramage in Los Angeles in February 1935, earned him $4,354. Roxborough and Black were elated for a different reason. Bojangles Robinson had brought in a posse of Hollywood stars to support Louis. Ramage was the local white fighter, but there was no mistaking the excitement which spread across the gleaming faces of Clark Gable, Bing Crosby and Mae West when Louis knocked out his wily opponent in the second round. He looked set for the big-time.

As they raced through the night to New York, even Blackburn had begun to believe it. If Joe could beat Primo Carnera before 65,000 people at Yankee Stadium, his claims as a credible chal-lenger would seem irresistible. But the stakes were wild and high. Roxy and Black said sixty grand for whipping Carnera would seem like loose change if he landed a championship fight. They were depending on Joe. Sometimes it felt as if just about every other Negro in America leaned on him.

The endless chug of the train soothed him. Joe drifted towards sleep. The hushed words faded into a whisper.

'Chappie,' Roxborough murmured to Blackburn. 'You sure he's ready for New York?'

'Yeah, he's ready for New York,' the old trainer growled, 'but New York ain't ready for him . . .'

A week later, just after dawn on Thursday 23 May, Jesse Owens swallowed a moan as they hoisted him into the car's rumble seat in Columbus, Ohio. His eyes glazed as he turned his head to the side, thinking he must look like one of those shock-haired fellas laid low by an electrifying Joe Louis combination. They all wore the same sickened face when they tried to lift themselves from the canvas. Jesse now knew how they felt.

'You OK, Shorty?' Dave Albritton asked as he strapped Jesse into the Hupmobile.

'Just about, champ,' Jesse said.

At six foot one, Dave was only a few inches taller than Jesse, but it was enough of a difference for him to milk it. It was 'Shorty' this and 'Shorty' that wherever they went. Dave had been his best friend for years. Jesse forced himself to shift position again. They were in for a long ride. Still, if anyone could make the journey bearable it would be Dave and Mel Walker – Ohio State University's two spring-heeled Negro high jumpers. With his stilt-like legs, the six foot five inch Mel was by far the tallest of the three. Like Jesse and Dave, he wore a crimson track-top with a big O in the middle.

The trip was meant to mark the next big step in Jesse's climb. That coming Saturday he would compete in the annual Big Ten Western Conference championship in Ann Arbor, Michigan. His folks could hardly believe that a poor Negro kid from Alabama was about to reach such dizzying heights. Contested by teams from the ten leading universities in or surrounding the Mid-West, the Big Ten provided the most searing competition outside the national track-and-field finals. The western conference of universities had, throughout its forty-year history, defined the ethos of amateur inter-collegiate sport by insisting that their athletes were 'bona fide full-time students who were not delinquent in their studies'. There were further restrictions. Athletes at the Big Ten universities could not be financially rewarded while their team coaches had to be 'appointed at modest salaries'. The Big Ten showcase was meant to epitomise everything glorious about amateur sport.

All month the boys had had their fun with newspaper predictions that Jesse could make history by winning four championship events. Then he messed up. He was joshing around late that Monday afternoon, wrestling a couple of guys after playing touch football on the tiny front lawn of their boarding house in Columbus. Suddenly, with two of them hanging on to him, a slashing pain tore down the length of his back. He was screaming when he hit the ground.

Jesse was still hunched over in agony an hour later when Larry Snyder came to see him. The coach shook his head in disbelief: 'What the hell happened?'

'We were just foolin' round, coach. I'm sorry. It was real dumb.'

'Let's start acting smart,' Synder said evenly. 'You better stay off your feet until we decide what sort of shape you're in.'

They worked on his back in the training room every day that week, massaging the damaged area and applying various heat treatments until Jesse could at least stand up straight. Although the pain had moved towards the base of his spine, it had barely dulled in intensity. In addition to a slipped disc, the vertebrae were swollen and out of joint. A doubtful Snyder allowed him to travel, while stressing that he would make the final decision on Jesse's fitness.

The 150 miles they'd cover in slow convoy from Columbus to Ann Arbor, with a stop-over in Toledo, would take six hours. Sixteen athletes, Snyder and his assistant, Tucker Smith, squeezed into three old cars – Snyder's white Hupmobile, a black Sterns Knight and a creaky grey Packard.

Jesse, Dave, Mel and the fourth Negro on the team, Fred Thomas, were usually in the Packard. It never picked up more than a rattling crawl but that didn't stop the wind howling through them. Frayed green curtains hung over the missing side windows as they travelled across icy roads and snowbound states. Without an indoor track of their own, Ohio State spent every weekend of the winter season on the road. Dave said it was a miracle none of the black boys had been frozen white behind those green curtains.

The bitter weather spread into spring. A cold May morning offered no comfort to Jesse's back, but his injury did win them a reprieve from the Packard. They were travelling with Snyder while some of the white fellers took their overdue turn in the curtained car. The Hupmobile swung out at the head of the parade at six-thirty that morning, with Jesse propped next to Snyder. In the back, alongside Tucker Smith, Dave, Mel and Fred settled down for a snug ride. Dave winked at Mel as he tapped on the sealed glass.

'These sure are nice windows, coach,' Dave noted. 'Real glass.'

Snyder joined in the easy laughter. He liked the coloured boys. They worked harder and listened more closely than the white athletes. He thought they would try anything to please him and to better themselves. Snyder had more than a strong hunch that, led by Jesse Owens, Negroes were about to dominate the sport.

The convoy slid down Columbus's empty High Street. They passed the Blue Moon. You could order a T-Bone steak, a baked potato and three vegetables, with dessert to follow, for 45 cents at the Moon. The offer did not extend to Jesse, Dave, Mel, Fred or any other Negro in town. Like every other restaurant on High Street, the Blue Moon was only open to white customers. If they fancied a break from their own meagre cooking, the best athletes at Ohio State had just one option: the old Union Building, where hot dogs were the perennial special of the day, was the only place in town where blacks could eat in public.

They drifted past the three main movie theatres. Each building was dark in the dim morning light. When they opened again that evening they would be reserved for '*Whites Only*'. The solitary movie-house which admitted Negroes was on the far side of Columbus. Even there, the crumbling Rex only sold 'cullud seats' in the top six rows of its dingy balcony.

None of their white team-mates seemed to notice. Almost a quarter of the track team was black but they were part of a Negro population which amounted to less than a hundred out of a student body of 14,000 at Ohio State. Unless they were Jesse Owens sprinting down a track or Dave Albritton and Mel Walker rolling over a high bar, black students in Ohio were meant to be invisible. They were not allowed to stay on campus. Jesse, Dave, Mel and Fred shared the top floor of a boarding house at 236 East 11th Street.

Dave sometimes called Columbus a cracker town. Jesse pointed out that there were far worse places on the road. 'I know that,' Dave said, 'we just about been to every bad town going in Ohio and Illinois and Indiana and Michigan. It still don't make any of this right.'

Jesse remembered the day in 1933 when he and Dave had driven through Indiana. Dave had a special knack of managing to borrow a car whenever they needed one to scout the best of the twenty-eight colleges chasing Jesse. On their way to Indiana University, in Bloomington, they stopped at a town called Kokomo. They did not stay for long once they heard that a young Negro had been lynched the day before. His body was strung up and left to dangle in the wind as the citizens of Kokomo picnicked around the tree.

Jesse and Dave had lived four miles apart in Alabama. On Sunday afternoons, when they were aged five and six, they would watch their older brothers play baseball against each other in either Oakville or Danville, home to the Albrittons. Dave remembered Prentice Owens, Jesse's eldest brother in a family of eleven, clearest of all. They called Prentice 'Big Leg' because he lifted his left leg unbelievably high whenever he pitched.

Both families had moved north, to Cleveland, where Jesse and Dave were old enough to hook up at Fairmount Junior High in 1928. They became even closer at high school, at East Tech in Cleveland, and were regarded as inseparable at Ohio State – once Dave, a few credits short of the required university entrance in 1933, had joined Jesse in Columbus in the fall of 1934. Eight months on, Dave was still a freshman which meant, under strict Big Ten regulations, he could only travel on the track-and-field team as an unofficial member.

Jesse and Mel had become pals in their own freshman year. Mel came from Toledo. As a favour to him they were stopping off in his hometown later that morning to help inaugurate a new YMCA. The two other cars were heading straight on past to Ann Arbor. The white boys dealt with a different kind of establishment. Whenever they made an overnight stop they would check in at a white hotel while the Negroes headed for the local Y. Life had always been that way.

They chugged through Delaware and Marion and headed up towards Findlay. It was far from the prettiest stretch of Ohio. They had been through trouble round these parts before. Jesse just hoped that Snyder did not pull into one of those roadhouses where some hillbilly would refuse to serve them. Dave could not stand it much longer. Besides being a high-jumper and a

hurdler, he also boxed for Ohio State. Dave was a decent technician in the ring, packing a wallop in both hands. There was no
telling what might happen if he cut loose on the next guy who
sneered, 'We don't serve no niggers!'

Findlay was halfway between Columbus and Ann Arbor.
They arrived in time for a late breakfast. The Hupmobile eased
into the parking lot of the first eating joint they saw. Snyder cut
the engine as the two other OSU cars drew alongside them. The
white students clambered out and walked towards the small
restaurant.

'Perhaps we could eat in the car,' Snyder said.

'Whatever, coach,' Jesse murmured. The others sat in silence.
Jesse could imagine the twitch in Dave's cheek as he clenched his
jaw tight.

'OK,' Snyder said. 'Egg sandwiches and coffee sound all
right?'

Jesse nodded. Tucker Smith opened his door. 'C'mon, Larry,'
the little trainer said, 'I'll give you a hand with the plates . . .'

The four black athletes watched the white men walk away.
Inside the diner, some of the Buckeye boys had already sat
down. The place was half-empty. There would have been enough
seats for all of them. Dave said nothing, burying his head in the
sports pages while they waited for their wilted sandwiches.

Jesse knew how to lift the mood. 'So,' he said casually, 'what's
the news of Joe?'

A week after his arrival in New York, Joe Louis was about to set
up camp in Pompton Lakes. Primo Carnera had already begun
training in New Jersey. The fight was a month away; but the
papers were full of the coming battle.

Jesse felt for Joe. He had looked frightened when the train
steamed into Grand Central last Wednesday morning. You could
see it in every photograph. His eyes were wide and startled like
a big beautiful deer pinned down by the glare of a thousand

searchlights. The only time he smiled was when the Red Caps, the Negro railway porters, broke forward to lift him up on their shoulders. They carried Joe across the shiny station concourse, the white people parting around them in creamy waves.

Joe had struggled at the press conference his promoter, Mike Jacobs, had arranged for the 'young Negro sensation'. All the New York writing stars were there – from the jazzy and nation-ally-syndicated likes of Damon Runyon and Paul Gallico to old Grantland Rice, the inky scourge of Jack Johnson. The blood rushed to Joe's face as they pressed in on him.

Joe knew Carnera was Italian but that didn't mean he had some kind of handle on world affairs. He'd heard nothing of a threatened war between Italy and Ethiopia. Who the hell was Benito Mussolini? And Haile Selassie? He couldn't understand why the fast-talking New York reporters kept pitching him those crazy names. Joe kept his mouth shut, waiting for Roxy to rescue him, which he did when some old buzzard in glasses asked him if his fight against Carnera 'symbolised the likely conflict between the world's only independent black country and fascist Italy?' He could not even guess what kind of answer he should give to that stuff.

Joe was bewildered. All he could do was promise, slowly and respectfully, that he would do his best to knock out Carnera within five rounds. He was more relaxed with the black reporters. They ushered him up to Harlem.

The *New York Amsterdam News* gushed at his reception. 'Surrounded by admirers on Wednesday in front of the Renaissance Grill, where he had tucked away five pork chops and a quart of milk, he doubled up a fist as big as the hoof of a Missouri mule and as hard as rock and demonstrated what he would do to Primo. He swung his fist in a playful spirit, but such is the magic which surrounds a hero that the onlookers showed their teeth and told each other: "He'll do it too." Detectives Webber and Brown of the West 125th Street station, who have been assigned to guard Louis during his stay in town, had all they could do to keep the rabble from piling in the fighter's lap. Those in front wanted to examine his new brown suit, his natty green tie and his pearl grey hat. They gazed admiringly at his sturdy legs, at his sizeable feet, encased in size twelve shoes which seemed to hug the sidewalk like a pair of grippers. A pencil which fell out of his overcoat was almost the cause of a little riot.'

Back in the Hupmobile, Jesse forgot about his back as they discussed the reports from New York. There would be no stopping the Brown Bomber once he stepped into the ring with Carnera. The whole country would then see something special in Joe Louis.

'Boy,' Dave sighed. 'I'd love to meet him one day . . .'

'We will,' Jesse said. 'I know we will.'

Ann Arbor, 25 May 1935

The sun shone on Ann Arbor that warm Saturday morning as, just after eight, Jesse lowered himself into a steaming bath. The heating pads they had placed on his stomach and back in the night, using a thin towel to wrap them around his midriff, had only partly eased his stiff body. Jesse sank into the water. He lay there for thirty minutes.

At noon, with Jesse again in the rumble seat, the Hupmobile rolled towards Ferry Field as tenderly as it had ever travelled. They were quiet as they neared the stadium. Jesse stared up at the red brick and ivy-covered walls of the field-house where Tucker Smith had worked on him before the heats the previous afternoon. He did just enough to qualify. Yet the rambling pain had moved again overnight. As Jesse climbed the iron staircase he felt it in his upper right leg.

He stretched out on the rub-down table in the visiting

dressing-room. Tucker massaged Jesse's back and legs with pure alcohol before he applied thick swaths of eye-watering Wintergreen cream. The trainer dug in and began the kneading. After half an hour he reached into his bag and opened a new jar of red pepper rub. Tucker ground the potion into Jesse's spine, starting at the base of his neck and moving methodically downwards. The heat rose from Jesse's shimmering skin.

At 2.15, Jesse pulled on his running gear and a thick warm-up suit. The temperature outside had climbed into the high seventies. He walked with Dave down the tunnel to the edge of the field. The arena was crammed with 12,000 people. Jesse headed for the nearest flagpole. His usual routine consisted of a jog around the 440-yard circuit, followed by ten minutes of stretching and then another five of practice starts. Jesse did not feel even close to normal. He sat down on the grassy verge and leaned against the white pole. It was warm against his back. He watched the others skim the track in languid circles. His first race, the 100-yard final, was at 3.15.

Jesse looked across at the main stand. In the front row he picked out the shock of white hair belonging to his first coach, Charley Riley. 'Pop' was down from Cleveland. After a few minutes he stood up, waved and began walking towards Jesse. This was the kind of day they had dreamed about years ago. The old coach used to make Jesse stare at a concrete alleyway which stretched along the length of a church in east Cleveland. Every morning, before school, they trained on that holy runway.

'Imagine,' Riley would always say, 'you're sprinting over a ground of burning fire.'

Ever since then, whenever he ran, Jesse flew with the lightest of steps, as if his feet would be scorched if he did not lift them up quickly and deftly. The way Riley taught him to keep his head still and his body relaxed lent his running a fluidity as marked as his speed. Riley had discovered Jesse when he was a spindly kid who looked as if he needed a decent feed just to survive the winter. Yet Riley, who was partially deaf, saw something miraculous in that stuttering fourteen-year-old boy.

'Now Jess,' Riley scolded as he neared the flagpole in Ann Arbor, 'don't you get up. I've heard all about that back . . .' He knelt down, his knees cracking. 'You'll be all right,' he promised. 'Just go out there and run – run like we know you can.'

When Riley headed back to his seat with a steady step, Jesse was not sure he would reach the 100-yard start in similar fashion. He decided not to risk moving until the last possible moment. His form throughout May, before the accident, had been almost eerie. On 11 May, he had become the first American to jump over 26 feet, leaving him a quarter-inch short of the world mark held by Japan's Chuhei Nambu. Dave loved the fact that the prodigious leap came against Notre Dame, a university which barred black students.

The following week, in Evanston, Illinois, he equalled Frank Wykoff's world record of 9.4 seconds for 100 yards. An hour later, between victorious long jumps, he raced over 220 yards in 20.7, only a tenth of a second slower than the world best. He then broke the 220-yard low hurdle world record, clocking 22.9 seconds in his final event of that memorable afternoon.

In the *Los Angeles Times* that Wednesday, 22 May, Braven Dyer considered the impact of Owens and his contemporaries: 'Say, those darktown strutters down on Central Avenue are really goin' to town these days as the papers continue to be filled with the exploits of this Negro athlete and that one. A guy can't get a word in edgewise what with the shine-boys, locker-room attendants and janitors proudly relating the feats of strength and skill and speed performed by their "cullud" brethren. My favourite bootblack can rattle off more of Jesse Owens's records than I can, and that's supposed to be my business. Jefferson High's ebony antelopes completely dominated the Southland cinderland classic; Jimmy LuValle once again regained his stride; Jesse Owens broke one world mark and tied another; Joe Louis looms as Max Baer's most dangerous contender – to mention the most important Negro headlines. Well, anyway, Africa won't win the Davis Cup.'

Jesse felt a nervous twinge as Willis Ward sprinted past the long jump pit. Ward was also an outstanding football player for the University of Michigan – when he was allowed to play. Southern colleges banned him from their stadiums. He was a Negro.

In 1934, Ward had set a western conference track record by scoring eighteen points with two victories and two second places in the same championship meeting. That February, in an indoor meet at Ann Arbor, he'd trounced Owens over sixty yards and in the long jump. He now concentrated on his jumping. Ward hoped he might beat Mel Walker and capture the Big Ten high-jumping title he had long coveted. He was also gunning for Jesse in the long jump.

At three o'clock, Larry Snyder walked briskly towards the flagpole. He wore white trousers, a white shirt and his Buckeyes tie. Snyder was young and ambitious. He knew his name as a coach could be made by Jesse Owens – and nowhere more decisively than at the 1936 Olympics. The Berlin Games would be far more crucial than a Big Ten final.

'I don't think you should chance it today,' Snyder said. 'It's not worth the risk.'

'Please, coach,' Jesse said, 'let's try the 100. If I look bad you can pull me straight out of the jump and the 220.'

Back and forth they went until, at last, Snyder relented. At 3.05 Jesse swung his arms and stretched them above his head. The heat from Tucker's red pepper rub spread across his back. He could feel himself perspiring. The applause began to swell as he approached the group of sprinters who had gathered near the starting line.

The man with the gun wore a black jacket and a white hat. He stood a few feet from the six runners. Jesse nodded to each of his five white rivals. He shook hands with his most serious opponents, Bob Grieve of Illinois and Sam Stoller of Michigan. Grieve had pushed him close in a couple of races that year while the nineteen-year-old Stoller, two years younger than Jesse, was considered the most promising young white sprinter in America. Stoller and Grieve, along with Owens and a dozen others across the country, were chasing the dream of a place on the US Olympic sprint squad the following summer.

Grieve, with hands on hips, flexed the muscles in his neck by rolling his head round in a slow circle. It was one way of easing the tension. Stoller chose instead to talk softly to Jesse, asking him how he felt. Jesse smiled wryly. Everyone knew about his injury by now.

With the trowel given to him by Pop Riley, Jesse dug small holes in the cinders for his feet. His mind was suddenly as uncluttered as if he had just begun work on a patch of garden one lazy Sunday afternoon. There was a gentle scuffing sound as he opened up the grey cinder. The others joined in the digging.

A minute later, they were almost ready. Grieve bent and stretched one last time while Stoller ran on the spot, lifting his legs to an exaggerated height to crank up the adrenaline. Jesse stood completely still. They were seconds away from his first Big Ten final.

A stillness settled across the arena. Everyone always stopped to watch Jesse Owens run. Eddie Tolan, the reigning Olympic champion, studied the runners from the stands. Tolan had felt a bond with Owens from the moment they'd lined up alongside each other in the 1932 Olympic trials. Owens, then a schoolboy, had drawn the prime position in lane four. Tolan, struggling with a strained leg muscle that day, was tucked away on the inside. His lane had been badly scuffed during the 10,000m heats. 'Let's swap,' Owens said. 'I haven't much chance of qualifying anyway.'

Jesse Owens was now expected to win every race he ran.

When he carefully placed his fingers just behind the white paint, and extended his legs, his black track shoes found the holes. Jesse was in the slot. His head lowered as the starter, W.J. Manilaw, walked down the line, checking that no one could claim even a finger-nail's advantage. Jesse breathed in deeply.

Manilaw cleared his throat. '*On your marks*,' he said.

Jesse Owens let the breath slide from his lips. Manilaw spoke again: '*Set . . .*'

The runners' heads lifted and their backs arched. Manilaw liked to prolong this moment, daring a flyer to break early. Owens held his position in the silence.

Manilaw pulled the trigger. The blank fired. They were away first time.

Grieve made the best start, followed closely by Stoller, Owens and Andy Dooley of Iowa. There were only inches between the leading four runners as they churned through the first twenty-five yards. Yet Owens found his customary rhythm as his body straightened into a smooth and majestic line. His head was held high and perfectly still. Owens's arms pumped effortlessly, the fists of his delicate hands turned inward in a light clench. His legs flowed beneath him, his feet lifting fast from the cinder. At the fifty-yard mark, and in the lead, he turned on the burners.

Owens accelerated away with astonishing ease, giving the impression that the track beneath him had turned into a moving runway. The others rocked and heaved as if they were running across sinking sand. The newspaper photographers near the finish leaned over into the outside lane so that their whirring cameras could frame the flying leader. They only pulled back when Owens, in the adjoining lane, was almost upon them. He sped past in a blur and snapped the tape, five yards clear of Grieve. Owens's face was expressionless as he slowed to a canter. He waited for the flaring pain. Yet his back felt great. His legs felt loose and supple.

Each of the three time-keepers stared at his stopwatch. They moved into a huddle and compared times: 9.31; 9.33; 9.34. Philip Diamond, the leading official, checked that his assistants had only snapped the thumb down after Owens's back foot had crossed the line. Diamond was a stickler, a man who argued vehemently against the modern push to stop the clock as soon as a sprinter breasted the tape. He was emphatic that, especially in regard to a world record, the holder of the previous best time should be favoured, so as to avoid any doubt when an obviously faster time was recorded.

Diamond conferred with Ted Canty, the track announcer, advising him that Owens's time should be confirmed at 9.4. It was considered correct, again in deference to the record-holder, to round up the three different times to the higher tenth of a second. For the second week running, Owens had officially equalled the world record Frank Wykoff had held since 1930.

Eddie Tolan made his way down to the field. He knew what Owens had done even before the clock-watchers did. With his heavy-rimmed glasses and dark suit Tolan could have passed for a bank clerk – except that there were no black tellers in Ann Arbor. Tolan was trying instead to make a living out of running, sprinting for money in exhibitions from Europe to Australia. They called him the 'Michigan Express'. As Tolan pushed his way towards the edge of the track, he wished he could be back on the cinders with this kid. The Olympic champion, however, was condemned to the wilderness. As a professional, he was banned from competitive athletics.

After he had accepted Tolan's embrace, Owens turned to the long-jump pit. He had been jumping brilliantly all year, and usually only needed one leap to win an event. Owens depended on the same routine in Ann Arbor. His 220-yard final was less than thirty minutes away, and the 220 low hurdles just fifteen minutes after that. His back might only last one jump.

In anticipation of his clash with Ward, the local favourite, the Michigan officials had decided earlier that week to move the site of the long jump from the far end of the stadium to a prime position in front of the main grandstand. A new board and pit had been installed six days before the final. The runway, however, was now just a stretch of old grass which had been cut short, watered and rolled in an attempt to approximate the more traditional strip of cinder.

The long-jump final had begun twenty-five minutes earlier and Ward held a comfortable lead. He had sailed past 25 feet in both of his first two tries. He was saving his third leap until after Owens had jumped.

'Welcome to the world's 100-yard champion,' Ted Canty hollered through the crackling megaphone as Owens approached. Despite the disadvantage of that grassy runway, Owens had decided to stick to his plan. At 3.22, seven minutes after his 100-yard dash, he nodded to Tucker Smith who measured out the mark and placed a white handkerchief deep in the pit, 26 feet and 2½ inches from the point where Owens's feet would leave the ground. Canty called dramatically for silence. When the hush came, he confirmed that Owens was about to attempt another world record. There was a whooping roar and a clattering scramble as spectators rushed from their seats and on to the field in an attempt to find the best possible viewing position for this latest slice of track-and-field history.

'You on a roll or somethin'?' Ward cracked as he cocked an eye at the sandy hanky.

Owens grinned and walked to the start of his run-up. By the time he turned around he was 108 feet from the take-off board. Hundreds of people surrounded the long-jump pit and hundreds more lined either side of the thin grass channel down which he would sprint. He barely heard the officials instructing them to stand clear as he prepared himself.

Owens rocked gently in a half-crouch, his legs bent and his back almost parallel with the ground. His head tilted forward slightly as if he was already being pulled towards the pit. He looked down and then, swallowing hard, lifted his head again. Everything depended on the speed he could reach before he hit the board. His back lowered fractionally and his legs tensed. And then, suddenly, he began to run, faster and faster, past the rows of screaming faces. Exultant spectators flooded the runway behind him. It looked like he was running from a sea of people as he closed in on the take-off strip.

His front foot hit the board and, with a simple kick, Owens began his leap. His legs pedalled smoothly through the air, while his arms stretched towards the mark that no other human had ever reached. Owens landed in an explosion of sand and noise, then made another small leap forward, to ensure that he did not disturb any part of the freshly-raked pit behind him.

A little white boy was waiting for him, an autograph book trembling in his hand. Even before he could take the book or look back at his mark in the sand, Owens was mobbed by the yelling throng. He knew it had been a huge jump. He had flown past the white handkerchief, its fluttering now a certain sign of surrender.

The official announcement made even Jesse Owens shake his head in astonishment: 26 feet, 8¼ inches. He had shattered Nambu's world record by six inches.

Owens was pulled away by Snyder, grinning like a madman. 'Jesse,' Snyder yelled above the noise, 'how's your back?'

'Coach,' he said, 'I reckon I should have backache more often. I feel great.'

Dave Albritton and Mel Walker forced their way through the crush. Jesse hugged his friends, but they did not celebrate for long. He was already being summoned to the start of the 220-yard final, where he would face Bob Grieve and Andy Dooley again. Grieve, his fiercest competitor at the Big Ten, had made the most of his twenty-five minutes of recovery time from the 100-yard final. He had purposely stayed away from the long-jump pit in an attempt to concentrate on his own best event.

Grieve hardly looked at Owens as they once more went through the ritual of making footholds in the cinder.

Owens flew from the holes first but he still held back over the first hundred, watching Grieve on his right, waiting to see what the Illinois man might have left after his earlier defeat. He decided not to hang around after the halfway point. Owens ran the second hundred like a dark and speeding train. He was over the line in 20.3, ten yards ahead of Dooley and three-tenths of a second faster than the world record set in 1924. Grieve was a distant third.

The Michigan spectators, forgetting their rivalry with Ohio State, jumped up and down in jubilation. Their pursuit of another Big Ten team championship seemed less significant than the fact that they were witnessing the most incredible string of individual performances ever seen in international track-and-field.

Larry Snyder tried to control himself. He knew that, in the twelve minutes left before the 220-yard hurdles, he had no chance of persuading Owens to withdraw from his final event. Snyder looked anxiously at the glowing figure in front of him. 'OK, Jesse,' he murmured. 'Take it easy in the hurdles.'

If Owens never practised his long jump, both in an effort to protect himself from injury and because the event came so easily to him, he had recently begun to hurdle in training. He was still, however, a comparative novice, and his hurdling was the only aspect of his athletic repertoire that lacked a graceful polish. Albritton joked that 'Shorty' Owens just ran fast and hopped over the fences without ever considering anything as mundane as his stride pattern or hurdling technique. Owens had still broken the world record in the 220-yard low hurdles the week before.

At four o'clock, he joined the five other finalists. Ten sets of wooden hurdles, two-and-a-half feet in height and twenty yards apart, stretched out before them in a series of straight lines down the home straight. Owens, in the outside lane, had the worst draw. It didn't matter. He took the lead after the third barrier and then hurdled with a speed and timing which he had never before achieved. Owens was six yards clear at the end. His time of 22.6 was another record. The white tape wrapped around his chest. In the space of forty-five minutes he had broken three world records and equalled another. He kept running. It felt like he could run for ever.

Chapter Three

The Press Gang

They drove through the night. Jack Clowser hunched over the wheel while, in the back seat of his spluttering Cadillac, the old white man and the young black man bounced side-by-side. Charley Riley and Jesse Owens were both talkers but, as midnight darkness engulfed the road to Cleveland, they were silent. They were exhausted. It had been an afternoon of miracles. Afterwards, wherever Jesse turned, people wanted to touch him. It was as if they believed his skin would transfer some of the magic which made him run faster and jump further than anyone on earth.

Clowser wished he was already at his desk in Cleveland, writing up the incredible story. The thirty-five-year-old reporter looked over his shoulder at the kid. Although his eyes were open, Jesse's head bumped softly against the side window. He was too tired to lift it from the glass. Clowser doubted if the significance of the day had sunk in yet. By morning Jesse's name would be splashed across America.

Clowser knew that Babe Ruth had hit the last three home runs of his amazing career that very afternoon, smashing a trio straight out of Forbes Field in Pittsburgh. Babe was retiring from baseball. An American legend had run its course. Jesse Owens, 'the coloured comet', took off that same day.

An Associated Press hack had told Clowser that his agency piece from Ann Arbor was being run as front-page news in every major Sunday paper in the country. The *Los Angeles Times* had spread the story across page one of their sports section. A single column on Babe Ruth was tucked away to one side: 'Homer Orgy By Bambino'. Owens had also relegated the Babe to the bottom of the page in *The New York Times*.

Clowser, who had followed Jesse since his earliest junior-high meets, was the only Cleveland reporter in Ann Arbor. He grinned when Riley asked if they could catch a ride back with him. They had to sneak Jesse out of the stadium first. He was barricaded in the dressing-room while people tried to force their way inside. Tucker Smith helped Jesse escape through a window. When he hit the ground he was only a few feet from Clowser's gunning car. Jesse jumped in and the Cadillac surged past the crowd at the main gate.

They were sixty miles past Toledo by midnight. Clowser swung east towards Cleveland. Travelling along the gleaming shore of Lake Erie they reached Sandusky. Jesse looked out at the darkened holiday town.

'Only place open at this time of night,' Clowser said as he pointed to the light of a roadside diner. 'And this one's fine, Jesse.'

Clowser's recommendation had nothing to do with the merits of the menu. The handwritten sign outside said as much: *All Welcome!*

They found three seats near the back. At an adjoining table a group of white kids slurped their sodas and flicked through the first edition of Sunday's *Cleveland Plain Dealer*. Clowser read the huge front page headline: JESSE OWENS BREAKS 3 WORLD MARKS – *Cleveland Boy Makes History, Also Ties All-Time Speed For 100 Yards.*

Clowser had found the perfect end to his own story as he listened to the kids chattering beside him. 'Completely unaware that Owens was seated a few feet away,' Clowser wrote later, 'one of them said: "Boy, would I like to see that guy run! He must be a great kid." Jesse just winked at me. He never made a move to identify himself.'

They each picked up a copy of the paper before they left. Clowser had to check the copy of his rival, Al Silverman, Jesse needed one for his scrapbook while Pop just wanted to relive the day in print. His deafness meant that he had missed the awe-struck exchange between Jesse's latest admirers. He studied the report silently while Clowser paid for their meal. Riley only lifted his head once to read aloud.

'Listen to this, Jess,' he said. '"The name of the twenty-one-year-old Owens is being read this morning by untold thousands in London, Stockholm, Berlin, Geneva, Tokyo and other world capitals. Chuhei Nambu, Japan's outstanding athlete, is proba-bly reading that his world broad jump record has been broken by a youth from Cleveland, Ohio, USA. And in Berlin members of the crack German Olympic squad, reputed to be close to *Reichsführer* Adolf Hitler, are scanning the information the United States has found a sensational record-breaker who will make a profound difference in the 1936 Olympics."'

As Jesse listened to the tremor in Riley's voice, he remembered the most vivid moment of the afternoon – when, soon after his fourth victory, he and Pop held each other.

'How about that, Pop?' Jesse had said.

He had been expecting Pop to give him the usual big rah-rah of a speech about the need to keep his head, but Riley could not find the words. His head slumped on Jesse's shoulder as he began to cry.

Charley Riley was fifty-seven years old, the same age as Jesse's father, Henry. He had two sons. Jesse knew that the eldest Riley boy hated sport while the youngest had been born a cripple. Pop Riley, who had always yearned for an athletic son, came from an

Irish family in Pennsylvania. Henry Owens had been born into slavery in Alabama. Pop had become a teacher at Fairmount Junior High in Cleveland. Henry had been a sharecropper in Oakville, Alabama. Unlike Pop, he was not a garrulous man. Whether moving low and slow through the fields of cotton or watching his fingers fiddle with the tattered brim of his hat, Henry could not bear to look a white man in the face.

Henry's father had been a slave. Born in 1878, Henry soon discovered as harsh a destiny in sharecropping. It needed a rare harvest for money to be made after he paid Jim Cannon, the white landowner, the rent for his shack, a mule, equipment and a forty-acre stretch of dry earth. In 1896, at the age of eighteen, Henry had married Mary Fitzgerald. Everyone called her Emma. Her parents, too, had been slaves. Henry believed, 'It don't do a coloured man no good to get himself too high, 'cause it's one long drop back to the bottom.' Emma yearned for a better life.

They had nine children in their first sixteen years of marriage. A further three pregnancies ended in miscarriage. On 12 September 1913, their tenth and last baby was born. Emma had a secret name for James Cleveland Owens. She called J.C. her 'gift child'. But, as a small boy, J.C. suffered from repeated bouts of pneumonia – or 'the devil's cold' as his momma called it. Strange growths sprouted all over his body. In desperation, Emma stuck a kitchen knife into the fire. She used the scorched blade to hack away at a growth in J.C.'s chest. Blood, so dark it looked black, poured from the wound.

J.C. grew stronger. He ate beans, onions, tomatoes and the corn his momma grew in the front yard. He loved running more than any game. One wintry afternoon, J.C. ran for almost an hour. With gulping breath, he reached a rocky outcrop near the border of Joe Steppart's patch. Joe was as black as Henry – and even unluckier. His wife's three babies had all died in childbirth. J.C. never stared too closely at poor Joe. Each year he seemed a little thinner and wilder.

J.C. ducked behind a rock when he saw his mother and father. He could hear their voices clearly as they walked. Emma had decided. It was time to head north – for Cleveland.

Her next words were lost in a yelp. Jim Turner, who also lived alongside the Stepparts, came hurtling towards them. 'It's terrible! Terrible! Joe Steppart and his missus was jus' found. They both hung themselves.'

The Stepparts had had enough of a raw black life. A few weeks later, early in 1923, Emma won her argument with Henry. Nine miles separated the farmlands of Oakville from the closest town of Decatur. They walked that dirt road for the last time. J.C. saw the white cross which marked the Stepparts' grave. Henry and Emma trudged ahead, leading a straggly line of children towards the promised land.

In Cleveland, Henry found work in the steel factory. They lived on the east side of town, in a mixed neighbourhood of Poles, Jews, Italians and Negroes. J.C.'s limited ability to read and write dropped him down a school year. He felt stupid and gawky as his legs tangled with the tiny desks. J.C. burned with embarrassment when his teacher misheard his Alabama drawl as he tried to tell her his name. His J.C. became her 'Jesse'. The name stuck.

By the time he reached Fairmount in 1927 he was confident enough, as a fourteen-year-old, to change his sweetheart's name. Minnie Ruth Solomons, a pretty black girl from Georgia, dazzled Jesse. He loved her smart clothes and shining face. But no girl of his could be called Minnie – especially not when Cab Calloway was jumping from every radio with a hit called 'Minnie the Moocher'. J.C. and Minnie became Jesse and Ruth.

Riley spotted Jesse's speed during a physical education class and set about persuading him to devote himself to the track. Jesse resisted, using his afternoon job in a shoe-shine parlour as a reason not to train. Riley persisted, eventually convincing Jesse to meet him an hour before school every morning. When they were not sprinting down the concrete walkway, Riley took him to the school's tiny gymnasium. He strapped Jesse into a leather harness attached to an iron ring on the wall by a thick rope. As he sprinted on the spot, Riley tried to perfect the way Jesse moved his arms, legs and feet. Sometimes Riley made Jesse run as if he was balancing a glass of water on his head; more often he encouraged him to skim the ground by repeating that image of hot coals scalding his feet.

Riley chose a moment of defeat, a rare loss in a schoolboy race, to teach Jesse a lesson. He took the boy to a racetrack just outside Cleveland. They studied the horses as Riley reminded him how he had wasted energy by trying to intimidate his opponents with a mocking look. Riley showed Jesse how the losing nags snorted and bared their yellow teeth. In contrast, the winning horses looked beautifully composed. The expressionless way in which Jesse ran came partly from that memory.

When he moved to East Tech High in 1930, his new school allowed him to be trained by Riley. Their results were staggeringly consistent. Owens won seventy-five of the seventy-nine races he ran in high school. In Cleveland's *Call and Post* he was 'a sensation and a marvel – a one-man track team'.

Jesse was only eighteen, and Ruth not quite seventeen, when she gave birth to Gloria in August 1932. 'Ruth's going to stay home, work and save money so we'll have something when I get out of school,' Jesse told the *Call and Post*. 'Of course I'm going to save all I can too . . .'

He took a job pumping gas at Alonzo Wright's service station on the corner of East 92nd Street and Cedar Avenue in downtown Cleveland. It made them some cash – and gave him time to flirt with girls. The *Cleveland Gazette* suggested coyly that Jesse was distracted 'by the spectacle of feminine pulchritude on parade' near the gas station. He was also tempted by conflicting college offers. Jesse leaned towards Ohio State, primarily because they promised to find work for both him and his father.

Ever since the Depression hit, and Henry lost his job, he sat on his bed and stared at the wall, day after day.

Ohio State was one of the country's more reactionary colleges, and so Jesse's decision assumed national implications. The *Chicago Defender* argued in an editorial that, 'Owens will be an asset to any school. So why help an institution that majors in prejudice?' Their open letter warned him against 'sanctioning hate, prejudice and proscription. You must realise, Jesse, that in the age in which you are living, a militant spirit against prejudice in all its forms must be shown. The day has passed for turning the cheek. We must fight or perish under the iron heel of the oppressor.'

Jesse didn't read the papers much, so he stumbled into Columbus, Ohio. It turned out that there was no job for his father; and his own work was as an elevator-operator at the State Office in Columbus. They gave Jesse the dark shift. While white OSU footballers manned the public elevator at the front, he operated the freight-elevator from four in the afternoon until twelve-thirty at night.

Jesse had since moved up in Ohio's cloistered world, swapping his elevator grind for work as a page at the state's House of Representatives. He preferred running around and delivering letters to pushing the freight buttons. It was more like white work.

As the Cadillac reached East Cleveland at 2.30 that Sunday morning, Jesse knew his family's wooden frame house would feel more welcoming than the black boarding lodge in Columbus. He would be back at Ohio State by Monday afternoon. Until then, after such a surreal day, home would offer some refuge. Jack Clowser's car shuddered to a stop outside number 2178 on East 100th. The house was dark.

Six hours later, at 8.30 the next morning, people gathered in their street. 'Where's Jesse?' a man shouted. 'We want the champ!'

Emma stepped on to the porch. 'J.C.'s comin' to see y'all, he's comin' . . .'

In his bedroom, Jesse looked at himself in the mirror. He wore a brilliant green suit. He was ready. The wooden porch was heaving by the time he joined Emma and Henry out front. His momma sat quietly in her rocking chair as everyone surrounded him.

'Thanks a lot,' Jesse kept repeating, 'it's awful nice of you to say that . . .'

Henry looked at his son in bewilderment. At least the old man had begun to talk again, telling anyone who passed that he still remembered when 'Buster', the name he always gave Jesse, 'was just a skinny little kid in Alabama'.

The *Cleveland Plain Dealer* arrived at ten. Their reporter, Alvin Silverman, had covered Jesse's exploits for years, almost as long as Jack Clowser. Silverman, however, had decided not to make the journey to Ann Arbor. He had assumed that Jesse's injury would prevent him from competing. An agitated Silverman followed the story from his office as the Associated Press wires fell into his steel in-tray. The only way he could rival Clowser's exclusive for the *Cleveland News* would be to write a sparkling piece from the Owens family home that Sunday morning.

Jesse, as ever, was happy to supply the quotes for Silverman's story. 'I'm telling you, Al, I was plenty worried before the meet started. I had real pain. Our trainer rubbed me down but it still hurt when I came out for the hundred. But from the time the gun fired until the meet was over I didn't think about it again. In the 100-yard dash, around the halfway mark, I turned on the old juice. I won easily enough, I guess. But I want to tell you something if you won't think I'm getting swell-headed.'

'Go ahead,' Silverman prompted.

'Well, Al, I really believe I can run the 100-yard dash in 9.3 seconds. I'm not bragging but I got a bad start. Frankly, I'm a little disappointed.'

'How about the broad jump?' Silverman asked.

'Now I am really proud of that. I took only one jump but I didn't want to take any chances. I put a handkerchief out at 26 feet and a couple of the fellows laughed and kidded at my confidence. But I didn't say anything.'

'Say, Jesse,' someone asked, 'how does it feel to be the world's fastest human?'

'I think the praise is a little too high,' Jesse laughed.

'You looked real good in the 220,' Silverman said.

Jesse paused and then, with a look which Silverman took to be one of disgust, said, 'I was just crazy in the 220! Why, darn it, I just trotted the first 100. I don't know what got into me but I was losing and the field began to pull away from me. I figured I had better get going and I'll tell you right now I never ran a faster 100 in my life than I did then.'

'How about the hurdles?' Silverman asked.

'I was a little tired from the 220 and besides, you know, I am not a very experienced hurdler. I broke with the field and we all hit the first hurdle together. I felt a bit better so I stepped up just a little. Y'know, it's a funny thing, but I thought to myself, these fellows ain't so tough! I dug in and I won.'

Silverman knew he was onto a huge story. Apart from Owens's charm as a local boy, Silverman argued that his performance was 'probably the most extraordinary achievement in the history of organized track athletics, a history which dates to Ancient Greece'. He described Owens as 'a credit to himself, his city, his school and his race'. Silverman wrote his accompanying feature – *Friends Jam Porch, Hail Jesse Owens As Hero* – with gathering passion. 'Jesse has the heart of a champion. Once he lost a race in the state scholastic finals of 1931. I saw him crying in a corner of the Ohio State locker room and went over and said, "Listen, Jesse, don't be a hard loser." "I am a sore loser," he said. "I hate to lose. I get so sore at myself that I can't help crying. I'm not sore at anyone but myself – but it burns me up that I'm not better."'

'Owens today is just as modest as he was when he was a seventh-grade Fairmount runner. He seems unable to comprehend that he is *the* Jesse Owens everyone talks about, and at the same time fears constantly that someone might think he has gone "high hat". What does he want to do? Often I have asked him this question, and always he has replied: "I want to help America win the 1936 Olympics. I want to break every record that has ever been heard of in my events."'

Al Silverman pictured his readers in the suburbs of west Cleveland on Monday morning. He could imagine them, in their white shirts and sober ties, shaking their heads. Who would have thought a twenty-one-year-old Negro kid from East 100th Street could pull off such a trick?

For John Roxborough and Julian Black it was a delicious coincidence that, apart from ending the pariah status of Negro sportsmen, Louis and Owens mirrored each other so clearly. The description of Owens as 'a credit to his race' echoed the white approval they needed for Louis. Without that support their fighter would be just another nigger.

'We're not exactly crusaders,' Roxborough said later that day, 'but we feel Joe will bring honour and respect to the coloured race.'

A reporter from the *Chicago Daily Tribune* turned to the silent fighter in Pompton Lakes, where he was training for Primo Carnera. 'Do you smoke or drink, Joe?'

'No,' Louis confirmed, 'I do not.'

'And is there a little girl in Detroit waiting to become Mrs Heavyweight Champion?'

Joe paused, thinking of Marva Trotter, a nineteen-year-old Chicago beauty he was crazy about, despite his clandestine sessions with the Harlem showgirls.

'No,' Roxy interrupted. 'Joe hasn't shown much interest in girls. He likes to dance, and he occasionally takes a girl to a dance.

He likes movies when he's not in training, but seldom takes a girl. He is not a night-time performer. No, Joe is a *good* boy.'

Joe gave the writer his best deadpan look. To avoid any link with Jack Johnson, he churned out a cosy platitude about his mother: 'Ma's the only gal for me.' His artful managers, meanwhile, spun heart-warming stories of how Joe had bought a new house for her in Detroit while she, in turn, had presented him with a Bible when he left for New York.

Newspaper editors portrayed Owens in similarly chaste fashion. The front page of the *Los Angeles Times*'s sports section featured a large photograph of Owens sitting on his front step in Cleveland with his plump and bespectacled mother. *Meet Jesse's Girl, His Ma!* trumpeted the headline while the caption below read: '"I owe it all to my mother," said Jesse Owens yesterday, as he told Mother Owens how he shattered three world records.' No mention was made of either his girlfriend Ruth or their two-year-old daughter.

It was easier for whites to see Owens in that soft haze. Louis had to escape Johnson's shadow. The break from 'Papa Jack' would be made irrevocable, Roxborough suggested, by the 'Seven Rules' they laid down for Louis. The Roxborough Commandments were printed by delighted newspapers:

(1) Joe Louis will never have his picture taken alongside a white woman.
(2) He will never go into a nightclub alone.
(3) There will be no soft fights.
(4) There will be no fixed fights.
(5) He will never gloat over a fallen opponent.
(6) He will keep 'dead-pan' in front of the camera.
(7) He will live and fight clean.

Roxborough and Black were too smart to shackle their fighter in private. They trusted his discretion. Since arriving in New York, low-key Joe had taken his pick of the girls lining up for him. But even in Harlem, where he was mobbed continually, he kept his intimate adventures quiet.

There were other furtive dealings. Roxborough and Black were invited to the Cotton Club by Carnera's manager, Oweny 'The Killer' Madden. Despite murdering six rival mobsters, Madden had only been convicted of the slaughter of Patsy Doyle. Paroled after an eight-year stretch in Sing Sing, The Killer had moved into boxing with 'Big Bill' Duffy, Frenchy DeMange and Jack 'Legs' Diamond. The sudden presence of Madden and Duffy at Carnera's side suggested that the Italian's first manager, the tiny Frenchman Leon See, had accepted their offer of insurance against having his legs broken.

Only the heavy company surrounding 'The Man Mountain' had ensured his ungainly rise. Carnera's alternative nicknames – 'The Ambling Alp', 'The Gorgonzola Tower' and 'Old Satchel Feet' – confirmed his massive limitations. But The Killer and his crew fixed everyone and everything, including most of Carnera's fights. By the summer of 1933 they had achieved the impossible. 'Da Preem' had been transformed into the heavyweight champion of the world. Carnera held the title for almost a year, eventually being outclassed by Max Baer in June 1934.

Madden got down to business as soon as Roxborough and Black arrived at the Cotton Club – which he also owned. At his celebrated venue, the performers were black and the audience was white. It did not matter, Madden suggested, that they were of a different colour. 'I don't discriminate against no one,' The Killer said softly, as if he would blow away anyone who crossed him. They were all men of the world. He wanted a slice of Louis's contract and, rather than hurting anyone, he would give them $50,000. 'I'm feelin' charitable,' Madden said. The numbersmen pledged to return before the end of the week.

'Don't keep me waiting, boys,' The Killer warned.

*

Jack Johnson travelled to Louis's training camp at Pompton Lakes, an hour's drive from New York, with a plan. He was out to catch the Bomber. Jack carried his cane and wore the blue beret, red tie, striped blazer and riding breeches he performed in at Herbert's Museum on 42nd Street in New York. It was one of his more reliable gigs – earning him $12.50 a day for standing on a small platform while he told his life-story to anyone who stopped long enough to listen. The words flowed from him in the rich British accent he used for his speaking engagements. He was a show-stopper. The freaks around him didn't stand a chance of holding a crowd like he did – not even Madam Catalina, the hissing snake charmer, nor Professor Renato, the moustached sword swallower, could divert people's eyes from Papa Jack. He lit up the place. Johnson would captivate Joe Louis in the same way.

He had sensed trouble from the moment he first saw the young fighter. The thought of Louis ruining his role as the world's sole black champion turned Johnson cold. Nobody really knew how much he had endured during his reign. They hated him too much to acknowledge that he was the most audacious fighter, and the most skilful defensive boxer in ring history. He ended up fighting bulls in Barcelona and taking on all-comers in a flea-circus. And now, five years later, stuck in Herbert's at the age of fifty-seven, it looked as if some dark kid from Alabama could walk away with his title.

Johnson was determined to find a way back into the story. Jack Blackburn was in the kid's corner – the same scarred Blackburn he had never liked. Blackburn had never been a world champion. He'd never been to Paris or London. He'd never worn a beret or straw boater his whole damn life. He gave Louis no class. Papa Jack saw himself riding to the rescue.

Louis loved clothes – you just had to look at his new black-and-white shoes, broad-brimmed hats and those striped suits to know that Louis cared more than most about the way he looked.

It was one of the few things Johnson liked about the poker-faced dummy. But Louis needed polishing. Black Jack was ready to do the spit and rub.

He slipped into Louis's impressive hideaway. The spread was owned by Joseph Bier, a white doctor. Bier had resisted threats from the Ku Klux Klan in New Jersey and welcomed Louis and his black entourage to Pompton Lakes. The white colonial mansion was draped in ivy and set against the Ramapo Mountains. Away to the left, and down the sloping lawns, Johnson could see a lake and a single-storey building which served as the gym.

He breezed through the open doorway, waved at the startled New York detectives and sauntered over to the next room where the sound of clinking pool balls told him he was heading for the fighters. Johnson picked out the Bomber instantly.

Joe was exhilarated. Jack Johnson stood in front of him, beaming and twirling his cane as he said, 'You lookin' good, young Joe, real good.'

The two fighters headed for a log cabin adjoining the gym. Johnson moved nice and slow. He wanted the kid to absorb the fact that he was with the man who had ruled boxing for seven years. Johnson talked in a beguiling voice, telling Joe he was behind him every step of the way.

'It's real important, Joe, that you train hard and think clear,' Johnson said with a restraint that surprised even himself. 'Don't even look past Carnera. The rest will come when you're good an' ready . . .'

Roxborough rushed to break it up. In less than two hours the press would descend on Pompton Lakes. Roxy could imagine what they would make of Jack Johnson whispering in the ear of his young Negro contender. He knew what the sly old nigger wanted – to become Joe's trainer.

Roxy caught his breath just before he opened the door. He did not want to startle Joe, not two weeks before the most important fight of his life. He walked in casually, shook hands with

Johnson and reminded Joe that an early lunch was waiting. 'It'll give me and Mr Johnson time to get better acquainted,' he said to his departing fighter.

Roxborough was tougher than he looked. He and Julian Black had dealt with Oweny Madden. As soon as they left the Cotton Club, Black took up a favour owed to him by one of the heavy boys in the Purple Gang. They only needed that one phone call to Detroit, and Madden withdrew his interest in Louis. If they could handle The Killer, what could a broken man do to them?

'There ain't nothing for you here,' Roxy said to Johnson.

'That's where you wrong,' Johnson grinned. 'I can do a whole lot for your boy.'

'Go back to the flea-circus, Papa,' Roxy sneered. 'That's where niggers like you belong . . .'

Later that afternoon Roxborough told reporters: 'Johnson has approached me three times with propositions to cut in on Louis. We want no Johnsons in our outfit. He threw a fog over the coloured race that has been a long time blowing away. In fact, it hasn't even dissipated yet. As long as Joe stays with Julian Black and myself, he'll not be misled.'

Bill McCormick of the *Washington Post* was convinced: 'It looks as if Roxborough, Black and Louis are destined to play a greater part in the future of their race than Booker T. Washington. Roxborough and Black are well-educated, gentlemanly and very personable fellows who have what many of their brethren lack – race pride.'

Louis's blackness dominated almost every description of him. It began with the nicknames dreamed up for him by sports-writers eager to show off their racy and alliterative wit. The Chocolate Chopper, The Dark Destroyer, The Dusky Downer, The Mocha Mauler, The Mahogany Maimer, The Panther With The Pin-Cushion Lips, The Saffron Sphinx, The Shufflin' Shadow and The Tan Tarzan Of Thump were followed by

Murder Man Of The Maroon Mitts and K.K.K. (Kruel Kolored Klouter).

The pattern had been set three months earlier when Mike Jacobs, his promoter, brought a train-load of writers from New York to Detroit to cover a Louis fight for the first time. Caswell Adams's report in the *New York Herald Tribune* on 30 March 1935 was typical: 'Stalking the ring as a lion does the jungle paths, Joe Louis, local Negro slugger, used Natie Brown as another sacrificial lamb.' By the time Louis reached Pompton Lakes, Adams saw him as a killer who 'has stalked through the heavyweight ranks like a reaper through a wheatfield'.

When Paul Gallico turned his gaze towards the 'fat-faced, *café-au-lait* coloured, sloe-eyed' Louis, he saw 'something utterly vicious and pitiless. Not once is there a glimmer of sympathy or feeling on Louis's face.' Gallico, acclaimed as America's finest sportswriter, resorted to sinister caricature. 'There will never be any complaint that Joe Louis is too nice a kid to be a fighter. He isn't. He is a splendid, vicious male animal, completely destructive. He was made for fighting and nothing else . . . Louis's handlers, Roxborough and Black, remind me more of animal trainers than fight managers. They gentle their animal around until feeding and fighting time, and then they turn him loose.'

Gallico still praised Roxborough and Black for 'a marvellous camp' where 'they go about in snappy riding clothes with fine-fitting, shiny brown leather boots'. He liked Roxy's little touches, such as his tendency to gather the reporters and Louis around a large table lit by a single candle. The flickering light fell across the darkened gym in a way Gallico described as 'picturesque'. The fighter was mostly silent but his sisters, 'who all look like him and have marvellous names like Vunies, Eulalia and Emmarell', would be 'shrieking and banging pool balls around in the next room'. Gallico noted that 'Louis paid little attention to them and none to his mother – the dark coloured woman in a corner looking in utter bewilderment at her son.'

Louis concentrated on maintaining his guard in front of the press and letting his punches fly between the ropes. Jack Blackburn's expert tutelage became increasingly evident with each new day of sparring. In his frayed black trousers and a white vest saturated with sweat, Blackburn cared nothing for the managerial niceties of image. He was consumed instead by a need to drive his fighter to an even higher and more brutal level of skill.

Carnera could turn the fight into a brawl. The hulking Italian often tried to stand on his opponent's feet and lean on him so that he bore down on the usually smaller man with his full weight. Bill McCormick claimed in the *Washington Post* that Carnera's elbows would pin the other boxer's arms to his side while 'he works on their muscles with his gloved hands. Carnera has a very strong grip and he inserts his four fingers and thumb and literally tears them to pieces.'

If Blackburn dismissed the habitual exaggeration with a snort, he knew Carnera's size and awkward style had to be countered. Louis worked best from close range, throwing short but withering punches with both hands. He liked to keep the action crisp and clean, avoiding unnecessary clinching and mauling. Against Carnera, whose freakish reach allowed him to box behind a pawing but elongated jab, Louis would have to fight more on the inside. His previous efforts at infighting, most notably when failing to nail Natie Brown during the veteran's protracted periods of holding, had been the least convincing facet of Louis's otherwise considerable repertoire. Blackburn then devised a simple strategy for Louis to fight the Italian on the inside without becoming embroiled in a wrestling match.

Despite his flat-footed appearance, Louis was quick and elusive. He went after his gargantuan sparring-partners and, feinting and ducking beneath their punches, pounded them to the body with fast hands and remorseless zeal. His blows made them sag and, on Blackburn's barked cue, he would switch his attack and 'go upstairs', throwing lefts and rights to the jaw and head. The journeymen's mournful attempts to smother him were greeted by laughter from the thousands of spectators who came from Harlem to watch the Bomber train.

If the sparring was unremitting, the atmosphere in the grounds outside was more akin to a carnival. Massed crowds of revellers would descend on Pompton Lakes and picnic on the lawns surrounding an outdoor ring. Makeshift stalls sold hot dogs and iced 'Joe Louis Punch' while hawkers hustled and emptied their trays of souvenir hats, Brown Bomber key-rings and Ethiopian flags.

Even the cautious coterie around Louis had accepted that the fight against Carnera symbolised a deepening international conflict. The build-up had been punctuated by images of Benito Mussolini draping an enormous black shirt around Carnera while Harlem embraced both Louis and Haile Selassie's visiting son. Italy was just weeks away from invading Ethiopia.

Westbrook Pegler, the esteemed New York columnist, warned that 'the principals in this prize-fight are Joe Louis, a young American Negro, and Primo Carnera, the Italian military reservist. The Yankee Stadium lies just across the Harlem River from the greatest Negro city in the world, where riots have flared twice in recent weeks.' The *Newark Daily Star* demanded the fight's cancellation rather than risk race riots spreading to New Jersey.

Edward P. Mulrooney, New York's Police Commissioner, dismissed the gloomy speculation. He argued that 'the American Negro is by nature law-abiding, kindly, well-behaved. He is also happy and fun-loving. If Louis wins, there will likely be singing and shouting and dancing in the streets of Harlem.'

Yet Mulrooney was not about to risk anything. *The New York Times* reported that, with 'an unprecedented 15,000 Negro ticket-holders' in a crowd of 60,000, 'the largest detachment of police ever assigned to a pugilistic affray will form a cordon around Yankee Stadium. Fifteen hundred members of the force,

including two emergency squads equipped with tear gas bombs
and other apparatus, and more than 300 detectives mingling
with the throng inside the enclosure, make up the detachment. A
thousand patrolmen on foot, one inspector, seven captains, nine
lieutenants, seventy-three sergeants, a group of motor-cycle men
and fifty-nine mounted men stand poised at 158th Street, on
either side of the stadium, ready for any emergency.'

Yankee Stadium, New York, 25 June 1935

Inside the muted dressing-room, Jack Blackburn stretched out a
callused hand to stroke the back of his fighter's neck. 'Chappie,'
the old trainer said, 'we do everything we done these past six
weeks and we in for a real easy night . . .' Joe nodded as the
noise echoed from the crammed arena above their heads. Buddy
Baer, who had won the final preliminary bout by an early
knockout, was about to leave the ring.

John Roxborough walked restlessly around the room.
Although he wisely let Blackburn take charge of Joe during those
gruesome last minutes, Roxy could not shake from his head
some of the words he had read earlier that day. He'd tried to
hide his shiver when Shirley Povich wrote in the *Washington
Post* that, 'I want to see if Joe Louis can take it. I want to know
what will happen when that awful right uppercut that Primo can
throw lands against the chin of the guy who hasn't been asked to
take a stiff punch since turning pro . . . his build-up has me
wondering and I'd like to know what he will do if the battle goes
against him, because he's never been behind in any of his fights
yet. I want to know if he's the same cool sharpshooter they say
he is when a big left hand has been sticking in his face for a few
rounds. I want to know how he'll react when Primo pushes and
mauls and shoves and holds and hits and steps on his toes. Will
he keep his head?'

Joe's face was expressionless as they waited. Jack Blackburn kept up his softly-spoken mantra, repeating his instructions with an almost hypnotic calm. 'You go to the body first,' he said, 'an' the head will follow. Body then head. Nice an' easy.'

At 9.53 a sharp rap came on the dressing-room door. 'Two minutes, Louis, two minutes!'

Blackburn lifted the purple robe from a metal hook. The room was quiet. Blackburn eased Joe's gloved fists through the satin sleeves. He pulled the robe over Joe's shoulders and then, wanting to keep in the heat, tightened it around the fighter's chest.

'OK, Chappie,' Blackburn said, 'let's go.'

Blackburn led them out into the night and towards the square blaze of the ring. Around a third of the crowd was black, seated high up in the bleachers, but the roar for Joe came from every section of Yankee Stadium.

Joe punched Blackburn's back with feathery blows. The trainer felt them with a grunt of satisfaction. Joe repeated the routine before every fight. People reached out to touch him but Joe looked straight ahead, his stare burning into the back of Blackburn's white T-shirt. His little punches kept coming until they reached the wooden steps and climbed through the ropes. The noise, now, was frightening.

Carnera was booed as he approached the ring. Joe was a big man but, sitting on a stool in his corner, he looked like a little boy as the Man Mountain trudged towards him. His mouth was dry. Chappie had once told him that fear made a man thirsty. Joe licked his lips instead of asking for a slug of water. He would be all right once they were fighting.

The dapper little ring announcer, Harry Balogh, moved to the centre of the ring. He pulled down the silver microphone which hung from the darkness above. 'Laideezzzz an' genlemennnn,' he shouted, his voice booming across the stadium, 'before proceedin' with this most important heavyweight contest

I wish to take the liberty of callin' upon you in the name of American sportsmanship, a spirit so fine it has made you, the American sporting public, world famous. I therefore ask you that the thought in your mind, and the feeling in your heart, be that, regardless of race, creed or colour, may the better man emerge victorious.'

Balogh lifted his head to the night sky and spread his arms wide, as if in relief that he had got the words out. The time had come. Arthur Donovan, the referee, called the fighters and their trainers together. Louis's bowed head almost touched Carnera's chest as Donovan told them to defend themselves at all times during the fifteen-round bout.

They turned back to opposite sides of the ring. Blackburn helped Louis out of his robe. The Bomber wore black trunks and shoes. 'OK Chappie,' Blackburn said, 'show this guy what you can do.'

The opening bell's jangling ring was swallowed by a bellow from the crowd. Both men moved quickly towards each other. Louis slid around Carnera and circled him. He threw a couple of jabs, as if to measure the distance between him and the giant. Carnera barrelled towards Louis and wrapped his huge arms around the young fighter. He clubbed the back of Louis's head while pressing down hard in an attempt to intimidate him. Louis did not try to escape. Instead, in a surprising show of strength, he forced Carnera backwards, as stoical as a butcher moving another massive slab of fresh meat into his freezer. Carnera snarled and, as they broke, tried to push Louis away with a clumsy shove.

Louis, his impassive mask intact, had already drifted back to the centre of the ring. His feet were planted on the canvas but his fists and torso twitched with sly little feints and ripples. Carnera went to counter the expected jab but Louis, instead, threw a fast overarm right which smacked into the Italian's half-open mouth. Such speed and power made Carnera open his eyes wide in shock. He would not make the same mistake of charging Louis again. Carnera watched him warily, more intent on working out from where the next blow might be launched than tagging Louis with anything other than the inoffensive jab he waved in the air. Louis stalked him methodically, waiting for his moment. It came after less than a minute when, having driven him to the ropes, Louis opened up with a vicious flurry of punches. A right cross split Carnera's upper lip. Blood seeped from his mouth as Louis hurt him with a left hook. Carnera's guard dropped and Louis targeted that immense head with precise combinations.

'Good work,' Blackburn said as Louis returned to his stool. 'That was easy, Chappie.' He wiped his fighter's face with a white towel before adding a note of criticism. 'Now forget the head-hunting. Remember what we worked on. Whack the body. Chop him down like he's some big old tree.'

After another right cross re-opened the gash above Carnera's mouth at the start of Round Two, Louis settled into his percussive body-punching rhythm. Again and again, controlling the middle of the ring, he would feint to the left or right and then step straight inside to hammer home his combinations. He rattled Carnera's ribs with both fists and drilled punches into the gut and chest as if looking for a way to get the big man's heart.

Carnera, his lips crusted in red, fought back briefly in the third, but a furious skirmish in which Louis was caught by a ringing right to the head did little to change the tenor of the fight. The Bomber rarely missed a punch and his numbing jabs and cruel hooks and crosses began to swell the Italian's already battered face. Carnera sought the refuge of the ropes. It was a mistake. Louis trapped him and rope-burns spread across Carnera's enormous white back. The Gorgonzola Tower began to melt in the searing heat.

Midway through the fifth round Carnera clinched desperately after another left from Louis almost dropped him. Although outweighed by sixty-four pounds, Louis lifted Carnera off his feet and twirled him around. 'Oh . . . oh . . .' Carnera moaned. 'I should be doing this to you.' Louis remained silent, his only answer coming in another sustained series of blows to both the body and head. The blood now spurted from Carnera's mouth.

Jack Blackburn knew the end was near. Just before the sixth he growled the command to Louis: 'Go get him.'

Poor Primo did not even see the short right cross that felled him. Instinctively, he attempted to pull himself up from the canvas but his legs collapsed beneath him. Louis, his arms resting against the top of the ropes, watched the Italian try again. Carnera finally made it to his feet with a slow shake of his head.

Even though many of his fights had been fixed, Carnera was a brave man. Without any hope of being rescued by the Mob this time, he could have stayed down. But Carnera tried to fight on. He stuck out his jab defiantly before, with Louis closing on him, he was reduced to hitting back wildly. Louis ghosted out of range and then ducked inside to connect with another crashing right cross. Carnera went down for a count of four. As he stood up and swayed helplessly, his corner urged him on. The Bomber, fast and deadly, razed him for the third and last time with a straight right and then a left hook. It was over. Arthur Donovan pulled Carnera away to safety.

Joe reached out with his right glove and touched Primo gently. The beaten man was too dazed to notice the hand on his back. Donovan led him towards his wooden stool. In the opposite corner, Chappie Blackburn reached out to hug Joe. Their embrace was perfunctory; and both men remembered not to smile.

Harry Balogh brought Joe back to the middle for the official announcement of his win. Holding him tightly by the wrist, the ring announcer shuffled him around the ring like a clockwork soldier so that Joe could acknowledge each section of the stadium. Bowing stiffly, Joe looked out into the dark arena, his face lit by the glare of flash bulbs as the cameras snapped and popped.

Joe wanted to cry with relief. He wanted to shout out his elation. It was the sweetest night of his life. People were on their feet, screaming his name, telling him that the world belonged to him. He had done it. He had won his first big fight in New York. He had crushed Carnera. Nothing could stop him now. Joe could feel the joy surging through him. But on the outside, even in exhilaration, his face was frozen.

At ringside, scratching away in ink or pounding at their typewriters, four hundred reporters went to work. They claimed to have witnessed the rise of a terrifying force in, as Davis Walsh wrote, 'the strange, wall-eyed, unblinking Negro'. Walsh, of the International News Service, filed his report faster than most. His opening words were already spitting down the wires to newspaper offices around the world: 'Something sly and sinister and perhaps not quite human came out of the African jungle tonight to strike down and utterly demolish Primo Carnera, the giant . . .'

Chapter Four

The Rivals

'If athletic greatness was a gift to be bestowed at will,' Bill Henry wrote in the *Los Angeles Times* after the fall of Carnera, 'the coloured race couldn't have chosen two more remarkable men than Jesse Owens and Joe Louis to be its outstanding representatives. Owens is being hailed as the greatest track-and-field athlete of all time . . . same thing goes for "Dead Pan" Joe Louis whose decisive defeat of Carnera has sent the scribes scurrying to the dictionaries seeking superlatives of greater scope than any they've used before.

'Being as famous as these two young men is a pretty tough test for the character of anyone. And it's sudden fame, too. The kind that will sweep you off your feet unless you're very careful. First Owens, only a few weeks ago, suddenly arrived at the threshold of notoriety achieved by few young men. Now Louis, another Negro, is thrust in front of the gawking, critical, staring world eager to hail him, spoil him and, if possible, ruin him.'

Jesse's life had changed utterly after Ann Arbor. The *Pittsburgh Courier* suggested that, like Joe Louis, 'the name of Jesse Owens is now as familiar as the name of the President of the United States . . . in no other way, except on the athletic field, would the name of a single Negro travel the circuit of general knowledge so rapidly'.

Although he and Mel Walker were the only Negroes on the Ohio State squad touring California that month, Jesse had been elevated to the role of track captain. For the *Call and Post*, one of the black newspapers which had questioned Owens's choice of Ohio eighteen months earlier, his 'election to the captain's office in his junior year is testimony that some progress has been made'. The paper thrust yet more responsibility on to the twenty-one-year-old. 'Admitting the presence of prejudice at Columbus, we say that Owens and the rest of the coloured squad must smash it from within.'

Jesse was more concerned that his only suit was laundered and pressed in time for the trip. Mel, however, needed a new suit. And while he had found the perfect grey tailored outfit in downtown Columbus, it would set him back $22.50. 'How much you got?' Jesse asked.

'Fifteen dollars,' Mel said mournfully.

Jesse reached into his pocket and counted out $7.50. 'Go get it, Mel. We gonna knock 'em dead in Cali' . . .'

On their first afternoon in Los Angeles, Ohio State shared training facilities with the University of Southern California's track team. Both sets of athletes stared in surprise at the crowd which had turned out at Bovard Field. It did not take long to see the reason for their appearance at a mid-week jog and stretch session. Jesse was hemmed in at the main entrance. Bill Henry reported that 'a motley mob, several hundred strong, composed of kids, students, newspapermen, photographers, track fans – even a bevy of Senegambian sirens from Central Avenue – surrounded this beautifully modeled grinning kid. He was pulled, hauled, shoved, ordered around, questioned and pestered until you'd think he'd get sore and swing on somebody. But at the end of the day he was the same smiling kid, with nothing in his appearance to indicate that on one afternoon a couple of weeks ago he ran and jumped into athletic immortality.'

Amid the jostling Jesse saw Quincella Nickerson. He had met

her at the station early that morning when she and another young beauty, Maggie-Mae Fleming, swanned to the front of the welcoming horde. They showed up again at the Sigma Chi fraternity house where Jesse and Mel were staying after a downtown hotel had refused them a room. Quincella and Maggie-Mae breezed over the familiar insult for they were members of the 'Club Sophisticates', a select group of black debutantes. In honour of Jesse, the Sophisticates had planned a cabaret evening at the swish Club Araby.

Quincella was outrageously pretty and flirty. She was the twenty-two-year-old daughter of William Nickerson Jr, the president of the Golden Life Insurance Company, and part of a West Coast Negro dynasty. Jesse had always been a sucker for a well-dressed girl and Quincella wore clothes of such elegance that he wanted to reach out and touch them.

She knew nothing about the more pungent world of the track, but Quincella picked her moment at Bovard Field. After they had swapped a friendly wave she allowed the reporters to get Jesse first. The snappers came next. Jesse's red Ohio vest and white shorts gleamed in the sunshine, and he thrilled the photographers by lying on his stomach, propping his chin on his hands as he grinned into their lenses.

Quincella moved closer when the pack around him dispersed. Jesse laughed when she asked if he always caused such a stir. They did not make quite the same fuss of him in Columbus.

She pointed demurely to her powder-blue sedan. 'That's my car,' Quincella said. 'Would you like a lift?'

He asked if Mel could join them. 'Of course,' Quincella said. 'C'mon, I'll take you two home for tea. My brothers will never forgive me if I don't introduce you.'

His week in LA developed a pattern. Every day, after training, Quincella picked up Jesse and Mel. They visited her father's office, went shopping and stepped out for afternoon tea. Jesse reciprocated by inviting her to join them for lunch with Will

Rogers. Hardly a day went by without another movie star dropping Jesse a line to say 'congratulations' or 'how about a drink?'. He liked meeting Mickey Rooney and Jack Oakie, and especially Clark Gable who turned out to be just a regular guy. Clark and Jesse spoke in intricate detail about the take-off techniques and body angles which provided the height necessary for the very longest leaps. Jesse thought that, outside of Larry Snyder and Charley Riley, he had never engaged in such an intelligent discussion of jumping. But he got the biggest bang of all in meeting Will Rogers. Beyond rope tricks and cowboy movies, Will knew a whole lot more than he did about life.

After lunch, Jesse and Quincella drifted off on their own. They went window-shopping – and a camera clicked as they admired a jewellery display at the front of a large department store. Jesse had already heard the whispers. Only the night before, a girl had joked that he and Quincella were becoming 'a hot item'. Jesse laughed. He and Quincella were friends. He had told her about Ruth and baby Gloria. Quincella, in turn, made him feel like one of her family. Jesse enjoyed dinner at the Nickerson home almost as much as all the parties. It was a house where he felt he could learn much about success.

William Nickerson was a formidable man. He made Jesse think that, once his track days were over, he too should move into business. Nickerson, however, embarrassed Jesse when, after their meal, he read aloud a lengthy article from that Friday morning's *Los Angeles Times*.

'"Mr Jesse Owens,"' Nickerson boomed, '"is polite, calm, confident and apparently not the least bit conceited. That's saying a good deal for any college boy. Owens is very conscientious. Coach Snyder never worries about his training. Owens wants to be a great athlete – and he expects to pay the price of living a reasonable life. He doesn't eat trick food. He likes to live a good wholesome life. He's a prime sleeper and he gets to bed pretty early. He never stays out after nine-thirty at night, except on Saturdays when he can roam around as much as he wants to.'''

Nickerson looked at his watch and roared. 'You've not got long to go before your Friday-night curfew, young man!'

A few hours later Jesse was the prime attraction at the Hollywood Legion's 'Celebrity Night' of boxing. He sat next to Mae West. He thought she would be loud and brassy, but they had a stimulating ringside conversation while watching the meaty fighters punch each other in the head. Afterwards, a group of them went out to her house in the Hollywood hills. Mae was kind to all of them but she paid most attention to Eddie O'Brien, a handsome 400m runner who came from one of the richest families in Ohio.

The next day, on 15 June, Jesse pulled off the old four-card trick. He won his usual quartet of events against the country's leading team, the Southern Californian Trojans, in front of 40,000 at the Los Angeles Coliseum. The sweetest moment came soon after he stepped on the cinder. Two little white girls raced across the track. They were pursued by a hefty security guard. The first girl brushed her fingers shyly against Jesse's arm while her friend offered him a paper cup to sign.

'What's your name?' Jesse asked as he reached for her pen.

'Maureen Foley,' the eleven year old whispered.

He wrote the words – *For Maureen Foley, with best wishes, Jesse Owens* – on her soda cup.

The stadium guard caught Maureen's pal. 'Well,' the freckled girl said defiantly, 'I got to touch him . . .'

The girls made the Sunday papers, as did the first photographs of Jesse and Quincella strutting round town. He only began to feel uneasy when he was told that a reporter had prised a quote from Quincella that she and Jesse were soon to be engaged. The *Pittsburgh Courier* were planning to print their 'exclusive' in the next few weeks. Jesse tried to shut it from his mind.

It worked – at least for a while. On 22 June he won four national collegiate titles. Before a crowd of 18,000 at Berkeley University, his victories in the 100-yard and 220-yard sprints, the 220-yard low hurdles and the long jump matched his Ann Arbor sweep. He scored forty of Ohio State's forty-one points – which gave them second place behind Southern California. Owens's dominance meant that, on his own, he earned more points than forty other college teams – including the giants of Michigan, UCLA, Notre Dame, Princeton, Yale, Harvard, Stanford and Temple University. The *Los Angeles Times* claimed that 'the human antelope Jesse Owens' had produced 'the most amazing display of individual prowess ever witnessed in the fair west'.

San Diego, 26 June 1935

Four nights later, at his last track meet in California, Jesse and his great rival, Eulace Peacock, clashed again. Eulace was one of only two sprinters in the world who could still unnerve Jesse. The other was the imperious veteran Ralph Metcalfe. An Olympic silver medallist in 1932, Metcalfe was ferociously competitive. Laidback Eulace was more like Jesse, and they became close friends.

Born a year after Jesse in 1914, Eulace was another Alabama boy. He came from Dothan and the same history of slavery. The Peacocks migrated north to Union, New Jersey, around the time Jesse's family moved to Cleveland. Eulace began running and jumping just when Jesse did – and they broke the same schoolboy records in different parts of the country.

In 1933, in New Jersey, Eulace set a new junior world best in the long jump by leaping 24 feet 6 inches. He was ecstatic when he told his family the news. After they had drunk a couple of bottles of pop to celebrate, Eulace switched on the radio. A few minutes later he heard a sports-flash. Jesse had just jumped even further in Cleveland. 'It's because of you, Owens,' Eulace moaned, 'that I only held that damn record for two hours . . .'

Their battle for supremacy was unresolved. They had swapped victories throughout the 1935 indoor season, and were already looking towards the Olympic Games. Owens had a year left to find a way of mastering Peacock; but he seemed to be inching ahead. In their first encounter of the summer, during the college nationals at Berkeley, Owens beat Peacock easily in the long jump with a leap over 26 feet. In the 100-yard sprint, he led from the start but Peacock closed him down. With ten yards left Peacock looked as if he was about to power past Owens. Yet Peacock's unstoppable surge never came. The gap remained at half a yard.

Ben Ogden, Peacock's coach in Philadelphia, had tried to persuade Owens to join Temple University in the summer of 1934. But Ogden believed even more in Peacock. At six foot, and 180 pounds, Peacock was stronger than Owens. Rather than floating across the track, he propelled himself down the cinders with driving aggression. If he could refine that style, Ogden was certain that Peacock would dominate the sprints.

Ogden and Peacock spoke in hushed tones as they limbered-up on a sultry evening in San Diego. Peacock looked more determined than ever. Jesse's stomach tightened. How could *he* concentrate? Ruth's letter lay in his bag at the side of the track.

Jesse had recognised her girlish handwriting with a strange ache. Seventeen nights had passed since he arrived in California. He had not found a moment in all that time to escape the whirl and call Ruth. That morning he had slit open the back of her envelope with growing dread. He could tell without even reading. Trouble was coming; the kind of cold hard trouble you had to write down rather than say out loud.

The ten-line letter was terse and wounded: *I've heard nothing from you . . . the newspaper . . . these photographs . . . this Quincella Nickerson . . .*

As they walked to the starting line, Eulace glanced at him. Jesse seemed strangely quiet. 'Good luck,' Eulace said.

'You too, champ.'

It would be Jesse's eighteenth event since Ann Arbor. He had won all seventeen of his sprint, hurdles and long-jump competitions over that past month and a day. The 100 yards in San Diego would be his last test before the US Nationals. He needed one more big run to dent Peacock's confidence.

Owens was out the holes first, but it was a smaller lead than usual. Peacock was on his shoulder at the forty-yard mark, charging down the track with a mighty flow. He drew level with twenty to go. They ran for the line, stride for stride, as if joined by an invisible stretch of twine. And then came the break. Peacock seemed to burst through the tape first.

They turned to look back at the officials gathering in a frantic huddle. Jesse gulped down another breath. He was drained. His streak could not last for ever. He walked towards his bag, where his track-top covered Ruth's letter. Life had just become a little more complicated.

The announcer conferred with the officials. 'Ladies and gentlemen,' he eventually crackled into his microphone, 'we've just witnessed one of the tightest finishes ever seen in San Diego. It's not been easy to separate these two great young runners, but we do have a winner of the 100-yard dash.' He paused dramatically. 'JESSE OWENS!'

Eulace offered his hand. 'They could have gone the other way,' Jesse said.

'It's OK, Jesse. We'll do it again next Saturday. Maybe I'll get you then.' And Eulace slipped away, in search of reassurance from Ben Ogden.

'Hey, Peacock!' a voice shouted. Eulace recognised one of the officials. The man ran towards him and took Eulace by the arm. 'I'm not sure I should be telling you this, Eulie, but you won that race. They'd already carved Jesse's name on the trophy – that's why they were talking so long. Because it was so close they went with the name already on the cup. They didn't want no big fuss – so they gave it to Jesse.'

Peacock absorbed the news silently before he nodded. 'It don't matter who they say won. The important thing is I *know* I can beat Jesse.'

They met again in Lincoln, Nebraska, the following Tuesday. Jesse and Eulace were both preoccupied as they prepared for the most significant track event of the year – the AAU National Championships. The finals of the 100m and the long jump were scheduled for that Thursday, 4 July. The seriousness with which Owens regarded Peacock's challenge was made plain by his decision not to enter the 200m or the 220-yard hurdles. Although he was the defending champion in the jump he had failed to win either the 100 or 200m titles in 1934 – losing to Ralph Metcalfe who had clinched the sprint double for his third consecutive year.

Jesse's mind was on Ruth. The *Pittsburgh Courier*'s front-page story on 29 June had featured a startling photograph of Quincella staring adoringly at Jesse. He knew it had been taken on the station platform just before he caught the train from Los Angeles to San Francisco. Quincella was one of a gang who had come to wave him goodbye. A photographer had asked if he could take a pic of Jesse and his young lady. 'Sure,' Jesse said. He had nothing to hide. Quincella laughed as he pulled her in close. The camera caught her smile and the ring on the finger. *Wedding Bells?* asked the *Courier*'s headline.

Their LA reporter, Bernice Patton, was unequivocal. 'Jesse Owens, the world's most famous track-and-field athlete, who is scheduled to represent America during the 1936 Olympics in Berlin, Germany, startled Los Angeles when he high-jumped into the matrimonial arena with the authentic, informal, public announcement that he and Quincella Nickerson, pretty Angel

City socialite, are engaged to be married. This writer received an exclusive interview from Miss Nickerson who blushingly accepted congratulations and related interesting events about the galloping romance ... Affirming the love-on-first-sight romance, Miss Nickerson said, "Really, there isn't much to say other than Jesse and I are engaged to be married. I don't know when we will marry. We have no definite plans. Everything happened so suddenly."'

Jesse had phoned Ruth long-distance soon after his arrival in Lincoln, calling the beauty salon in Cleveland where she worked. He tried to convince her that the whole story was based on nothing more than gossip and a throwaway joke Quincella had made to a woman who turned out to be a reporter. Quincella was already engaged to someone else, a fellow who just happened to be out of town when Jesse was in LA. She was nothing more than a friend, one of many he and Mel had made on tour. Ruth should speak to Mel. He would tell her there was nothing in it.

Ruth was a patient woman; but she had waited a long time for Jesse. She was his sweetheart. She was the mother of Gloria, their little girl who was only a month away from her third birthday. She could take the hurt entailed in living in Cleveland while Jesse ran from his base in Columbus and roamed the country as a dashing young buck. She could take almost anything as long as she knew he would be coming back to her. But, Ruth said evenly, she would not be shamed. She would not stand by quietly while he played some game with a hussy who had the dumbest name she had ever heard.

If Jesse's anguish was locked inside him, Eulace Peacock's pain was reflected across America. It had nothing to do with running; and everything to do with race. In Lincoln, he told Jesse another familiar story. Eulace knew that Jesse, more than anyone, would understand the way he told it. Glad of the diversion, Jesse sat and listened.

On the long journey from California to Nebraska, Eulace and the Temple University boys had taken the train from Los Angeles. All five of them were Negroes, so they found an empty carriage at the back of the Pullman. They were not looking for trouble. When the white conductor checked their tickets they lifted their hats and spoke politely. They explained that they were on their way to the national championships.

'So I won't hear a peep out of none of you boys – right?'

'Right,' Eulace smiled.

'OK,' the man nodded.

The first few hours passed peacefully. Then the train shuddered to a stop. When they heard voices outside, Eulace pulled down the window and inched out his head. He picked out the conductor moving along the outside of the train, rapping on windows and passing on the message that there had been a real bad storm thirty miles away. Trees, hit by lightning, had fallen on the track. It would take all night to clear them. At the next crossing, they would take a looping diversion. They would head deep down into New Mexico and follow the track which ran along the border with Texas. By dawn they would be clear into Oklahoma and heading back up in the right direction through Kansas and then on to Nebraska.

Eulace closed the window. 'You hear that?'

'Yeah,' Eulace's friend Al Threadgill grunted. 'It's real Dixie country down there.'

The train began to move. They closed their eyes, and were soon asleep. Eulace was not sure how many hours slipped by before they hissed to a halt again. They tried to doze on but, this time, the voices and crunching feet were much closer to the rear of the train. A railway guard approached the conductor. In the darkness of their carriage, they listened quietly.

'You got some niggers on this train?' the guard shouted. All five of them sat up, suddenly alert.

'That's right,' the conductor answered. 'Five coloured fellers at the end.'

'You know you're on the Lubbock line, dontcha?' the guard said.

'Yeah, we had to take this route because of a storm way back. We're switching to the Wichita track soon.'

'Niggers ain't meant to ride on white trains out here.'

'These boys are from a top college back east. They're athletes – even competing in the national championships in a couple of days.'

'They still niggers,' the guard insisted.

'So what do you want me to do?'

'Get 'em off this train.'

There was a long pause. Eulace and the others tensed in the sweltering carriage.

'You do it,' the conductor finally said. 'If you want them off, you go right ahead.'

The silence seemed endless. Eulace could imagine the two men staring at each other. He was ready for whatever happened next.

'Go on, get outta here,' the guard snapped abruptly. 'Take your niggers with you.'

Jesse noticed how his friend laughed when he said 'your niggers'. Eulace delighted in his own imitation of a Texan accent, but that laugh also covered the pain and fear he had felt on the train. It was the same hurt Jesse had been through more times than he could count. He had been kicked off trains and buses. He had felt white hands cover his face and push back hard when he tried to step through restaurant doorways. He had been refused permission to run in South Carolina, just like Eulace had been banned from a meet in Louisiana. He began to laugh, too. It sure was better than moaning or crying.

Even at the Nationals they were not clear of those same white voices. Eulace told Jesse about the latest joker. 'There's this kid from Georgia running in the heats for the hundred tomorrow. He's walking round the dressing-room saying that if any nigger beats him, then he's gonna quit running.'

'Well,' Jesse said, 'I guess we won't see him on a track after tomorrow . . .'

Lincoln, Nebraska, 4 July 1935

Jesse woke that morning to more grim news. Most of the papers carried the latest Associated Press story about his turbulent love life: 'Jesse Owens, the sensational sprint and broad-jump champion, denied vehemently on Thursday the published rumours that he had become engaged to a beautiful young Los Angeles "deb". The young Clevelander asserted that Miss Minnie Ruth Solomon of his home town and to whom he had been betrothed for more than a year was the only girl whose name might be authentically linked with his . . . He said Miss Quincella Nickerson was a most charming young woman. "However, how could I have become engaged to her?" he asked rather bitterly. "Why, there was never any sentimental discussion between us. I only knew her for three days and certainly one could not grow so serious in so short a time. At least I couldn't. I'm not that sort of chap."'

The *Cleveland Plain Dealer* was more ruthless, sending a newsman to meet Jesse six hours before the 100m final. The reporter asked Jesse if he planned to marry Ruth.

'Yes, of course. We're engaged.'

'When are you going to marry her?'

'As soon as these championships are over I'm heading back to Cleveland to sort it out.'

The *Plain Dealer* man spoke curtly. His editor was planning a front-page story on Jesse and Ruth. The paper would feature a snapshot of the couple's little girl, Gloria, and highlight the fact that she had been born out of wedlock. The *Plain Dealer* would then address the 'Quincella issue'. As far as the news hack could tell, his editor would only change his mind if Jesse gave him an exclusive 'good news' story.

'I've already told you,' Jesse said despairingly. 'I plan to marry Ruth.'

'It would be even better news if we could inform our readers this weekend.'

Jesse had already sent a telegram to Ruth telling her that he would return to Cleveland's Union Terminal at 5 p.m. that Friday. But that was his business. 'I've got nothing more to say,' he told the reporter. 'Right now, I've got a race to think about.'

He travelled alone to the University of Nebraska's Memorial Stadium, and tried to focus on his more immediate task. At two o'clock that afternoon he would race both Ralph Metcalfe and Eulace Peacock over 100m. The winner would be proclaimed the fastest man in America. Metcalfe had been the country's premier sprinter for four years. He'd routinely beaten his younger rivals. Peacock would invariably shrug his shoulders and say, 'The big old lug beat me and Jesse again – jus' like he's our daddy.'

Yet Metcalfe could not dominate sprinting indefinitely. The week before, in a warm-up, he had lost to Bob Packard, a seventeen-year-old Rockford High schoolboy. The momentum had swung towards Jesse. Peacock, however, was closing fast. It was too tight to call.

Inside the concrete arena, with the heat reaching 102 degrees, Jesse was no longer sure he cared who won. He wanted the race to be over so that he could return to Ruth. Jesse set about his preparations mechanically, hardly lifting his head as he stretched and practised his start.

The last hour dragged but, finally, they took their positions in the centre of the track. Metcalfe was in lane three, Owens in four and Peacock in five. Owens wiped the corners of his mouth.

They were flecked with dry white saliva, which made him look more nervous than he felt. He just longed to get away.

There were eleven false starts, two of them caused by Owens. While they crouched for the twelfth time, the incredulous starter, Johnny McHugh, saw Owens twitch again. He made them rise, so saving Owens from disqualification. 'Come on, boys,' McHugh said irritably. 'Let's try once more.'

They went down again. This time they made a clean start. Peacock, the coolest of the trio during the incessant interruptions, was away first. Metcalfe, a notoriously slow starter, was already second, ahead of Owens. They held that position for thirty, then sixty, then ninety metres. Five metres from the tape, Peacock arched his back and thrust out his chest. He was over the line and, within seconds, racing into the arms of one of his Temple team-mates. 'You beat Jesse, Eulie!' his friend yelled, 'you damn well beat Jesse!'

'Where's Metcalfe?' Peacock panted more anxiously.

Peacock beat Metcalfe, with Owens running a dismal third, in a time of 10.2. It would have been a world record, but AAU officials ruled that a light wind made his mark ineligible. Peacock didn't care. He had beaten Metcalfe for the first time in his career – and he had whipped Owens.

An hour later, and still flying, Peacock challenged Owens in the long jump. Owens led after the first round with an ordinary leap of 25 feet 9½ inches. With his fourth jump, he hit a more typical mark of 26 feet 1¼ inches. Owens was still seven inches short of his world best.

Peacock saw his chance. For his last jump, he hit the take-off board squarely and hurled himself through the air. Peacock ploughed two deep furrows into the far end of the pit. It was his first-ever jump over 26 feet. Peacock danced when the exact measurement was announced: 26 feet 3 inches. He was in the lead at last. Owens had one more jump.

Fifteen thousand pairs of eyes watched the champion. Owens

began to run, his stare pinned to some distant point in the freshly raked sand. He flew from the board. Owens landed amid a tense roar. He dusted himself down and watched the tape measure stretch and quiver. The track announcer, the excitable Ted Canty, confirmed that, for the first time in history, two men had cleared 26 feet in the same competition.

'Jesse Owens has just leaped an incredible 26 feet and . . . 2¼ inches! He is three-quarters of an inch short of our new champion. From Temple University, and also the new 100m champion of America . . . *Youuulaceee Peeeecock*!'

Jesse left Lincoln early the next morning. His loss to Peacock mattered little. He was going to marry Ruth, just like he had always said. She was the girl who had stood behind him on those icy mornings when he sprinted down the pavements of east Cleveland. She was the first girl he had ever kissed. She was the woman he wanted.

Jesse longed for his old life where it had been just him and Ruth – and the track. So he allowed the *Dealer* their scoop. On Saturday 6 July 1935, on their front page, they printed their exclusive: 'Jesse Owens, Cleveland's world famous coloured track star, was married last night at 9.30 to Miss Minnie Ruth Solomon, less than four hours after he had returned to the city from a series of track events in the west. He went to his home at 2178 East 100th Street, showed his mother and father a watch he had won at Los Angeles, changed into a fresh suit of clothes and, accompanied by a newspaperman, went calling on Miss Solomon. "Well, Ruth, are we going to get married tonight?" Jesse asked. "If you got the ring," Miss Solomon replied. Jesse did not have the ring. He did not have a marriage license and no minister had been arranged. He found the ring at home, a friend persuaded Frank Zizelman, marriage clerk of the Probate Court, to issue a license at 7.30 pm and Miss Solomon persuaded Rev. Ernest Hall of East Mount Zion Baptist Church to leave a choir practice to perform the ceremony at the bride's home of 9113 Beckman Avenue. Jesse, before walking into the living room to face the Rev. Hall, pinned a white carnation into his button-hole and hummed *I'm Heading For The Last Round-Up*. Miss Solomon, meanwhile, arranged the train of a peach-coloured chiffon dress. "Do you take this man for your lawful wedded husband?" intoned the Rev. Hall at the conclusion of the ceremony. "Yes," the bride said, "yes . . .'"

Ten hours later, just as the *Plain Dealer* hit the streets, Jesse left Cleveland. He headed east this time, a twenty-one-year-old husband forced to leave his new wife and child for yet more track meetings in Ontario, Buffalo and New York. Running had started to feel like work; and unpaid work at that.

On the day after his marriage to Ruth he lost to Peacock in the 100-yard dash at Crystal Beach in Ontario. Owens led for the first seventy-five yards before Peacock blazed past him. Two days later, on Monday 8 July, at the Buffalo Police Games, Peacock won the 100m in 10.5, after an inadvertent mid-track collision slowed Owens. Peacock was cleared of any illegal use of his elbow. On a wet Tuesday night, twenty-four hours later, Peacock winged his way down a soaking Ohio Field track in New York to beat Owens by half a step and take the last 100-yard dash in 9.7 seconds.

In the space of six days, Peacock had beaten Owens on five successive occasions. Lawson Robertson, confirmed as the head coach of the US Olympic team in Berlin, insisted that 'Peacock is the fastest and most consistent starter of all our sprinters. He also has a better finish than Owens.' Jesse's hero as a schoolboy, Charley Paddock, the 1924 Olympic champion, saw Peacock as the only sprinting certainty for Berlin. 'Owens is pretty much burned out,' Paddock wrote. 'If he specialises in the 200 metres next year, and leaves the 100 metres and the low hurdles, he might still figure. He certainly cannot continue to run in three events and the broad jump as well and hope to make the grade. As for the short dash, the Ohio State boy is far too slow off the marks to do much good in the hundred.'

In New York, the day after his fifth straight defeat, Owens sounded equally downbeat. 'Of course I'm a little worn down,' he told the writer John Lardner. 'I've been doing a lot of running this summer. I need to lay off now and take a little rest. But Eulace is a great runner – and a very good jumper. This boy has been right behind me for quite a while. It looks as though he's more than caught up now.'

Owens was even more open with the *New York Amsterdam News* columnist Marvel Cooke: 'It's going to take a special man to defeat Eulace Peacock. You see, I've already reached my peak. Peacock is just now reaching his. He's a real athlete. I don't know whether I can defeat him again.'

Chapter Five

When Jesse Met Joe

Joe Louis looked at Jesse Owens and he saw himself. It felt good. It felt eerie. They were twenty-one years old. They came from Alabama. They moved north. They beat the stutter. They made it on the track and in the ring. They made it with the girls. They made the papers. They became part of the same damn headline. Joe shook his head at the kind of sad story his sisters loved to read on the front page of the *Pittsburgh Courier*: *'You'll Never Know,' says Joe; Jesse Owens in Triangle!*

'The handsome Jesse Owens, whose winged feet have won him the appellation of the world's fastest human, is entangled in the meshes of love. Two lonely female hearts beat as one for the great sprinter, as he stands ready for the greatest race of his life . . . the matrimonial track. Joe Louis, the fighting Adonis, who brought the world to its feet when he knocked out the Man Mountain Carnera, is also reported to have been stung by the love bug and is on his way to connubial bliss.'

Joe didn't know what they were banging on about most of the time. He liked plain words. Words that anyone could understand. But the *Courier* was sneaky. 'Dame Rumor has it that the Brown Bomber is engaged to Miss Elsie Roxborough . . . the *Pittsburgh Courier* interviewed the beautiful Elsie yesterday.

When asked was there any truth in the reported engagement she said, "At the present time, I cannot tell you anything definite, but as soon as I am ready to make a statement, I will let you know." When approached on the same question in New York, stoical Joe declared: "If there is someone, you will never find it out."'

At least they got the last part right. Joe now knew what Jesse had been through with that girl out west.

Roxy and Julian Black sat opposite him. They had spread two different editions of the *Courier* in front of him. Their managerial faces wrinkled as they watched. Joe was a slow reader. The first piece, about him and Jesse, came from the 6 July 1935 edition. The second had been published that very Saturday, 20 July, and it told another tale.

'Joe Louis, heavyweight sensation, has discovered that there's no ring as devastating as the love ring. The Brown Bomber's enlightenment came after a cute little red brick, hurled through his shiny Buick, did plenty damage to his automobile and feelings. The hurler is said to be Miss Elsie Roxborough ... It was at the Club Plantation, during the Blue Hour, when Freddie Guinyard introduced the young fighter to Bennie Mitchell, former chorus girl with the Brownskin Models and crowned *Queen of Detroit's Night Clubs* last February.'

Joe almost smiled at that one. Freddie, the soft-hearted shark in the sharp hat, had been his best buddy since he moved to Detroit in 1926. They used to steal fruit from the Eastern Market before they picked a more legit trade. They were still schoolboys when, late in the afternoons, they began to deliver blocks of ice across Paradise Valley. Joe, the strong lug, did the lugging; Freddie, the skinny punk, collected the dough. It was great business. Few black homes in Detroit owned a fridge. Joe and Freddie drove a horse-drawn carriage with a burlap draped over the ice to slow the melting.

On one of their ice trips, Joe told Freddie his hottest secret.

He had just had sex with a girl. Bennie Franklin, apart from being a year older than Joe, was his eldest sister's step-daughter.

'So what?' Freddie laughed. 'I'm tellin' nobody.'

Seven years on, Freddie and Joe were still keeping secrets. Bennie had changed her name back to Mitchell – her real mother's name. Bennie and Joe had been lovers for more than six years. There was a whole lot of stuff about him that the *Pittsburgh Courier* would have loved to know. But they were getting nothing of the real story.

'What's happening, Joe?' Roxy asked. 'How come these stories keep popping up?'

Joe shrugged. The papers were Roxy's business.

'I'll deal with Elsie,' Roxy promised. 'You just forget this other girl. If people start saying you're the new Jack Johnson we're in trouble.'

'They did it to Jesse Owens,' Joe mumbled. 'They set him up.'

'Yeah,' Black grunted. 'And the white papers wanna nail you more than Jesse Owens. When it comes to the heavyweight championship we're on their turf.'

'Look,' Roxy said, 'this thing will blow over in a day or two. By then we'll be in Cleveland.'

For Roxborough and Black, the *Courier*'s latest love-saga had been a mild diversion. Both girls were coloured. Even the awkward presence of Elsie, in a curious way, worked to their advantage. Where Jack Johnson had swaggered around with white prostitutes, Joe had only got involved in a mix-up with his manager's niece. But the canny pair hated even a trace of scandal. The Cleveland trip, and a meeting with Jesse Owens, was a chance to get back on track.

On the night Joe fought Primo Carnera, a giant electric billboard shone down on Harlem. High above the entrance to the Savoy Ballroom, on Lenox Avenue and 140th Street, the words gleamed: MEET JOE LOUIS IN PERSON TONIGHT! Twenty thousand people thronged the streets outside just before midnight. The crazy ones up front tried to break down the doors, and the 250 extra policemen bussed in to deal with the post-fight crush struggled to hold them back. Dozens more emergency patrol wagons poured across the city – only to be blocked as far away as 125th Street.

Men and women hung from apartment windows along Lenox and Seventh. While they waited for a glimpse of the Bomber they cheered the raucous scenes below. On Seventh Avenue, in-between dancing the Shim-Sham Shimmy and the Lindy Hop, black couples kissed and cried openly. A siren-screaming truck, followed by twenty-five police motorcycles, climbed the sidewalk on Lenox. Terrified people were pushed back against the tenements. A narrow lane opened up, but small boys kept jumping in front of the traffic. They punched the air and shouted, 'That's the way Joe did it!'

Joe was locked in an office at the back of the Savoy. The journey from a friend's apartment on 153rd Street had been agonising – despite fooling a crowd expecting him to parade in from the opposite direction. Inside a darkened car, Joe had gazed blankly at streets which streamed past like mysterious rivers of light. Only the fight felt real. The rest was a hazy dream.

But it was a great dream. Joe had conquered New York.

At the Savoy, however, he'd waited listlessly while a New York City police inspector, John De Martini, told Charlie Buchanan, the ballroom manager, that 'It'll be murder if Joe steps in front of that mob outside.' John Roxborough soothed Buchanan by suggesting that Joe show his face on stage before departing swiftly by the route they had come. They would also waive his $2,000 appearance fee. That did the trick.

By 3 a.m., Joe was deep in sweet honey. Tucked away in a corner of the Cotton Club, he smiled at the gorgeous women surrounding him, the fight fading from his mind with the touch of silky skin. He pulled down the deadpan face and slid back out into the city via a side exit – a couple of girls in breathless tow.

Joe Louis had become a headline and an icon. No matter how long he lived, he would never be seen as an ordinary man. Yet to white America he was still a nigger. Some hacks, like Jack Cuddy, followed Louis on his weekend break to Atlantic City. On 30 June 1935, Cuddy's UP agency report was printed across America: 'Young Joe Louis, Michigan Mahogany Maimer, entrained for his Detroit home tonight after capping his first professional invasion of the East with a promenade down the world's most famous boardwalk. This five-mile stroll down the "silky way", where the world and his missus come to show off, was a greater triumph for Shuffling Joe than his six-round victory over gigantic Primo Carnera. It satisfied a life-time aspiration of the erstwhile Alabama pickaninny. It transformed the deadpan dynamiter into a laughing jubilant chap – a jungle man on parade.'

Roxborough and Black had worked him hard. From his debut on 4 July 1934 to the New York extravaganza on 25 June 1935 he had fought twenty-three times: a fight, on average, every sixteen days. Joe needed a break, so he went back to the people who mattered most to him.

Joe swamped his family in Detroit with presents. His mother, as strong as she was plump, gave him the best gift in return. Lillie treated him like he was still the same old Joe, just one of the fourteen kids she and his step-father, Pat Brooks, called their own. Not everyone, however, was immune to his fame. On his second day at home, Joe's sister Eulalia watched him walk down a Detroit street. People rushed out to see the Bomber. The elation was addictive. Eulalia sprinted after the others, only stopping when she suddenly realised she was chasing her little brother: 'What the hell am I running behind *him* for?'

He headed next for Chicago. Marva Trotter worked as a stenographer at the *Chicago Defender*. She was too pretty to be a writer, and far too smart. Joe allowed her to bring along a girl-friend to act as chaperone whenever they went out. He moved carefully with Marva. But he allowed himself one indulgence when he got back from New York – he bought her a car worth $7,200 just to show how much he loved her. She smiled and breathed the loveliest 'yes' when he said it was time for them to get real serious.

Cleveland, 23 July 1935

That Tuesday morning, at exactly seven o'clock, Jesse Owens arrived for work at Alonzo Wright's Service Station in east Cleveland. His short-sleeved shirt and canvas shoes were sparkling white. The cocked cap on his head was the same navy blue as his trousers. It was his third summer at Alonzo Wright's. The bespectacled Mr Wright, who called himself a 'Negro entre-preneur', said the fastest man in the world had a place on the pump for life. Jesse hoped for a little more but, in the meantime, there were worse ways to earn a buck.

Most of the time he rushed around doing everything for little or no pay. Encouraged by Larry Snyder, he had just spent a couple of days allowing a black professor of anthropology, William Montague Cobb, to put his body through a detailed examination to determine whether or not his speed and jumping ability were rooted in 'racial characteristics'. Jesse didn't mind having his legs, arms and torso X-rayed, measured and analysed by a fellow as decent as Dr Cobb. But he already knew the answer to that Howard University study. It was simple – he had worked his butt off for seven years.

Dr Cobb reached the same conclusion. He argued that 'pseudo-scientific conjecture', such as the assumption that a longer heel-bone, said to be characteristic in Negroes, ensured greater sprinting power and jumping leverage, was meaningless.

Jesse's heel bone was no longer than that of an average white man. Cobb also suggested that Jesse had 'a typically Caucasian' calf muscle – unlike Frank Wykoff, the fastest white man in America, whose muscles were more classically 'Negroid'. Jesse Owens's athletic prowess, Cobb stressed, was due to 'industry, training, incentive and courage'.

Jesse walked up and down the forecourt, humming some nameless tune while his eyes swept restlessly across the street outside. As soon as a car turned into the filling station, he was over in a grinning flash.

'Yes sir?' he would smile, his rag-filled hand moving fast over the hood of the car. 'What'll it be today, sir? Gas? Engine check?'

By the time the other pump-hands had yawned and stretched, Jesse would have polished another car, filled it with gas and topped up the oil and water. As long as he was busy, and on the move, life was great. And, that morning, life was better than ever. Alonzo Wright had given him permission to knock off early. It was not every day, after all, that Joe Louis came to Cleveland.

Jesse stepped out just before noon in a beige gabardine suit with a matching silk handkerchief flouncing out of his tuck-pleated breast pocket. His brilliant white Florsheim shoes clicked on the sidewalk as he crossed over Central Avenue and turned on to East 55th Street. People called out his name and car-horns hooted in greeting as he strode past with a smile as broad as the lapels on his suit.

He felt nervous. Jesse admired Joe Louis with an intensity that made him feel like a fan rather than an equal. He was unsure what the fighter would make of him when they finally met. Joe did not come across as a fellow who would waste time on the cheerful banter Jesse normally reeled out in strange company.

Joe and his entourage were at the Majestic Hotel on East 55th. John Roxborough had left word at reception. As soon as

Jesse skipped up the front steps, he was taken to Joe's suite on the top floor. Roxborough opened the door with a flourish. '*Jesse Owens!* C'mon in, Joe's itching to meet you!'

Joe Louis walked towards him with a little smile and a large outstretched hand. 'Jesse,' he said quietly, 'how ya' doin?'

'I'm doing great,' Jesse beamed.

Jesse and Joe stood in the centre of the room and shook hands vigorously as if neither was quite sure what to do next. 'Wow, champ,' Jesse eventually joked, 'it's great to shake hands with the most famous man in America.'

'Ain't that you?' Joe laughed. 'You look a king in that suit . . .'

Jesse looked at Joe's tan gabardine suit and bright white Florsheims. 'How about that?' Jesse said as his eyes swept across their almost matching outfits.

Joe introduced him to Jack Blackburn and Julian Black. They were friendly, but there was an edge to the old trainer and the slick manager which suggested they had seen more in life than Jesse ever would. They were not the kind of men he would like to offend.

'We're letting the *Plain Dealer* take a couple of shots of you and Joe together,' Roxy said. 'Is that OK?'

'Sure,' Jesse said.

Joe, who was less keen on photographers, remained silent as a chattering man was shown into the large room. It may have been nervous energy on his part but neither Jesse nor Joe had ever heard anyone talk so fast or loud. Joe ambled out on to the balcony for a breath of more tranquil air. Jesse and the photographer followed him.

They peered over the balcony. A few hundred people pointed and waved at them. Jesse waved back. Joe stood motionless as his name was shouted.

'They're calling you, Joe,' the photographer confirmed. 'Must be a swell feeling . . .'

'Yeah,' Joe said. 'Real swell.'

Joe looked blankly at Jesse. The runner felt as if his own face had frozen.

'Boy,' the photographer whooped as he peered through the box-shaped lens, 'that's nice an' moody . . .'

Roxy kicked him out five minutes later. Joe immediately relaxed. He and Jesse talked about clothes as they leaned against the brick wall at the far end of the balcony. Joe dug out a card from his trouser pocket and handed it to Jesse:

BILLY TAUB

By Special Appointment

TAILOR TO THE ROYALTY OF SPORTSDOM

Duke Ellington, Joe said, had introduced him to Billy Taub, who made suits for Babe Ruth, Kid Chocolate, Dizzy Dean, Bojangles Robinson and, of course, the Duke himself. Joe had a plan. He and Bojangles would take Jesse down to 40th and Broadway to meet Billy.

Jesse felt giddy. Joe spoke of Duke Ellington as coolly as Jesse might mention Pop Riley. And Bojangles Robinson was one of his best pals. Jesse was even more surprised by the warmth of Joe. Who would have thought it? They spoke easily and openly. Jesse told Joe about California and the newspaper saga, glad that he had a happy ending in Ruth. The fighter responded with his own snappy breakdown. 'I don't wanna give up foolin' with the other girls,' Joe admitted, 'but I wanna get Marva.' Jesse smiled and nodded.

An hour later, deep in Skurdy's Restaurant, across the road from the Majestic, the fighter was surrounded by jostling men and women. The people crowding around Jesse were far more polite. There was none of that desperate craving that threatened to swallow up Joe. The big man did not allow it to disturb him. Joe's right hand did the work of signing autographs and pumping hands. He kept his left hand free so that he could use a spoon to shovel soup into his mouth. Jesse wrote his own name across napkins and shirts.

The crush became almost unbearable. Sergeant Jim Cunat and Patrolman Warren Stainbrook, assuming that a riot had ripped through the restaurant, radioed for emergency back-up. They then forced their way through the fevered mob – only to discover that Joe Louis was taking a spot of lunch before he and Jesse Owens headed out to the city's Parade of Champions. The policemen relaxed and waited their turn to get the signature of the future heavyweight champion of the world.

Joe looked at Jesse and winked. He knew Jesse understood the madness. They started laughing as they shook their heads at each other. What could they do? They might as well take on America together. Roxy had it all mapped out. After New York and LA, Chicago and Cleveland, the capital itself would be the next to fall. Jesse and Joe were heading for Washington. They were thrilled. The girls down on U Street in DC, so they'd heard, were more than fine.

Washington DC, 26 August 1935

'The Improved Benevolent and Protective Order of Elks', a countrywide organisation dedicated to values of 'charity, justice, brotherly love and fidelity', was still separated by the old divide. Prevented from belonging to the same group as their white counterparts, the coloured Elks had invited Jesse and Joe to their annual convention in Washington. They would be awarded medals of achievement and lifetime membership of the Elks.

Joe didn't care about the Elks. He was more taken with Jesse's tie. 'I like them colours,' Joe nodded approvingly at Jesse, who had chosen an even brighter tie to lift the same suit he had worn in Cleveland to meet Joe. The Bomber was dressed casually in a checked sports shirt, red braces, plaid trousers and white shoes. Joe pulled Jesse close to him. He wrapped a big arm around the runner's shoulders as the cameras flashed. Jesse grinned broadly while a tentative smile opened up Joe's face. They looked like old friends.

Bojangles Robinson, sliding down the banisters, diverted attention away from the young athletes. Joe looked over his shoulder. The entire press contingent had moved across the room to watch the tap-dancer's amusing antics. 'Hey Jesse,' Joe said, 'I got a story for you.'

Joe told Jesse how, the day before, he'd decided to spoil himself. He went out to buy himself the snazziest car in Detroit. At the Buick showroom a fawning salesman steered him towards a sleek black limo with white-wall tyres. Joe was impressed most by the mahogany bar built into the back of the car. Like Jesse, he never drank alcohol. Yet he still imagined driving around in his best Billy Taub suit while sipping a bottle of pop from that incredible bar.

The salesman was called away to assist another client. Joe walked slowly around the car, occasionally leaning over to run his fingers along the gleaming mahogany. It was a treat to touch. By the time the man returned Joe had made up his mind. He had to have it.

'Well, sir,' the seller said quietly, 'the lady has already purchased the car for you.'

Joe's eyes followed the direction of the quiet nod. It was the same white woman the Buick man had just rushed over to help. She was a good-looking blonde. As Joe ambled over, Roxy's warnings tumbled through him. *'Never be on your own with a white woman . . . never have your photograph taken with a white woman . . .'*

Apart from the salesman, no one else was around. Joe said hello. She said hello. Her eyes told him more than words could have ever done. Joe took the car, offered her two tickets to his fight against Max Baer and agreed to drive over to her house later that day. She knew the meaning of discretion.

'Wow,' Jesse said, 'that's some pick-up.'

'What about you?' Joe asked. 'You having fun in Cleveland?'

'Lately,' Jesse sighed, 'I been having more trouble than fun.'

Two weeks before, on 12 August, Jesse had appeared before an American Amateur Athletic Union commission to answer a charge that he had received $159 while working as a page at the Ohio State House in Columbus. His official wage at the State House during term-time was $3 a day. The AAU was incensed to learn, via an anonymous tip-off, that Jesse's payment included the months of June and July – even though he had not worked in Columbus during the university holidays. Jesse was suspended from all competition and accused of using his amateur track credentials to make a profit. He offered to return the amount in full – but there were men in the AAU who longed to bring him down. If found guilty he would be barred for life from amateur athletics.

Joe could not believe it. He had made $60,000 against Carnera and then, on 7 August, he'd earned another $53,000 for a first-round knockout of Harry 'Kingfish' Levinsky, a former fishmonger. Two minutes after the bell, having been knocked down for a third time, Levinsky pleaded to the referee: 'Don't let him hit me again.'

Joe told Jesse, almost with embarrassment, that he'd just signed a $240,000 contract to face Max Baer. It meant that, for three fights in the space of three months, he'd pick up $353,000. Meanwhile, a cheque of $159 for three months' pay in Columbus threatened to end the career of America's greatest athlete.

Three days in Washington with Joe, however, offered Jesse some relief. He also gained perspective by witnessing the hysteria when they drove down U Street. Men, women and children screamed out Joe's name as if they knew he could change their lives. The longer they drove, the more Jesse felt for Joe. He carried a terrible burden. Even the Elks press conference turned into a one-man show as a reluctant Louis fielded questions about his next fight. Asked about the prediction that Max Baer would swarm all over him, Louis said simply, 'He ain't crazy. But one thing I know – if I hit him solid, he'll stay hit.'

'It was Jesse Owens's misfortune yesterday,' Shirley Povich suggested in the *Washington Post* on 27 August, 'to be cast in the company of Joe Louis, current idol of the coloured race. In his excursion through Washington's Harlem with Louis, Owens commanded no more attention than if he were Mr Average Man doing the average thing in the average way, fearful lest he wasn't maintaining his average. The gasps, the ahs and the ohs were for Joe Louis alone. They had eyes only for the strapping, dark brown prize-fighter; ears only for a boast that might drop from his lips. Owens slid in and out of the company like some flunky who knew his place.'

However, for Povich, 'every comparison of the two men, aside from the physical, favours Owens. The mob may sing to plaudits for the nut-brown young giant whose lethal fists have projected himself to the forefront of the world's heavyweight challengers, but there is room for belief that the smiling little track star will contribute more to the uplift of the Negro race.'

Owens offered white liberals a more accommodating presence than Louis. His words rang with hope. 'When white folks see that we dance as well as they,' Owens said breezily, 'when they see that we eat and drink the same things, and laugh and cry over the same things, they begin to realise we are human beings. All this bleating about being downtrodden doesn't do any good.'

Joe ambled into New York two days later. His gaze kept being snared by newspaper adverts which featured black women who could have passed for white.

QUICK! EASY! HERE'S THE SURE WAY TO GET WHITER SKIN! – NADINOLA BLEACHING CREAM. *While you sleep it works*

*wonders. Soon your skin grows whiter, shade by shade.
Your friends find you more charming, more attractive
than ever.* FAN TAN BLEACH CREAM WHITENS SKIN TO GRAND
AND GLORIOUS LOVELINESS! *– A skin you can rightfully be
proud of and happy to own. Let a new, lightened skin
bring you success in love, business and social popularity.*

Joe couldn't understand why a black girl would want to look
white. It was as crazy as him wanting to look like Primo
Carnera. Marva had no hang-up about being black. Nineteen,
slim and foxy, standing five foot four in her bare feet and weighing 118 pounds, she liked to dress in black. Sometimes she wore
white gloves. Size six gloves. Size five shoes. Her favourite per-
fumes were Gardenia and Evening In Paris. She did not use
skin-whitening creams. Joe thought it strange that he knew so
many little things about Marva. But it told him why he wanted
to marry her.

Joe could be shy, but he could also be, as Marva said, 'awful
bold'. He put the call through to Chicago and asked her straight:
Would she come to New York and see him fight Baer? And, by
the way, would she marry him? She said the word he wanted to
hear, and she said it twice: 'Yes . . . Yes . . .'

Joe could not wait. He wanted to be a married man by the
time he faced Baer. They would get hitched a few hours before
he headed out to Yankee Stadium. Julian Black set it up. He and
Roxy knew Joe could take Baer. And they knew, with even more
certainty, that marriage to a respectable young black woman
would remove 'the Jack Johnson problem'.

With his tutor, the black journalist Russell Cowans, Joe read
the papers every day to improve his reading. A week before the
fight he was hurt by an article in which Jack Johnson accused
him of being 'a flash in the pan'. His 'dogs', or feet, were slow
and his stance was wrong. Papa Jack claimed that, at the age of
fifty-seven, he would have made shorter work of Carnera.

Johnson's shadowy legacy remained – for Max Baer still played the race card. In March, while still world champion, Baer admitted that, 'I told my mother long ago that I wouldn't fight a coloured man. But if Louis continues to clean up in the division until I'm the only one between him and the championship then I'll fight him – if there was enough money in sight.'

Baer had since lost his title to Jimmy Braddock – and the unbeaten Louis now offered him the chance of a lucrative comeback. 'Louis has everything,' Baer said after watching him beat Carnera. 'But we still don't know whether he has the fighting heart. I saw Carnera hit him twice and he didn't look too good. He blinked his eyes and that means something.'

Louis was determined to stop Baer. He trained rigorously at Pompton Lakes. Some of the New York writers struggled to contain their distaste. Paul Gallico again described Louis in bestial terms: 'I felt myself strongly ridden by the impression that here was a mean man, a truly savage person, a man on whom civilisation rested no more securely than a shawl thrown over one's shoulders, that, in short, here was perhaps the perfect prize-fighter. I had the feeling that I was in the room with a wild animal . . . He lives like an animal, fights like an animal, has all the cruelty and ferocity of a wild thing. What else dwells within that marvellous, tawny, destructive body? The cowardice of an animal? The whipped lion flees. The animal law is self-preservation. Is he all instinct, all animal? Or have a hundred million years left a fold upon his brain?'

New York, 24 September 1935

Joe woke from a restful sleep in Harlem. It was just after 6 p.m. He took his time getting out of bed. He thought a lot about Marva, and only a little about Baer. Joe showered and pulled on a white shirt and a dark grey suit. He looked everywhere for his damn tie before deciding to do without it. The smart but casual look suited his mood. He was ready for the biggest night of his life.

Joe and his managers walked down a short flight of stairs to a larger apartment in the same building on Edgecombe Avenue. The Reverend Walter Trotter, Marva's older brother, opened the door. Joe felt more nervous than he did when stepping into a ring. Fifteen minutes later, at exactly 7.45, the service began. Julian Black, playing the part of best man, stood on Joe's right while Marva's sister, Novella, led the bride into the reception room.

Marva wore a white silk gown, its long train trimmed with ermine. She carried some lilies. Marva looked more beautiful than ever. The vows and prayers slipped by in a blur. Joe just had time to kiss his wife before the next call came. It was eight o'clock. 'I got a date with a fellow named Max Baer,' he cracked.

At exactly ten o'clock, amid a record 95,000 crowd at Yankee Stadium, Marva sat at ringside in a black hat and a pale green suit ringed with fur on the collar and sleeves. Joe's stare settled instead on Max Baer. The ring announcer, Joe Humphreys, began his shout: 'We'll be brief because you want action. I'm here for that poipose – to give it to ya. Main event. Fifteen rounds. Principals – presenting the sensational Californian and former world's heavyweight champion . . . *Max . . . Baer*! His worthy opponent – the new, sensational pugilistic product. Although coloured he stands out in the same class with Jack Johnson and Sam Langford. The idol of his people . . . none other than . . . *Joe . . . Louis*!'

They both wore black. Baer's trunks were distinguished by the yellow Star of David he wore in deference to his Jewish heritage. He was five years older, an inch taller and eleven pounds heavier than Louis. It counted for nothing. After a few cursory jabs, Baer missed with an overarm right. Louis was waiting. He ripped into Baer with his opening quartet – a straight right, a vicious uppercut, a left cross and another hard right. Baer crumpled a little beneath the jolting accuracy and hurtful speed.

Louis then switched to a more basic form of boxing brilliance. Dominating the ring and dictating the pace of the fight, Louis drilled his jab into Baer's big handsome face. It was a particularly personal form of cruelty towards Baer, a man who seemed to care most about the way he looked. Just before the fight started, the boxer they called 'fun-loving Maxie' had even stood in his corner of the ring and used his glove to brush his gleaming black locks into a neater side-parting. Baer was now far more concerned about the damage being done to his face by that withering jab. Near the end of the first round, as a despairing Baer tried to bully him against the ropes, Louis responded with a barrage of twenty-five punches. Only two missed their target.

Baer came out apprehensively for the second. He hitched up his trunks and then went back to the same dark feast where he did little but eat the jab that Louis kept sticking into his face. Whenever Louis felt like switching the method of torture he would sink his left hook into Baer's head and gut. He was almost ready to reel him in. Baer struck out blindly, hitting Louis twice after the bell. The Bomber just turned away.

Halfway through the third, after jabbing Baer into another daze, Louis was finally tagged by an uppercut. He hit back with heavy combinations, forcing Baer to the ropes. Baer was wide open, his head already lolling in surrender. A short right unbalanced him further. His left foot lifted from the canvas in an involuntary jerk as Louis landed another crackling right against his unprotected temple. Baer fell as if electrocuted. His hair stood on end while he took the count on one knee. He finally pulled himself up and, forlornly, waited for Louis to hit him again. Baer did not even try to punch back as a left and a right uppercut were followed by three left hooks. They came in a chilling row, each landing squarely against Baer's jaw. He hit the canvas even more heavily this time. He was on his hands and knees at the bell.

They should have ended it then, but Baer came out for the fourth. He endured another two minutes and forty seconds before a hook to the body, a right and a short left finished the fight. Baer sank slowly, as if imploding from the inside.

'I could have struggled up once more,' Baer said later that night, 'but when I get executed people are going to have to pay more than $25 a seat to watch it.'

Joe and Marva spent their first night together in an apartment on Edgecombe Avenue in Harlem. They sealed the door and the sixth-floor windows but, still, they could not block the ecstatic noise which filtered up from the street below.

An aspiring young black writer witnessed the same reaction which erupted simultaneously through Chicago's South Side. Richard Wright's first published writing, for a socialist newspaper called *New Masses*, described a scene familiar to every major American city that night. 'The area between South Parkway and Prairie Avenue on 47th Street was jammed with no less than 25,000 Negroes. Clasping hands, they formed long writhing snake-lines and wove in and out of traffic. They seeped out of doorways, oozed from alleys, trickled out of tenements and flowed down the street, a fluid mass of joy. White storekeepers hastily closed their doors against the tidal wave and stood peeping through plate glass with blanched faces. Something had happened all right. And it had happened so confoundingly sudden that the whites were dumb with fear. They felt – you could see it in their faces – that something had ripped loose, exploded. Something which they had long feared and thought dead ... The younger Negroes began to grow bold. They jumped on the running boards of automobiles on 47th Street and demanded: *"Who yuh fer – Baer or Louis?"* In the stress of the moment it seemed that the answer to the question marked out friend or foe. A hesitating reply brought waves of scornful laughter. "Baer, huh?" That was funny. Now hadn't Joe Louis just whipped Max Baer? "Didn't think we had it in us, did you? Thought Joe Louis was scared, didn't you? Scared because Max talked loud and made boasts. We ain't scared either. We'll fight too when the time comes. We'll win, too."'

That Sunday, Joe took Marva to the Calvary Baptist Church in Detroit. He became the centrepiece of a fiery sermon preached by the Reverend J.H. Matson.

'Joe Louis is doin' more to help our race than any man since Abraham Lincoln!' the preacher yelped.

'Amen to that!' boomed the congregation.

'He don't smoke!'

'Amen!'

'He don't pour no red-hot liquor down his throat!'

'No, sir!'

'He fights clean and he shall stand before the King! That's what the Bible say!'

Joe flushed as the words flamed down. He just wanted to fight, make some money and have fun with pretty girls.

'He is one of the chosen!' the preacher shouted. 'He shall make the whole world know that our Negro people are strong, fair and decent! He will lead us from bondage!'

Joe looked down. Jesus Christ, he thought, am I all that?

Chapter Six

The Fight

On Friday 15 November 1935, two sixteen-year-old black boys were dragged towards an old oak tree in Altair, Texas. Ben Mitchell and Ernest Collins cried as they were wrenched across the ground by a group of white farmers wearing overalls and carrying ropes. Hundreds of people ran to keep up as they neared the tree.

Mitchell and Collins had only been taken to jail the night before. Although the sheriff had yet to find any evidence linking them to the death of a nineteen-year-old white girl, Geraldine Kollman, he felt compelled to make an arrest. The boys had been accused of 'looking close' at the victim earlier that week. It was customary in the South for Negro suspects to be imprisoned prior to a trial – for their own safekeeping. Sixty per cent were still lynched before they reached court.

A news agency report on the Altair lynching revealed that, 'one coloured man, fair enough to pass for white, stood on the edge of the mob as the boys were being strung to the tree. "They'll never get away with any Scottsboro case in Texas," he overheard one of the leaders say. "This is the way to treat them – kill 'em off." The coloured man reported that "The mob was composed of the best citizens of this county. My heart sickened as I watched them. There seemed to be no conscience among either leaders or followers. The murder of these two boys was no more to them than the driving of a nail to a fence. They were not even that serious about it. There was not an expression of sympathy. Tears stemmed from the eyes of the two boys who kept crying, "We didn't do nothing like that, boss. We ain't guilty. You're wrong, mister."'

That same night, in Cordele, Georgia, police began a widespread hunt for five black men who had used shotguns to scatter 'a mob of infuriated whites intent on lynching eighteen-year-old Frank Horn, whose alleged crime against society was that he was too "sassy".' The gun-blazing quintet were tagged 'The Joe Louis Five'.

Across the border, in Alabama, the Scottsboro case had returned to court for a fourth trial a day earlier. The nine black 'Scottsboro Boys' were charged with raping two white women, Victoria Price and Ruby Bates, aboard a freight train in March 1931. They had been saved twice from Death Row by Supreme Court rulings that the verdicts were unjust as Alabama excluded blacks from their juries. A new eighteen-man jury included a token black member. The Scottsboro Boys again faced execution – even though Ruby Bates had reversed her original testimony to insist that the attacks never happened. She had since disappeared.

The first death sentence had been passed in Decatur, nine miles from Jesse Owens's birthplace. With the case making national news, the rise of two Alabama Negroes in Owens and Louis prompted the *Chicago Defender* to speculate that the runner and fighter 'could do much to promote anti-lynching bills in the North and wipe out this beast-like reign of terror in the South. Frankly it is hard to see how whites that greet our star athletes with wide-open arms can turn around and wish to lynch, or see lynch, the brothers of these same youngsters who do not happen to be athletically-inclined.'

That December, Louis made history by becoming the first black man to be voted America's Athlete of the Year. In an annual poll of the country's sportswriters, Owens came third with Eulace Peacock two places behind him. Yet even the fact that three out of America's top five athletes were Alabama Negroes could not mask a stark truth. The Tuskagee Institute in Alabama confirmed that twenty Americans had been lynched in 1935, five more than the previous year. Eighteen were black.

Max Schmeling came from a country where racial genocide defined government policy. In Adolf Hitler's first public statement, in 1919, he wrote that Germany's aim should be 'the removal of the Jews altogether'. Speaking a year later, the Austrian-born Hitler, a member of the then obscure National Socialist German Workers' Party, sounded even more threatening: 'Don't think that you can combat racial tuberculosis without seeing to it that the people [are] freed from the causative organ of racial tuberculosis. The impact of Jewry will never pass away, and the poisoning of the people will not end, as long as the causal agent, the Jew, is not removed from our midst.'

In one of *Mein Kampf*'s most chilling passages, Hitler claimed that a million German soldiers would have been saved if, before World War I, 'twelve to fifteen thousand of these Hebrew corrupters of the people had been held under poisoned gas'.

By January 1933, when Hitler was invited by President von Hindenburg to form a coalition cabinet, six million Germans were unemployed. The real tally, counting temporary workers and hidden unemployment, was considered to be 8,750,000 – or half the German work force.

Max Schmeling had a job. He was a fighter skilled enough to have become world heavyweight champion in June 1930. Schmeling was embraced by Berlin's cultural elite – a fluid collective of film-makers, artists, actors and writers who enjoyed the less cerebral company of showgirls, racing drivers and husky torch singers. When Schmeling was first drawn into the circle, and met the director Josef von Sternberg, the satirical artist George Grosz and writers like Heinrich Mann, the elder brother of Thomas Mann, he felt he was 'yet another exotic presence for them, a kind of mythical animal'.

Schmeling was neither an intellectual nor an artist. He was as bewildered by German Expressionism as he was by the chance to buy some early and modestly-priced paintings by Picasso. 'I would never hang this type of picture on my walls with that kind of head, a guitar and everything else,' he admitted bashfully. 'I'm not ready for all this.'

He married Anny Ondra, an actress from Prague, who was soon at work with Alfred Hitchcock on his first 'talkie', *Blackmail*. As Schmeling moved between Europe and America his confidence grew in tandem with an expanding group of influential associates. He posed for paintings by Grosz and sculptures by Rudolf Belling while, in America, he was championed by the exiled von Sternberg, Ernst Lubitsch, Bertolt Brecht, Marlene Dietrich and Fritz Lang.

Before the Nazis seized control of Germany, Schmeling's friends had partied in Berlin with an abandon born of the feeling that catastrophe might erupt at any moment. The impetus was emotional rather than political. Hitler's marching followers provided just another eccentric backdrop to the city's surreal cabaret bars and clubs.

Schmeling was used to living amongst the freakish. In 1925 he'd spent a month travelling with a circus while he taught boxing to the son of 'The World's Strongest Woman'. The gargantuan Frau Sandwiener could bend horseshoes straight while a line of cars drove over her. Schmeling liked her; just as he liked the Berliners who ignored the goose-stepping Nazis.

Heinrich Himmler, one of Hitler's highly-educated deputies, argued that 'intellect rots the character'. On 10 May 1933, at universities and city squares across Germany, hundreds of thousands of books were burned on bonfires. 'Here sinks the intellectual basis to the ground,' gloated Joseph Goebbels, the Nazi Minister for Propaganda at a roaring Opernplatz in Berlin where 20,000 books by 'corrupt enemies of a racially pure Germany' were set ablaze. The poet Heinrich Heine, whose own 'degenerate' work lay in the blackened pile, warned that, 'where books are burned, in the end people are also burned'.

Crude signs were plastered over Jewish shop windows in Berlin: GERMANS DEFEND YOURSELVES AGAINST JEWISH ATROCITY PRO-PAGANDA: *Buy Only at German Shops*. Nazi gangs enforced the message with brutal intent.

In April 1933, three months into his new position, the Reich Chancellor summoned Schmeling to a private dinner. Schmeling was flattered; even as world champion he had never been invited to the Reichstag.

Hitler had extolled the virtues of boxing in *Mein Kampf*: 'No other sport is its equal in building up aggressiveness, in demanding lightning-like decision, and in toughening the body in steely agility.' He believed that sexual attraction between Aryan women and Jewish men would be negated if more Germans took to the ring. 'The maid should know her knight. If beautiful bodies were not completely placed in the background by our foppish modes, the seduction of hundreds of thousands of girls by bowlegged, disgusting Jew bastards would be quite impossible.'

Hitler knew that his country's best fighter, Schmeling, was also the most famous German in America. Schmeling was then about to return to New York to fight Max Baer. The fact that Baer was partially Jewish mattered less to Hitler than the opportunity to portray, through Schmeling, a more urbane face of the new Germany to the world.

Schmeling was beguiled by the polite man who greeted him. 'Good day, Herr Schmeling,' Hitler smiled, 'how good of you to come . . .'

Hitler, accompanied by two back-slapping cabinet ministers in Göring and Goebbels, engaged Schmeling in chit-chat about boxing and Berlin. Just before the boxer left the Reichstag, Hitler said casually, 'I hear you're going back to America. If anyone over there asks how it's going in Germany, you can reassure the doomsayers that everything is moving along quite peacefully.'

Schmeling had been managed since 1928 by Yussel 'Joe' Jacobs, a small, wise-cracking Jewish New Yorker whose parents had emigrated to America from Hungary. Jacobs, despite his clumsy attempt to launch Schmeling in America as 'The Black Ulan of the Rhine', had emerged as a shrewd hustler who spouted some memorable catchphrases. He'd coined that immortal sporting lament, 'We wuz robbed!' when Schmeling lost his world title to Jack Sharkey in 1932.

Jacobs had few qualms about travelling regularly to Germany with Schmeling. They shared a similar attitude. Even when confronted with anti-Semitism, they reacted as if it was an aberration which should be ridiculed. In early 1935 Schmeling reserved a room for his manager in one of Berlin's more fashionable hotels. When Jacobs tried to check in, Schmeling was called aside by the desk manager. 'I'm afraid we won't be able to accommodate him,' the man said. 'Herr Jacobs is . . . you know, don't you?'

'You mean you can't give him a room because he's a Jew?' Schmeling said.

'You have to understand the new situation,' the manager shrugged.

'When this shows up in the New York papers,' Schmeling warned, 'you'll have seen your last American guests. Is the room available or not?'

The man silently pushed the registration forms across the desk to a grinning Jacobs.

The little manager also responded wryly when Schmeling's

defeat of Steve Hamas in March 1935 was greeted by 25,000 Germans leaping to their feet to sing *Deutschland Über Alles* and give the Nazi salute. In the middle of the ring, Jacobs mechanically lifted his own right arm. He then turned towards Schmeling and winked. At the end of his raised arm, blue smoke curled from a fat cigar.

Within days, Schmeling was ordered to meet the officious new Minister of Sport, Hans von Tschammer. The forty-eight-year-old Tschammer, an ardent follower of Hitler since 1922, was rarely seen without his peaked cap, a military jacket covered in medals, brown riding britches and high leather boots. His desk was covered by news clippings featuring photographs of Jacobs's ironic pose. 'You really should box more in Germany, Herr Schmeling,' Tschammer said. 'Our youth needs role models to inspire them.'

'Fight locations are decided by whoever makes the best offer, *Herr Reichssportführer*.'

'You shouldn't be so short-sighted, Schmeling,' Tschammer threatened.

A letter arrived later that week. Tschammer informed Schmeling that he and Goebbels had studied the scandalous photographs of Jacobs. They considered the entire affair to be shameful. Schmeling was the only German sportsman who still worked with a Jew. The matter had to be rectified.

An incensed Schmeling requested an appointment with Hitler. He was invited to tea the following afternoon, with the instruction that his wife should accompany him. The reason soon became clear. While he ignored Schmeling, Hitler flirted awkwardly with the blonde, blue-eyed Anny: 'Would the gracious lady prefer tea or coffee?' the *Führer* simpered. 'Tea? How nice, Frau Schmeling. I also only drink tea – and it can never be too strong! Which sort of cake would you like, gracious lady?'

While Hitler slurped his tea, Schmeling praised his Jewish manager. 'I really need Joe Jacobs. I owe all my success in

America to him. Herr Jacobs is competent, respectable and correct.'

Hitler said nothing, only gesturing angrily when Schmeling said he wished to retain Jacobs because 'loyalty is a German virtue'.

After a studied pause, Hitler turned towards Anny and resumed his cake-chatter. He soon stood up and shook her hand: 'It was so pleasant seeing you again. How is the film business?' Before she could reply, Hitler nodded to one of his guards. Schmeling saw the flash of SS insignia as they were ushered away.

He would keep Jacobs as his manager. The *Führer* had more significant work on his agenda. While Schmeling travelled to New York to watch Louis fight Baer, Hitler addressed 300,000 of the party faithful in Nuremberg. On 15 September 1935, beneath a black sea of swastikas, lit by brilliant searchlights, the Nazis passed the Citizenship Law, the Blood Law and the Flag Law. Jews were stripped of their German citizenship. Only those of 'German blood' could be considered countrymen. Jewish political rights were abolished. Marriage, and even sexual relations, between Jews and Germans were prohibited by the need to ensure the survival of a 'pure' Aryan race.

Hitler tried to temper his rhetoric with softer words aimed at the outside world. He was acutely aware that a summer of random savagery against Jews had jeopardised the 1936 Berlin Olympics, with America leading the call to boycott the Games. Hitler spoke vaguely in Nuremberg of 'perhaps creating a basis on which the German people might possibly be able to find a tolerable relationship with the Jewish people'.

For Hitler, the final solution to 'the Jewish Question' could wait until his Olympic dream had been fulfilled. With the three Nuremberg laws in place, the *Führer* turned his attention towards America. He needed Max Schmeling more than ever. Hitler instructed Arno Breithaupt, from the Reich's Sports

Ministry, to call Schmeling. Breithaupt spoke persuasively to the fighter: 'You know America well, Max. Could you go over there and exert a positive influence on the right people?'

The right man, at least as far as the Nazis were concerned, was Avery Brundage, the President of the American Olympic Committee. Brundage had consistently advocated that America should ignore the 'Jew–Nazi altercation' and even spoke of a 'Jewish-Communist conspiracy' to force America's withdrawal from the 1936 Olympics. After visiting Germany, he insisted that 'certain Jews must understand that they cannot use these Games as a weapon in their boycott against the Nazis'.

Brundage's friend and counterpart on the German Olympic Committee, Theodor von Lewald, asked Schmeling to personally deliver an official letter which promised a fair and open Olympics for all athletes, whatever their colour or religion. It would give Brundage another promotional puff to swing the AOC vote his way and ensure America's presence in Berlin.

After handing over the letter in New York, Schmeling concentrated on Louis. On 13 December 1935, he watched the Bomber destroy Paulino Uzcudun in four rounds, with Louis using his exquisite left jab to set up a straight right which drove two of the Spaniard's teeth through his bottom lip. It was a terrifying punch, but Schmeling retained his composure. 'Joe Louis is the hardest puncher I've ever seen,' he admitted. 'But I don't think it's impossible to beat him.'

'Tell us, Max,' an American writer taunted, 'how do you plan to pull off this miracle?'

'I saw something tonight,' Schmeling said cryptically.

'What did you see, Max?'

'I saw something,' Schmeling repeated.

Having demanded that Schmeling provide him with a first-hand account of his meeting with Brundage, Hitler was shocked when the boxer confirmed that he had signed a contract to fight Louis in New York in June 1936. The idea that Germany's greatest fighter would be crushed by a black opponent haunted the Nazis.

Five months later, and seven weeks before the fight, Schmeling returned to America. He dismissed the idea that the *Führer* might have wished him luck before he left Germany. 'Why should he come down to the boat to see me off?' Schmeling asked. 'He is a politician.'

Schmeling set up camp in Napanoch, in the Catskills, seventy miles upstate from New York. He chose to train at a Jewish country club. Schmeling and his trainer Max Machon, as well as the two detectives assigned to guard him, spent the rest of their time a few miles away in a secluded cabin in the woods. They lived a Spartan existence. Schmeling woke early every morning and ran for six miles up the tree-lined mountains to strengthen his thirty-year-old legs for the looming battle. And then, both before and after sparring at the country club, he slept, ate and played cards. Sometimes, Schmeling reached for a gun and went walking alone amid thickets of scrub and prettier stretches of mountain laurel. It was then, while hunting, that he thought most clearly about the grainy images he had watched in a darkened room in Berlin.

It had been a long German winter. Schmeling's weeks and months in Berlin had been occupied by the suitcase of film he had brought back with him from America. Inside that brown leather case were reels of film, each enclosed by a steel canister marked in black ink: *Louis–Ramage, Louis–Carnera, Louis–Levinsky, Louis–Baer, Louis–Uzcudun.* Schmeling studied his opponent again and again. Eventually, in an attempt to break down Louis's style, Schmeling and Machon ran the film backwards, frame by frame, following a blow from its point of landing back to the instant it was thrown.

A small mistake in Louis's stance became more glaring the longer they watched him. They were not the first to notice. Jack

Johnson, for all his slithery envy, could still focus on a fighter with deadly accuracy. He had spoken for six months about Louis being a sucker for a right hand. To Johnson it was such an obvious flaw that he couldn't believe anyone thought Louis might become the greatest fighter of all time. That title belonged to *him*.

Schmeling and Machon were more considered in their judgement. By studying Louis's punches in isolation they created a complete picture of the fighter. It was an often frightening exercise. The films proved how hard Louis hit the men in front of him. His defence and control of the ring were no less shimmering on screen. Schmeling thought Louis came closer to boxing genius than any fighter he had ever seen. His lone weakness was exposed far less than Johnson claimed. Schmeling thought it barely noticeable to the naked eye but, reverse frame by reverse frame, there were fleeting examples when the left side of Louis's face was unprotected. The opening only emerged when Louis threw three or four left hooks in succession. He would then leave his left hand low for a second before sliding back into his impregnable pose.

To take maximum advantage, it was imperative that Schmeling's short, devastating right should be unleashed just as the last Louis hook connected. The older man knew he would have to take some of Louis's most hurtful punches so that, from close range, he could fire the right. He would have to train at a pitch he had not previously endured. It was the only way his body might survive the battering which would precede the moment when his greatest strength, that right hand, tested Louis's resilience.

Schmeling planned to build his intensity steadily. Louis's supporters in the press were scathing when they cast a lazy eye over Schmeling. 'Up at Napanoch,' Al Monroe jeered in the *Chicago Defender* on 30 May, 'we saw a pitiful sight that answered to the name of Max Schmeling. We saw a big German boy overawed by his own importance but below expectations as a fighter. We saw a fighter overweighed with age and slow in the timing of his punches.'

The world champion, Jimmy Braddock, was a more detached judge. On 3 June he said, 'Max looks pretty good. He's in tip-top physical condition and he's hitting better. He's sharpened up his right since I saw him.'

Five days before the fight, on Saturday 13 June, *The New York Times* reported that, 'A complete reversal of form was shown by Max Schmeling today. In his ring work on Thursday the German was unimpressive, but today he appeared to excellent advantage – so much so that there was a general return of confidence among his followers.'

While opponents like Levinsky and Baer had become desperately jittery just before they fought Louis, Schmeling seemed spookily calm. 'Why should I be afraid?' he asked. 'This boxing is my business, my trade, my profession. I have been hit before and I did not like it, I admit. But I was not scared then and I will not be scared when Louis hits me.'

After he watched the German at work during the final week of training, Mike Jacobs took Schmeling aside. 'If you beat Joe,' the Bomber's money-man said gruffly, 'I want you to be with me, Max. I've got a contract I want you to look at.'

A month earlier, on 13 May 1936, Joe Louis's twenty-second birthday, the world champion had tracked down the young Bomber. 'What's the matter with you, fellah?' Jimmy Braddock asked. 'Are you tryin' to duck me? I'm the champion and you oughta be chasin' me, but since you won't do that I'm comin' after ya . . . so how about it, kid? Do we fight or do we fight?'

Joe looked at Braddock, suddenly forgetting the giant birthday cake he had just been given by Roxy and Black on his opening day of training. 'Sure I'll fight you, Jim,' Joe said. 'As soon as I smack down this Schmeling, I'm your man.'

The fact that he turned up to train for Schmeling twenty pounds over his usual fighting weight hardly mattered. He accepted a large slice of cake while Braddock and everyone else sang a loud and off-key version of 'Happy Birthday'. Joe had five weeks to get himself back into shape – in a new camp.

Roxborough and Black chose Lakewood, sixty miles from New York, in Jersey, because its larger grounds could accommodate more paying customers to Louis's daily training sessions. According to the black *Chicago Defender*, Lakewood 'is a place where Jewish aristocrats come in winter time. It is no place for your and my race. Lakewood is pretty and yet it isn't ideal. Thousands of pine trees, with resin dripping, and a blistering hot sun make the place uncomfortable and keep it so until the wee hours of the morning.'

Joe was more interested in having a good time. His last fight had been a one-round demolition of Charlie 'Let's Laugh' Retzlaff on 17 January 1936. During his subsequent hiatus he and Marva took a delayed honeymoon in Hollywood, where he starred in *The Spirit of Youth*, a ham-fisted boxing film based on his life. Apart from setting up some discreet liaisons with starlets like the Norwegian ice-skater turned actress Sonja Henie, Joe indulged in his latest passion – golf.

There were still some, like Mary Knight, who depicted him as a barely comprehensible jungle boy. After her visit to Lakewood on 14 June, the *Washington Post* printed her attempted reconstruction of Louis's drawl, with the deliberate misspellings supposedly adding to the impression that she had just met a primitive moron: 'Joe Louis confided to me today his only fear. It's water! He was playing golf when we met. Immediately our conversation drifted to sport in general. "Fighting's fun," Joe said. "Just like everything else – golf, tennis or . . ." "Or swimming," I added, trying to be helpful. "No ma'am," he replied quickly. "Hit sho' ain't nuthin' like swimmin'! Ah don't never fool wid no water. Ah' skairt o' water. Ain't nuthin' else in di' world Ah's got a fear of cep water. But Ah sho' is a-feared o' dat stuff."

Jack Blackburn, as usual, kept his eyes on the ring. Joe's sudden interest in golf disturbed him. 'Chappie,' the trainer warned, 'all this golf ain't good for you. The timing's different. And them muscles you use in golf, they ain't the same ones you use hitting a man. Besides, being out in the sun don't do you no good. You'll be all dried out.'

Louis ignored Blackburn. For once he believed he knew more about boxing than the hard man in his corner. He based his assessment of Schmeling on seemingly logical principles. The German was eight years older than him, and on the slide. Whereas Louis was unscathed after two years as a pro, Schmeling had lost seven fights in a dozen years. Schmeling was lighter, shorter, slower and far less versatile than Louis. Baer, who had stopped Schmeling easily, had been smashed by Louis; Uzcudun, an equally hapless KO victim of Louis, had survived three fights against Schmeling, one of which was drawn, without being knocked down.

'Max is very foolish,' Uzcudun warned. 'That fellow Louis is likely to kill him.'

Louis had little difficulty believing in his own indestructibility. The *New York Amsterdam News* reported 'a strange indifference to his work . . . his interest is much more rapt in playing baseball, fishing and golf'. Louis, watched by crowds of 4,000 at every training session, was scathing in response. 'What do these people want for half a dollar,' he asked, 'a homicide?'

Blackburn, although concerned by the lacklustre approach, argued that 'all this noise about Joe being out of shape is just ballyhoo to make Schmeling's chances of winning look better'. But Louis, whipped on by Blackburn, regained some of his sharpness. On 13 June, the same day they reported on Schmeling's marked improvement, *The New York Times* suggested that 'there is no longer even a lingering doubt that Joe

Louis is right at the top of his form and ready to step into the ring against Max Schmeling as finely conditioned as he has been for any fight'.

Joe and Chappie knew different; but it was time for another big night in New York. They just needed one more win before Joe Louis fought for the heavyweight championship of the world.

The Nazis withdrew their endorsement of Schmeling. In an editorial for the party's *ReichSport Journal*, Joseph Goebbels denounced the fight while the same paper insisted that there was 'not much interest' in a contest involving a black man. Controlled by Hans von Tschammer, the *Journal* attacked any Germans who wished to travel to America to support their fighter. Under a headline demanding IS THAT NECESSARY? the Nazi broadsheet insisted that 'we cannot feel much enthusiasm for the plan to arrange an excursion to the Max Schmeling–Joe Louis boxing match. Although such a trip in itself might be agreeable, it would suit us better if the Schmeling–Louis fight had not been chosen as the reason for making it.'

On Thursday 18 June 1936, before a seething House of Commons in London, the British Foreign Secretary Anthony Eden announced the end of sanctions against Italy as the best way to avoid a great European war. Amid angry cries of 'Shame!' and 'Resign!' the British Prime Minister, Stanley Baldwin, rose to defend Eden's announcement. The principal power in Europe, Baldwin argued, was Germany rather than Italy. And it was time for Britain to reconcile herself with the new Germany.

Baldwin echoed Hitler's assertion that the Nazis had saved Germany from Communism. He also suggested it was 'no wonder, considering the desperate troubles Germany had gone through, that her people now worshipped ideals of force and violence. Yet Chancellor Hitler has told us he wishes for peace, and if a man tells me that I wish to try it out . . . the part

Germany can play for good or evil in Europe is immense, and if we believe the opportunity is presented let us do what we can to use it for good.'

Europe was opening up to Hitler. The fate of a lone German fighter in America could be underplayed. The Nazis sent only one reporter to New York to cover the bout for the newspaper *Volkischer Beobachter*. Arno Hellmis had been instructed to make the most political gain from a bleak personal scenario for Schmeling. While admitting that 'America is in a boxing fever', Hellmis claimed, 'the racial factor is strongly placed in the foreground, and it is hoped that the representative of the white race will succeed in halting the unusual rise of the Negro. In fact there is no doubt that Max Schmeling, when he enters the ring on Thursday evening, will have the sympathy of all white spectators on his side, and the knowledge of this will be important moral support for him.'

American press reaction to Schmeling was overwhelmingly positive. One reporter believed that 'almost every sportswriter in this country likes Max, who is good-natured, gentlemanly, sportsman-like, polite, thoughtful and every good thing imaginable'.

The depictions of Louis as a man were more typically derisive. In a *New York Times Magazine* feature, printed the Sunday before the contest, Meyer Berger claimed that Louis 'says less than any man in sports history including Dummy Taylor, the Giants pitcher, who was a mute. Dr William Walker, who examined Louis before the Carnera fight a year ago, was amazed at the man's silence. "Closest thing to a wooden Indian I ever saw", said the doctor ... Another physician who has observed the Louis routine compares the Bomber to a primordial organism; in temperament, he is like a one-celled beastie of the mire-and-steaming-ooze period.'

On the morning of the fight, Joe Louis took the 09.10 train from Lakewood to New York. There were sixteen people in his party. Joe joked and laughed with all of them before, his mind turning towards Schmeling, he became more thoughtful. He played a soft blues on his harmonica while staring at the crowds thronging every station they passed. By the time they reached New York, Joe was asleep.

Schmeling's car had left Napanoch just before nine. Accompanied by his cornermen Max Machon and Otto Petri, Schmeling was driven to New York by a gloomy policeman, Sergeant Jim Hopkins. They followed the lead car, carrying his manager Joe Jacobs, who had made the seemingly solitary prediction of victory for Schmeling by a ninth-round knockout. The mountain roads were treacherous beneath the slanting rain. It was a slow and mostly silent journey.

The weigh-in was scheduled for noon at the New York Hippodrome. Louis arrived on time, amid raucous scenes. The Schmeling convoy was thirty minutes late. Both fighters noticed a lingering stench in the packed arena. It was a reminder that they had replaced the animals who had performed for a season at the Hippodrome, alongside Jimmy Durante, in a circus musical called *Jumbo*. Yet the German felt strangely elated as he approached the stage where he would strip down for the ceremonial stepping on the scales.

Schmeling's gaze locked on Louis as he ambled up the wooden staircase. 'Hello Joe,' Max said, 'how do you do?'

'Fine, Max,' Joe replied with mild surprise. 'And you?'

'Very good, Joe. Thank you.'

Schmeling, five pounds lighter than Louis, called out after his weight had been announced: 'Good luck this evening, Joe!'

The Bomber nodded. Soon after they had pulled on their clothes, a conservative suit for Max and a Billy Taub special for Joe, Mike Jacobs spoke to the boxers. Although the rain had eased, a torrential downpour was forecast for that evening. The fight would have to be put back a day.

As they drove to the Hotel Theresa in Harlem, Joe turned to

Jack Blackburn and said, 'That German sure was a pretty cool bird.'

'Chappie,' the trainer murmured, 'it looks like you got a fight on your hands this time.'

Schmeling settled down to wait in his room at the Plaza. The view was panoramic. New York spread out before him. Through the misty cloud, the city looked beautiful and ominous. Yankee Stadium, in the distance, made a ghostly outline.

Just before ten that night, at the precise moment when he should have been walking from his dressing-room to the ring, the fighter lay still in his huge hotel bed. The room was dark and quiet. Max Schmeling was already lost in a deep and dreamless sleep.

New York, Yankee Stadium, 19 June 1936

Twenty-four hours later he sat on a wooden table. He had not fought for eleven months, but the experience Schmeling had gained over twelve years helped him control his fear. He listened to the noise of the crowd as the door to his dressing-room opened. Tom O'Rourke, a former promoter and one of the grand old men of American boxing, had arrived to wish him luck. The eighty-three-year-old put his hand on Schmeling's arm. 'I know you can win, Max. You've just got to be careful and use your head.'

'Thank you,' Schmeling said.

Moments later, O'Rourke slipped soundlessly to the ground. His unblinking eyes stared up at the boxer. They carried O'Rourke away. Max Machon and Otto Petri tried to convince Schmeling that he had just seen a man faint. The fighter knew different. Old Tom was dead.

They were soon summoned to the ring. The black clouds rolling over New York, and an attempted boycott of the fight, organised by Jewish shops protesting against the Nazis, restricted the crowd to 45,000 – half as many who had watched Louis's demolition of Baer the previous September.

Schmeling, his hair slicked back, wore a patterned robe of black and grey. Louis was dressed in a blue gown with red trim. The American looked serene as he cocked his head at the motionless German during referee Arthur Donovan's instructions. They went back to their corners. Louis, his back propped against the wooden post, rested his arms on the top rope. His feet did a little dance of four fast steps. Schmeling spat one last time into his trainer's bucket. He bit down hard on his mouthguard and then scuffed his shoes on the canvas to test their traction. The fighters were surrounded by blackness, but the ring was hot and glaring.

They began slowly and warily. Schmeling, typically European in his upright stance, watched his young rival intently, his eyes alert to the feints and swivels which the Brown Bomber had used so devastatingly against Carnera and Baer. Louis's respect for Schmeling, however, had grown over the last thirty-six hours. He worked behind a measured jab, content to take a long and careful look at the canniest opponent he had yet faced. Louis still took the opening round comfortably – for Schmeling's most meaningful act was to trudge forward and bury his head in Louis's chest whenever more than one stinging punch was thrown his way.

'You're still alive,' Max Machon snorted in Schmeling's corner as his fighter sat on the small stool.

'Louis can punch,' Schmeling said quietly. The tender skin beneath his left eye had already reddened.

'Yeah?' Machon sneered. 'And you can't?' He slapped his hand against Schmeling's right glove. 'Give him your calling card – show him what's he's up against.'

Louis maintained his steady rhythm in the second, following a series of crisp jabs with a left hook. Schmeling took the punch and, remembering his strategy, fired a right over Louis's lowered guard. The punch caught Louis, making him gulp inadvertently. It felt as if he had swallowed his mouthpiece, such was the jolting impact. Although his brain was clouded, he instinctively snapped five unanswered jabs into Schmeling's face. Louis had won another round; but he'd also been hurt for the first time in more than a year.

Schmeling returned for the third with fierce determination. He did not even wait to counter Louis as he connected early with two more hard rights to the jaw. Louis responded with sharp body punching before, once again, his jab snaked into Schmeling's face. He dominated the rest of the round, out-boxing the German so thoroughly that Schmeling looked confused and discouraged at the bell. The first three rounds had gone to Louis, with the last amounting to a skilful beating. For Schmeling, his right eye swollen and closing, a desolate night seemed certain.

'C'mon Maxie,' Joe Jacobs yelped in Schmeling's corner, 'what's happenin'?'

Machon silenced the agitated manager with a stare. He turned back to Schmeling and, speaking in German, said simply: 'You caught him with a good one early on. He really felt it. Keep patient – you'll get your chance to unload that right again.'

The fourth opened quietly. Both fighters prodded and feinted for thirty seconds, their faces glazed with concentration. They could hear each other's rasping breath and the smothered grunt whenever a punch landed cleanly. Schmeling was the first to back away, taking three, four, five steps as Louis followed him in a half circle. Retreating smoothly until he faced Louis squarely again, Schmeling planted his feet firmly on the canvas to add leverage to his hitting. Louis pumped out a left jab. It grazed Schmeling's face just as, in that same instant, the German threw the punch he had dreamed of for six months.

The overarm right swept past Louis's drooping left arm, like a wave crashing over a rock, and smashed into the side of his head. Teetotal Joe stood still for a moment and blinked, as if he had just swallowed his first almighty hit of bourbon. He staggered sideways, his eyes wide as his legs almost collapsed beneath him. Schmeling recognised that stricken weave. He tore into Louis, throwing punches from a variety of angles before cracking another right to the temple. Louis sank towards the ropes, ducking a left but falling straight into the next right cross which dropped him for the first time in his professional career.

Clem McCarthy, the gravel-voiced radio commentator broadcasting to America and the world beyond, jumped up at ringside, his microphone pressed to his mouth as he growled in disbelief. *'Schmeling has sent Louis down! Joe Louis is down!'*

Instead of taking the eight or nine seconds he had to recover, Louis hauled himself up immediately. He looked lost and small as he flexed a wobbly right leg and tugged at his shorts. Schmeling closed in on Louis. McCarthy, staring up at the young American just above his head, ground his words together in a jagged rush: 'He did not wait for the count. He got up on the count of two. Schmeling came back at him and gave him another right. Schmeling is pouring in now and Louis for the first time is getting the real test.'

Louis clinched desperately. The referee forced them apart and Louis, reaching deep into himself, started to jab again. At the bell they were fighting at close quarters, with Louis firing the last shot of the round. Jack Blackburn climbed between the ropes. His fighter was in trouble.

'OK Chappie,' he said as he sponged down Louis's face and the back of his head, 'listen to me. You're still in there, but you gotta keep your guard up. You took that right hand 'cause you were wide open after your hook.' He wiped away the sweat and excess water as he calmly repeated his key instruction: 'Whatever you do, Chappie, *keep that guard up*!'

Four times in the opening minute of the fifth, Schmeling hit Louis with his overarm right. Louis, despite his trainer's urging, was too groggy to block the fast and looping blows. Even when he began to string his own punches together, Louis's combinations lacked the impact of Schmeling's isolated but far more telling power-shots. Louis was struck again by a right moments after the bell. Schmeling was warned by the referee, but more damage had been done.

Schmeling had taken control. He was not the same worn fighter who had lost to Baer, Sharkey and even a journeyman as mediocre as Steve Hamas. Schmeling had uncovered a freshness of purpose and a capacity for hard and accurate hitting unlike anything Louis had ever confronted. The Bomber's left cheek was distorted by the rights that kept pounding into him.

In the middle of the sixth round his mother was led from her seat by Freddie Guinyard: 'My God, my God,' Lillie Barrow wailed. 'Don't let him kill my child . . .' Marva Louis, whispering, '*Joe . . . Joe . . . Joe . . .*' in horror, had to be restrained from also fleeing the stadium in tears. She was persuaded that, as millions of his followers around America prayed, her husband might still stage a miraculous recovery.

He gave reason for hope in the seventh as, cajoled by Blackburn, he switched his attack to the body. Louis sank left hooks into Schmeling's midriff and flank. The German was in need of respite. He gave up on the round early and, for the first time in almost ten minutes, went on the retreat. 'Louis is apparently out of danger,' McCarthy rumbled at ringside, 'having learned to take that right hand. Now Louis is trying with his left. He's got his own plan of attack. Blackburn has rallied him and it's going to be a real fight.'

Louis doubled-up on his jabs and hooks and clipped Schmeling repeatedly to the head to take the round – his fourth out of seven. Yet Schmeling, even with his right eye closing, looked untroubled.

He was more honest in his own corner. 'This guy still hits like a bull,' Schmeling sighed to Machon.

'Concentrate, Max!' the trainer said angrily. 'You've got to get back on the attack.'

Schmeling blocked Louis's opening assault in the next round and rocked him with an uppercut. The Bomber was disorientated further by two rights and a left from Schmeling. As he began to totter, Louis flung a low left. He apologised by placing both hands on Schmeling's shoulders but his very next punch, on the bell, was almost as far south. Louis seemed to have lost all sense of direction and hope.

'Louis is a very tired fighter,' McCarthy confirmed. 'C'mon in, Ed Hill,' McCarthy said, as he turned to his between-rounds analyst.

Edwin C. Hill, who hosted the influential *Human Side of the News* on national radio, tried to sound more upbeat. 'I've told you about the fairness of the fighters,' Hill said, 'and now I want to tell you about the fairness of this crowd. We've got oh, I suppose, 45,000 people here in this great, immense Yankee Stadium. But there isn't a trace of that which so many people have been afraid of – racial feeling or anti-Nazism or anything of that kind. These people realise that we're watching two great athletes. One may be a little darker than the other, perhaps, but there's no question of anything else.'

In the ninth and tenth, Schmeling's ceaseless right hand hammered the twenty-two-year-old until his legs slowed to a crawl. Louis's courage remained intact. His fists kept up their own mournful tempo, but they lacked their usual venom. John Roxborough was perspiring heavily at ringside, while Julian Black glowered from the corner. Their glorious plan looked suddenly empty and futile.

'Louis has got to try for a knockout,' McCarthy insisted.

After an even but pedestrian eleventh, Schmeling rushed from his corner at the start of the twelfth round and opened up with two more rights. Louis was warned for another low blow before they settled into a typical exchange – left jabs for the slow-shuffling Louis and a right cross and uppercut from Schmeling. With two minutes gone, another right and a left hook drove Louis to the ropes. He was badly hurt. Four more rights and a left followed as Louis stumbled across the ring. Schmeling was merciless, dropping one heavy right after another on the Bomber.

Louis faltered near Schmeling's corner, his puffy face glazed with the certainty of coming darkness. Schmeling steamed in, attacking both body and head. A right uppercut smacked against Louis's chin. He was helpless then, his hands lolling at his side, his face exposed. One last savage right cross sent him crashing down. Louis was on his knees. His gloves clawed the ropes as if he was a baby struggling to hold himself upright against the bars of his rocking cot.

Louis slid to the canvas and lay on his side. He shook his head. There was no mistaking that moment of terrible realisation. Louis repeated the same slow shake as if to say a silent 'enough'. And then, agonisingly, he rolled over. The count, sounding like a faint and eerie whisper, reached ten. Spreading his arms wide, the referee nodded twice. Joe Louis had lost. Joe Louis had lost.

Jim Hall, a black man, died of heart failure in a New York tenement when he heard Clem McCarthy's final hoarse cry: *'The fight is over! The fight is over!'* He was not the only black fatality – sixty-year-old Robert Gannt, in Columbia, South Carolina, and sixty-six-year-old Josephine Tandy, of Madison, Indiana, had also collapsed and died while listening to McCarthy's blow-by-blow account.

A few minutes after the count a black teenage girl walked into a drugstore in Harlem. She picked up some poison and tried to drink it. And the music stopped around America that Emancipation Day as bands and singers walked off stage.

At Cincinnati's Moonlight Gardens, Lena Horne was meant to be singing with Noble Sissle's Orchestra. She was backstage instead, with the rest of the band, crouched around a radio, listening to McCarthy's parting words. Lena was almost hysterical. The musicians around her were crying. Joe Louis had been beaten up by a white man. And there was nothing any of them could do to help either him or themselves.

'How dare you!' Lena's mother raged at her. 'You have a performance. The show must go on. You hardly even know this man.'

'I don't care,' Lena yelled back. 'He belongs to all of us . . .'

They covered Joe's head in a white towel as they led him from the ring. He was barely conscious when they laid him on a rubbing table. Jack Blackburn, his face heavy with sorrow, pulled off Joe's boots. He massaged his damaged fighter gently, as if his own fingers might bring the light back into Joe. After a few minutes of silent ministering, Blackburn reached for the smelling salts. He waved them vaguely under Joe's nose as if he hated the idea of bringing his boxer round to the hard truth of defeat.

In the shower, water ran down Joe's swollen face. He could not wash himself. His hands hurt so much he cried aloud when he tried to make a fist. When the fighter turned to look at himself in the steamed mirror he just said, 'Oh God, my face . . .'

Dr William Walker was called in to examine him. Joe looked bad, but nothing was broken or bleeding. Both thumbs were badly sprained and the bloated bruising around his mouth and eyes would take weeks to heal. He looked away to the wall. Joe could not face anyone. He cried for a long time, eventually turning to stare into Blackburn's own filled eyes. 'What happened?' Joe asked.

'Nothing tragic, Chappie,' the trainer said. 'You just got knocked out. It happens.'

*

Young black men rioted that night in Chicago and New York. Outside Yankee Stadium a white spectator was shot and another was kicked unconscious. Buses were stoned and cars were turned over. Jack Johnson, who had placed a sizeable bet on Schmeling, had to be saved by the police as a crowd pursued him in Harlem. They were ready to lynch him for gloating over their unbearable loss.

As his car drove through the Bronx, Max Schmeling saw bricks and bottles being hurled at any vehicle heading downtown. The German car picked up speed as it raced towards the safety of Manhattan.

Joe Louis's most virulent critics had already begun their mockery. O.B. Keeler, in the *Atlanta Journal*, derided 'the Pet Pickaninny' while Davis Walsh of the International News Service hailed the 'white master' who made 'the black avenger revert to type and become again the boy who had been born in an Alabama cabin'. For Jack Dempsey, the former world heavyweight champion and Louis's boyhood hero, 'Schmeling's victory is the finest thing to happen to boxing in a long time. Who did Louis fight anyway? Baer, who was scared to death, Uzcudun and Carnera. The big bubble broke tonight. Joe Louis will be licked by every bum in the country.'

In the Plaza, in a hotel room filled with flowers, Schmeling tried to understand what he had just done. As the night finally edged towards light, the telegrams were read out. Beyond Ernst Lubitsch, Marlene Dietrich, George Grosz, Primo Carnera and Douglas Fairbanks, two names rang out. Joseph Goebbels wrote: 'Congratulations, I know you fought for Germany. Your victory was a German victory. *Heil Hitler.*' The *Führer* himself offered, 'Most cordial felicitations on your splendid victory. Adolf Hilter.'

As black America mourned, Germany rose to a different dawn. Arno Hellmis's radio commentary of the fight had electrified the country, with his descriptions of Schmeling's destruction of *der Neger* reaching across the sea to embrace the Nazi myth of racial grandeur. His delirious fight report followed quickly. 'All America is enchanted by the great achievement of the German. How much this has accomplished for the German cause should not be underestimated.'

Chapter Seven

August in Berlin

The SS Manhattan, *15 July 1936*

Jesse Owens stretched out, face-down, on the narrow bunk-bed, and propped himself up on his elbows as he looked around Cabin 87 on Deck D. His home for the next nine days was below the water line. He and the other Olympic athletes were deep down in Third Class while the team officials cruised up above in First. Jesse didn't care. He was surging across the vast dark sea to Europe. He was heading for Germany. He was closing in on Berlin.

Jesse picked up his slim pocket diary. He breathed in the smell of new leather as his cheek pressed against the smooth black surface. The words on the front were printed in gold:

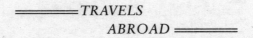

He opened the diary and wrote his name on the white inside cover in the same way he signed every autograph: *Jesse Owens, Ohio State University*. He skimmed the next thirty pages of small print which offered 'Suggestions and Information for Your

Enjoyment and Travelling Comfort'. The notes covered everything from 'Dining Reservations' to 'Sea Sickness', 'Deck Tennis' to 'Fog Signals'. They even told you to address a King as 'Sire' and the Pope as 'Holy Father'. There was, however, no mention of the correct form of address should he meet the *Führer*.

Jesse settled down to write his first entry. He filled in the date and next to the space reserved for a description of the weather he opted for 'Clear'. In his curvy handwriting he began his Olympic diary.

Left the city of New York on pier 60 on the morning of July 15th. There were many people there to see the boat sail. Before the boat left there were photographers and radiomen aboard taking pictures and interviewing different people. I was one of those chosen to speak. Said goodbye to my friends and retired to my cabin.

Jesse looked up at the tiny travel clock Ruth had given him. He flipped back to the *'Difference In Time'* section in his diary. Five p.m. in New York meant it was eleven at night in Berlin. Jesse was moving into another world, a world of shadow and strife. He had been asked repeatedly about the Nazis and the Jews. Jesse wanted to speak from the heart. 'If there is discrimination against minorities in Germany,' he'd said on the radio in November 1935, 'then we must withdraw from the Olympics.'

Larry Snyder went crazy when he heard that interview. Did Jesse want to spoil everything? The AAU had then just cleared him of the charge that he used his reputation as an amateur sportsman to make $159 as a page at the State Office in Columbus. His suspension had been lifted and he was free to concentrate on the Olympics. It did not mean, Snyder thundered, that he should start giving voice to vague political ideals. Anyway, the coach demanded, who exactly would they be helping if they allowed the German sprinter, Erich Borchmeyer, to win the Olympic 100m for Hitler?

Jesse agreed to avoid all future political discussions. Snyder, instead, spoke bluntly in public. 'Why should we oppose Germany for doing something we do right here at home?'

Julius Streicher, the publisher of *Der Stürmer*, a rabidly anti-Semitic newspaper, asked a similar question after he had ridiculed international reaction to the trauma of Martha Dodd, the daughter of the American Ambassador in Germany. Dodd had watched Jewish men and women being held down in the streets of Nuremberg while their heads were shaved. 'We do not mind if the daughter of a foreign ambassador witnessed such scenes,' Streicher said. 'I would like to suggest to foreign countries that, rather, they report about lynch justice in America. Such a report would be worthwhile. We pay no attention to Negro executions, so people should not bother when we lead racial offenders through the streets.'

The black press also considered the similarities between Nazism and the lynchings which terrorised the southern states of America. The *Pittsburgh Courier*, the *Chicago Defender* and the *Call and Post* were convinced that black life in the South constituted the bleaker fate. For the *Courier*, 'There isn't an upright Negro in Mississippi who wouldn't swap places with a Berlin Jew and pay him a bonus. There isn't a Jew in Germany who, having agreed to come to Mississippi and live as a Negro, could be compelled to keep the bargain.'

Rather than turning over that little riddle in his head, Jesse had been overwhelmed by a more personal struggle. No sooner had he escaped the AAU suspension than Ohio State University removed him from their athletic squad for the entire 1936 indoor season, from January to April, because of poor exam results. The OSU administrators gave Jesse an additional warning. Unless he showed a marked academic improvement at the end of that coming term, he would also be excluded from the summer championships and ruled ineligible for the Olympics. Mel Walker was given the same ban.

Jesse had not run or jumped competitively since the disastrous defeats to Eulace Peacock the previous July. He was condemned to hibernation while Peacock sharpened his Olympic preparations. Ralph Metcalfe, meanwhile, produced some typically authoritative indoor performances. Conrad Jenkins, Metcalfe's coach, turned up the heat. 'Jesse Owens will never beat Ralph Metcalfe,' Jenkins insisted. 'Last year they held Owens out of the 200m at the Nationals – and Peacock, too. They were afraid of Ralph. They're still afraid of him.'

Jesse was finally given permission to compete as an independent athlete at an 'open' meet, the Butler Relays in Indianapolis, on 23 March. It was his first appearance in eight and a half months. The OSU squad set out that Monday morning in their usual convoy. Jesse, Mel and Dave Albritton took up the rear in the battered 1914 Model-T Ford they had saved long and hard to buy for $32.50.

It was the same old story. When they pulled into a roadside eatery on the outskirts of Indianapolis, they stayed in the car while Larry Snyder tried to get permission for them to eat inside. In brilliant sunshine, the coach looked increasingly agitated as he and a waitress shook heads at each other.

When Snyder returned to the Model-T, Mel asked: 'What'd they say this time?'

Snyder shrugged in embarrassment. 'Something about the owner being out. She says she can't take the responsibility . . .'

Ten minutes later, their team-mate Charlie Beetham delivered their food. They dug in, eating with hungry intent, knowing this would be their last meal before they ran and jumped later that afternoon.

Dave reared back as a face pressed against the side window. A big man with a heavy paunch lifted his head and yelled to the restaurant manager, 'Guess who we got here!'

'You were paid, weren't you, mister?' Dave said as he rolled down the glass.

'We don't want nigger money!' the man shouted. He reached through the open window and banged his fist down hard on Dave's plate. Eggs, bread and a plastic cup of lukewarm coffee flew into the air. The athletes sat in shock while the fat man, his breath hissing through clenched teeth, grabbed hold of the empty plate and wrenched it from Dave's grasp. Dave and Jesse climbed slowly out of the Model-T. Their clothes were stained by coffee and flecks of egg. The man stared at them, his face flushed and quivering.

Jesse gripped Dave's arm. 'No, Dave, no,' he whispered.

Dave tried to pull away, but there was a wiry strength in Jesse. At last Dave relented. 'OK,' he said bitterly. 'What's one more time?'

The white man walked away with Dave's plate. 'We'll get something from the next place,' Jesse eventually said. 'We've still got time.'

'Shit,' Dave snarled. 'This is about being empty in *here*!' His fist thudded into his chest. 'Aren't we ever gonna fight these bastards?'

'We are fighting,' Jesse said, thinking how weak he sounded.

Jesse felt stronger that afternoon. 'I'm gonna run my balls off today,' he said. Dave just grunted but, afterwards, his eyes glittered when he hugged his friend. Jesse had won the indoor 60-yard dash in 6.2 seconds, the 60-yard hurdles in 6.9 and the long jump with a leap just under 25 feet. Dave cleared 6 foot 7 inches to take the high jump.

Five nights later, on Saturday 28 March, Jesse ran in another unrestricted meeting. At the Cleveland Public Hall he faced Eulace Peacock in a 50-yard sprint expected to be the first in a chain of encounters culminating in an Olympic decider over 100m at the Berlin Games. They each won their respective heat in 5.4 seconds. As the fastest qualifiers, Owens and Peacock had drawn the two middle lanes in the final. At the gun, while Owens came up with a graceful burst, Peacock's crude wooden starting block slipped. He recovered his balance but, in such a short dash, Owens sprinted to an easy win.

When Owens realised what had happened, the Cleveland *Call and Post* reported that he offered 'one of the grandest exhibitions of sportsmanship ever witnessed . . . he immediately put his arm around Peacock's shoulder and led him back to the starting line. He insisted that the race be run again. After a brief rest, Jesse further showed his sportsmanship by changing lanes with Peacock. This time both runners got off to a clean start but Peacock beat Owens to the line by inches.' His victory marked his sixth straight defeat of Owens.

There was some relief for Jesse. Snyder negotiated his return to the track in the spring quarter, for Jesse's results at OSU had shown a slight improvement. The next showdown with Peacock was scheduled for 25 April and the first major outdoor event of the year – the Penn Relays. With that date in mind Jesse set about reclaiming his form, believing that the winter break had allowed his body to recover fully from the world-breaking rigours of the previous year.

Peacock, however, was a victim of his own success. Injury and fatigue had set in during the summer of 1935 when he followed his triumphs over Owens by running and jumping for an AAU invitation team during an extended European tour. Peacock had damaged his hamstring in Italy and, at the Penn Relays, the problem returned with cruel timing. During a meaningless 4×100m heat, Peacock tore the same hamstring. He clutched at his leg as his head bobbed in despair.

The next day, in his absence, Owens easily won the 100m final, the long jump and, as the anchor man for OSU, the relay. His roll began. Over the next five weeks he broke records wherever he went. The most significant saw him smash the world mark in the 100-yard dash with a 9.3 run on 16 May in

Wisconsin. A week later, before his home crowd in Columbus, Owens repeated his 1935 Big Ten championship sweep by winning the same four events.

On 4 July, with his right thigh 'taped up like a baseball bat', Peacock lost both his AAU national titles to Owens. He was trounced in the long jump, leaping three feet short of his best, and broke down in the 100m. He was running a distant third behind the imperious Owens when, after eighty-five metres, the muscle popped again.

Peacock was given a 'special invitation' to the final trials on 11 and 12 July, the weekend before the American team sailed to Berlin. It was hopeless. He limped to the line in last place. His jumping was just as futile. In contrast, with decisive victories over Metcalfe in the 100m and 200m, and a big win in the long jump, Owens was the only athlete to secure himself more than one berth on the American team.

The day had been made even more memorable by the high-jump final. Minutes after Cornelius Johnson set a new world record with a leap of 6 feet 9¾ inches, Dave Albritton duplicated the feat. Like Jesse he was now a world record holder – and on his way to Berlin as one of nineteen Negroes on the US team. Although all the southern states had refused to host a trial including Negroes, the *New York Amsterdam News* suggested that 'those who mourn the defeat of Joe Louis . . . can find not only solace, but also genuine pride and appreciation in the results of the Olympic selections'.

Three days later, on Deck D of the *Manhattan*, Jesse's gaze drifted across the pages in his diary reserved for HIGHLIGHTS OF THE TRIP. He looked away. Anything could happen. He only had to think of Eulace and Joe to know that he, too, might still fall.

When the team gathered for dinner on their first night aboard the boat, Jesse went to his assigned table. His reputation for diplomacy had preceded him. He was expected to eat every meal alongside three loud white Southerners – Forest 'Spec' Towns, Jack Torrance and Glenn Hardin. Jesse tried to move to another table, only to be ribbed unmercifully by the southern boys.

On their second night, far out to sea, they hit a wild and pitching storm. *The boat really rocked*, Jesse noted in his opening entry on the HIGHLIGHTS pages. But, after he got over his sea-sickness and a light cold, life on the *Manhattan* settled into a tedious rhythm. In the mornings Jesse worked out on deck and wrote letters to Ruth. Most afternoons he slept or hung out with the other sprinters. He filled a page of his diary just before dinner every evening and, afterwards, there would be a movie or a game to play. He usually returned early to Deck D so that he could, as he wrote in his diary, kiss a photograph of Ruth before he fell asleep.

On 20 July, Jesse revealed that *the day was very uninteresting. There wasn't much going on and therefore most of the day was spent in my cabin*. Two days later it was even worse. *It rained, and the day as a whole was very dreary and nothing exciting happened. Had a dance that night but didn't go. That's all*. Jesse had made a conscious decision to endure the boredom. He would not be diverted from the task awaiting him in Berlin.

The team's resident femme fatale, Eleanor Jarrett, took the opposite route. Only Jesse could claim to be more famous than the beautiful and husky-voiced twenty-two-year-old swimmer from Brooklyn who 'trained on champagne and cigarettes'. If her taste for the fast life was indisputable, so too were Jarrett's swimming credentials. She had already swum in two Olympics and, four years previously, had slashed three seconds from the world record while winning gold in the 100m backstroke. Eleanor had since earned a Hollywood contract and married the bandleader Arthur Jarrett. Apart from setting new world records over every distance in backstroke, she toured with Jarrett's band, crooning torch songs, and took acting lessons with Josephine Dillon, Clark Gable's first wife.

The leading sportswriters on the *Manhattan* – Paul Gallico, Alan Gould and Joe Williams – were smitten with her. They described Eleanor as a 'statuesque beauty' and 'the glamorous Brooklyn mermaid'. They invited her to join them in the First-Class bar every night. Eleanor flirted and drank champagne, smoked and told jokes, sang songs and drank still more champagne.

After she had been reprimanded on board by Avery Brundage, Eleanor responded with haughty panache. On the last night before they reached Germany, she returned to the upper deck and partied even harder than before. Eventually, one of the women chaperones saw her staggering back to her cabin. The team doctor and the ship's physician were called in to examine her. As everyone already knew, she was smashed on champagne.

Early the next morning, Brundage announced her expulsion from the Olympic team. Eleanor cried alone in her cabin. Her sobbing promise – 'I swear I'll never touch another drop' – was dismissed by Brundage. He was bent on removing any athlete who questioned his autocratic rule. Eleanor Jarrett would not be the last Olympian he'd banish to the wilderness.

On Saturday 18 July 1936, fourteen days before the opening of the Olympic Games, the German Labour Front announced *A Week of Mirth and Happiness*. 'Prior to the strain of the Olympic weeks, Berliners should take stock of themselves. Then, with merry hearts and friendly expressions on their faces, receive their Olympic guests. None should miss the chance.'

The militant Nazi journal *Der Angriff* (The Attack) instructed its Berlin readers that 'we must be more charming than the Parisians, more easygoing than the Viennese, more vivacious than the Romans, more cosmopolitan than London, and more practical than New York'.

Hitler and Goebbels suspended all 'Nazi activities'. Aware that soaring morale at home would be bolstered further by a successful Olympics, they wanted desperately to legitimise their regime around the world. The Berlin Games would provide a magnificent stage for the Nazis. Hitler sneered at fears that the stadium and village were too colossal in their design – complaining instead to architects like Albert Speer that 'everything is far too small'. The monumental size of the eventual constructions was matched by an intricate concentration on the tiniest details of the Olympics.

But Hitler was forced to buckle on one central tenet of Nazism. Earlier that year Henri Baillet-Latour, the Belgian President of the International Olympic Committee, had been horrified by the anti-Semitic posters he saw while travelling across Germany. On 4 February, the eve of the Winter Olympics, he told Hitler that such menacing messages were not conducive to 'a festival of international sport'.

In a barely controlled rage, the *Führer* declared that it was 'ridiculous and unjustified' that 'a question of the highest importance within Germany' should be hidden beneath 'a small point of Olympic protocol'. Baillet-Latour threatened the immediate cancellation of both the Winter and Summer Olympics. Hitler seemed to fall into a trance. For a few highly-charged minutes he ignored Baillet-Latour and the translators. Finally, he succumbed. 'You will be satisfied,' Hitler muttered as he walked quickly out of the room.

Anti-Jewish slogans disappeared as walls were whitewashed and shop windows were cleaned. Public persecution of Jews was forbidden before and during the Berlin Games. For a few summery months in 1936 it became possible for Jews to hope that they had survived the Nazi assault. Goebbels even tried to remove the worst anti-Semitic publications from shops and street kiosks. He specifically barred Julius Streicher from selling *Der Stürmer* during the 'festivities'.

Larry Snyder warned Jesse to expect taunting from the Nazis. As they walked down the gangplank in Hamburg on 23 July,

Jesse was more intent on looking good. Apart from being voted the second most popular man aboard the *SS Manhattan*, Jesse had won 'The Best Dressed Man' award. He disembarked in his straw boater and light blue pin-stripe suit, a small suitcase in his hand.

He had been inspired most by Ralph Metcalfe. The night before, while Eleanor Jarrett knocked back the champagne up top, Metcalfe met the black athletes on Deck D. He spoke with serene conviction to the eighteen men gathered around him. There was no turning back. They were moving into Germany the next morning. They would be watched by the whole world as they ran and jumped beneath the scrutiny of Hitler and the Nazis. None of that would matter, Ralph said softly, if they remembered why they loved being athletes. They all wanted to do their very best. They all dreamed of winning. If they stuck to those simple truths, Ralph promised, they would remain strong. They would win plenty of medals.

Ralph stared at each of them in turn. 'OK,' he said, 'you all look great. Let's show them what we can do.'

They travelled from Hamburg to Berlin by train, and were taken by bus to the City Hall for a public reception. It was then that Jesse heard the first mysterious chants: '*Yess-say . . . Oh-vens . . . Yess-say . . . Oh-vens . . . Yess-say . . . Oh-vens . . .*'

'Whaddya think they're shouting, champ?' Jesse asked Ralph, as they walked near the head of the team.

Ralph shook his head. 'Man,' he murmured, 'I can't believe it, but I reckon they're singin' your name.'

Jesse Owens's renown in Germany had survived even those newspaper reports which, charting the rise of '*Das Negerfest*' in American sport, had attributed his speed and jumping power to 'animal qualities'. Some papers printed a photograph of an ape alongside Owens, but his record-breaking feats had made him the most famous international sportsman in Berlin.

Even the German officials ceded to public demands that Jesse should travel in full view on top of the open-decked bus. Jesse grinned at the cheering faces and snapping cameras, lifting his hat whenever he heard his name. Berlin gleamed beneath his gaze. The streets were clean and wide and the huge old buildings seemed impossibly grand. Wherever he looked there were flags. A few were white, with five Olympic rings in the middle. But the swastika dominated the city.

The bus followed a marching band up Unter den Linden to the City Hall steps, where the Mayor of Berlin awaited. As he stepped off the bus, Jesse was mobbed by young Germans.

By the time the US team arrived in the Olympic Village late that afternoon, Jesse was exhausted. There was no let-up. Members of the Hitler Youth, who looked like Boy Scouts to Jesse, greeted the Americans with fawning politeness. Jesse and Dave were more startled by a particular ritual as they were led through the village. Any German they passed immediately snapped to attention, lifted his right arm in a stiff salute and barked: *'Heil Hitler!'*

'Boy,' Dave breathed, 'ain't that some kind of hello?'

'If you don't mind us asking,' Jesse said to the Nazi youth assigned to look after them for the duration of the Games, 'why do those fellows keep doing that?'

'It is a tribute to the *Führer*, of course,' the German boy explained in accented but perfect English. 'But it is also a welcome to Germany. We want you to feel at home while you are here.'

The village lay in the middle of a magnificent forest of birch. Exquisite lawns rolled down to an artificial lake and a small cluster of blue ponds. Their German guide pointed out some of the village amenities, including a hospital, a library, a theatre, a restaurant, a swimming pool and a barber shop. Winding pathways led them back to the gigantic houses which had been built for the male athletes. There were 160 in all, and every thirteen-roomed house could host twenty-six men. Each house would be catered for by German stewards fluent in the language of that particular group of athletes. They would act as guides and messengers. Every team would also have their food prepared by chefs specialising in that country's cuisine.

The village had been designed by Wolfgang Fuerstner, a brilliant officer in the German army. When his partly-Jewish background was discovered, shortly after the completion of his masterpiece, Fuerstner was quietly replaced as Village Director and stripped of his German citizenship. In order to deflect press attention, Fuerstner was kept on in the village as an 'assistant'. His fate would be decided as soon as the Games ended.

Although Jesse wrote in his diary that *the weather in Germany is somewhat funny – in the morning the sun is shining beautiful and suddenly it will rain*, he loved the fact that he could eat *steak, and plenty of it, as well as bacon, eggs, ham, fruit and juices*. On his second day in Berlin he *met many people from strange lands and most of them could speak English*. Jesse liked the Australians most of all. *After a bull session with some of their boys*, he wrote admiringly, *what liars they are!*

They ventured out into the city that night. He and Dave were hoping for a break from the hand-pumping and back-slapping persistence of the other Olympic athletes, but it was even more frenetic in Berlin. The Germans were fascinated by the colour of their skin.

Jesse and Dave made it to Shelbini's Bar where they listened to a black jazz trombonist. It was a special night. Dave had his first taste of champagne – 'Boy,' he told the abstemious Jesse, 'this stuff is just like ginger ale!' – and they danced with German girls. A number of men even asked if the two athletes would dance with their wives. The boys were happy to oblige.

Two days before the Games began, the Nazis paraded Max Schmeling around the Olympic Village, taking special care to saunter through the American quarter as if they wanted to remind Jesse Owens how far his friend had fallen at the hands of a German.

After his defeat, Joe Louis had gone underground. When he eventually emerged, two nights later, dark glasses covered his damaged eye while his coat collar was pulled up high so that it partly concealed his swollen cheek and puffed mouth. Joe slipped into Penn Station. Only a few photographers were waiting for him when he arrived in Detroit. Joe covered his face with a straw hat as he ducked into a taxi.

Even more devastating news awaited. His family had not dared tell him, but two days before the fight against Schmeling his fifty-eight-year-old step-father had suffered a stroke. A grieving Joe sat beside his mother as they watched Pat Brooks take his last breath at home in Detroit on 9 July 1936. The Brown Bomber had never been so vulnerable.

Der Weltkampf, a German monthly, argued that America and her allies 'cannot thank Schmeling enough for this victory for he checked the arrogance of the Negroes and clearly demonstrated the superiority of white intelligence'. *Das Schwarze Korps*, the newspaper published by the SS, Hilter's elite *Schutzsstaffel*, or Protection Squad, gloated that 'Schmeling's shattering fist has smashed all adversaries of National Socialism' and 'saved the prestige of the white race'.

Hitler chose to ignore the fact that Schmeling was still managed by 'the Jew' – Joe Jacobs. The *Führer* had arranged for the boxer to travel in the captain's cabin on the *Hindenburg*, the German Zeppelin which left America soon after Schmeling beat Louis. When it landed in Frankfurt fifty hours later, Schmeling saw that 'the ground was black with people'. Hitler summoned him to the Reich Chancellery that day. Dismissive of the fighter two months earlier, Hitler now showed exaggerated courtesy. In an almost ceremonial manner, he expressed the thanks of the German people and asked an embarrassed Schmeling if he had really believed he would knock out *der Neger*.

The *Führer* was ecstatic when Schmeling revealed that he had brought back a film of the fight. Once the reels had been collected from customs, Hitler, Goebbels and Schmeling watched the destruction of Joe Louis. Hitler provided a running commentary, pounding his thigh in delight. 'Goebbels,' he ordered, 'this film must be shown as a main feature throughout the entire Reich!'

When Schmeling entered the Olympic Village, the fight footage was still being screened in cinemas across the country. It was billed as *Max Schmeling's Victory – A German Victory!*

Jesse agreed to face Schmeling, but he did so reluctantly. He felt heavy with thoughts of Joe. Jesse knew he could not stand any celebration of his defeat. But Schmeling surprised him.

'Jesse,' Max said, 'I am honoured to meet you. I have heard a lot about you.'

'Hello Max,' Jesse said icily.

'How are things for you here in the village?'

'Pretty good.'

'You know, Jesse, coming back to Germany, I looked forward to three things. One was to see my wife, two was to do a little hunting and three was to see you win some gold medals.'

'I'm going to try my best,' Jesse said.

'I think Joe will also be listening out for you,' Max said after a pause. 'He is a great fighter – and a great man.'

'I know – he's my friend.'

'I would like to become friends with Joe one day,' Max said.

'Well,' Jesse responded more warmly, 'anything's possible with Joe.'

The Nazis watched from a discreet distance as the two men talked for five more minutes.

'Schmeling seems OK,' Dave Albritton said later that night.

'Yeah, Max is all right,' Jesse confirmed. 'But Joe'll whip him next time.'

*

Hitler officially opened the Olympic Games on Saturday 1 August 1936. Before an exhilarated crowd of 110,000, each country's team marched past the Nazi leaders seated at the heart of an enormous grandstand. Hitler wore a nondescript brown uniform while Göring, in a pale blue Luftwaffe outfit, and Goebbels, in his white lounge suit, were dressed more dashingly. As they passed Hitler's box, many teams gave the Nazi salute, or its Olympic variation which involved a disconcertingly similar lift of a stiff right arm. The British party opted for an understated 'eyes right' gesture towards the *Führer*. The Americans were more defiant. They refused to dip their flag or offer any form of salute. The crowd's whistling derision soon turned to mass hysteria as the USA were followed by the last group – Germany.

Richard Strauss, the composer, led his orchestra through a stirring *Deutschland Über Alles*. The arena soared in united song. As the last notes faded, the stadium choir were on their feet. And then, after a chilling pause, 110,000 right arms lifted in unison as the mantra boomed across the arena: '*Sieg Heil! Sieg Heil!*'

When the mania subsided Hitler, for once, made a concise speech. 'I announce as opened the Games of Berlin, celebrating the eleventh Olympiad of the modern era.'

On the fringes of the track, boys from the Hitler Youth opened their small wire cages. Twenty thousand white doves flew up into the sky. A distant battery of guns hammered out a twenty-one gun salute. In the eventual silence a lone runner appeared from the tunnel below. He was blond and beautiful. He held a torch above his head as he ran across the track and up the steps which led to a marble platform. And, there, he lifted himself up on his toes and plunged the torch into a concrete bowl. Flames leaped from the cauldron. The crowd, seemingly hypnotised until they saw that burst of fire, erupted.

Berlin, 2 August 1936

They left the Olympic Village early that cold and drizzly
Sunday morning. Jesse wore a black beret, a buttoned tweed
sports jacket over his blue USA training top and white trousers.
Dave Albritton's head was bare and, without a jacket of his
own, the three letters, USA, stretched across his brawny chest.
On the western side of the village they walked through the tall
iron gates. It was just after eight o'clock. Neither Jesse nor
Dave had slept much the night before. In the dark, they had
spoken for hours about the coming day. Jesse faced his opening
pair of heats in the 100m. Dave had the more demanding task.
By late afternoon the high jump would be decided. Dave would
then know what colour medal, if any, he would receive from
Hitler.

The bus crawled towards the stadium. They had avoided the
same forty-five-minute trip the day before, preferring to relax in
the village rather than attend the protracted opening. Jesse's
nerves were not soothed by the hundreds of thousands of
Germans, walled in by troops, lining the streets. They waited
feverishly for Hitler's sleek black convoy.

Inside the Olympic arena, 50,000 people were already seated
by 9 a.m. Jesse ducked into the American dressing-room. To the
dismay of Larry Snyder, he had drawn the twelfth and last heat
of the 100m. As soon as Jesse ran his race at 11.55 he would
have to rush back to the bus which was due to depart for lunch
at the village. Another return journey to the stadium later that
afternoon would do little to help him recover for his second
heat. Snyder was indignant that the team officials, meanwhile,
avoided the inconvenience of travelling by bus. They drove
around Berlin in a convoy of American cars the AAU had
shipped over for their exclusive benefit.

Snyder resorted to clandestine methods to help his star athlete. He stole the rub-down table earmarked for the Spaniards

who, in the midst of civil war, had withdrawn from the Games. The coach then set about finding a bed which Jesse might rest on between races. He was emphatic that Jesse would stay in the arena as much as possible.

Just before he stepped out on to the track, at 10.30 a.m., Snyder prepared Jesse for an antagonistic reception. They had heard the roar which engulfed the stadium when the German squad arrived.

'Block them out, Jesse,' Snyder said as they walked down the tunnel.

'OK, coach,' Jesse murmured.

He turned towards the far end of the track to begin his warmup. The first heats were only thirty minutes away. Ralph Metcalfe and Frank Wykoff were set to run in the seventh and ninth heats. In the race between them, Erich Borchmeyer was expected to win heat eight. The German champion was the first to greet Jesse.

'Jesse,' Borchmeyer asked, 'do you remember me?'

In 1932, when Jesse was still a schoolboy, he and Borchmeyer had raced over a hundred yards before a crowd of 60,000 at the Coliseum in Los Angeles. Owens won in a time of 9.6. Borchmeyer told the American press then that 'this Owens is unbelievable'. He also asked Jesse for a signed photograph.

'I still have that photo,' Borchmeyer reminded him. 'I always keep it. One day I shall show my children.'

Jesse was distracted by Borchmeyer's coach. The old German circled him, his eyes fixed on Jesse's legs. As Snyder suggested later, 'He studied them like a scientist studying a rare specimen of fauna.'

Jesse noticed how, wherever he looked, cameramen seemed to have their lenses trained on him. They all worked for the strikingly attractive but formidable German woman who'd introduced herself to him earlier that week. Leni Riefenstahl, the young film-maker, had risen through the ranks of German cinema to make *Triumph of the Will* – a fiercely luminous depiction of a Nazi rally in Nuremberg. She had been commissioned by Hitler to provide a record of the Berlin Olympics. Riefenstahl chose eighty of Germany's finest cameramen and, making unprecedented use of aircraft, cranes, wheelchairs, trolleys and narrow dug-outs buried in the track itself, aimed to provide both panoramic and intimate footage of the Games. She had already zeroed in on Owens as one of the key personalities in Berlin. His black skin revolted the Nazis; but Riefenstahl, despite her close relationship with Hitler and Goebbels, observed a graceful beauty in his lithe body and the flawless symmetry of his running.

The German crowd saw something similar. They began to chant again as Owens jogged around the perimeter of the track: 'Yess-say . . . Oh-vens . . . Yess-say . . . Oh-vens . . . Yess-say . . . Oh-vens . . .' He lifted his arm in acknowledgement.

When the heats began, Owens practised his start in an attempt to familiarise himself with the German commands. The starter, Fritz Miller, was a bulky, balding man who wore a white coat and held his gun high in the air. His voice was quiet but clear as he said *'Auf die Plätze . . . Fertig . . .'* before he pulled the trigger. On the edge of the grassy interior of the track, Owens crouched down as the other sprinters went through the ritual for real. He broke cleanly every time the gun fired and ran a few strides before easing back so that he could watch the rest of the race.

Metcalfe, Wykoff and Borchmeyer all won comfortably. Yet the fastest time was recorded by a runner Owens had never seen before – Martin Osendarp, of the Netherlands, in 10.5.

Owens, in a white vest bearing a small American flag, a diagonal flash of red, white and blue piping and the number 723, waited for the gun in the outside lane of his heat. Only the first two finishers, in a field of six, would qualify for the quarter-finals.

The Japanese runner, Naoki Sasaki, was away fastest, leading Owens for forty metres. They were level at fifty, and then Owens slid past Sasaki with almost absurd ease. Fifteen metres from the tape he looked casually to his left. The others were far behind. Owens crossed the line in 10.3, equalling the world record.

He barely had time to pull on his tracksuit before he was called away to the bus. On the journey back to the village he stared out of the window, amazed by the size of the crowds gathered around the loudspeakers blaring from most street corners. For the millions of Berliners who had failed to get tickets to the Olympic arena, live commentary was broadcast across the city.

When he returned to the stadium early that afternoon, the mood bordered on delirium. Hitler had just arrived. The *Führer* was accompanied by Göring, Goebbels, Himmler, Hesse and Julius Streicher. Clearly visible in his box overlooking the home straight, Hitler made a great show of demonstrating his involvement in the competition unfolding below. The crowd responded, echoing his delight as German athletes began to dominate.

Germany had never won an Olympic gold medal before but, by three o'clock that afternoon, they had triumphed in the first two events of the Berlin Games. Hitler leaped to his feet, laughing and clapping like a demented seal as Tilly Fleischer and Hans Woellke set new Olympic records in the women's javelin and the men's shot-put. He soon invited both victors to his box – where he congratulated them in ostentatious style. Hitler did the same when Ilmari Salminen, a tall blonde Finn, won the 10,000m final ahead of two of his countrymen.

At 4.15, Jesse Owens ran the second quarter-final of the 100m. Hitler shifted in his seat and focused his binoculars on the runners. Owens was in lane two. Takayoshi Yoshioka, the Japanese sprinter, posed the major threat. The wiry Yoshioka, an Olympic 100m finalist in 1932, was famous for his explosive technique at the start. No man on earth could match his getaway.

Yoshioka had tied a white scarf in a thin band around his head. He looked like a warrior.

Owens started well, and was just behind Yoshioka after twenty metres. He did not even glance to his right as, absorbed in the smooth rhythm of his own running, Owens accelerated decisively. Unlike his morning heat, he ran hard at the tape and won by five metres. A demoralised Yoshioka finished fifth. Owens's time was announced as 10.2. – a new world record.

The crowd rose to him; but the Nazi commanders remained seated, offering restrained applause instead.

Hitler turned intently to Erich Borchmeyer, running in the final quarter-final. Squat and powerful and with a receding shock of black hair, Borchmeyer looked nothing like the elegant Owens and Metcalfe. But he could run, and he surged forcefully over the line in a time of 10.5. Hitler stood up and snapped out a Nazi salute in tribute of Borchmeyer. The German spectators answered him in unison, raising their arms and shouting 'Sieg Heil! Sieg Heil!'

Out on the field, Dave Albritton, following Jesse's advice to slow the tempo of the high jump, had dogged Cornelius Johnson all afternoon. The bar had risen gradually as the sky over Berlin darkened. To keep out the cold both Americans wore tracksuits as they jumped. They had reached the crux of their battle when, despite the drizzle, Johnson sailed into the lead again with a jump of 6 foot 7^{15}/$_{16}$ inches. The pressure on Albritton was intense as, having clipped the bar on his second try, he prepared for his final attempt.

Jesse watched anxiously as his friend ran and jumped, rolling over the wooden bar before his back leg dragged it down behind him. Albritton's failure gave Johnson the gold medal. The rain intensified while Albritton, locked together at 6 foot 6¾ inches with his white team-mate Delos Thurber, steadied himself and won the jump-off to secure silver. Hitler and his contingent departed hastily.

'It isn't for your correspondent to question the movements of the German leader,' Arthur Daley wrote in *The New York Times*, 'but the fact remains that his abrupt departure after reviewing virtually the entire afternoon programme caused the wagging of many tongues ... Five minutes before the United States jumpers moved in for the ceremony of their Olympic triumph, Hitler left his box. Johnson and Albritton are Negroes. None of the other winners were. Press box interpreters of this step chose to put two and two together and arrive at the figure of four.'

Late the following afternoon, at 4.55, the rainy cold made Jesse shiver as he stripped down to his vest and shorts for the 100m final – the most prestigious event of the entire Olympiad and the defining moment of his life. Hitler was once more in his box, hoping that Borchmeyer might somehow defeat the Negro sprinters and win the title of the World's Fastest Man for Nazi Germany.

Jesse had spent the morning resting on the small bed Larry Snyder had set up for him in their dressing-room. Just after 12.30 p.m. he ate the cold steak sandwiches and drank the milk and the coffee Snyder had brought for him in two Thermos flasks. Three hours later he won the first semi-final, streaking away from Wykoff and Hans Strandberg of Sweden. The damp and scuffed cinder felt heavy beneath his feet, even if he seemed to run as effortlessly as ever. Jesse's time, comparatively slow for him at 10.4, reflected the deterioration of the track. He had already lost his world record from the day before, having been informed that his 'wind-assisted' 10.2 in the quarter-final had been ruled inadmissible. Jesse didn't care about breaking the record. He just wanted gold.

Ralph Metcalfe was equally determined. He won the second semi-final in 10.5 which meant that, of the six finalists, only he and Owens had yet to lose a race in Berlin. His ambition was deepened by the disappointment he had suffered in the 1932 Olympic final. Metcalfe was convinced that he, rather than Eddie Tolan, should have been given the gold medal after they finished in a virtual dead-heat. If the twenty-two-year-old Owens still had the 200m and the long jump to come, and perhaps other Games in the future, the 100m final offered Metcalfe his last chance of an Olympic win.

Owens, in the inside lane, clasped his hands in front of his face when his name was announced first. He thought of Charley Riley as he looked down the length of the track. He could hear Pop's words in his head, as if they were back in Cleveland staring at the concrete alley which ran alongside the old black church: *'Imagine you're sprinting over a ground of burning fire.'*

At 4.58 the six men dug their foot-holds in the cinder. Silence descended over the Olympic stadium. The crowd scanned the runners as they lined up alongside each other. Owens, Strandberg, Borchmeyer, Osendarp, Wykoff and Metcalfe. Hitler leaned forward excitedly, his right fist banging lightly against the railing.

Jesse Owens knew that ten seconds would determine the outcome of eight years of dedicated training. He crouched down and placed his fingers just behind the white line. He stretched out his legs to find the holes he had just dug with his trowel.

The starter's soothing voice steadied Owens's twitching legs. *'Auf die Plätze . . .'*

Owens lifted his head. His eyes misted in concentration as he stared at the finish line.

'Fertig!'

Owens raised himself from his haunches. His mind went blank.

The gun cracked loud and flat in the immense stillness.

Owens was out the holes first. The sound of the others, and of the suddenly roaring crowd, dropped away. He was surrounded by silence once more. Owens was lost to the world. He was already racing. He was flying. With his head held high and almost perfectly still, his arms and legs blurred inside their rhythmic pumping. His feet, as always, barely seemed to touch the track.

Owens had opened up a clear lead after thirty metres, ahead of Strandberg and Osendarp with Metcalfe trailing badly after an appalling start. In the adjoining lane, and already a metre down, Strandberg clawed at a muscle in his leg as if he could no longer stand the strain of racing Owens. The Swedish sprinter kept running but Owens glided further ahead, sweeping soundlessly through the halfway mark. With Osendarp now second, Metcalfe began to impose himself. He powered past the outclassed Borchmeyer and the grimacing Strandberg before closing on Wykoff.

Two metres in front, and with only twenty to run, the race belonged to Owens. He flew serenely towards the tape. Metcalfe, however, was now hurtling down the track, charging towards the finish as he moved into second place ahead of Osendarp. The gap between Metcalfe and Owens had narrowed to a metre, but it was too late. Owens snapped the tape and kept running, only slowing as he rounded the bend at the end of the straight. It had looked easy; but a sudden trembling rippled through him. He put his hands on his hips and began to breathe again, gulping fast and hard as he heard the now familiar chant: '*Yess-say . . . Oh-vens . . . Yess-say . . . Oh-vens . . .*'

When Jesse eventually stood on the winners' dais and looked up at the giant results board – *100m Lauf Männer Entscheidung: 1 Owens (USA) 10.3; 2 Metcalfe (USA) 10.4; 3 Osendarp (Holland) 10.5* – three blonde women approached the podium. Before Jesse received his gold medal, a laurel wreath was placed around his head while one of the women presented him with a small potted oak from the Black Forest, given to every winner as a gift from Germany. Jesse and Ralph stood to attention while the 'Stars and Stripes' resounded around the arena. The young German women turned to the American flag and lifted their arms in the Nazi salute.

Hitler watched the scene below him. He, in turn, was studied by the American and British reporters, curious to see whether he would respond positively to their criticism that he had snubbed Cornelius Johnson and Dave Albritton. Henri Baillet-Latour was another caustic observer waiting to see how the Nazi leader might react. The IOC President had held an emergency meeting with Hitler the night before to insist that the *Führer* should shake the hand of every winner – or none at all. Hitler, making no gesture towards Owens, seemed to have chosen the latter course.

Although he did not publicly congratulate the German hero of the day, Karl Hein, who broke the Olympic record in the hammer throw, rumours circulated that Hitler had arranged to welcome all the German medallists in a private room somewhere in the stadium. A former Nazi Youth leader, Baldur von Schirach, tried to convince Hitler he should at least be photographed alongside Owens. 'These Americans should be ashamed of themselves for letting their medals be won by a *Neger*,' Hitler yelled. 'I would never shake the hand of one.'

Even without knowledge of that exchange, the American newspapers reached the same conclusion. The *Los Angeles Times*, in a story headlined as DARK SHADOW FALLS OVER HERR HITLER AS NEGRO ATHLETES DOMINATE OLYMPICS, focused on the *Führer*'s 'depression' in the face of 'a darktown parade'. The Cleveland *Call and Post* chose an even more graphic angle and a banner headline: HITLER SNUBS JESSE!

On the third day of the Games, 4 August, Owens faced his most gruelling stretch of competition. The heats for both the 200m and the long jump began at 10.30 a.m. Owens shattered the world record in the third race with a time of 21.2. He pulled on his top to keep warm and then headed immediately for the jumping pit.

After he had greeted his German rival, Lutz Long, who had

sought him out earlier that week in the Olympic Village, he jogged down the length of the runway. In such an obvious warm-up Owens did not even attempt a leap as he crossed the take-off board. He looked back in disbelief when a red flag was raised. His first 'jump' had been ruled illegal by the German official.

Ten minutes later Owens sprinted down the same lane – this time for real. He hit the board and sailed far beyond the qualifying mark of 23 feet 5 inches. Again, he stared in shock at the red flag. The same official pointed at Owens's feet to indicate that he had over-stepped the marker. Larry Snyder shook his head in fury as Owens rubbed a weary hand over his face. If he made one more mistake he would be disqualified.

Lutz Long walked towards him. The blond and blue-eyed German champion represented one of Hitler's most cherished Olympic dreams. Yet, as Jesse told the story later, Long tried to help him. In front of Hitler, the German offered advice as rudimentary as his English. Jesse was such a great jumper, Long said, he would easily clear the required distance if he took off even six inches short of the board. Jesse smiled and nodded.

The American journalist Grantland Rice watched Owens prepare himself. 'I was searching for some tell-tale sign of emotion. But, calmly, he walked the sprint path to the take-off board and then retraced his steps. Studying the situation for a moment, the American athlete anteloped down that runway and took off at least a foot behind the board. He still landed two feet beyond the qualification mark.'

At 3.30 p.m., Owens repeated his morning feat by winning his second 200m heat in the identical time of 21.2. He could now concentrate on his jumping.

An hour later, the final pared down to a riveting battle between the Negro and the Aryan. Owens took an early lead but the slender Long poured everything into his second leap. He pumped his legs in mid-air as if furiously pedalling an invisible bicycle. It was another big jump. He and Jesse grinned at each other. 25 feet 10 inches. They were level. Hitler did his own crazy jump for joy as he leaped to his feet to applaud Long.

Owens responded within minutes. He bent his knees, arched his back and sprinted down the runway. At the board, his legs started their climb. Without any of the striving which had propelled Long's leap, he flew high and far. On impact, he clasped his hands and leapt once more in the pose of a swimmer plunging into clear blue water. Owens had become the first man in Olympic history to jump past 26 feet.

The German crowd, entranced by the quality and intensity of jumping, were now on their feet, stamping and screaming their support for Long as he walked to the end of the runway. Hitler rocked back and forth as the chant for the German – a low bellow of 'Lutz Long . . . Lutz Long . . .' – reverberated around him. Goebbels and Hesse stood up in anticipation. Hitler, still seated, kept rocking as he trained his binoculars on Long.

The German stared for fifteen seconds at the sandy pit. Then he began to run, his feet kicking up cinder as he moved faster and faster. He jumped with one last massive effort before landing and falling forward onto his stomach. Long looked back quickly as he rose, for the hissing groan of the crowd was unmistakable. The red flag confirmed that his foot had crossed the take-off board. They did not even measure the length of his leap.

Jesse Owens had won his second gold medal, but he still had one more jump to come. He would make it the most memorable of all. Grantland Rice wrote that 'he seemed to be jumping clear out of Germany' as he shattered the Olympic record with a leap of 26 feet 5 inches.

Lutz Long was the first to congratulate Jesse, stepping into the pit to embrace him. They walked past Hitler, arm-in-arm, talking and smiling as the applause rolled down from the grandstands.

While they waited for the medal ceremony, Lutz and Jesse relaxed together in the middle of the grassy arena. They stretched out on their stomachs and spoke a little more. The bond between them was obvious.

Jesse visited Lutz in the Olympic Village that evening. Despite Lutz's fractured English, and Jesse's non-existent German, they communicated over the next few hours. Two apolitical young men had much in common. They had both been born to poor rural families who had moved to the city in search of work. They were also married, with a child each. They agreed to remain in touch after the Games. They were, Jesse said, two uncertain young men in an uncertain world.

Jesse was exhausted when he woke after that emotional night. He did not quibble when the American coaches announced that he would not be called upon to run in the sprint relay. The US team would consist of Frank Wykoff, Foy Draper and the only two Jewish runners on the American team – Sam Stoller and Marty Glickman.

The German press, meanwhile, were becoming increasingly embittered towards the 'black auxiliary tribes' of America. Martha Dodd, the American Ambassador's daughter, was confronted by an aide to Joachim von Ribbentrop, the Nazi Foreign Minister. He accused the United States of relying on 'non-humans like Owens and other Negro athletes'.

On a cool cloudy Wednesday evening in Berlin, with Jesse having ambled through his 200m semi-final in a sweatshirt and a winning time of 21.3, he readied himself for one last push. They lined up for the final at 6 p.m. – Osendarp, the 100m bronze medallist from Holland, Paul Haenni of Switzerland, Lee Orr of Canada, Wynand van Bevern of Holland and Owens and Mack Robinson from America. The two Negroes dominated the race from the start but, soon after they hit the straight, Owens turned up the flame. He raced away to win his third gold in a world record time of 20.7. Robinson picked up silver in 21.1 seconds.

For Jesse, Olympic glory was meant to end there. But, two days later, the American coaches, Lawson Robertson and Dean Cromwell, dropped Stoller and Glickman from the relay. The Jewish sprinters had come first and second in the trial race the Americans had run earlier that week to decide the line-up. Their sudden demotion appeared to smack of anti-Semitism.

Glickman, in particular, reviled the pompous and bow-tied Cromwell. During a vitriolic team meeting, he brushed aside Cromwell's claim that the AAU had just heard that a supposedly 'crack German squad' had been 'training in secret'. Glickman and Stoller stressed the significance of running, and winning, as Jews, in front of Hitler.

'Let Marty and Sam run, coach,' Jesse urged.

Cromwell pointed furiously at the triple gold medallist. 'You,' he seethed, 'will do as you're told.' Owens and Metcalfe were in; Glickman and Stoller were out.

On Saturday 8 August, with Owens running the first leg, the USA equalled the world record in their morning heat. Late that afternoon, in the final, Owens opened a lead which Metcalfe stretched even further. Paul Gallico suggested that 'they put the team so far out in front that the white boys to whom they turned over the baton could have crawled in on their hands and knees'. But Draper and Wykoff ran hard – and the Americans crossed the line with a fifteen-yard lead and a new world record of 39.8 seconds. A more permanent mark on history had also been made. Jesse Owens had become the first athlete in Olympic history to win four gold medals.

Television, attempting to cover the Olympic Games for the first time, had been less successful. As pictures of the relay were beamed back to the village and to eighteen halls around Berlin, *The New York Times* reported that, 'the results are very close to zero. All that you can see are some men dressed like athletes but only faintly distinguishable, like human beings floating in a bath of milk.' White runners, in particular, 'were divined rather than seen, as vague blurs in the milky mess'. The black athletes were more recognisable. And, on the giant smudged screens of Berlin, Jesse Owens stood out clearest of all.

Chapter Eight

Christmas in Havana

Tropical Stadium, Havana, Cuba, 26 December 1936

The rain finally eased as they reached the track. It had fallen in a slanting drizzle ever since they'd arrived in Havana, twenty-four hours earlier, on a miserable Christmas Day. The weather made Jesse think of Cleveland, and of Ruth and four-year-old Gloria waiting for him at home. This was meant to be the best Christmas of their lives. But here he was – back on the dirt.

It felt as if twenty years, rather than twenty weeks, had passed since Berlin. As he neared the starting line he looked up, for the small break in cloud had widened into a patch of clear Cuban sky. Jesse had not run since 15 August when, on an unusually sunny Saturday afternoon at the White City stadium in London, he'd cruised through the third leg of a routine American relay victory over a slow British quartet. He knew this race would be very different.

Jesse glanced at his Cuban challengers. The small man, J.M. Contino, who had been introduced as 'Pepe', stared at him with a grim face which might have been carved from cold white stone. Jesse nodded uncomfortably. Contino ignored him. Jesse's attention switched to Julio McCaw. He was bigger than any sprinter Jesse had ever seen. Julio McCaw was huge.

According to the Cuban Sports Commission and the irre-
pressible Marty Forkins, Jesse's new agent, Jesse Owens vs Julio
McCaw would be the definitive *Race Of The Century*.

Jesse wore his white Olympic vest. Only the number – 723 –
had been removed. The little flag and the slash of red, white and
blue remained, running diagonally across his chest and down the
sides of his shorts. Before the gun fired, the newspapers wanted
a photograph of the Olympic champion and his latest challenger.
Jesse was more obliging than Julio. He dropped down into his
customary starting pose. Jesse lifted his head and gazed into the
cameras, for once without smiling. Julio McCaw loomed over
him as the shutters whirred and clicked.

They were surrounded by thirty men and young boys who, in
their excitement, had run on to the field. Forkins and the Cuban
organisers had boasted that a crowd of 10,000 would throng the
small stadium. They were wrong. Less than 3,000 people would
watch Jesse Owens race Julio McCaw during the half-time interval of a drab football match between the Cuban Athletic Club
and the local Marines.

At last they were ready. Jesse dug two holes in the cinder with
the same trowel he'd used in Berlin. He hunkered down, feeling
the old calm descend as he waited. Then, instead of gazing
serenely down the track stretching in front of him, Jesse turned
to the left to take another look. Julio McCaw and the starter
stood on the far bend, 140 yards from the tape.

The world's fastest man had been given a forty-yard start.
Jesse was given another unexpected boost at the loud bang of
the starter's pistol. The sudden sound startled Julio McCaw.
Jesse sprinted gracefully into an even greater lead. He was back
in the groove, planing smoothly over the rutted surface, his feet
lifting fast and light as he sped away.

Fifteen yards from the finish, he heard the first sounds. Julio
McCaw was closing on him like a thunderous storm. Rather
than following the full curve of the track, Julio McCaw had

taken a short cut across the pitch. He had veered straight over the hard grass so that, by the time he hit the cinders again, he'd made up almost twenty-five yards on the slighter figure flying in front of him. It was too late. Jesse crossed the line first. Seconds later, Julio McCaw pounded past in a blur of dust and cinder.

People moved towards the winner, holding out their programmes for Jesse to sign. They were still cheering in the stands beyond the low wire fencing. Jesse Owens lifted his arm. He had won another race.

Julio McCaw was no ordinary horse. In the Havana newspapers they called him a thoroughbred. He was a five-year-old gelding, ridden by Pepe Contino, one of Cuba's leading jockeys. Contino was scathing. 'He had all the luck at the break,' the jockey said of Owens. 'We'd have run right over him if the race had been a few yards longer.'

Jesse was on happier terms with Julio McCaw. He posed for photographs with the horse, stroking its glistening neck as he grinned cheerfully. The reporters asked him how he felt about running 100 yards in 9.9 seconds. 'Since I haven't competed for a long time,' Jesse said, 'and considering the condition of the track, I am satisfied with my showing.'

'Would you ever race a horse from an even start?' an American journalist wondered.

'I would be willing to race a horse without a handicap,' Jesse said carefully, 'provided the animal selected is not remarkably fast.' He turned back towards the track. 'It sure is good,' he sighed, 'to get out on the cinders again . . .'

Four months earlier, in Berlin, an hour after he had won his fourth gold medal, Jesse Owens turned despairingly to Larry Snyder. 'Coach,' he said softly, 'they just told me I'm going to Cologne.'

'Who did?' Snyder asked in surprise.

Jesse pointed at the departing figures of Dean Cromwell and

Lawson Robertson. 'They want me to run in some meet there – and in about ten other cities as well.'

Snyder guessed that Avery Brundage, the AAU President, and his deputy Daniel Ferris were behind the idea of a barnstorming tour across Europe. Brundage and Ferris were too powerful for him to tackle alone, so Snyder chased after Robertson and Cromwell, confident that he could persuade the US team coaches to fight for the welfare of their star athlete.

They listened silently as he argued for the need to rest Jesse. After ten Olympic races in seven days, and his arduous struggle in the long jump, Jesse had lost twelve pounds in weight. He was physically and emotionally drained.

Yet the AAU were determined to wring as much money as they could from him. They had struck a deal with track administrators across Europe. The AAU would receive 15 per cent of the gate from every exhibition meet they attended – on the condition that Owens performed in the sprints and the long jump.

'It's out of our hands,' Robertson said. 'The contracts have been signed.'

'Anyway,' Cromwell sneered, 'it'll give your boy a chance to see some more of Europe.'

After Snyder had told him the bad news, Jesse sent a five-word telegram to Ruth in Cleveland: *Love, home Sept 16. Jesse.* He counted out the days in his head. Thirty-nine more days on the road. Thirty-nine days until he saw Ruth. It sounded endless.

The next morning, on Sunday 9 August, Jesse woke to his own pile of cablegrams. Most were congratulations from his friends while some were invitations from community organisations to celebrate his achievements once he returned to America. He stared in disbelief at one of the last he opened. A Californian orchestra offered him $25,000 to appear with them for a two-week season. The cablegram did not say what he was meant to do on stage or suggest any dates for his performances. Jesse didn't care. He could barely lift his eyes from that *$25,000.*

At the Olympic stadium, while Jesse watched the last day of track competition, Snyder spoke to sympathetic reporters. Stressing that his role as adviser would be 'financially platonic', Snyder said that 'it would be foolish for me to stand in Jesse's way. He's absolutely at the height of his fame now. Nothing that he could do in his remaining year at college would lift him to a higher peak. Under the circumstances I believe he is justified in accepting offers to turn professional so long as they're the right kind.'

American track administrators, however, needed Jesse to retain his amateur status – at least until they had completed their European jaunt. When they'd sailed across the Atlantic, Dan Ferris, in his position as the AAU's Secretary-Treasurer, had casually outlined a plan for a brief tour after the Berlin Games ended. The details were deliberately vague, and athletes like Jesse were too immersed in their Olympic dreams to pay any real attention. They thought only of Berlin. They did not even hear the whispered names of Cologne, Prague, Bochum, London, Stockholm, Oslo and the rest. They knew nothing of the $30,000 debt the American Olympic Committee needed to clear as a matter of urgency.

Jesse returned to the village at 4.30 that Sunday afternoon, looking forward to a last night in Berlin. He would do the rounds with Dave Albritton as they said their farewells to their new friends from around the world – the most important of whom, for Jesse, was Lutz Long. But he had hardly stepped off the bus when Ralph Metcalfe raced towards him. 'Forget the packing, Jesse,' Metcalfe said. 'Just grab your spikes and togs. We've got a train to catch.'

Metcalfe had just been told that they were leaving for Cologne that evening while a different party, including Dave and Larry Snyder, would depart for Dresden early the next morning. Dave was still at the Olympic stadium so Jesse, having tossed a few things into a bag, left a note for his friend, asking him to take the rest of his gear to Dresden.

The next night, on 10 August, before a crowd of 35,000 in Cologne, Jesse won the relay as well as the long jump. In the 100m final, he raced into a two-metre lead over Metcalfe and seemed certain to crack the world record when he suddenly slowed and allowed his friend a consolation win. The meet lasted from 6.00 to 8.30 p.m. – and, immediately afterwards, Jesse was ordered to attend a banquet which dragged on until midnight with people milling ceaselessly about him. His popularity in Germany was such that the *New York Amsterdam News* suggested that 'many Germans know but two English words and they are "Jesse Owens". Many of those who know four will greet you with "Jesse Owens, Joe Louis".'

Early the next morning he travelled alone to Prague where he was due to join another American party of athletes led by the runner Glenn Cunningham. Jesse had no money when he arrived at the airport. He had to rely on a fellow passenger who bought him some milk and a sandwich. The plane was delayed and Jesse arrived in Prague at 4.30 p.m. He was driven straight to the stadium for a 6 p.m. start. Over the next three hours he won the 100m heats and final, as well as the long jump, though with performances that barely matched his best schoolboy efforts.

The following day, on Wednesday the twelfth, he flew to the German town of Bochum, eating his first meal at four o'clock that afternoon. Two hours later he ran 10.3 for the 100m, equalling the official world record. In the long jump, the unheralded Wilhelm Leichum beat an exhausted Owens by nearly a foot.

An hour later, reunited with Snyder, he was on his way to the town's tiny airport where the Americans boarded a small plane for another bumpy journey – this time to the even less glamorous setting of Croydon, on the south-west fringes of London. They arrived just before midnight and were forced to sleep on mattresses in an empty hangar at Croydon Airport. Even that dismal rest was broken by the early-morning arrival of Albritton and the others who had left Hamburg eighteen hours earlier and only reached England after a nightmarish trawl across a stormy Channel.

In the wan morning light of Croydon, Snyder and the fourteen athletes around him ate stale sandwiches. They at least had a couple of days to settle in a hotel in central London and prepare for another exhibition at White City on the Saturday. Snyder was furious – America's greatest athletes, he said, were being 'treated like trained seals'.

Jesse was equally forthright. 'Somebody's making money somewhere,' he told *The New York Times*. 'They are trying to grab everything they can and we can't even buy a souvenir of the trip.'

Jesse was bolstered by the offers flying in from America. The most exhilarating rumour was that Eddie Cantor, the comedian, was apparently ready to pay $40,000 in exchange for Jesse appearing on his nationwide radio show and alongside him on stage as a dancer. While Snyder sent a return cable to Cantor, requesting more information, Jesse struggled to rationalise the kind of money they were dangling in front of him.

'But Larry,' Jesse eventually said, 'I ain't so hot as a tap dancer.'

'With your sense of rhythm,' Snyder reassured him, 'you'll soon master it.'

Al Jolson was apparently ready to offer $20,000 to the Olympic hero while Mike Jacobs, the ingenuous promoter of Joe Louis, sent a cable asking Jesse not to commit himself to anyone until they met in New York. Less famous names were even more cavalier:

DON'T DO ANYTHING UNTIL YOU TALK TO ME. I WILL DEPOSIT $25,000 IN YOUR ACCOUNT *Jack Bryant, JB Associates*

HOLLYWOOD CONTRACT AVAILABLE. APPOINT ME YOUR REPRESEN- TATIVE *Ed Sykes (Booking Agent)*

HEY MR SPEEDY! LET'S TALK TURKEY! *Norm Dillard, Businessman*

Jesse just laughed. Yet, like the rest of the team, he was broke. The prospect of running before a crowd of 90,000 at White City, and so making thousands more for the AAU, fronted by a millionaire in Avery Brundage, made him bitter. And bitterness, however fleeting, was a strange and unsettling emotion for Jesse Owens.

It seemed as if they had been treated better by the Germans than their own people. The AAU men were like wizened old vultures. Owens and Snyder were on the brink of defying them in London when, late on Friday afternoon, they were given plane tickets to Stockholm by a man they had never met before. He supposedly represented the Swedish promoters of an exhibition meet on Monday night. Stockholm, they were told, would mark the start of a week-long Scandinavian tour.

Refusing to accept the Stockholm tickets, Snyder decided to confront the greed and hypocrisy of the national union. Jesse was thrilled. They were going home. He was, at last, going to make something from everything he had worked so hard for on the track.

Although he did not know it then, he ran his last amateur race the next afternoon. Frank Wykoff, Marty Glickman, Owens and Metcalfe romped away with the White City relay.

While the rest of the team left the hotel just after dawn on Sunday, Owens and Snyder stayed in their rooms. It did not take long for Snyder's phone to jangle. Daniel Ferris was on the crackly line from Berlin, demanding to know why they were not on their way to the airport.

'It's tough for a coloured boy to make any money,' Snyder said of Owens. 'What kind of friend would I be to stand in his way?'

'You know I'll have to suspend him,' Ferris threatened.

'You can't suspend him in the Big Ten,' Snyder insisted, 'that's one organisation you and Brundage don't run. Listen, you're spending money on a call that could be spent making up those Olympic deficits of yours.' Snyder slammed down the phone.

Brundage and Ferris summoned the press in Berlin, on that last day of the Olympic Games, just as Hitler began his final sweeping parade towards the stadium. 'We had no alternative under the circumstances but to disbar Owens,' Ferris told the astonished journalists. 'It is an open and shut case of violating an agreement. It means Owens will not be able to engage in any competition controlled by the AAU or in college meets either. Owens has failed to fulfil his contractual obligations. And so the suspension is automatic. He is barred from this moment onwards.'

When Jesse met with reporters in the hotel lobby that rainy Sunday afternoon, he spoke with uncharacteristic anger: 'This suspension is very unfair to me. There's nothing I can gain out of this trip. All we athletes get out of this Olympic business is a view out of a train or airplane window. It gets tiresome, it really does. This track business is becoming one of the biggest rackets in the world. It doesn't mean a darned thing to us athletes. The AAU gets the money. It gets all the money collected in the United States and then comes over to Europe and takes half the proceeds. A fellow desires something for himself.'

The following Wednesday Jesse and Larry caught a train to Southampton, from where they would sail to New York aboard the *Queen Mary*. Jesse read the *Daily Mirror* as they clicked and clacked through the English countryside. On page fifteen the tabloid headline screamed: SHE SHIRKED THE HANGMAN'S JOB AT A NEGRO'S EXECUTION! The report was from Owensboro in Kentucky and detailed the events of the previous Thursday, 14 August 1936, when '15,000 people – a typical country carnival crowd – saw Rainey Bethea, a Negro, hanged here shortly after dawn. More than 2,000 of them sat on specially constructed wooden stands round the gallows. They had been invited by the authorities. Others watched from windows, roofs and other points of vantage. It was just another execution – of a Negro – but the fact that a woman might have to act as executioner in her official capacity as Sheriff of Davies County drew thousands to the scene. They were cheated at the last moment. The woman, Mrs Florence Thompson, delegated the task of hangman to a local policeman. Many Owensboro citizens gave all-night "hanging parties" at which beer and sandwiches were consumed, and just before the hanging many were drunk. A section of the crowd got impatient. "Bring on the nigger. We're tired," they shouted. Then, when the nigger was brought on, and the trap-door opened and he dropped to his death, they cheered and yelled.'

That same morning, as Jesse and Larry neared Southampton, a body was found in the Olympic Village. Wolfgang Fuerstner, the German Army Captain whose Jewish background was discovered just before the Games, had shot himself. On 20 August the London *Times* confirmed that 'Captain Fuerstner was found dead in his room in the village yesterday morning. He is credited with having originated the idea of meeting the temporary needs of the Olympic athletes with a village which would be of permanent usefulness to the German armed forces.'

As the athletes left the Olympic Village for the last time, machine-gun fire rattled in the adjoining fields. German soldiers were preparing for war.

Ruth Owens and Jesse's parents, Henry and Emma, travelled from Cleveland to New York on Sunday 23 August. The *Queen Mary* was due to dock early the next morning. In the two weeks which had passed since the Olympics they had been interviewed frequently about Jesse's exploits. Emma attributed her son's speed to his docile father. 'Henry,' she said, 'was a naturally fast runner and could beat any of the young men who lived in our section of Alabama about forty years ago.'

Henry accepted the compliment humbly but, buoyed by the

acclaim Cleveland's black preachers had bestowed on Jesse, he spoke with unusual conviction. 'My son's victories in Germany,' he said, 'force me to realise that I made the best move of my life by moving out of the South. Jesse was always a rather shifty little fellow and was always on the go. When we came to Cleveland he started to box his own shadow and naturally I figured he wanted to be a prize-fighter. I never questioned him about it but I later learned from one of his sisters that he was boxing the shadows to develop some sort of foot movement Mr Riley, his coach, had told him about. I now hope my boy and Joe Louis will go to the end of what they started and make a creditable showing not only for themselves, but for our race.'

Ruth had never heard the old boy say so much in a single mouthful. He was normally a one-word kind of man – a 'yep' or a 'nope' being enough to break his silence. She felt even prouder of Jesse. 'If love were money,' she told reporters, 'Jesse and I would be very rich. I'm very happy and have never been jealous of Jesse's athletic achievements which have kept him from me. Both his mother and I just want him to come home and rest. As for me, my lone ambition is to become a perfect wife.'

Once Ruth and Jesse's parents reached New York, they were refused entry to four different hotels – the Biltmore, the Lincoln, the McAlpine and the New Yorker. Herman Finckle, a Cleveland councillor, saved them from wandering the streets further in search of a coloured hotel. Finckle checked out of the New Yorker and reserved rooms both for him and the Owenses at the Hotel Pennsylvania.

At the front of the massed crowd who gathered at the harbour before 8 a.m., hucksters jostled with gamblers for the quickest path to the world's fastest man. They reckoned without Bojangles Robinson. At fifty-eight, the grand old tap-dancer was the same age as Henry Owens, but he had the energy of the twenty-two-year-old Jesse. Bojangles, even at the height of his celebrity, was always searching for publicity.

Aware of the need to squeeze out the hustlers before they snared Jesse, Bojangles made a 'shore-to-ship' call. He was through to the runner in minutes and, with typical zest, persuaded Jesse to say nothing to the press until they'd had time to talk. Bojangles also slipped in the news that, as the unofficial 'Mayor' of Harlem, he'd organised a welcoming committee to usher Jesse from the boat to his own apartment where, the showman cackled, 'the celebrations shall commence'.

Beneath the grinning bonhomie, Bojangles was a tough old dog. It had been decided that the only way to avoid an unseemly crush would be to anchor the *Queen Mary* offshore for an hour. The Coast Guard would then take the most notable luminaries out to the ocean liner to greet Jesse. There was limited seating on the small boat and a fight broke out between rival political groups. Bojangles, followed closely by the Owens clan, swept to the front. They were the first people Jesse saw as he waved down at the Coast Guard cutter bouncing across the waves.

'Gangway for Mrs Owens,' Bojangles roared when the boats linked together. Three hundred newspaperman watched Ruth run to her husband. Jesse wore his pin-striped suit while she dazzled in her black velvet coat and red fox fur. He kissed Ruth, repeating the scene over and over for the salivating photographers. Eventually his mother forced her way into his arms. 'Yeah man, Jesse!' she whooped. 'My baby, my wonderful boy! I'm so proud o'you!'

The rest of the gang joined them – Bojangles, Henry Owens, Jesse's brother Sylvester and Charley Riley. Jesse hugged them all. He was remarkably composed when he addressed the press. Larry Snyder had predicted every question they would ask and, on the journey back from England, he helped Jesse polish his answers. 'I have another year at Ohio State and I want very much to earn my degree,' Jesse said. 'But I cannot afford to reject all the generous offers that have come my way. I am going to take my time before I decide the right course for me. I'm not going to do anything foolish.'

As for his refusal to tour Scandinavia, and his subsequent ban, Jesse said, 'I was simply too tired after the Olympics and felt I couldn't give of my best. Why, I participated in four meets in a week with only a single day's rest. I lost weight and I could no longer do justice to myself. And besides, I never signed anything promising to go on tour. If I had done, I would be there rather than here.'

Jesse refrained from criticising either Avery Brundage or the AAU. 'As a man, Mr Brundage is fine. I have nothing to say against him or the AAU.' Even Hitler was spared. 'I don't think Hitler snubbed me,' Jesse said. 'Please remember he is a very busy man. It seemed that each time I finished running he was scheduled to leave. That's fine with me. And after one of my wins I had to hurry up to reach the radio booth. I passed the Chancellor as he stood up. He waved his hand at me and I waved back at him. I think the writers showed bad taste in criticising the man of the hour in Germany.'

'Let's have no more political questions,' Bojangles snapped, as he steered Jesse away. Bojangles had organised a police escort as they headed for Harlem. There was no need. As the *Columbus Dispatch* noted, 'Owens and his party reached Bill Robinson's apartment at 2588 Seventh Avenue, at 149th Street, shortly before 11 a.m. No one was there to greet them except a bevy of bluecoats assigned in mistaken anticipation of a large crowd of Harlemites.'

Later, the rich and the famous, all associates of the beaming Bojangles, swept through his home. Jesse and Ruth could not help but be seduced – especially when Bojangles's manager, Marty Forkins, outlined the opportunities which awaited.

'You should hook up with Marty,' Bojangles said, 'he'll set you up for life.'

When Jesse, Ruth and his parents arrived at Grand Central

that evening to catch the overnight train to Cleveland, a glittering future seemed assured. He had no need to return to Ohio State. Marty and Bojangles would take care of everything while the money simply rolled their way. The party mood spread to the next morning when they were welcomed home to Cleveland. The streets were teeming with fans. The motorcade wound through a fifteen-mile procession which took in both their East Side ghetto and the white neighbourhoods of the west. Where Harlem had been oblivious to his arrival, the black quarter of Cleveland rocked with pride as streamers and confetti fluttered across the slow parade.

The *Chicago Defender* reported 'another orgy of welcoming' three days later when Jesse and Ruth arrived in Columbus. As if to match the fervour of Cleveland, all state offices were shut for two hours that morning so that people could be at Union Station to greet the Buckeye Bullet. They followed him through the same streets where Negroes were not allowed to live or eat. But, just for one day, the town belonged to Jesse.

It felt as if the whole world would soon be his when he and Marty Forkins signed the contracts which bound them together as 'entertainer' and agent on 1 September. Forkins spoke suavely to the press of pulling together a variety of deals which could net Jesse $100,000.

'Even if I make only $25,000,' Jesse said, 'that'll be fine. When you've had practically nothing all these years that would make a pretty start . . .'

The American track squad arrived back in New York on the morning of 3 September. They were joined by the rest of the Olympic team, headed by Owens, and set off on an emotional pageant through the city. The reception on Broadway was rapturous but, as the *Chicago Defender* observed, 'by the time the cavalcade had reached the fringes of Harlem, word had gone forward that the mighty Jesse Owens and other Race luminaries had been huddled together in two cars, literally Jim Crowed in the parade of honour ... men, women and children unmistakably showed resentment and soon the little tots had developed a tune: *"Jesse Owens Jim Crowed, Jesse Owens Jim Crowed"*. It was a cruel sight. It appears that the advance guards, like the Olympic torch-bearer, had gone ahead, sounding the alarm, because by the time the parade reached the middle of Harlem, the streets were practically deserted. As the band played blatantly along the way, the few spectators who lined the sidewalks hissed loudly, women being the most vehement. Citizens throughout the country are waiting breathlessly to see how the great Jesse Owens is to be treated on his swing around the country on a vaudeville tour. Whether he will demand to be treated like all other American citizens in decent hotels or be shunted into black belts or in shanties along railroad tracks remains to be seen.'

Jesse was soon immersed in the world of big business. He and Ruth got a kick out of being taken to swanky restaurants by company executives who planned to 'do a deal' with him. They were mesmerised by the parties and soirées staged by the rich friends of Bojangles and Marty Forkins. However, the appeal, at least for Ruth, waned. Jesse could tell she was getting edgy. Days turned to weeks and still there was nothing but airy talk of how he might begin earning some of the money that had been promised him.

Like most other offers, Eddie Cantor's $40,000 turned out to be worthless. The proposal had been made by one of Cantor's agents rather than the comedian himself. And whenever Jesse tried to follow up another possible agreement, the next entrepreneur in line would slide away. While he was still hot, it made good copy for them to be seen with Jesse. His more permanent commercial value was still open to question.

By mid-September the Cleveland *Call and Post* commented that, 'a few weeks ago it seemed as if he couldn't get here fast enough to take advantage of all the offers that were pouring in on him. Today he needs a Sherlock Holmes to find a bona fide offer that he can cash in on.' These early setbacks, the paper suggested, had left Jesse 'a sadder but wiser man'.

While the *Chicago Defender* admired the fact that Jesse was 'still gay in voice despite the disappointments', the *New York Amsterdam News* warned that 'Negroes are hoping that the professional promoters of the Ohio lad will not exploit him to the point where they burn him out; that they will not turn him into a mere clowning buffoon just for a few paltry dollars . . . can't an athlete, a sprinter, become professional without turning clown?'

Ruth had seen enough, and returned to Cleveland. Jesse stayed on in New York – to take tap-dancing lessons from Bojangles. If all else failed, Forkins said, he could get a gig as a nightclub performer. Jesse, while professing enthusiasm for his new career, wished he could return to the track.

Larry Snyder began the campaign for an AAU reprieve. 'Jesse is building for the future,' he told the *Los Angeles Times*, 'but becoming a professional entertainer does not mean his days as an amateur athlete are over. He's not going to get money for his running or track work – but as an entertainer.'

Jesse put his own case for reinstatement to the Cleveland branch of the AAU. 'I'm no professional. I haven't received any pay. My status is the same as it's always been. I'm getting good and tired of being kicked around.' His hometown officials argued for the ban to be lifted. Brundage and Ferris were unimpressed. Brundage stressed that an athlete had to be suspended for at least a year after announcing even his intention to turn professional. 'There is no misunderstanding,' Ferris added. 'We wish Owens luck in his new venture.'

At least there was easy money to be made from politics. Jesse was essentially apolitical, but the Republicans confirmed that they would pay him between $10,000 and $15,000 to campaign on behalf of Alf Landon, their presidential challenger to

Roosevelt. The chance to finally earn some money mattered more to him than the fact that Roosevelt had not publicly acknowledged his Olympic achievements. Fearing a backlash from Southern voters, the President rejected a personal plea from the Reverend Ernest Hall, who had married Jesse and Ruth, to officially receive Owens at the White House.

While the *Pittsburgh Courier* claimed that Landon 'is notoriously prejudiced against the coloured race', Jesse spoke more cheerfully on the Republican stump. 'I am not a politician and there are many people here old enough to be my mother or father. I will not attempt to tell them how to vote. But I will tell you that I have met Governor Landon and I think he is one of the finest men in the country.'

If hardly inspirational, Jesse was a far superior political orator to Joe Louis. The boxer had succumbed to desperate overtures from the Democrats and had agreed to lend his support to Roosevelt. When he rose to address the United Coloured Democrats in Jersey City on 8 October, he took the microphone nervously. After clearing his throat and peering at the packed hall, Joe got some words out. 'I wish I could talk as loud as I punch,' he mumbled. He paused before he tried again: 'Although I have trained in New Jersey it is the first time I have been here in Newark ... uh, I mean Paterson.' As the audience laughed, Joe fidgeted with his collar. It felt awful tight. 'Jersey City, I mean . . .' he said at last.

Having abandoned the idea of winning over the AAU, Jesse allowed Marty Forkins to nail down some endorsement deals with black companies and arrange for him to appear at functions and ball games. The money began to grow. He was soon able to start spending. Jesse bought himself a new Buick sedan and a $6,000 eleven-room house for his parents in Cleveland. He spent a further $2,000 on furniture for his parents and put down the deposit for a new Chevrolet to replace Charley Riley's wheezing old Model T Ford.

The large deals still kept slipping away – the latest being the decision in early December not to cast Jesse as the lead in the Hollywood movie *Charlie Chan Goes to the Olympics*. He stayed in Cleveland, for Joe was in town to fight Eddie Simms. The bout, on 18 December, did not last long. One punch, a devastating left hook after eighteen seconds, left Simms a quivering wreck. He tottered up as Arthur Donovan's count reached six.

'How are you, boy?' the referee asked anxiously.

'Let's go someplace,' Simms muttered drunkenly. 'Let's get out of here. Let's go on the roof.'

'Jesus,' Donovan said after he had waved the fight to an end after twenty-six seconds, 'he must be out of it if he thinks I'm some girl.'

Jesse still topped the bill in his home town. 'Of all the persons who took part,' the *Cleveland News* reported, 'the one who received the heartiest applause was a man who did not draw on a boxing glove, and who has never drawn on one in a professional match. Jesse Owens is his name. The former Ohio State track star and Olympic winner literally brought down the house when he was introduced from the ring. Owens climbed through the ropes, straightened up and smiled his winning smile. The ovation was deafening – and even after he had returned to his seat, the demonstration continued.'

Joe was more restrained. 'C'mon, Joe,' a photographer begged after his fast win, 'give us a big smile.' Joe's lips moved slightly. 'Aw, I said a *big* one!' the man yelled. Joe's lips twitched again. The photographer shrugged and brought down the shutter.

Havana, Cuba, 31 December 1936

Two weeks after he had succeeded Joe Louis as only the second black man to be voted America's sportsman of the year, in a landslide Associated Press poll, the AAU decided that, at least in their world, Jesse Owens was no longer America's leading athlete. Even four gold medals could not hold off the challenge of Glenn Morris, a Denver car salesman who had won the decathlon in Berlin.

'Stop kidding me,' Morris said when told that he had narrowly beaten Owens into second place for the AAU's Sullivan Trophy – awarded each year to the country's outstanding performer in track-and-field.

When the Associated Press reached Jesse in Havana, he laughed at the result. 'That's funny,' he said, 'but I'm glad the best man won.'

As Jesse prepared for a long-jump exhibition during the half-time break of an American Football game in Havana on New Year's Day, Marty Forkins made his indignation public. 'This is incomprehensible,' Forkins fumed. 'Ferris is now going too far. He's persecuted Owens ever since the Berlin Olympics. We will demand Ferris change his attitude or else we will institute legal action against the AAU.'

Beneath the tirade, Marty was ready to 'wager any amount' that Jesse Owens would defeat the fastest race horse in America from an even start over 100 yards. The *Washington Post* reported further that 'Marty Forkins, his New York manager, announced in Havana that ice skaters and greyhounds will serve as competition for Jesse Owens during a forthcoming tour'. It would not end there, the *Post* predicted, for Forkins 'believes his coloured star can conquer most members of the animal kingdom in short races'. The circus had begun.

Chapter Nine

King Joe

Joe Louis pulled on his running shoes and zipped up his black tracksuit. With half-open eyes and a body still heavy with sleep, he covered his head with a flat woollen hat to blunt the chill of another pale daybreak. Of all of the afflictions a fighter has to endure, from giving up sex to being smacked in the head so hard it feels like the blood might pour from your ears, this tested Joe the most. He would never get used to the shock of being shaken from his bed at dawn and made to run ten miles along a cold and empty road.

Fifteen minutes later, at 5.15, Joe turned away from the beautiful Spanish-style villa in Chiwaukee and ran wearily down the high dunes overlooking Lake Michigan. He headed inland. They were five miles from Kenosha, in Wisconsin, and another fifty-five from Chicago where later that month, on 22 June 1937, he would fight for the heavyweight championship of the world.

During the first two weeks of May, before Jack Blackburn even arrived in Wisconsin, Joe had done most of his running at Kenosha Stadium, circling the cinder track alone. The end of each fourth circuit meant that he had clocked up another mile. Joe went round and round, feeling like a big rat on a slow wheel. It made him understand why Jesse loved the sprints. When they swung into a more serious routine on 14 May, six weeks before fight night, Blackburn moved him from the track to a road which snaked through the undulating ridges and wetlands of Chiwaukee Prairie.

Joe still felt as if he was on the wheel. Chappie Blackburn and Carl Nelson, Joe's bodyguard, made sure he kept his measured pace as they followed him in an old Model T, clocking off one long mile after another. They said little apart from the occasional grunt and call of *'C'mon!'* and *'Pick it up, Chappie!'* He ran through the quiet countryside. Joe didn't think about much at first, losing himself in the sound of his own steady pant and the thudding of his feet.

Gradually, as his head cleared, the fight rose up inside him. He saw the Cinderella Man, Jimmy Braddock, the reigning champion, weaving towards him, his fists flying as he tried desperately to stop Joe taking away his title and the fortune it held. Even as his legs ached and his feet burned Joe imagined himself in the centre of the ring, cutting down the angles as he moved in and hacked down Braddock. He felt good then.

Joe had not forgotten Max Schmeling. Sometimes it felt as if he could hardly stop thinking about him. When Chappie eventually allowed him to turn around and head for home, just as the pain of the run began to bite, it was Schmeling who drove him on. With the sweat rolling from him, Joe thought of 'Smellin'', as he called the German, and ran a little harder. He remembered how he had cried the night he lost. It was his own fault. He hadn't trained. He hadn't listened to Chappie. He hadn't shown any respect. He thought he could just turn up and Smellin' would fall at his feet. It ain't ever happening again, he told himself. Braddock and the title would come first; and then, best of all, it would be Smellin'.

In the distance, he picked out the yellow-bricked mansion Roxy and Black had hired for their camp. It was the kind of place, they said, the future champion of the world deserved. Joe valued their faith. They'd stood by him, never giving into doubt. Schmeling was supposed to get the first shot at Braddock, but Roxy and Black had manoeuvred past the German and secured Joe his crack at the title. It was a momentous feat. Twenty-nine years had passed since the last black man challenged for the championship – when Jack Johnson chased Tommy Burns all the way to Australia in 1908.

Johnson was hunting Louis now. It had gone on for two years. Johnson had backed Carnera and Baer and Schmeling against Joe. He even chose Jack Sharkey in August 1936: 'Sharkey looks good,' Johnson smirked. 'He should beat Louis. Sharkey is faster and knows how to use both hands. Louis is a sucker for a right hand and after they are through teaching him how to avoid it he will be a sucker for something else.' After Louis's easy win, Johnson turned to his next opponent. He offered to be in Al Ettore's corner. Another Louis victory did little to convince 'Papa Jack'.

'I'd like to say Louis is a great fighter because he is one of my race,' Johnson said, 'but if I did I would only be kidding myself and anybody else who might be interested. Louis not only has marked mechanical flaws but he's not a bright boy.' Apart from claiming that Schmeling would beat Louis 'every day of the week', Johnson argued that Braddock would be too experienced for the challenger. He offered to guide the champion from the corner. Braddock turned him down.

Joe felt he should hate Johnson but, as he ran up the sandy dunes towards the early morning calm of his camp, he almost felt sorry for the old boy. Johnson had no peace from either the memories of his own greatness as a boxer or the fear that Louis might take his place in history. Only seven months before, Johnson had challenged him to a three-round fight. The Bomber declined the chance to punch a fifty-eight-year-old fool into oblivion.

He forgot Johnson as he stood beneath the hot shower in a

large and gleaming bathroom. It was some house. Every bedroom contained two private bathrooms. Each of the ten rooms
was filled with rare antique furniture while more modern con-
veniences, like a swimming pool and a ping-pong table, were
found downstairs. Their original choice of location had been a
house in Lake Geneva, a holiday town in Wisconsin – but the
Geneva Lake Owners' Association protested. A black boxer and
his entourage were not the kind of clientèle they favoured.

Joe was left alone in Chiwaukee. He liked it that way. He fell
back into bed and slept for another three hours, until just after
ten. Breakfast was a grand affair. He drank a jug of chilled
orange juice and then settled down to his prunes and oatmeal
before moving on to a big plate of liver and lamb chops. Joe
took it easy for the rest of the morning before, around two, he
and Chappie walked over to the gym.

On their first day together in Wisconsin, Chappie had spoken
curtly as he smeared Vaseline over Joe's high cheekbones and
eyebrows. 'All right, you son of a bitch,' Chappie growled, 'you
made it this far. Now I'm gonna make sure you go all the way.
When I finish with you, you're gonna be a fucking fighting
machine . . .'

Blackburn believed Louis was the best fighter in the world; he
also understood that Joe was young and new to the trade.
Schmeling had exposed him. But Joe rarely made the same mistake twice. They were a year further down the track. Joe had
won his last seven fights, even if he had not always shimmered.
In January 1937, Bob Pastor ran for ten rounds. Joe won the
fight clearly but there were doubts at ringside that he could ever
adapt to the tactics of supposedly smarter boxers like Schmeling
and Pastor.

Chappie knew different. Joe was learning fast and, with the
steely spirit he brought to Wisconsin, Blackburn was certain
they would take the title. He made Joe concentrate on his
defence, forcing him to do little but keep his gloves up, step

back, sway out of reach and then reply with a disciplined counter. It was colourless work, and so the pressmen had to spice up their repetitive stories. On 14 June, eight days before the fight, the *San Francisco Examiner* claimed that 'Louis Still Lacks Fire'. A day later, the *New York Daily News* agreed that 'Louis's Blows Still Lack Sting'; while on the sixteenth, the *New York Sun* suggested 'Louis Still Unable to Avoid Rights to the Jaw'. On 18 June, with four days to go, *The New York Times* offered a more hopeful, if moderate, headline: 'Louis Fast and in Superb Shape – but Fire of Early Bouts is Gone'.

The reports suited Mike Jacobs. They were part of his pitch to sell the fight. He had placed press agents in the camps of both Louis and Braddock to drum up conflicting publicity which would suggest that the balance had swung from the challenger to the older and less magnetic champion. Joe just did as he was instructed – only occasionally breaking orders. He was told to pull his punches, and so save his hands for the fight, which accounted for the lack of drama in his training. Joe could not keep it up. When one of his sparring partners, the lanky Leonard Dixon, clipped him with a right to the chin, Joe responded with chilling intent. Dixon was knocked cold.

Jimmy Braddock, the Cinderella Man, had held the belt for two years. This would be his first defence. He had waited and waited for a big money contest, and Joe Louis was *the* money fight. Braddock helped make it happen by wriggling out of a bout with Schmeling in September 1936 on the basis that he was suffering from arthritic hands. The rearranged match was set for June '37 and, as a supposed sign of his commitment, Braddock coughed up $5,000 as a guarantee to the New York Commission that he would fight Schmeling. Five grand was peanuts compared to the dough he could make against the Brown Bomber.

Louis yearned for a rematch with Schmeling, but the German turned down a $300,000 offer from Jacobs. Schmeling knew that Braddock was the easier opponent. Victory over Braddock would also earn Schmeling his second heavyweight crown and give him an even stronger bargaining position when he came to negotiate his purse for the inevitable rematch with Louis.

Roxborough and Black campaigned relentlessly for Louis; but another force was involved. The Nazis believed the heavyweight championship would add credence to their beloved myth of Aryan superiority. They actively supported Schmeling's bid to entice Braddock to fight in Berlin for $350,000.

Mike Jacobs, hounded by Roxborough and Black, saw his chance. Stoking American fears that the world championship could be lost in Germany, where it seemed plausible that Hitler would engineer a way of holding on to the title indefinitely, Jacobs also undermined the prospect of Schmeling meeting Braddock in New York. With the backing of his allies in the Anti-Nazi League, whose vice-president was Fiorello LaGuardia, the Mayor of New York, Jacobs convinced Braddock and his manager, Joe Gould, that a fight against Schmeling would be ruined by a boycott.

Jacobs also guaranteed Braddock that he would be paid four times more than Louis. In the event Braddock lost, Jacobs promised Gould ten per cent of his own earnings from all future Louis fights. It sounded terrific to Gould, but Jacobs thought he would find a way out once it was all over. The promoter had already opened up a hole in Braddock's contract with Madison Square Garden and prised the champion away. Jimmy Johnston, the Garden's irate matchmaker, took Jacobs to court. He lost. Judge Guy T. Fake ruled in favour of Jacobs. 'What a name,' Joe said of the judge, 'what a guy.' Louis–Braddock was on.

Schmeling and Johnston, with the backing of the New York Commission, appealed against the decision. An absurd situation ensued. While Braddock prepared to face Louis on 22 June, Schmeling continued training for his own doomed contest against Braddock on 3 June. On the morning of his scheduled challenge, even though he knew that the appeal had failed and Braddock had no intention of fighting him, Schmeling attended a mock weighing-in session. The State Commissioners went through the charade, instructing their doctor to examine the German to ascertain whether he was fit to fight that night.

After a strained silence, while they waited for the missing champion, the Commission President, General John Phelan, stood up and said, 'Gentlemen, you have seen what has happened here. Mr Schmeling has, as per regulation, been weighed and declared fit. His opponent, Mr Braddock, however, has not appeared. Therefore the Boxing Commission declares that the current world champion may not participate in this match and is fined a further $1,000.'

Braddock dismissed the small fine as 'a mosquito bite'. He pointed out the financial incentives of fighting Louis. 'I'm not ducking Schmeling at all,' he said. 'I'm ducking poverty. Poverty has been with me nearly all my life. Now I have a chance to beat it for good. Do you know the difference between the purses I'd have got with Schmeling and what I figure to get in Chicago? Me and Joe Gould will be disappointed if we don't leave with $400,000 after the Louis fight. After Joe and the taxman take their cut I should still end up with $250,000. I'd only have cleared $25,000 after tax against Schmeling.'

Back in May 1935, when he made his own title challenge, Braddock was asked whether he'd ever been on welfare. 'Sure,' Braddock said, 'sure I was. I'm not ashamed of it either.' He explained that, in September 1933, he'd picked up his first welfare check of $21 a month. His career as a boxer, which had been defined by his disappointing loss to Tommy Loughran in a light-heavyweight title contest in 1929, had hit an awful slump. With a weakened right hand which had been fractured repeatedly, and never enough money to look after himself and his family, Braddock was rarely in decent condition. He lost eighteen out of his next thirty-three fights. Braddock was slipping away. While on welfare he finally landed another scrap in the summer of 1934 against a hot prospect from Georgia – a kid called Corn Griffin.

Braddock knocked out Griffin in three rounds, making $200, and went on to win a decision that November over a more talented young black fighter, John Henry Lewis. Even with that $700 purse he still couldn't pay the seven months' rent owed for his apartment on 31st Street. The boxer came to an arrangement with the owner. He and his family moved from the fourth floor to the basement, where Braddock would work as the janitor.

Early in 1935 he had earned $2,000 against Art Lasky. 'I gave $300 to the relief funds of Union City,' Braddock said. 'That covered the $240 I got, all told, when we were on relief. It was the only fair thing to do.' He paid off the rent and, with his wife and three kids, moved back up to the fourth floor. More significantly, his victory over Lasky opened up an unexpected path to the heavyweight title. In an impoverished division he was one of the few opponents available to the clowning champion Max Baer. His subsequent decision over Baer in a mediocre fight was one of the biggest upsets in boxing history.

'Listen,' Braddock said when asked how he felt about facing Louis, 'I used to fight tough guys for ten bucks. I got my nose broken, an eardrum busted and my eyebrows laid open in a fight that paid me eight lousy bucks. I can't miss three hundred grand for this one. And nobody will ever tell me that Louis is three hundred thousand tough . . .'

'The big fight is to be held at Comiskey Park, home ground of the Chicago White Sox, right in the depths of the worst cesspool of vice and crime known to America,' the *New York Enquirer* gasped. 'It is in "Little Hell" that the toughest elements in the Middle West hole in for the plottings of their nefarious crimes. Already thousands of outside blacks have come from Detroit, Memphis, St Louis, Birmingham and New York. Numbers racketeers, *agents provocateurs*, scallywags, street walkers, nymphs, panderers, demi-mondaines and cadets are operating openly. The remnants of the Detroit Purple Mob and the still-strong Capone combination, coupled with Egan's notorious St Louis "Rats", are having a Roman holiday ... Civic leaders expressed frank fear as to the probable result should black spectators at the fight get out of hand. At the last mixed title bout held here, two spectators were slain and scores wounded. With the eyes of the world on Chicago, the better element does not want any race riots.'

Although 10,000 policemen had been assigned around the ballpark, and 4,000 special deputies would patrol the 'black belt', the mood in Chicago was sanguine. Braddock had done much to defuse the racial tenor of the fight. Unlike most of his predecessors as world champion, Braddock seemed without prejudice or malice. He showered and ate alongside his black sparring partners as if he hardly noticed their colour, and refused to supply the press with their usual stream of racy quotes.

Louis, a 3–1 favourite to beat Braddock, was on the brink of history. Yet doubt still swirled around him. He was about to confront some demons from his past. Hype Igoe speculated in the *New York Evening Journal* that, 'the shellacking he got from Schmeling has made him a little gun-shy. It is only natural that any twenty-two-year-old youngster who had to absorb a right hand drubbing such as Max inflicted won't laugh it off in a day, especially a rather proud individual like Joe Louis. I'm positive that Schmeling left his brand on Joe, but how deeply did it sear?'

In an attempt to reduce the tension before they left for Comiskey Park, Jack Blackburn discarded the pre-fight ritual of locking his fighter away for the afternoon in a barren hotel room. After the lunchtime weigh-in, where Braddock's manager kept shouting out Schmeling's name as a way of trying to unsettle him, Joe was allowed to return to his own apartment in

Chicago. He was accompanied by a small posse of solemn men – Blackburn, Bill Bottoms and Carl Nelson.

At three o'clock that afternoon, while Chappie and Joe played cards, Bill Bottoms went to work. It did not take long. At 3.15, Joe's chef laid out a last meal before the fight. Joe ate well, devouring a large steak and salad, before he knocked back a quart of milk and a cup of green tea. He then climbed into his bed and slept. Carl Nelson, acting as time-keeper as well as his bodyguard, woke him at exactly seven. 'C'mon, champ,' Carl said softly. 'Time to go . . .'

Comiskey Park, Chicago, 22 June 1937

The large dressing-room had been divided into two by a thin wooden partition. Braddock and his people were on one side, the Louis camp on the other. They could hear each other as they waited. Joe stayed silent, remembering the moment earlier that day when, as they were about to leave for the weigh-in, the package arrived. It was addressed to him and delivered by special messenger. Chappie ripped it open. They found a record inside. The song was called 'You Can't Take That Away From Me'. The heavyweight champion of the world had scrawled his name across the sleeve: *James J. Braddock*.

Louis played his own game just before the fight. He sat and waited until Braddock, growing prickly with impatience, gave in and left the dressing-room before him. The Bomber soon followed and, before Braddock had even ducked through the ropes, Louis was behind him. He stared blankly at the white Irish shamrock planted in the middle of the champion's green robe.

The fighters were called to the centre of the ring. Louis, dressed in a purple gown with a silk trim of burnt orange, looked at Braddock. His team crowded around him. Only Julian Black appeared distracted as the referee repeated his instructions. The manager nervously shuffled one of his gleaming two-tone shoes across the canvas as if he might step on some luck.

'Boys,' the ref said at last, 'shake hands and come out fighting. May the best man win.'

As they broke away and headed for their corners, Blackburn slid the gum-shield into Louis's gaping mouth. The trainer wrapped an arm around his fighter. 'Don't get careless, Chappie,' Blackburn urged. 'Keep those hands up.'

Braddock came out fast and swung a huge right which Louis ducked. They exchanged punches to the body, with Louis digging a left into the ribcage. Braddock, standing tall, began to work more cautiously behind his jab. He was a decent stylist, but it was difficult for him to hold off Louis. A jolting straight right hurt Braddock and backed him against the ropes. Hard combinations thudded into him. Louis seemed ready to cut loose and do serious damage, but then he missed with an overarm right which, as he stumbled forward, left him wide open to the counter. Braddock reacted instantly, cracking an uppercut against Louis's exposed chin. He had not even seen the punch. Louis was hurt. Louis was down in Round One.

Before Blackburn could yell at him to take a count, and give himself time to recover, Louis jumped up. The referee had not even reached 'two'. Louis veered away from Braddock on rickety legs. He had made the same mistake against Schmeling when he leapt up too quickly after being floored the first time. Braddock moved fast, driving Louis into a corner. Louis avoided another scything right. His head felt surprisingly clear. He connected with a left and a right cross just before the bell.

Blackburn was in the ring as soon as Louis reached his stool. 'OK,' the old man said, 'take it easy. This guy's game and he knows a lot. But he'll come apart after five or six more rounds. Keep sticking that jab in his face. Don't get in too close. OK?'

'OK, Chappie,' Louis nodded.

Braddock steamed out for the second, but a more composed Louis matched him jab for jab. When Braddock whacked a left to the gut, Louis responded with his own hook to the head. The older fighter moved deftly inside and worked the body, but Louis fired back with three successive rights. Braddock winced in surprise. The Bomber hit hard.

Joe boxed patiently in the third round as Braddock kept after him with the right hand. Louis took a few, and he took them well, before settling into his jabbing and shuffling routine. Despite the fast pace, he fought with restraint. The weeks of training, and the warning of that early knockdown, helped him maintain his discipline.

The exchanges were even for the first half of the fourth until Louis began to make his power tell. He was now punching with such accuracy and authority that Braddock had begun to moan softly whenever he was hit. The champion's eyes were puffed and bruised, and there was a small cut above the right brow.

'You're taking over,' Blackburn said, 'but let's wait another round or two. You just take it easy in there, Chappie, you wait for me to tell you when . . .'

After an exceptionally quiet fifth round, as Braddock took a breather behind his own jab, Blackburn upped the tempo again. 'OK,' the trainer said, his black eyes glittering, 'start throwing that right hand now. Give him a real taste.'

Braddock tried to regain the initiative in the sixth. He moved and punched with more conviction while Louis, mindful of Blackburn's command, looked for an opening for his right. A minute passed before Louis saw his chance. A chopping right hand split Braddock's upper lip while another right smashed into the side of his head. Braddock's eyes blurred but his legs held him up. Lefts and rights cascaded from Louis as a crouching Braddock reeled away. In desperation he started hitting out wildly, but Louis countered coolly. 'Hang on, Jim,' Joe Gould yelped from the corner as the bell rang.

Braddock rose slowly for the seventh, the eight-year age gap between him and Louis suddenly looking much wider. He had to keep punching if he was going to stem the next onslaught. His delivery, however, was awry with most of his punches being hopeful swings which could be evaded easily. Louis's jab, in comparison, was sharp and his combinations were precise. He also increased the volume of his punches so that Braddock was given no respite. The Cinderella Man may have known what it felt like to have 'my nose broken, an eardrum busted and my eyebrows laid open' in a fight, but Louis was hurting him like he had never been hurt before. This was a new and dark kind of suffering.

With each hurtful blow, Braddock seemed to sag a little more. 'Hands up,' Gould screamed midway through Round Eight, 'hands up!' He might as well have been telling his fighter to surrender rather than protect himself.

Louis followed a sneaky hook, which knocked down Braddock's left hand, with a brute of a right. It crashed against Braddock's jaw. Louis knew it was over even before Braddock hit the floor. As if he was trying to pump the breath back into the stricken champion, the referee moved his hand up and down, close to Braddock's face, as he neared the end of his count. 'Six . . . Seven . . . Eight . . . Nine . . .' Braddock lay in a curled heap. They could have counted to a hundred, and Braddock would still not have moved.

As Braddock's cornermen hauled him away, Jack Blackburn and Julian Black made it through the ropes. Louis placed an arm around each man as they embraced him. A blue horde of policemen rushed into the ring to stop any black or white invasion. Deadpan Joe was surrounded by forty uniformed men as, with his hand raised high, the announcement was made: *'The winner and new champion of the world – Joe Louis!'*

In the streets outside, across Chicago and all of America, they had clustered around radios and loudspeakers. When they heard those magical words – '*and new champion*' – they shouted out his name again and again and again. '*Joe Louis! . . . Joe Louis! . . . Joe Louis!*' They danced around bonfires and climbed on top of taxis and street cars. '*Joe Louis! . . . Joe Louis! . . . Joe Louis!*' They raced down alleys and avenues and beat out his name on dishpans and dustbins. '*Joe Louis! . . . Joe Louis! . . . Joe Louis!*'

'Joe Louis,' Jimmy Braddock told reporters as he left the ring, 'is some hitter. Man, I could've stayed down three weeks from that last punch. Joe's left jab feels like somebody is jamming an electric lightbulb in your face and screwing it in. His right hand is even worse – it feels like somebody is nailing you with a crowbar.' Braddock shuddered. 'My face was all ripped and bruised when Louis threw that last right. It just about blew half my head off.'

King Joe felt unbearably light in his body. The moment was too much. He fainted in his dressing-room. Chappie brought him round. He had done it. He was the champion of the whole world. Joe allowed Chappie to pull off his gloves.

'I'm gonna take this one,' Blackburn murmured as he held the right glove close to his chest. 'I reckon I earned it.'

Joe nodded blearily. His hands ached. He wanted to see Marva. He wanted to hold her close. But, first, he had to face the press. They closed in on him, asking him how he felt and what it meant to be only the second black champion in history.

'I want Smellin', Joe said in a daze. 'Bring him on.' His hands throbbed even more. 'Don't call me champion until I get that Smellin'. I want Smellin' . . .'

Max Schmeling, seething with frustration after his legitimate challenge for the title had been blocked by the resourceful team around Louis, tried to dismiss the new champion. Rather than watching Louis demolish Braddock at Comiskey Park, he had flown to London in an attempt to arrange a fifteen-round contest against the British champion, Tommy Farr. 'The Chicago result simplifies the situation,' he told the International News Service. 'It makes my forthcoming fight with Farr the logical world title contest. I have no intention of putting myself in the position of challenger. Louis has got to come to me if he wants to fight. I have already beaten Louis and there is no reason why my fight with Farr should not be for the world championship.'

Schmeling, who had not fought since beating Louis, had rejected Mike Jacobs's offer of the challenger's usual twenty per cent cut of the gate for the rematch. He used his considerable contacts in European boxing to persuade the British and French boxing authorities to join the German Commission in announcing their intention to ratify a proposed bout against Farr as a 'world championship' decider. It was always going to be a hollow title, and Farr was soon lured away by Jacobs who guaranteed him $60,000 to fight Louis. 'That's almost double what Schmeling's people have promised me,' the former Welsh coalminer said. 'So guess what? I'm off to New York to fight this Louis feller.'

Schmeling had once again been out-hustled and humiliated by the Americans. He sailed to New York in a state of near despair as he tried to work out how he might reclaim some of the territory he had lost in the fourteen months his career had been dormant. With his thirty-second birthday bearing down on him, Schmeling needed to settle on a fight date with a champion who was eight years younger than him. Although he had told Jacobs that he would not consider anything less than a thirty per cent slice of a title contest against Louis, he could no longer afford to be pedantic.

Soon after the boat docked, Schmeling and his trainer Max Machon travelled to Pompton Lakes to watch Louis train on 25 August 1937. The fight against Farr at Yankee Stadium was five days away. Although he hovered near the back of a large crowd, Schmeling made sure he had a clear view of the ring. He needed to see for himself if Louis had improved as dramatically as the American press claimed.

In contrast to his own infuriating hiatus, Louis had fought and won eight times since losing to Schmeling. The benefit of those thirty-six rounds of boxing was obvious, for Louis moved beautifully and landed his punches with impeccable timing. His sparring partners quaked with the kind of look which suggested they knew that, if they roused him, he would smack them into oblivion. Schmeling was undeterred by such one-sided sparring. Yet he could not fail to be struck by the fact that, as world champion, Louis now had an even greater aura about him. He seemed to burn and glow in the ring.

Two more American icons stood together at the front as the new champion pounded away. Jesse Owens and Babe Ruth, king of the track and king of the diamond, nodded approvingly whenever Joe looked down at them.

'Watch this, Jess,' he said near the end of a round, 'watch this home run, Babe.' And then Joe wheeled round and let fly with a screamer which knocked Tiger Hairston to the ground.

'Done,' Babe growled as Jesse flinched. 'You just better save one of those for Yankee Stadium.'

For all his exuberance in front of Jesse and Babe, Joe bit down hard on his gum-shield when he saw the Germans whispering to each other.

'Do you see 'em?' Joe asked softly as Blackburn wiped the sweat from his eyes.

'I see 'em,' Blackburn said. 'Forget it.'

Joe grunted. This guy was different to any other opponent. Smellin' got under his skin.

After Joe had pummelled George Nicholson, as if it was Schmeling they had put in front of him, Marva joined him in his changing-room. She was still haunted by the memory of sitting helplessly at ringside, staring and crying as, a few feet away, her husband was taken apart by Schmeling, bit by broken bit, in that slow and dreadful beating. It was just the same as if they had put her in a room and made her watch Joe being tortured. The fight gave her nightmares. Sometimes she woke up screaming.

'You OK?' she asked Joe as Chappie unwrapped his hands.

'Yeah,' Joe murmured. 'I'm goin' to see Smellin'.'

'I'll come with you,' his wife said.

Joe was impressed all over again with Marva. She was cool. She was strong. She pitched it exactly right with Schmeling. Marva was polite and sweet as the three of them talked. No one would have ever guessed how many tears, and how much sleep, Schmeling had cost her. But she framed her chat in a businesslike box. It was just formal enough for the German to know the battle was not yet over. Without saying anything out loud, Marva told Schmeling her man was still gunning for him.

Schmeling was friendly and respectful. But, like Joe, the German had the look of a fighter who believed deeply in himself. Schmeling would have been even more interesting to Joe if it had not been so personal. He was too obsessed with Schmeling to admire his fighting conviction.

Still, alone with Marva, he softened as she expressed her surprise. 'I liked that quietness in Schmeling,' she said. 'He was more gentle than I expected.'

'Yeah,' Joe agreed. 'If we wasn't fighting, I might almost like him.' Then the deadpan shutter, the mask he hardly ever showed to Marva, slid down again. 'But I want to fight Smellin',' Joe said. 'I want that more than anything.'

Jesse and Ruth Owens had left Pompton Lakes an hour earlier. They were unusually pensive as their Buick moved slowly through the late afternoon traffic heading back to New York. Jesse remembered how Babe Ruth had button-holed him at a banquet a few days before he sailed to Berlin in 1936. 'You gonna win those Olympics, Jesse?' Babe had asked in his high voice.

'Gonna try,' Jesse promised.

'Tryin' don't mean shit,' Babe had sneered. 'I don't *try* – I succeed.' He launched into a long and dirty-mouthed speech which
culminated in his certainty that he could hit sixty home runs a
year because 'I fuckin' know I'm gonna hit a homer every time
I swing that fuckin' bat'. The Babe's laugh had rumbled up from
his fat belly. 'So, Jesse,' he'd said, 'you gonna succeed in Berlin?'

'Sure,' Jesse nodded with a broad smile. 'Sure I am . . .'

It was a good memory. But Jesse noticed that, in Pompton
Lakes, Babe didn't ask him about the races he ran these days. He
was almost relieved. On 9 June, thirteen days before Joe beat
Braddock, Jesse had sprinted against Sweet Harmony in
Cleveland. He was a slick, but nervous, greyhound. Jesse edged
home at the tape. He still felt empty inside. It was hard to get a
rush out of beating a dog.

Ruth worried about him. She and Marva had enjoyed the
sight of their husbands joking and laughing together for an hour
before sparring began; but Ruth knew that, deep down, Jesse
wished it was him who was in training for another massive
sporting event. She hated the fact that he was racing dogs and
horses instead.

Jesse squeezed her hand. He was all right. They were OK. He
had started the year with a bang. With the help of Bojangles
Robinson, he and Marty Forkins finally nailed a big deal. Jesse
signed a contract worth $75,000 with Consolidated Radio
Artists to lead a twelve-piece band on a tour across America.
Jesse couldn't play an instrument or dance like Bojangles. So he
stood up front and announced each new number in a string of
snappy anecdotes. They also persuaded him to sing a little. That
was a horrible mistake.

On the opening night at the Savoy in Harlem, Jesse did his
thing in front of a packed house. Afterwards Cab Calloway,
Louis Armstrong and Jimmy Durante came backstage to say
hello. They did not seem worried about any competition from
him and his band. At least he looked good in his white suit, and

he and Ruth had a hoot meeting big Cab. They told the chuckling Calloway how his hit – *Minnie The Moocher* – had made Ruth drop her real name of 'Minnie'. There were other special moments. The *New York Amsterdam News* was amongst the sympathetic Negro papers who suggested Jesse was 'charming' and that he 'acquitted himself like a veteran'.

The rest of the tour was harder. They did a long series of one-night stands. It was rough and dangerous. They played black theatres and nightclubs in small towns and crowded cities. It felt like hell. Bottles flew through the air and knife-fights spread across the floor. At the end of some gigs the promoters ran off with the dough. Jesse was soon sick of it. When he came down with a throat infection he took the chance to quit.

He had since set up his own travelling basketball team, the Olympians. Jesse was also trying to establish a pro sprinting circuit where he would run for money against Eddie Tolan and Ben Johnson. In the meantime, he was hanging out with Ben and Eulace Peacock in New York. Eulace was running and jumping again in Big Ten and AAU events. That hurt Jesse. He missed the intensity of competition for it had given his life a shape and a purpose he had never regained. He knew why he had looked so closely, almost with envy, when Joe and Max had faced each other at Pompton Lakes. They were locked in a battle which felt more real than anything else in ordinary life.

Nine months later, on 11 May 1938, Louis and Schmeling signed the contracts for a fight that would decide their consuming rivalry. Louis would take forty per cent of the gate, double the amount guaranteed to Schmeling. The rematch was set for Yankee Stadium on 22 June, a year to the day since Louis had won the title. Before they began the harshest six weeks of training either of them would ever endure, both fighters claimed to be psychologically ready.

'I been trying to get that guy in a ring ever since the night he whipped me,' Louis muttered. 'Now it's gonna come.' Louis had dressed for the occasion in an aquamarine sports coat, a pea-green sweater, a red tie, a white shirt, canary-yellow trousers and two-tone shoes. The champion had also grown a light moustache.

Schmeling wore a dark business suit. His words, however, were meant to have a real cut and dash: 'I will defeat Joe Louis again,' he promised, 'because I have placed in his mind a sense of fear. Always now, in the ring, he anticipates danger. Fear is something he never knew before. It has caused him to talk more than usual. He has been trying to explain what happened in our first fight for two years now and he is still no nearer the solution.'

'Suppose Louis knocks you out this time, Max,' a reporter said. 'You're a hero in Germany. Will there be any change in the way your country looks upon you?'

'No, no,' Schmeling said. 'What difference would it make? It's just a prize-fight. Nothing else.'

Yet, as Schmeling realised privately, the wider political symbolism of the fight threatened to overwhelm him. He was now regarded by many Americans as an official representative of Hitler. The Nazis had already annexed Austria, encouraging a wave of savage attacks on Viennese Jews, and had begun to mass their troops on the Czechoslovakian border in readiness for another invasion. 'The aim of German policy,' Hitler said, 'is to make secure and preserve the racial community – and then to enlarge it so that we have ample living space for our Aryan people.'

Earlier that year, when Louis was invited to the White House, Franklin D. Roosevelt had turned to the fighter during a staged photo-call. 'Lean over, Joe,' Roosevelt instructed, 'so I can feel your muscles.' As the Brown Bomber offered him a bunched arm, the President cracked, 'Joe, we need muscles like yours to beat Germany.'

If there were still calls for America to remain neutral in the event of war spreading across Europe, a world championship fight between Louis and Schmeling engendered a fierce nationalism. It also united a country fractured by race. Rather than describing the fight as a contest between a Negro and a white man, as many of them had done only two years before, newspapers now depicted it as a struggle between an American and a German. The American symbolised freedom; the German represented fascism. Joe Louis, at last, belonged to America. Max Schmeling, once he had taken a licking from Mighty Joe, could run straight back to Hitler.

Schmeling had noticed the change when he fought Harry Thomas at Madison Square Garden in December 1937. He was no longer 'good old Max' to the American sportswriters. He had become *Der Schlager* (The Butcher) and 'the Teuton'. The banners outside the Garden were even more personal: *Schmeling Go Home!*

Five months later, it was far worse. As he walked around New York, Schmeling was distressed when people flashed contemptuous Nazi salutes at him. He tried briefly to defend his countrymen: 'Germans are the fairest people in the world,' Schmeling protested to Jack Mahon in the *New York Daily News*. 'They mobbed that little fellow Jesse Owens when he was there with the Olympic team in '36 and he beat Germans, didn't he?'

Casting aside the frivolity of the Olympic Games, the Nazis had reverted to brutality. As the word *Jude* and the six-pointed yellow star were smeared against doors and windows across Berlin, the concentration camps began to fill. Schmeling himself had been affected. His friend and neighbour Josef Thorak was married to a Jewish woman. Thorak was trapped between his own ambition as a sculptor in the Third Reich and a more fearful loyalty to his wife. They eventually decided that, for the sake of his work, he would divorce her. However, secretly, she would still live with him and their three children. Such a furtive arrangement was never going to last in a Germany committed to a crackdown on *Rassenschande*, or 'race-mixing'.

The Gestapo, tipped off by an informer, began to monitor the sculptor's house. Thorak's close relationship with the Nazis' leading architect, Albert Speer, was the only reason why they did not storm through the front door. Yet Schmeling knew they would soon resort to more vicious tactics. He met with Goebbels to stress that Frau Thorak was 'an exemplary mother and a tremendous woman'.

'She's still a Jew,' Goebbels said.

In an attempt to save her, Schmeling told Goebbels that Frau Thorak encouraged her children to listen to Hitler on the radio. 'Please understand,' the fighter said, 'I see this purely in human terms.'

Although Goebbels arranged for one of his deputies to meet her, the outcome was limited. Frau Thorak escaped the concentration camps but she was forbidden to have any contact with her husband. While she fled into exile in England, Schmeling was watched more closely. When it was discovered that he had met other Jewish friends in Holland, he received an informal warning from the Ministry of Propaganda. Schmeling reacted angrily and was confronted by Goebbels just before he left for America.

'What are you thinking, Herr Schmeling?' Goebbels hissed. 'You come to the *Führer*, you come to me, and still you socialise with Jews!'

Unaware of the trauma Schmeling had witnessed, American reporters now regarded him as, in the words of the *New York Daily Mirror*'s Bob Considine, 'a sober and humourless person, often aloof from the infectious chuckles of his generous Jewish manager, Joe Jacobs. He sticks close to his invariable German friend and trainer, Max Machon, a friendly blue-eyed Teuton, and, occasionally breaking off an interview, will mutter earnestly in German to him while the sports-writers stand vacantly by, wondering what the blazes he's saying.'

Describing the German as an icy loner, Hugh Bradley wrote in the *New York Post* of a 'grim, even bitter Schmeling lurking in the background of a suave interior. When he talks politics he speaks pieces that might well have come out of a handbook of party discipline.'

The Anti-Nazi League, meanwhile, campaigned for a boycott of the fight. Picketing Mike Jacobs's office on West 49th Street, women protesters handed out pamphlets which emphasised that the bout would be exploited by the Nazis for 'propaganda purposes'. They also distributed copies of a photograph which showed Max and Anny Schmeling in conversation with Hitler.

'*Schmeling is a Nazi!*' the women chanted, '*Schmeling is a Nazi!*'

While Germans protested against America's 'unsporting propaganda', Schmeling was damaged further by Goebbels. According to the Nazi newspapers, who were acting on orders from Goebbels, Schmeling claimed 'the black man will always be afraid of me. He is inferior.' Those fabricated quotes had disastrous consequences for Schmeling's reputation in America – even though he insisted that 'I never said any of that. I'm not a politician. I'm just a fighter . . . and I am no superman in any way.'

Since their brief meeting at Pompton Lakes the previous August, Louis and Schmeling had each fought three times. The new champion had been stretched the full fifteen-round distance by Tommy Farr on 30 August 1937. Only five weeks had passed between his defeat of Braddock and that opening defence, and he'd fought with little inspiration in narrowly out-pointing a durable and awkward opponent. A long break rejuvenated him as, in February and April of a new year, Louis knocked out Nathan Mann and Harry Thomas.

Schmeling needed three rounds more than Louis to stop Thomas in eight, but he also moved confidently into 1938 with

decisive points victories over Ben Foord and Steve Dudas. He
described his recent work in the ring as one of the reasons which
would ensure him victory: 'I was in fine shape when I met Joe in
1936 but I hadn't fought for a year then. This time I will be
better because I have just had three fights in the space of four
months. I am so well conditioned and healthy that, even though
I am thirty-two, I am more like a man of twenty-three.'

Schmeling trained relentlessly through the heat wave in
Speculator, upstate New York. Hype Igoe of the *New York
Journal and American* suggested on 4 June that, 'Schmeling looks
like a Seminole Indian. Nearly three weeks of basking in the sun
on the edge of Lake Pleasant has turned the German to a
mahogany hue. He loves the place. "I began by doing one whole
week of road work," Schmeling said, "going from eight to ten
miles each day. My legs have never been in the condition they are
today. I could fight a thousand rounds and not feel fatigued."'

Two years before, in Napanoch, the German camp had been
cast in the shadow of the Bomber. Louis, then, seemed almost
invincible and Schmeling often felt worn down by questions
about his own fear. 'Are you having nightmares about Louis?' he
was asked in 1936. 'Do you worry about being seriously injured
in this fight?' The queries were more tedious than disturbing but,
piled one on top of the other, they had the cumulative effect of
sometimes making him lie awake at night as he wondered how
it would feel to be hit by Joe Louis. Schmeling had the courage
not to give into dread, but it now came as a relief to know that
the shadows had moved across Pompton Lakes.

Jesse Owens admitted to Russell Cowans, the sportswriter and
Louis's former tutor, that, 'I wish we could ban those reporters
from asking Joe if he's worked out a defence against Schmeling's
right hand. Before the first fight, I don't think he thought much
about Max. Maybe that caused over-confidence – but now it's
gone too much the other way. Almost every question they throw
at him has "Schmeling's right hand" in the middle of it. I actu-

ally think he's going to deal with Schmeling very effectively, but the way these guys are going on about that right hand, it's like they *want* him to have nightmares about it . . .'

Schmeling was encouraged. 'I hear that Jack Blackburn, who is a very smart trainer, has got Louis trying to box more cautiously,' the German said. 'So they must be very worried about my right hand. But if Joe plays safe he will be twice as easy for me. If he's too careful and anxious he cannot be dangerous. This is the best news I've had since I came back to America.'

The truth was more tangled. Rather than being preoccupied with Schmeling's right hand, Joe's mind locked on vengeance. As the days passed at Pompton Lakes, and the fight loomed ever closer, he began to speak with uncharacteristic venom. 'I am out for revenge. All I ask of Schmeling is that he stand up and fight without quitting. I'll give him enough to remember for life and make him hang up his gloves for all time.'

His grim words fitted the mood of the camp. Where Lakewood in the summer of 1936 had provided a celebratory atmosphere, as Louis trundled through training for Schmeling amid the streamers, silly hats and a jazz band playing jaunty ditties at ringside, Pompton Lakes in June 1938 was an austere place. Louis, seeing the rigorous schedule of sparring Blackburn had arranged for him, demanded that an additional two days be added to his work-load.

Blackburn ensured that the desire for retribution was framed by a methodical plan. He no longer had Roxy or Mike Jacobs hanging around him, as they had done before the Baer and Carnera fights, trying to persuade him to let Louis drop some unnecessary bombs on his sparring partners. Blackburn, then, had occasionally succumbed for he understood the significance in creating an image of young Joe as an awesome hitting machine in front of the jaundiced New York press.

Three years on, Blackburn was more interested in sharpening

the world champion's defence and expanding his already formidable arsenal of punches. 'Yesterday,' Sid Mercer wrote on 6
June, 'some 2,000 spectators saw Louis in a workout that was
too tame to suit them. He was trying out some new angles of
body punching and he didn't look so good . . . He sank some
powerful punches to the midriff, but seldom let go at the head
with his Sunday sock. There were no knockdowns. So many of
the folks present complained that they didn't get enough for
$1.10.'

Blackburn carefully stoked the fire in Louis and, gradually, he
increased the severity and speed of Louis's work. 'Pace is what's
going to beat Schmeling,' the watching Jimmy Braddock said on
14 June. 'If Joe sets the same pace against Max as he did this
afternoon, he'll murder the guy.'

Another former world heavyweight champion, the scholarly
Gene Tunney, sat in the row immediately behind Braddock. 'If
Joe keeps it up,' Tunney agreed, 'I don't see how he can lose.
He's a much better boxer now. He is more compact, keeps his
arms closer to his body and gets his right up to block punches.
He still doesn't roll with a punch, which is too bad. But Joe can
take a punch and counter – and when he does it won't be a fair
exchange.'

A familiar dissenting voice rose up the day before the fight.
On 21 June, in a UP Agency poll of the ten former world heavyweight champions who were still alive, only Jack Johnson tipped
the challenger. 'Schmeling has the technique,' Johnson explained,
'and technique in fighting is more important than strength or
punching ability. Max, at thirty-two, should be right at his peak.
I think Schmeling's cunning and strategy will win over Louis's
poor craftsmanship.'

Papa Jack paused and then, letting slip his famous 'golden
smile', he said, 'I said the exact same thing last time. I was just
about the only feller to say it. I wasn't wrong then . . . and I ain't
gonna be wrong now. You just watch. Louis is in for another

mighty fall.'

The following morning, in an article syndicated across the country, the ghosted voice of Joe Louis rang out: 'Tonight I not only fight the battle of my life to revenge the lone blot on my record, but I fight for America against the challenge of a foreign invader, Max Schmeling. This isn't just one man against another or Joe Louis boxing Max Schmeling; it's the good old USA versus Germany.'

Across the Atlantic, the Goebbels-controlled *Der Angriff* accused the United States of an 'organised campaign of lies' and of turning the contest into 'a racial question and political affair. Do Americans think so lightly of their world champion that even in the last few hours before the fight they are trying to destroy Schmeling's morale with such attacks? Max will be wise enough to give the yelpers the cold shoulder and permit nothing to destroy his composure and optimism.'

Joe Louis cut a picture of studied cool as he arrived for the 11 a.m. weigh-in at the New York Boxing Commission. He wore a cream Billy Taub suit, a polka-dot scarf, a white hat with a black band running round its base and a pair of sunglasses with two small and perfectly round dark circles for lenses. He and Schmeling, nodding curtly to each other, stripped down to their trunks. The German, weighing in at 193 pounds, was five-and-three-quarter pounds lighter than the champion.

After a late lunch of a steak and salad prepared for him by Bill Bottoms, Joe went for a long walk with Jack Blackburn and Freddie Wilson, one of his buddies who ran with him in the early mornings at Pompton Lakes. The three men strolled silently along the bank of the Harlem River. There was little to say. They were just trying to eat up the hours before they left for Yankee Stadium at 7 p.m.

'How you feel, Joe?' Freddie eventually asked.

'I'm scared,' Joe said.

'Scared?' Freddie replied, concern thickening his voice.

'Yeah,' Joe drawled. 'I'm scared I might kill Schmeling.'

Yankee Stadium, New York, 22 June 1938

Joe lay on the stretcher bed they had set up for him at the far end of the dressing-room. It was just after eight, two hours from the most serious fight of his life. He closed his eyes and, on cue, Blackburn, Roxborough, Black, Carl Nelson and Freddie Guinyard lowered their voices. Their whispering soothed him and, within minutes, Joe was asleep.

They gave him an hour before, at exactly nine o'clock, Blackburn roused him gently. 'C'mon, Chappie,' the trainer murmured, 'it's time we got ready.'

Twenty minutes later they were joined by Max Machon who arrived to watch Blackburn wrap Joe's hands. Although it was usual to have a man from the opposing corner observe the process, Joe could not stop his eyes sliding towards Machon. 'It's OK, Chappie,' Blackburn said.

Machon, monitored by Julian Black, had already taped Schmeling's hands. The German fighter now sat alone in his dressing-room. He had lost both his manager and his cut-man for the night. Joe Jacobs was suspended and barred from the corner after a protracted dispute with the New York Boxing Commission over another of his fighters, 'Two-Ton' Tony Galento, who had brought a keg of beer into the ring before a fight as a publicity stunt. 'Doc' Casey, who had worked on Schmeling's cuts and bruises between rounds for years, had been frightened by the threatening letters which had poured into the German camp. While Schmeling didn't blame Casey, an American, for his absence, he had never felt more alone as he waited for Machon to return.

Blackburn wrapped a fighter's hands better than anyone in the

1. Jesse Owens, Dave Albritton and Mel Walker in their Ohio jerseys in May 1935, *en route* to Ann Arbor and Jesse's greatest performance.

2. Jesse Owens and his coach Larry Snyder.

3. The Brown Bomber entourage: Julian Black, Jack Blackburn, Joe Louis, John Roxborough and Russell Cowans.

4. Deadpan Joe Louis was routinely described as either a 'wild animal' or the 'saviour of his race'.

5. Joe Louis gives a lift to his inspirational trainer, Jack 'Chappie' Blackburn, in early 1936.

6. Jack Blackburn, assisted by a New Jersey policeman, tapes Joe's hands at their Pompton Lakes training camp.

7. Jesse Owens settles down into his 'starting holes' in the freshly-dug cinder.

8. Jesse Owens and Eulace Peacock after their 100-yard race in New York in July 1935. Peacock had just secured his fifth successive victory over Owens in the space of six days. 'I don't know whether I can ever beat him again,' Jesse admitted.

9. While Joe Louis earned over $350,000 from three fights in the summer of 1935, Jesse worked as a part-time petrol-pump attendant in Cleveland.

10. Joe Louis in Harlem with his wife, Marva, the day after their marriage and his victory over Max Baer, before a crowd of 95,000, on 24 September 1935.

11. Jesse and Ruth Owens.

12. Joe and Marva Louis.

13 & 14. Joe Louis and Jesse Owens, pictured at the start of their lifelong friendship.

15. Jesse Owens and Dave Albritton eat their first meal at the Olympic Village in Berlin in late July 1936.

16. Jesse plays the sax while waiting for the US team's departure to Berlin.

17. Jesse Owens, Ralph Metcalfe and Frank Wykoff practise their starts on the deck of the *Manhattan* as it sails to Germany.

18. Jesse and his German long jump rival Lutz Long – Hitler's favourite Olympic athlete.

19. Jesse Owens at the start of the 200m Olympic final, which he won in a world record 20.7 seconds.

20. Jesse leaps to victory in the final of the long jump at the Nazi Olympics.

21. The Fastest Man On Earth: Jesse streaks to an easy win in the 100m final.

22. Naoto Tajima of Japan, Jesse Owens (centre) and Germany's Lutz Long offer different salutes on the podium after the Olympic long jump final.

23. Beyond his athletic heroics, Jesse was voted 'The Best Dressed Man' on the US team.

24. Jesse is kissed by his mother, Emma, and his wife, Ruth, as he disembarks from the *Queen Mary* in New York.

25. A tickertape parade on Broadway celebrated Jesse's Olympic triumph.

26 & 27. Shortly after the Berlin Olympics and his ban from amateur athletics, Jesse Owens was reduced to racing against horses – like Julio McCaw in Havana, Cuba, (top) in December 1936.

28. Joe Louis and his most formidable opponent, Germany's Max Schmeling, play a game of pool, staged for publicity purposes by their promoter Mike Jacobs.

29. Louis and Schmeling take to the scales just before their 1938 rematch in New York.

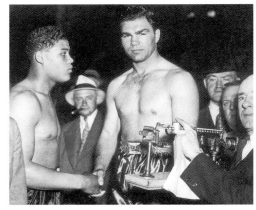

30. Schmeling backs away from Louis in the first round of that historic second fight.

31. The fight of the century: Joe Louis v. Max Schmeling, 22 June 1938.

32. Joe Louis, at the Fort Dix US Army camp, trains for his title fight against Abe Simon in March 1942. Louis donated his entire purse to the American Army.

33. Joe Louis's mother, Lillie, listens to a radio broadcast of his first championship defence after the war – a rematch against Billy Conn in June 1946.

34. Joe Louis, 1946.

35. Joe Louis on the ropes in his last fight – against Rocky Marciano, 26 October 1951.

36. The End: Louis on his knees against Marciano.

37. Jesse revisits the Olympic Stadium in Berlin in 1965.

38. Jesse Owens the orator.

39. Jesse Owens and Richard Nixon.

40. Jesse Owens, a 'special consultant' for Leader Cleaners in Chicago, serves another delighted customer in 1954.

41. A poster in Harry Edwards' office castigates Jesse Owens and Joe Louis as 'Traitors' after their opposition to the proposed boycott of the 1968 Mexico City Olympics.

42. Tommie Smith (centre) and John Carlos hold their fists high in a black power salute after the 200m Olympic final in Mexico City.

43. Boxing promoter Mike Jacobs with Joe Louis and Max Schmeling in 1973.

44. Jesse Owens, 1975.

45. Joe Louis, 1973.

trade and, as they went through the peaceful ritual, Joe felt himself relax again. He was almost ready.

When Machon left, Joe flexed his fingers before he clenched his hands into fists and began to shadow-box. As he shuffled his feet and snapped jabs and crosses into the muggy air, he turned his head towards Blackburn. 'In three rounds, Chappie,' he said, 'if I don't knock Schmeling out you better come in and get me because, after that, I'm through.'

'No, Chappie,' Blackburn said, 'you can go fifteen rounds.'

Joe, however, had decided. He was going after Schmeling straight from the bell. Nobody, not even Chappie, was going to stop him. He began to throw his punches with fast and mean intent, while feinting and ducking in a ceaseless weave. His breath quickened and the sweat shimmered on his skin. Joe normally shadow-boxed for ten minutes in his dressing-room. But this was no ordinary fight. This was the biggest night of his life. He kept moving for thirty minutes, losing himself in the heat and the flow of his phantom punches.

He pulled on a flannel robe to keep his gleaming body warm and then, to look the part, he allowed Blackburn to slip the blue silk robe over his shoulders and tie it round his waist.

Louis walked to the ring first. The noise of 70,000 people climbed to a fevered roar as they saw the hooded figure of the Bomber enter the crammed arena. Louis and his entourage were surrounded by a larger troop of uniformed policemen who held back the crowd. He slipped through the ropes to a howl of approval as, his feet touching canvas, he began his famous shuffle across the ring. This was the way Joe Louis danced. He threw more punches into the hazy night. He looked incredible. He looked invincible.

A different kind of sound greeted the unshaven and slick-haired challenger. It was more like a low bellow. The German pulled a towel over his lowered head as he was showered with fruit, cigarettes and paper cups. It looked as if he had covered himself with a shroud. When Schmeling finally reached the ring, Louis looked at the man who had plagued him for two years and three days. Arthur Donovan, the referee, summoned the fighters and trainers to the middle. His words were aimed mainly at Machon and Blackburn. 'I don't want anybody from your corners sticking his head through the ropes during this fight. It may cause serious trouble.' He made the fighters touch gloves and, wishing them luck, sent them back to their respective corners.

In the sudden hush at ringside, the distinctive voices of the radio commentators could be heard. The guttural chatter of Arno Hellmis, broadcasting live to Germany, was matched by the growl of Clem McCarthy. Hellmis stressed that, 'Max expects to fight before a hostile crowd. Because he is a German he has been at the centre of a storm of racial dispute and boycott. We believe it will not matter. Max will whip Joe Louis again. He will knock him out even quicker than he did before. He has the right hand and the courageous heart to do it.'

McCarthy's message was simpler. Broadcasting to 146 radio stations across the country, he spoke passionately to an estimated audience of 70,000,000 Americans, when he predicted that this would be 'the greatest fight of our generation'.

Louis danced slowly as he waited. The German struck a more curious pose. His arms hung limply at his sides while his chin jutted in the air as he stared across the ring at Louis. It was almost as if, his body exposed, he was daring the champion to attack him. Max Machon, leaning between the ropes, stroked Schmeling's left arm as he offered his final instructions. Louis looked more like a fretful little boy as he hitched up his black shorts.

Schmeling, wearing purple trunks, moved quickest at the bell. Brushing a glove against his brow, he skipped towards Louis, reaching the middle of the ring first. Schmeling backed away in a semicircle and Louis followed, forcing him to change the direction of his retreat towards his own corner. The first punches, two jabs and a short left hook, came from Louis. They were not especially hard blows but the speed with which they were thrown surprised Schmeling. He lowered his head and wrapped his arms around Louis. They clinched, Schmeling gratefully and Louis reluctantly. He showed his displeasure by cuffing Schmeling round the head with another left.

They broke and Schmeling held out a pawing jab in an attempt to hold off Louis. The Bomber feinted and then, leaping in with a giant stride, he landed with his next left. The two men both crouched at impact, their heads touching, before Louis straightened and nailed Schmeling with a combination of a jolting right uppercut, a left and a right. Yet another left and right followed before, at last, Louis missed with a punch – a swinging hook.

Schmeling moved away, his face etched in concern as he awaited the next assault. Louis had found the perfect strategy to unsettle him. While analysing film of the first fight, Blackburn and Louis had realised how much Schmeling struggled when he was pressurised. Even a groggy Louis had been able, in 1936, to force Schmeling to skitter backwards. And Schmeling was a fighter happiest when, given the time and space, he could systematically advance, pick his openings and set himself for that big right hand. Now, against a furious but controlled whirlwind like Louis, he seemed helpless.

He flicked out his left defensively before he threw his first real punch, a long right hand which missed. The only pause in the fight ensued. Louis, stalking Schmeling, waited and feinted for almost ten seconds, ignoring the left hand that the challenger stuck sporadically into the air. The ruse worked. Schmeling, threatened by the prowling Louis, tried to regain the initiative by careering forward into a clinch. The fighters rested their heads against each other for a second time, their cheeks almost touching, before Louis smacked home body blows which made Schmeling hunch over in pain. He tried to push Louis back but the American was already on the rise, throwing a left and a right as he moved away.

A few feet apart, they faced each other again before Louis, fierce and marauding, speared a jab into the older man's face. Peering through his own high guard, Louis hurt him with two more hard lefts. Schmeling, his back now close to the ropes, waved a few reticent jabs at Louis as if wary of antagonising him further. It no longer mattered what Schmeling did. Nothing could stop Louis as, in terrifying close up, he rocked Schmeling with an uppercut. A left and then a right cross crashed into the German with such force it looked as if his face would be permanently dented. Schmeling stumbled, as if in terrible shock, his arms wide and flapping like a stricken bird. He only managed to stay upright by grabbing hold of the top rope and hanging on. Louis measured him for the next punch by pressing his left glove against Schmeling's cheek. When he was sure of the trajectory, which took him all of a second, Louis drew back his left and, with a fast swivel of his feet, widened his stance and shifted his angle of punching so that the full weight of his body would be behind the next blow. The left hook ripped into Schmeling's midriff and made him lean over the rope in anguish, his back now half-turned towards Louis.

While Machon yelled, 'Move, Max, move!' Louis missed a left but then landed one of the most devastating punches ever seen in a ring. Schmeling twisted his trunk just as the paralysing right hand connected with his lower back. The force of the punch fractured two bones, driving Schmeling's third lumber vertebra into his kidney. Schmeling screamed. Louis hesitated, thinking he had heard a woman crying at ringside, but then drove another left to the body and a right cross to the jaw, a left and two more rights to the head. Schmeling dangled on the ropes, seemingly unable to even fall to the sanctuary of the floor.

Arthur Donovan stepped between the fighters, sending Louis

to a neutral corner. Schmeling looked out into the darkness of the baying arena and, seeing nothing, he let go of the top rope and lurched towards Louis. The referee, who had only shouted out a standing count of 'One . . . two . . .', had no choice. Donovan waved the champion back into action. Louis only needed one more punch, a right cross to the jaw, to finally drop Schmeling. He fell heavily on his side before, rolling over on his injured back, he somehow hauled himself up at another count of two.

Louis, with chilling calm, stepped towards his victim. Two jabs, a right cross, a left hook and another short right knocked Schmeling on to his hands and knees. The German, relying on drunken instinct, forced himself to rise again. Louis, once more using his left arm as a measuring stick, held Schmeling at a distance before clubbing him to his broken body with a right and a left. Schmeling, a forlorn and swaying figure, looked up as a brutal right cross smashed against his unprotected jaw.

Max Machon, fearing that his fighter might be killed, flung a white towel into the ring. Donovan bent quickly and threw the sodden towel back through the ropes, for New York regulations prevented a fight being ended by a trainer. His attention was dragged back to the sight of Schmeling trying to rise from the canvas.

The referee picked up the time-keeper's count – which was being echoed by Clem McCarthy as he cried hoarsely into his radio microphone: '*The count is five! Five . . . Six . . . Seven . . . Eight . . .*'

Machon, screaming at the referee to stop it, climbed into the ring. Donovan turned to push him away but then, remembering the ruined fighter at his feet, he suddenly spread his arms wide. It was over. Max Schmeling had been crushed in two minutes and four seconds.

The Nazis had already shut down the radio broadcast in Germany, pulling the plug on Arno Hellmis's commentary as soon as Schmeling went down the first time.

Across America, meanwhile, people ran from their homes. They ran into the black summer night. They took to the streets howling, '*Ah told ya so! Ah told ya so!*' They ran towards the giant banners unfurling from tenement blocks with the message printed in black and white: *Joe Louis Wins, Hitler Weeps!* And they kept running, hammering their hands on cars and banging sticks against dustbin lids as they screamed at everyone they saw: '*King Joe! Ah told ya so! King Joe! Ah told ya so!*'

Duke Ellington was one of many at ringside both bewildered by the speed of Louis's victory and ignorant of the extent of Schmeling's injury. 'I dropped my goddamn straw hat,' Ellington yelled. 'It was rolling around down by my feet. I was just trying to pick it up so I can sit down and watch Joe take this cat apart. And then all of a sudden they all start jumping and hollering. I can't fucking believe it. The goddamn fight is over.'

A few seats ahead of him, at ringside, Bob Considine banged out his report: 'Listen to this, buddy,' he typed, 'for it comes from a guy whose palms are still wet, whose throat is still dry and whose jaw is still agape from watching Joe Louis knock out Max Schmeling. It was, indeed, a shocking thing, that knock-out – short, swift, merciless, complete.'

In the same row of seats, Henry McLemore, the UP Agency newsman, was almost hysterical. 'Joe Louis is swifter than the chair,' McLemore wrote, 'quicker than the hempen noose. Only the guillotine can match him as a killer.'

Joe Louis was surrounded in his dressing-room. The sweat still gleamed on him. They pulled the gloves from his hands and stared in wonder at him.

'Well,' King Joe said at last, a ghostly smile lighting his face, 'I guess you can call me champion now . . .'

PART TWO

Black Days
(1939–81)

Chapter Ten

Bums and Clowns

East St Louis, 19 June 1939

Jesse and the boys reached the speakeasy just before midnight. Beautiful girls and snappy guys were dancing close and shouting out the blues as if they knew every single word of every song. Wednesday nights were always the same in this dark East St Louis house. The handwritten sign outside, which made Jesse and the ballplayers choose this place, had nailed its pitch in four words: *Joe Louis Tribute Nite!*

Jesse was into swing and big band jazz. He liked a smooth and mellow groove. This was raw and wild but here, on the banks of the mighty Mississippi, it was just what he needed. They were at the end of another night on tour. Some towns were better than others. St Louis was some town. Jesse took the back-slaps and the hand-pumps with a sweet grin. He was more famous in East St Louis for being a friend of King Joe than for anything he had done in Berlin three summers before.

'How's Joe doin'?' strangers yelled at him over the blaring racket. 'Send him down here soon as he decks that fat white boy!' Some voices wanted a more personal service. 'Jess! I got me a bet that say he KO Two-Ton Tony in three. Tell him, Jess, tell Joe I need the money.'

John Roxborough had told Jesse that, so far, he knew of ten Joe Louis tribute records. In East St Louis they played the same three songs over and over again: Memphis Minnie's *He's in the Ring (Doin' the Same Old Thing)*, Lil Johnson's *Winner Joe (The Knock-Out King)* and Carl Martin's *Joe Louis Blues*.

A few Wednesdays before, Sonny Boy Williamson had sung live on the stained barroom counter that doubled as their tiny stage. As soon as Sonny Boy got *Joe Louis and John Henry Blues* down on record later that month, the speakeasy would have a new song to make their Wednesday nights hum. Until then, they kicked off as usual with Memphis Minnie. Her black and blue voice, low and husky, crawled through the Mississippi night, refusing to be drowned by the roaring accompaniment from the floor:

> *Now ya people goin' out tonight*
> *Let's go an' see Joe Louis fight*
> *An' if ya ain't got no money*
> *Gotta go tomorrow night*
> *Cause he's in the ring doin' that same old thing*
>
> *I'd chance my money with him*
> *I'd bet anybody that pass my house*
> *In one round Joe would knock him out*
> *In that ring, mmmmmmm, doin' the same old thing*
>
> *I wouldn't even pay my house rent*
> *I wouldn't buy me nuthin' to eat*
> *Joe Louis said take a chance with me*
> *I will put you on your feet*
> *Now in the ring – he's still fighting – doin' the same old*
>   *thing*

Jesse steered clear of the drink. Quieter than most, he listened to the slurred words. When they were not hailing Joe as the saviour of the race, they were celebrating him as their safest bet in a crazy world. The sprightly piano intro to *Winner Joe* sprang up, as little Lil Johnson urged them to gamble on Joe:

> *Yeah man, I'm bettin' on Joe*
> *You got any money?*
> *I'll bet ya!*
>
> *We all heard about Primo Canary*
> *They thought he was so good*
> *But Joe started choppin' on his head*
> *Like a farmer chopping wood*
> *So Choppin' Joe*
> *You got to bet, go*
>
> *Then Joe walked up to the Man Mountain*
> *And kindly shook his hand*
> *Then Joe backed up a step or two*
> *And knocked him in the Promised Land*
> *So knock it Joe*
> *You got to bet, go*

Jesse could have done with a big fight bet to ease his own money blues. Six weeks had passed since he'd hit the bottom. On 5 May 1939, in a Cleveland courtroom, he'd listed his assets as being worth $2,050 while his liabilities totalled $8,891. He had declared himself bankrupt.

'I did that,' Jesse said of his bankruptcy plea to the *St Louis Post-Dispatch*, 'to avoid an unjust judgement. Three years ago I became the co-signer of a note for $20,000 which was to be used to produce a show in New York. Another co-signer took the money and disappeared.' The *Dispatch* gave him his due. 'The world's fastest human said that far from being broke or even

bent his circumstances were very good and he is perfectly satisfied with having turned professional.'

Jesse avoided talking about his dry-cleaning blues. It had been
a filthy business. Two men had promised that, with his name
and some upfront money, the *Jesse Owens Dry Cleaning
Company* would become something special. 'Leave it to us,'
they said, 'and we'll take care of everything. We'll split the profit
three ways.' So he gave them his name. And then away he
dashed to his next trick on the exhibition circuit.

In the summer and fall of 1938 he raced everything they put
alongside him. He'd already split with his manager Marty
Forkins and, after he allowed Joe to beat him in their Chicago
stunt, he ran in Louisiana and Pennsylvania, in Nevada and
Mexico, sometimes with only a stop-watch for company but
more often against an animal or a machine. Jesse took on polo
ponies and trap-horses, greyhounds and double-decker buses,
motor-cycles and steam-engines.

Jesse kept racing and smiling – especially when he compared
the $350 he made here and the $500 he pocketed there to the
empty purse he had carried as an amateur. Yet he knew he lost
something deep inside himself with every performance. It was
not really the speed, for he was still almost as fast as he had been
in the Olympics. His steely calm had eroded instead. Few could
see the change.

Whenever he got home to Cleveland he would drop by the
cleaning business on Cedar Avenue. The *7-Hour Service by the
World's Fastest Man* logo began to look tawdry in a deserted
store. He should have spent time checking the books or drum-
ming up more business, but Jesse could not bear the idea of
sitting in an office out at the back, studying his costs or the fluc-
tuations in customer numbers. He needed to keep moving. When
the inevitable crash came, in February 1939, his partners were
already missing. Jesse was lost again.

The first warning had sounded in October 1938 when the

government placed a lien of $746 against his new house. Jesse had failed to pay any income tax on at least $20,000 he had earned in the frantic months following his return from Germany. He went out and worked even harder in an attempt to make up the deficit. Before he joined the Negro baseball circuit, he managed his Olympians basketball team on another tour and picked up a job as a salesman for Calvert Distillers. Despite being teetotal he tried to sell whisky in each new town he visited with the Olympians. It did not move him back into the black.

The Cleveland *Call and Post* was one of many newspapers to hand down some lofty advice. 'Jesse is still young enough, if he is made of the right stuff, to take this defeat, and come back and justify the confidence millions of people have placed in him. It is a far cry from the adulation and cheers of the world to the ignominy of the bankruptcy court, but there is a trail that leads back. We hope Jesse will take this and in a new field establish himself in the good graces of the public.'

He was out on the road again, travelling with a black baseball team, his buddies in the Pittsburgh-Toledo Crawfords. They had made it to East St Louis late that afternoon and headed straight for the Belleville Athletic Field. Before the Crawfords faced the Belleville Stags, Jesse was expected to run against a horse for the entertainment of a small crowd. After the ballgame, he would give what the *St Louis Globe Democrat* described as a further 'demonstration of his ability. Owens will run a century against anyone who wants to compete, and will circle the bases against a relay of four players.'

It turned out to be one of his better nights. They decided to call off the horse race. The track was considered too muddy by the nag's fretful owner. Jesse had the less traumatic task of sprinting against players from both the Crawfords and Stags. He returned later to face the locals. Jesse made sure the crowd got what they wanted by tripping and falling so that a few small boys could dream of the night they beat the Olympic champion. And then, in the last race, against some of the St Louis bucks who fancied themselves on the cinders, he ran for real and won by more than ten yards.

Rather than climbing on the bus and rattling towards their next destination, the Crawfords spent the night in East St Louis. As Memphis Minnie and Lil Johnson belted out the Joe Louis blues, Jesse felt a glow as good as the buzz he promised you'd get from a hit of Calvert's whisky. A new deal had turned up a few days before. The Indianapolis Clowns, another black baseball outfit, had offered him an improved contract. He would be in work for the rest of the year. Slowly, week by blurring week, he was getting back on track.

A month later, trawling through the South again, Jesse rode with his new team. He sat up front in the old blue Chevy Sedan driven by Ed Hamman, the manager of the Indianapolis Clowns. Ed was white, the Clowns were black. His Chevy led the truck carrying the rest of the squad from Knoxville to Chattanooga. Ed had packed away the sign they usually placed on top of his car. On one side it read *Indianapolis* CLOWNS – *Baseball's No 1 Show Team*; on the reverse it advertised *Baseball Tonite Featuring 'Clown' Ed Hamman*. There was no need to draw attention to the presence of a Negro team driving across Tennessee at night.

After fourteen years on the road, Ed had travelled across the country more times than he could remember. He had begun his career as an eighteen-year-old, playing ball on barnstorming tours for a religious team called the House of David. To wear the House of David colours you had to grow a beard. Since then, in the company of his black friends, he had seen all the colour-bound inequities of America about as close as any white man could get. Ed was no politician or reformist. He just loved playing ball.

Ed was more than a manager. He was *the* Clown, the one player who smeared his already pale face in white greasepaint and drew big red lips around his mouth. Ed the Clown wore a loose jester's uniform, covered in red stars and dots, and a tin hat on his head. He used an enormous plastic baseball bat whenever it was his turn to take a hit. Ed could play a little but the others on the team, the black men, were not that far off the major leagues. The Clowns had won nine American Negro league titles over the years and had toured regularly alongside another colourful outfit – the New York Black Yankees.

Ed was convinced that, eventually, baseball would change. One day the white ball clubs would allow their curiosity to get the better of their prejudice. Joe Louis and Jesse Owens had lit up the ring and the track. Their Negro ball-playing equivalents were somewhere out there, turning out for the Clowns or the Crawfords or the Black Yankees. Some Major League team back East would finally scoop up a couple of black stars to help break a losing streak or make the play-offs. There would be hell to pay; but once the first white club opened their door, the rest of baseball would follow.

Ed was preparing for the day. He would need a new angle to keep the Clowns intact when Negroes were no longer a novelty in ballparks across small-town America. Ed had his plan mapped out. He would move deeper into the showbusiness and freak-show end of the market. He was already scouting around to see if he could find some midgets who could play ball at something near this level. He was an equal opportunity kind of guy.

Jesse gave them some lustre, and his running against horses always drew attention to the Clowns. The crowds in the South showed a particular affinity for the stunt. When Ed walked around the ground after every game, selling copies of his joke-book, Jesse and another horse would be led across the field. Ed cringed when he heard the muffled laughter. Jesse soon shut them up. There was an innate seriousness and elegant grace in everything he did out on the track.

Each night on tour, Ed and the Clowns would rig up his portable floodlights to a generator pumping from the back of their truck. He then sat down in his clown costume and watched Jesse run against some horse. It always started out as a charade; but the sight of Jesse Owens running through the night moved Ed like little else on earth. Beneath the dim lights and the fluttering moths, Jesse raced the horse as if he was on an Olympic track.

Ed and Jesse had worked out a way he could beat every horse he faced. They could even line him up next to a thoroughbred – as long as the horse was positioned close to the gun. When the loud bang came the horse would whinny in fright and rear up. Jesse would be a long way out of his holes by the time all four hooves were back on the ground.

On the road from Knoxville, they fell into talk about skits and tricks. Ed was fascinated by the japes Joe Louis's last opponent, 'Two Ton' Tony Galento, had pulled off. Galento, a squat five foot nine inch, 230-pound barroom owner, had sparred with kangaroos, wrestled with bears and apparently even choked an octopus to death. His doctor, Joseph Higi, reported that 'Two Ton' Tony 'is the thick-boned type [who] does not readily register pain. I doubt if any of the thousands of blows he has ever stopped really hurt him.' Galento claimed to train in Orange, New Jersey, on beer and hot-dogs. He could open the bottles with his teeth and eat ten hot-dogs in a sitting. Galento also relied on a singular repartee – which consisted of him promising that, 'I'll moider da bum!'

Galento also said, 'I'm gonna knock that nigger out,' before he challenged Joe Louis in New York. He tried to get even deeper inside Louis's head during the pre-fight instructions on 28 June 1939. 'Hey Joe,' he sneered, 'I'm gonna fuck your wife.'

Louis fought furiously and carelessly. In the third round, a wild left hook dropped him. The Bomber was hurt but he avoided the next batch of meaty swings and then pummelled Two-Ton Tony with bitter accuracy. For a man never meant to have felt pain before, Galento was a trembling wreck when the referee stopped the fight in the fourth round. Barney Ross, a great fighter who had just lost his world welterweight title to Joe's friend, the even greater Henry Armstrong, said, 'It made my skin crawl, that finish. Nobody who ever lived could stand much more of a beating like that. Galento won't be right for weeks. A beating like Joe gave him isn't something you get over with a night's sleep.'

Jesse and Joe went to a couple of parties after the fight. People hung on to Joe like leeches. The rich and famous were the worst. If Joe hadn't been the champ they would never have lifted their eyes to him. Jesse hated the way they now acted as if they were lifelong buddies of the Bomber.

'I worry about Joe,' Jesse told Ed. 'He could end up being hurt something terrible.'

The same thought crossed Ed's mind a few hours later, only this time he was thinking about Jesse soon after they pulled into a roadside diner. They stepped out into the night. At the door of the restaurant a white man blocked their path. 'We can serve *you* in front,' he said to Ed. He paused as his stare switched to Jesse. 'This nigger will have to go out back.'

They turned away. Ed touched his arm. 'Jesse,' he muttered, 'I feel so bad.'

'It's OK,' Jesse said. 'It's not your fault. Why don't you go back in and get us a couple of sandwiches? We can eat in the car.'

Early in 1940, after an extravagant banquet to honour the great and the good who had made their mark in sport the previous decade, Jesse and Joe were invited to another party. The teetotal boys said sure, as long as they could skip the drinking. The bar was heaving and, being in Chicago rather than Chattanooga, it was a mix of colours and cultures. People, as usual, gravitated towards them. It was easy for Jesse – most admirers just wanted to shake his hand or ask him to sign their beer coaster – but they acted more oddly around the world heavyweight champion.

Jesse always said he'd never have to race another horse if he got a buck every time some white guy came over to take a pop at Joe. They would saunter over to ask if they could have a crack at him. And, Joe being Joe, the champion would say, 'Sure.' He'd stand up and wait for the stranger to punch him. Usually, Joe's lightning hands would block the blow before it could connect. The puncher would exclaim in wonder, or whistle in admiration, when Joe gently opened his own hand to set free the man's bunched fist. It was like magic.

'You still got it, champ,' some would say, as if their punching speed was a true measure of Joe's quality as a fighter.

Jesse was accustomed to watching the ordeal but, that night, with the booze swirling through so many men crowding round the sober pair, the surreal custom seemed sinister. Jesse spotted another prospective puncher. He was in his thirties, as tall as Joe and even broader in the chest. His arms were thickly muscled and, unlike the rest of the drunken smilers, his face was blank.

'Looks like you got one more,' Jesse said as the man walked towards them.

Joe glanced up as he reached their table. 'You're Joe Louis, aren't you?' the man said.

The Bomber nodded as people around them laughed. Joe could look desperately shy in public.

'Mind if I throw one at you?' the man asked.

'OK,' Joe said as he stood up. 'Go ahead.'

A hard left came racing in towards the belly of the Bomber. Joe shot out an arm and easily deflected the punch. He was about to sit down when, as he turned to Jesse, the man threw a right with all his strength. Joe never even saw the punch as it smacked into his face. His eyes suddenly cold and violent, Joe moved towards his attacker. His hands closed into the familiar shape of his fists.

Jesse jumped in front of Joe to try to hold him back. As Joe pushed against him, Jesse turned and shouted, 'What did you do that for, mister?' He grabbed Joe's hands as the man stepped towards them.

'I like to get one of you niggers a week,' he jeered, the drink rising from his breath. 'And there's no nigger bigger than Joe fucking Louis.'

Jesse let go of Joe. He lifted an empty beer mug from the next table. He smashed it against the back of a chair. He held the jagged remains of the glass in his hand and moved a step closer. The room was now silent as the white man backed away.

It was Joe's turn to step in. 'C'mon,' he said, gently prising the glass from Jesse's hand. 'Let's go . . .'

As Joe prepared himself for another fight, against a bum called Johnny Paychek at Madison Square Garden on 29 March 1940, Jesse began work as a suit salesman at the Lyons Tailoring Company in east Cleveland. It wasn't quite the same as having clothes made for you by Billy Taub on Broadway – but it was a steady job. The men at Lyons were thrilled. Jesse's branch manager splashed an ad across the *Call and Post*. Above a photograph of Jesse wearing a snazzy three-piece suit as he posed in a sprinter's traditional starting position, the caption invited the people of Cleveland to, 'Come in and shake hands with the greatest athlete of all time. Jesse will be glad to show you the newest and smartest Spring patterns and colours in fine imported and domestic fashions.'

Six weeks later Jesse called Joe. Lyons had just sacked him. He was too easily distracted from his task. Whenever a gorgeous honey walked past the store the fastest man on earth chased after her. If Jesse had been pursuing the downtown strutters instead, trying to entice some suit-wearing fellers into the shop, his manager might have allowed such unprofessional behaviour. But Jesse always chose a pretty girl over a suit-sale. He had to go.

Joe Louis's career path was more clearly defined. After he had beaten Schmeling in 1938 he won his next four fights the following year by knockout. The first two matched the speed of his Schmeling KO: John Henry Lewis and Jack Roper failed to survive Round One. 'I zigged,' Roper suggested dolefully, 'when I shoulda zagged.' After the Galento massacre, Louis stopped a former opponent, Bob Pastor, in eleven. He was running out of credible opponents.

Nineteen Forty saw more of the same. On 9 February, Arturo Godoy, a durable Chilean, earned himself a June rematch after he survived fifteen rounds with Louis by clinching and crouching so low that the champion had neither the space nor the leverage to punch with his usual impact. Godoy was so relieved at the end that he gave Louis a smacker on the forehead. Deadpan Joe steamed with frustration. He did not enjoy being kissed by a guy. In the return, as he always did when fighting someone for a second time, Louis dominated. He dropped Godoy three times, and won by an eighth-round stoppage.

Another Louis victim, the hapless Johnny Paychek, could only mumble, 'It was the damndest feeling being hit by that guy. I can't describe it. I remember going down the first time, but after that I must have been asleep.'

'The Paychek fight was a vacation,' Louis said, with all the enthusiasm of a man who hates holidays.

Louis, fighting every month, remained the busiest champion in boxing history. His tour began in Boston in December and, over the first six months in 1941, it cruised through New York, Philadelphia, Detroit, St Louis and Washington before returning to New York. The losers – Al McCoy in December, Red Burman in January, Gus Dorazio in February, Abe Simon in March, Tony

Musto in April and Buddy Baer in May – became the 'Bum Of The Month Club'.

Joe faced a more complicated battle in the bedroom. His appetite for women was insatiable. 'I got a big appetite,' he explained. 'It's like I like steaks, lamb chops, chicken, apples and bananas. I like each at different times but I have to have them all.'

On fight nights, only a few hours after leaving the ring, Louis would duck into a hotel like the Theresa in Harlem. His secretary, Leonard 'Bearcat' Reed, would have Joe's 'lady-friends' waiting for him in different rooms. Joe knew all the dancers and singers and waitresses by name, and he would call Reed in the suite next door. 'OK, Bearcat, send in Gloria.' Fifteen minutes later he would be ready for a change. 'Send in Carmen,' Joe would say. After another twenty minutes, Reed's hotel phone would again jangle. 'This is swell, Bearcat,' Joe enthused, sounding only a little weary. 'Tell Lydia she can come see me now . . .'

Reed and Freddie Guinyard arranged for the girls he didn't see to be taken out for the night, with expensive gifts being provided as Joe's own apology. Most of the women, whether he saw them for twenty minutes or not at all, seemed curiously forgiving. They were invariably happy to turn up the next time Joe celebrated the end of his training camp abstinence.

Joe fell for glamorous and intelligent women. Few were as lovely or fiery as Lena Horne who had been a fan of his ever since she was a teenage Cotton Club regular who visited him at Pompton Lakes. Joe was smitten with the singer. They resumed their tempestuous affair in 1940 – even though Joe was seeing two famous actresses, Lana Turner and Sonja Henie, as well as a Cotton Club dancer called Ruby Dallas. Joe was mad about all of them. He was still married to the long-suffering but no less beautiful Marva.

While Joe insisted that his affairs with Turner and Henie

remain 'undercover', he was more brazen with his black lovers. He was fortunate that the Negro press believed the public had no right to know the steamy details of his private life.

Soon after he became champion, Joe and Marva had met up in Detroit with his friend Sunnie Wilson. While Marva and Wilson's date walked ahead, the men called out to say they would take a quick look at the fighter's new Mercury. They jumped into the car. While the unsuspecting women waited patiently inside the restaurant, Joe and Sunnie drove to Toledo where they knew they would find some chorus girls. From Toledo they followed the showgirls to Cleveland and Pittsburgh and Buffalo. Marva and John Roxborough were frantic as they tried to track down Joe. When he finally returned he was as laid-back as if he had been away for ten minutes rather than ten days.

Even the increasingly lonely Marva sometimes smiled at Joe's adventures. During a brief break from the 'Bum Of The Month' excursion, Clark Gable invited him to a fishing trip off the Baja Peninsula in California. Joe kept quiet about Gable's call. Instead, he volunteered to pick up some salt for Marva from the local store. He hit the road without another word. A week later, Joe made it home. He had not forgotten the salt. Joe silently placed it on the kitchen table as Marva stared at him in disbelief. And then, as if to make up for the delay, he placed a five-carat diamond ring on top of the box of salt. 'Sorry,' he eventually said, 'it took so long . . .'

When Marva found a letter from Lena Horne to Joe, she packed up his wardrobe and had it delivered by container truck to his training camp. In his usual style, Joe sent his clothes straight home alongside a stylish Dusenberg roadster he knew Marva loved. He was right. She was crazy about the wood-panelled interior of her new car.

Polo Grounds, New York, 18 June 1941

Joe Louis allowed Mike Jacobs to tack his bout against Billy Conn, the skilled and ambitious world light-heavyweight champion, on to the end of his bum-a-month tour, an escapade which had induced both fatigue and complacency into his usually methodical preparation. The Conn fight would mark the eighteenth defence of his title in less than three years. Louis had knocked out fifteen of those seventeen challengers. His symbolism outside the ring was just as sensational.

Where he had once been the Dark Destroyer, Louis was now acknowledged as a mighty force of cultural unity and political harmony. For Ed Sullivan, 'The fists of Joe Louis are the megaphones and microphones of his race . . . he is all the sorrows and joys, and fears and hopes and the melody of an entire race . . . Louis has done more to influence better relations between two races than any single individual.'

Yet Joe Louis was about to buckle under the weight of his own legacy. A year earlier, in July 1940, Conn and his manager, Johnny Ray, had predicted his fall. Bob Considine paraphrased them in the *Washington Post*. 'Joe Louis is ready to be licked by any intelligent boxer. Soft living, money in the bank, a distaste for fighting and the loss of his punch have made him a husk of his former self. If you or Joe don't believe this then you should listen to little Johnny Ray talk . . . "Sure, Louis was a great fighter," Ray readily agrees. "But everything's got to end. The greatest athletes in every sport fade eventually. It's hard for the average fellow to realise that champions always collapse . . . when Mike Jacobs first mentioned a Louis-Conn fight, a year ago, I hemmed and hawed. Billy weighed in the 160s then. But when Billy heard me hedging he threw his knife and fork down and yelled – 'What the fuck are you stalling for? I'll fight Louis tomorrow'."'

Ashamed of his size advantage, Louis agreed to a stipulation in the contract that he would weigh less than 200 pounds. He starved himself during the last days before the contest, while training harder than usual. Scaling his lowest weight in years, at half a pound below the 200 mark, Louis had severely weakened himself. Billy Conn was still twenty-five pounds lighter than him.

Louis coined an immortal line when he was asked if he would be able to cope with the younger man's speed. 'He can run,' the Bomber said of Conn, 'but he can't hide.'

The bulk of support in the 56,000 crowd was for the smaller man. Sentiment for Conn had been roused further by emotive press accounts of his mother's doomed struggle against cancer. Louis was cheered when he removed his white gown, but the reception for the Pittsburgh challenger was thunderous. Conn danced into work with brisk feet and flashing fists. After some quick combinations, he backpedalled as he threw a left. Conn stumbled and landed with an embarrassing bump on the canvas. The phlegmatic Louis stared at him as if he had just seen a glimpse of the future. The next time Conn went down would surely be at the end of his deliberate punching. Louis connected with two clubbing rights. He seemed to be planning an early end to another mismatch.

The champion dominated the second round. He backed Conn against the ropes and hammered his body. The boyish Billy surprised him. He swallowed his medicine with barely a wince and landed a hard left hook at the bell. From the third on, Conn slipped deftly in and out of range. He put bunches of punches together in pretty combinations as he made Louis look ponderous. The champion was reduced to using his weight to bear down on Conn as if he wanted to sap a little of the sting from those fast punches. Yet, even in the clinches, Conn often hit Louis round the back of the head before sliding away with an impudent grin.

Jack Blackburn spoke bluntly in the corner just before the

start of Round Five. It was time for Joe to 'take charge and lay some pain on this kid'. After he had been winded by a hard left and a right to the body, Conn slowed for the first time that night. He boxed more tentatively through the rest of the fifth and the sixth. But, during the next two rounds, he made Louis retreat as he clipped him with flurries of dazzling punches. Louis's left eye began to swell. He had not been in such a testing fight since losing to Max Schmeling five years before.

Conn took the next three rounds and, in the eleventh, switched from the head to the body and back again. His quantity and quality of punching, as well as his superior speed, began to overwhelm Louis. The unthinkable looked suddenly plausible. Conn was not only out-boxing Louis; he shook the champion with lefts and rights which had the force to earn a knockout. As the bell rescued Louis, Conn raised his hand in triumph. King Joe was ready to crumble.

A tottering Louis sank towards the ropes as Conn unleashed a furious barrage in the twelfth. Four big left hooks to the face and body, interspersed by a right uppercut, made Louis's legs wilt. He reeled forward and Conn wrapped his arms around Louis's ringing head. They did a dark samba together, with Louis's right leg flapping awkwardly in the air, before Arthur Donovan, the referee, stepped in and separated them.

'You're way down, Chappie,' Blackburn said glumly when Louis was ushered back to his stool. 'You gotta knock him out.'

If Conn could stay on his feet for another nine minutes, he would be the new heavyweight champion of the world. He had already decided to pursue a more glorious victory. 'This is easy,' he told Johnny Ray. 'I can take this son of a bitch out this round.'

'No, no, Billy,' Ray urged as they sponged his head with water to cool his ardour. 'You got the fight won. Just stick and run.'

Conn came out with renewed determination in the thirteenth. He would not stick or run. Instead he went toe-to-toe with the desperate champion in front of him. The crowd bellowed in a kind of ecstasy, both at the courage of the fighters and the even more electrifying prospect of a knockout win for Conn.

Closing in on the finish, Conn planted his feet and prepared to launch his favourite left hook. Louis saw his chance. Drawing on all his calm resilience and technique, Louis beat Conn to the punch and landed a short and vicious right to the jaw. He followed up with three right uppercuts which rocked Conn's head with sickening force. Louis threw thirteen successive and unanswered punches. Each landed with clinical accuracy before the last, another crushing right cross, knocked Conn to the ground.

Louis walked to a neutral corner. His expressionless face was bruised and bloated. As Arthur Donovan counted, Louis showed the only sign of his bottomless relief. He allowed himself a breath so deep that his chest rose and fell with a heartbreaking jump. Louis reached the ropes. He spread his arms across the top rung and watched Donovan lift another hand as the count reached six. 'Stay down, Billy,' an exhausted Louis whispered. *'Stay down . . .'*

Conn managed to lift his face from the canvas at the count of seven. He sat up at eight and began climbing to his feet by the time Donovan shouted 'Nine!'. Conn did not even shake his blasted head when the ref signalled the end. Donovan patted him gently on the back as if to tell him how close he had come to the championship.

They covered Joe Louis's head in a white towel. Inside the shroud the Bomber stayed still and quiet. There was no need for words. He had just saved himself.

Even after that terrible scare, Joe was addicted to his old life. And so, two weeks later, on 2 July 1941, his wife filed for divorce. Marva's lawyer said they would leave the amount of financial support she could expect to the court's discretion.

She did, however, point out that Joe Louis owned property valued at $400,000 and had annuities worth another $400,000. His annual income was estimated to be, at the very least, $250,000.

If those figures appeared correct on paper, they were different in reality. As a way of strengthening their hold on Louis, Mike Jacobs and John Roxborough had agreed to a series of loans over the years as the fighter maintained his outrageous spending habits. He was now $100,000 in debt to his promoter and manager – owing $59,000 to Jacobs and $41,000 to Roxy. He had also, following the advice of his hopeless accountant, Ted Jones, failed to pay anything to the IRS for years – in the erroneous belief he would be able to negotiate a settlement more easily on a larger sum. He already owed the tax-man $81,000 and, still, Jones advised him to stall his payment.

Joe didn't care about the money. He just wanted to keep everybody happy. So he went back to work. On 29 September he returned to the Polo Grounds to fight another dangerous young dreamer before a sell-out crowd. Lou Nova, who studied yoga in California and spoke of his 'cosmic punch', was considered by some to be an even more perilous opponent than Conn. John Lardner, one of the sharpest writers in American sport, confessed to 'a heavy heart' as he picked against Louis for the first time in six years.

The unease did not last long. Louis punched with such authority that even his mystical opponent admired both the artistry and the power of hitting. After he had been struck by a masterful left hook in Round Four, Nova staggered to his corner. His agitated seconds attempted to revive him. Big Lou was already lost. 'As I sat there and the handlers fussed over me,' he admitted later, 'I was thinking that I'd got hit with the most beautiful punch I had ever seen. I could feel everything in Joe's body behind the punch, right from the toes up. Wasn't that odd? I'd got hit by Joe and I just sat like a painter, admiring the fine work of another painter. Then the bell rang and we were on our feet and at it again.'

The champion painter splattered him over the canvas in the sixth. Nova simply beamed through his concussion. After the fight he described himself as a student of Far Eastern metaphysics and Hindu spirituality. The Brown Bomber was unmoved. 'I don't like all that mysterious shit,' he muttered.

Chapter Eleven

Soldier Blues

Early on 7 December 1941, hundreds of low-flying Japanese war-planes bombed Pearl Harbor, killing 2,335 American servicemen and sixty-eight civilians. Eighteen US naval ships and 170 American planes were also destroyed in the surprise attack. Within a week, after vowing vengeance against Japan, America joined the Allied Forces in Europe and declared war on Germany and Italy.

Joe Louis was ready to sacrifice himself as an ordinary soldier. He also agreed to Mike Jacobs's suggestion that he should donate the entire proceeds of his next championship purse to the Navy Relief Society. It would be the first time in history the heavyweight champion of the world risked his title for nothing in return.

In the *New York Daily News* the sportswriter Jimmy Powers pointed out that, 'You don't see a shipyard owner risking his entire business. If the government wants a battleship, the government doesn't ask him to donate it. The government pays him a fat profit . . . the more I think of it, the greater guy I see in this Joe Louis.'

The Navy, however, refused to draft Negroes. 'Coloureds' were not considered fit to serve as ordinary seamen. Wendell

Wilkie, the Republican's Presidential candidate in 1940, lamented the fact that Louis could never wear a Navy uniform 'because his skin is black. I don't think this is right in a free country.'

Rather than picking an easy opponent for the benefit – a Johnny Paychek or Jack Roper – Louis endorsed the selection of Buddy Baer. The six foot six inch Baer weighed 250 pounds. In their previous encounter in May 1941, a Baer haymaker knocked Louis through the ropes in the first round. The champion fought back and, in the sixth, he knocked Baer down three times. As the conclusive blow landed seconds after the bell, the fight ended in controversy.

'We got unfinished business,' Baer growled. Unlike Louis, the challenger would be paid for his efforts – a purse which amounted to 12.5 per cent of the gate. While Jacobs made much of donating his promoter's fee to the Navy, he kept quiet about the fact that he'd pocket the money for broadcasting and promotional rights.

Wilkie celebrated Louis's generosity a few minutes before the first bell. Speaking from inside the ring with quivering passion, Wilkie said, 'Joe Lou-eee, your magnificent example of risking for nothing your championship belt, won literally with toil and sweat and tears, prompts us to say: "We thank you." And in view of your attitude it is impossible for me to see how any American can think of discrimination in terms of race, creed or colour.'

Surrounded by the Navy's top brass, Louis moved fast and hit hard. When Baer went down for the third and last time in the first round, he clutched despairingly at the ropes. Louis looked unbeatable.

Two days later, Joe and Julian Black slid into a limousine and headed for Camp Upton on Long Island. Joe was about to become a soldier. He was dressed in his best suit, a cashmere overcoat and one of his favourite broad-brimmed hats. When they arrived, with newsreel cameras trained on him, Joe took off his hat as he sat next to an Army clerk in the mess hall. Hunched over his typewriter, the clerk maintained an appropriate formality. He gravely asked the first question on the induction form: 'Occupation?'

Joe hesitated for a moment, as if searching for the exact word. 'Boxer' was not quite right; and 'World Champion' sounded far too grand.

'Fighter,' he eventually said. The man began to type as Joe remembered to add what he'd been instructed to say for the benefit of the cameras. 'And let's get at them Japs . . .'

Private Joe Louis was assigned to Company C, a black regiment at the base. He had become part of a segregated Army.

On 10 March, at another glitzy dinner hosted by the Naval Relief Society, the uniformed Joe stood nervously at the speaker's podium. His friend Lucky Millander, the bandleader, had tried to bolster him as he faced the prospect of another speech. Lucky came up with a phrase which he persuaded Joe to use: 'We'll win because God is on our side.'

When Louis was alone at the dais, he spoke more from the heart than memory. 'I have only done what any red-blooded American would do,' he said. 'We gonna do our part, and we will win because we are on God's side. Thank you.'

Another friend, Billy Rowe of the *Pittsburgh Courier*, cajoled him for mixing up his words. 'You messed up, Joe,' Rowe exclaimed. 'You were supposed to say God is on our side – not we're on God's side. You got it wrong, you dummy!'

Newspapers, however, trumpeted the saying and Roosevelt sent a telegram from the White House to commend Joe's choice of words. Within days the Army had begun work on their latest recruitment poster. Over an image of Joe Louis wearing his uniform and carrying an Army rifle, their clarion call repeated his message: *We will win . . . because we are on God's side*.

'Who's the dummy now?' Louis coolly asked Rowe.

*

Jesse and Joe laughed in disbelief when they heard that some of the Bomber's words were being analysed by a crazy professor. Elmer Nyberg, of New York University's School of Commerce, taught a six-week course on the art of public speaking. During his seminars, the Professor insisted that, 'There is no one in the sports world today who compares with Louis for tactful public speaking.'

Joe thought differently. Out on the exhibition circuit, between races, Jesse could mesmerise a crowd while talking about his inspirational experiences at the 1936 Olympic Games. He reminded Joe of the finest preachers he had ever heard. And, with America at war, Jesse's memories of Berlin were imbued with even greater meaning. But he had grown weary of having to refute the old myth that Hitler had personally snubbed him – and only him. For years, Jesse had tried to explain the full story. He spoke about Dave Albritton and Cornelius Johnson, for they had been the first Negroes to stand on the winners' podium. Jesse said that the German people had been kind to him; and that he even thought Hitler had waved to him. Six years on, people wanted to hear another speech. They wanted to hear how he had single-handedly defied Hitler. They wanted to hear that his burning anger, after Hitler refused to shake his hand, had driven him to the greatest peak of sporting achievement.

Jesse could not bring himself to say those words. Neither rage nor indignation had won him gold in Berlin. The facts were more plain. He had an extraordinary capacity to run and jump but, more than that, he had given his life to the track. And so Jesse hardly ever mentioned the Nazis. He turned instead to his own roots in Alabama and to his family's move to the North. Joe Louis, he reminded everyone, had taken the same road. They were both Negroes in a white world. But the world was changing, and the chance had come for both of them. One day soon, Jesse promised, the opportunity would open up for everyone in America.

'They said I went to Germany to beat Hitler,' he boomed at the conclusion of his speech. 'Well, I just went to Berlin to run . . .' Jesse let his words hang and die in the air. He held the microphone close to his mouth, and looked quietly at them. The last words were said softly, but with such purity that they conjured up images of him flying alone across that Olympic track: *'. . . and run I did.'*

Like many black Americans who benefited from steady employment in the armament factories, Jesse's improved fortunes coincided with the onset of war. When Pearl Harbor was bombed, he was struggling as a mature student at Ohio State, having returned to university in an attempt to complete his degree. Jesse and Ruth had three daughters – Gloria, who had just turned eight, Beverly, aged three, and Marlene, their new baby. They had moved to the Hilltop, a black neighbourhood in Columbus. In his spare time, Jesse ran another dry-cleaning business on High Street and worked as an assistant to Larry Synder on the university track team. He also performed what Dan Burley described in the *New York Amsterdam News* as 'his now infrequent One-Man Track Shows' – either running alone against the clock or against a horse or a motorbike driven by a crazy daredevil called 'Smiling Jack' Hildebrand.

Little time was left for study. In December 1940 his poor exam results could have resulted in expulsion, yet OSU acknowledged that his personal circumstances made him a 'special case'. He battled on. A year later, his marks were no better. Jesse had no choice. He dropped out again. Two weeks later, in January 1942, Jesse got his break. John B. Kelly, a senior officer in the Department of Civilian Defense, asked him to manage 'the Negro side' of a new national fitness programme designed to boost the physical and mental health of all Americans as they plunged into war.

Jesse was based in Cleveland but, typically, he was expected to roam across the country as he organised fitness clinics and programmes of exercise for ordinary black Americans. He displayed his own physical prowess in exhibitions similar to those that had filled his life for five years. Yet, at its core, it was a stable government job with decent pay. Despite his exemption from the Army on the basis that he was a father of three, Jesse's new position involved him, another ardent patriot, in the war.

Jesse earned yet more acclaim when, on 28 March, he arranged for Joe to join him in Philadelphia for a joint session in which they spoke in front of an awe-struck audience and did some demonstration work on the track and the old punching bag. Jesse did the running and Joe the hitting. They made an irresistible team.

Watching from the sidelines, Chandler Owens, a black publicist unrelated to Jesse, hit upon an idea he sold easily to the Army. Chandler was given permission to prepare a pamphlet for the Office of War Information. *Negroes and the War* was aimed squarely at black Americans after the discouraging news of racism in both Army and Naval quarters. The emotional text centred around the threat of Nazism and described, in vivid detail, how Hitler had snubbed Jesse Owens in Berlin. Jesse's own words about Joe, who had been promoted to Sergeant by the time the booklet was printed, were quoted at the heart of the tub-thumping message: 'Under the lights at Yankee Stadium,' Jesse said, 'our champion knocked out the German champion in one round. Sergeant Joe Louis is now a champion in an army of champions. Joe Louis doesn't talk much, but he talks truly. He talks for thirteen million Negroes, for all American citizens, when he says: "We're going to do our part, and we'll win 'cause we're on God's side."'

The night before he joined Jesse in Philadelphia, the Bomber defended his world title in a second benefit bout – this time for the Army. Louis knocked out Abe Simon, another bum-of-the-month club member, in New York. He donated his entire purse of $45,882 to the Army. His clash with Buddy Baer had made $65,200 for the Navy. The combined total of $111,082 would have virtually cleared his IRS tax debt of $117,000. Even as the plaudits swirled around him, the IRS tightened their grip. Although Louis had given all the money he earned to the government, the IRS decided that both purses should still be considered as income and taxed at the normal rate.

He accepted the fact that his boxing career would be put on hold until the war ended – no matter how many years passed before both Germany and Japan surrendered. His steadiest form of income, until then, would be his Army salary of $28 a week. Joe had more painful emotions to confront. Shortly after the Simon fight, which Jack Blackburn had missed while ill in hospital with pneumonia, Joe received a two-word telegram: *Chappie's Dead*.

Joe was distraught. Chappie had been one of his closest friends, and the best teacher he had ever known. He had also lost his manager, John Roxborough, who was about to begin a three-year sentence at Jackson State Prison for racketeering. Joe's often distant relationship with Roxy's co-manager, the former embalmer Julian Black, had become increasingly strained over financial wrangles. He opted not to renew his contract with Black. No matter how dispiriting the circumstances, Joe had taken control of his life.

He contacted Truman Gibson, a black attorney from Chicago who served in the military as the chief assistant to the War Department's Head of Negro Affairs – William Hastie. Gibson granted Louis his wish to be transferred to Fort Riley, a cavalry camp in Kansas. While Joe found few opportunities to work with horses, he was diverted by the presence of another extraordinary sportsman in the Negro barracks – Jackie Robinson.

The little Joe knew about Jackie Robinson came from Jesse. Jackie's older brother, Mack, had won a silver medal in the 200m Olympic final. Even then, Jackie was on the rise as an athlete of exceptional brilliance. Apart from breaking some of Jesse's junior long-jump records, Jackie Robinson was a formidable boxer and college football player. He also played a little baseball.

It was impossible to miss Jackie Robinson at Fort Riley. He carried himself with a conviction and dazzle which told Joe that, even though Jackie was only four years younger, he was a new kind of black man. He was assertive in a way that eluded both Jesse and Joe. Jackie knew he had the ability to become a huge star in baseball, a black star, and he was ready to smash every obstacle in his way. He objected to the fact that, while he was allowed to play football for Fort Riley, he was banned from the camp's all-white baseball team. Whether in the Major League or a military camp, baseball remained the strictest enforcer of the colour line. Jackie still made an almighty fuss – and plenty of enemies. Joe liked him instantly. After a couple of months in Kansas, he put in another call to Truman Gibson.

'We've got this kid down here,' he told Gibson, 'Jackie Robinson . . .'

Jackie had applied for the Officers' Candidate School at Fort Riley. If he qualified he would train alongside white soldiers in an integrated environment. As usual, the Army turned down Robinson and all other black applications – on the basis that they lacked 'leadership qualities'.

Gibson came down to Kansas to meet the Camp Commander, General Donald Robinson. The irony of the General sharing the same name as the fiery Negro was not lost on any of them. Within days, Jackie Robinson and eighteen other black soldiers enrolled at the school for future officers in the American Army.

He was soon back in trouble. When a white officer yelled at a black soldier, calling him 'a stupid nigger son of a bitch', Jackie stepped in. He stood right in the officer's face. 'Sir,' he bristled, 'you shouldn't address a soldier in the US Army in those terms.'

'Fuck you,' the officer screamed at Jackie. 'That "nigger" goes for you too!'

Jackie had a violent temper. And he knew how to fight. He broke almost every tooth in the white man's head before they pulled him off. It took all of Gibson's diplomacy, and some lavish gifts from Joe, to persuade the commanding officer not to instigate a court-martial.

They sent Jackie to Camp Swift in Texas. One day, on an Army bus, the pistol-carrying driver turned to Jackie and said, 'OK, nigger, get to the back of the bus.' As Jackie hesitated the driver pulled the gun on him. It was a bad mistake. Jackie whipped the gun out of his hand and used it to break some more white teeth. After he produced an equally vigorous legal defence he was pardoned at the court-martial. That was Jackie – he was a tooth-breaking kind of guy. They would all hear of him again.

Another of Joe's young Army friends also went by the name of Robinson. Although he had been christened Walker Smith, the genius of a boxer from Detroit renamed himself Sugar Ray Robinson. Sugar Ray had idolised Joe for years, trailing him like an obedient pup. Joe preferred having Sugar Ray as his buddy rather than as yet another fan. The two fighters were both contracted to Mike Jacobs, and so they ran up some fun on their promoter's tab. They spent tens of thousands together in uniform, usually chasing girls. When it came to women, little Sugar was as sweet as the big Bomber.

In the Army they faced more humiliation. Once, while waiting for a bus in Camp Siebert in Alabama, Joe and Ray became twitchy. 'I'm sick of hangin' round here,' Joe said. 'I'm gonna call us a cab.'

'Hey, soldier,' a white military policemen shouted when he saw Joe pick up the phone.

'What's up?' Joe asked.

'Soldier,' the MP said as he walked towards the fighter. 'You coloured boys belong in the other bus station.'

'What's my colour got to do with anything?' Joe asked.

'This is a white bus station,' the MP insisted.

'I'm wearing an American Army uniform,' Joe said, 'just like you.'

'Down here,' the MP said as he poked Joe in his ribs with a wooden club, 'you'll do as you're told.'

'Don't touch me,' Joe warned.

'I'll do more than touch you, nigger,' the MP said as he drew back his arm.

The Bomber was just about to resort to his favourite old combination when Sugar Ray landed on the MP's back. He wrestled him to the ground as Joe fought two other armed military policemen. The battle was just turning brutal when another soldier yelled, 'Hey! That's Joe's Louis!'

That shout broke up the fight. For once the Army came down on the black side – although only after Louis threatened to call the White House. The MPs were officially reprimanded.

Wherever he travelled, Joe witnessed segregation in base camps around America. He called Gibson every week to report on the latest examples of discrimination. Gibson would take the evidence to the Under-Secretary of War, Robert Patterson, and demand another change. The worst case arose at Fort Bragg, in California. Rather than being made to sit at the back, blacks were not even allowed to board the buses. When Gibson passed on Louis's cold-eyed account, Patterson refused to believe such a situation could exist on the West Coast.

'Sir,' Gibson said evenly, 'Joe just tells it like it is.'

When Patterson called the Fort Bragg Commander he was horrified to learn the truth. From that point on, the US Army passed a resolution banning all forms of segregation in every camp, station and military posting across America. 'It's all down to you, Joe,' Truman Gibson praised the fighter.

While Louis enforced such dramatic shifts in military policy, he was seen in public as a stoical figure who would do anything for Uncle Sam's Army. He featured in two Hollywood war films – the frothy *This Is The Army* and Frank Capra's *The Negro Soldier*. Although Capra tried to sharpen a melodramatic script, he was enough of a realist to know his own satirical leanings had little place in a piece of propaganda which would be screened in 3,500 theatres across America. The film opened with a sermon preached by the young black scriptwriter, Carlton Moss. Footage of Louis fighting Schmeling in June 1938 filled the screen. 'An American fist won a victory,' Moss warbled. 'But it wasn't the final victory. Now these two men who were matched in the ring that night are matched again. This time in a far greater arena and for much greater stakes.'

Capra switched between images of the German and the American in military training. 'Max Schmeling,' the jerky narration continued, 'a paratrooper in the German Army, men turned into machines, challenging the world . . . Joe Louis training for the fight of his life. This time it's a fight not between man and man but between nation and nation. A fight for the real championship of the world, to determine which way of life shall survive – their way or our way. And this time we must see to it that there is no return engagement. For the stakes this time are the greatest that men have ever fought for . . .'

When Joe was discharged from the US Army on 1 October 1945, everything had changed. The war had been won; but the people who'd surrounded him for so long had all gone. He had lost both Marva and Lena Horne. Chappie was dead. Roxy was still inside. Julian Black was out of the frame. So much else had been ruined or remade in the forty-four months he been away from the ring. Even his most enduring nickname, the Brown Bomber, sounded off-kilter after Hiroshima.

Joe was happier reading the baseball reports than the front pages and, incredibly, baseball had also begun to change. In August 1945, Joe had heard his buddy, and one of the few sportswriters he bothered to read, Jimmy Cannon of the *New*

York Post, denounce baseball as 'a game of prejudice, played and dominated by bigoted men with Jim Crow for an umpire'. Good old Jimmy made his rant on ABC national radio. He was far from finished. 'Having Jim Crow as an umpire in organised baseball is laughable when you realise what a fine champion Joe Louis has been. As I have always said, Louis is a credit to his race . . . the human race.'

On 23 October 1945, his twenty-third day of freedom, Joe heard the unbelievable news. Jackie Robinson was on his way to becoming the first black man to play Major League baseball. Branch Rickey, the General Manager of the Brooklyn Dodgers, announced that Robinson would turn out first for the Montreal Royals – who doubled as a farm team for the Dodgers.

'This Robinson is definitely dark,' Al Parsley of the *Montreal Herald* noted. 'His colour is the hue of ebony. By no means can he be called a Brown Bomber or a Chocolate Soldier.'

Jackie Robinson had done it. Joe felt suddenly humbled. He remembered the day at Fort Riley when Jackie looked up at him. 'I got to tell you, Joe,' Jackie said. 'If it hadn't been for you and Jesse Owens . . . man, I wouldn't be here now.'

Joe had just heard from Jesse. The familiar uncertainty was back in his life. At the start of that month, just a few days after Joe got out of uniform, Jesse lost his job at Ford. It was not the first time Jesse and Ford had fallen out since he began working for them back in 1942. Ford had seemed the best thing to happen to him in years. Jesse had moved in on a lower management level before, in August 1943, he became the Director of Negro Personnel. He was the liaison man between the black section of United Auto Workers Union and the white board. When Jesse came down hard in favour of the workers, they fired him, before rehiring him to get everyone talking again. Six months later, they sacked him again; only to reappoint him within hours. His final axing occurred when Jesse was conveniently away from the office. They offered him a different job when he returned. Jesse declined. He'd had his fill of corporate politics. He was going back out on his own.

Jesse had at least decided against returning to the horse track. He had raced sporadically against horses for five straight years until, in 1943, he could no longer stand it. At a grubby little track in Freemont, northern Ohio, he had turned to face a horse he'd beaten six times previously. The organisers had hammered a handwritten sign into the ground surrounding the dusty race strip: *No dogs, no Japs*. If it had not been for their desire to see him race that snorting horse, they might have added *no niggers* to the list. There was an edge of violence in the air. The crowd let slip a growl as the man with the gun moved towards them. Jesse felt a curious kinship with the horse in that moment. He looked at his old rival. The horse, traumatised by the ritual, had opened its eyes wide in terror. White foam rolled from the sides of its mouth. The race seemed even more degrading than usual. Jesse lost for the first time to a horse that afternoon. He had not run against an animal since.

Joe, meanwhile, was $350,000 down. The numbers made his head ache. He had to get back in the ring. With Mike Jacobs pushing the rematch between him and Billy Conn, Joe could quit worrying. It would be OK. Jacobs announced that ringside tickets would cost an unprecedented $100 each – and he predicted that the fight revenue could top $3,000,000.

Joe had to get back into fighting shape. His bout against Conn, his twenty-second defence of the title, was set for the summer. Joe used to love training; now it was just a grind. The gym had lost the glow which once transfixed him. It became a room full of nothing but hurt and sweat. He no longer thrilled to the rhythmic sound of a heavy bag being hit or to the feel of his hands being wrapped. Joe was tired of being smacked in the face and, especially, of returning to the hell of the dawn run.

Yet he missed the rush of those big fight nights. So he kept working. When he and Billy faced each other at the weigh-in he had got down to 207 pounds, only five pounds over his best fighting weight. Billy was fifteen pounds over his own optimum mark. He had blown up into a heavyweight. And it had been as a light-heavy, with fast hands and feet, that Billy had troubled him so much five years before.

They had become friends during the war, and so Billy made him laugh after a couple of minutes in the ring at Yankee Stadium on 19 June 1946. 'Take it easy, Joe,' Billy sighed, 'we've got fifteen rounds to go.' Billy was twenty-eight. He fought like a man of forty. The long wartime break, and the excess weight, had squeezed all the vitality out of him. It was a relief for everyone when Louis pounded Conn into submission in the eighth round.

The whole night had been a let-down. A bored crowd of 45,000 compared poorly to the fevered 56,000 who had watched their classic first fight. And while Jacobs announced takings of $1,925,564 he was still more than a million down on his prediction.

Joe took a big hit himself. His purse of $625,000 was almost double his biggest previous payment. He still had to pay an immediate $115,992 to the IRS and $28,692 in New York State tax. There was more pain in the combined amount he owed Jacobs and Roxborough – but he coughed up the $204,000. His new manager, Marshall Miles, took a cut of $140,492. Joe had another $33,884 in expenses to settle and, although he and Marva were considering a second marriage, he still had to clear her alimony claim of $66,000. The total amount he signed away within forty-eight hours was $589,060. He had $35,940 left – and the IRS had yet to impose its own taxation demand on the fight for $246,055. At the final count, he would be $210,115 in the red from that single bout. Joe knew why they said some circles were vicious.

Yankee Stadium, New York, 25 June 1948

After an historic eleven years and three days as world champion, and an unprecedented twenty-four successful title defences, Joe Louis was ready to duck through the ropes one last time. Under the hot lights he would show the world he was still a fighter – even as a thickly-set and slightly balding thirty-four-year-old man. He was still the Brown Bomber. He was still Joe Louis.

This would be only his fourth fight since the war. After he stopped Billy Conn, Joe took on Tami Mauriello in September 1946. Tami made the mistake of clipping him to the jaw within a minute. Joe, who had planned a leisurely start, could feel the power surging through him as he went to work with his combinations. Tami fell as if he had been hit by a couple of sledgehammers. It was over inside a round.

With so much happening outside the ring he did not fight again for over a year. He had remarried Marva in June 1946 and, the following May, she gave birth to a twelve-pound son, Joe Louis Barrow Jr, whom they called Punchy for short. Joe had his perfect family: a beautiful wife, a little girl, Jacqueline, and his baby boy, but he wanted more. Joe still wanted to party away from home with his buddies. He still wanted all those gorgeous women. Joe and Marva would not last long in their rematch. When they were over in London he sent her off on a shopping trip. While she was out he brought in the two mouthy English girls he had met the day before. The three of them spent the afternoon together in the bedroom. As he sent them on their way with another kiss each, he saw Marva watching him. 'How long have you been back?' he asked his wife. 'Long enough,' Marva said sadly.

His life also soured in the ring. On 5 December 1947 he fought Jersey Joe Walcott at Madison Square Garden. Walcott had been one of Jack Blackburn's fighters before Roxy convinced him to give up everything for Louis. Walcott was black and he knew how to fight but, over the years, he'd lost his way. They had used him as a sparring partner before the first Schmeling bout and then he was knocked out by Al Ettore and Abe Simon – white mugs whom Joe had handled easily.

The press heaped abuse on Walcott as a championship challenger. He was older and lighter than Joe. He was a has-been who had never made it. They even mocked the fact that Walcott's real name was Arnold Cream. They made their little cracks. Guess who's gonna be creamed in the Garden? It was never going to be quite so simple. Jersey Joe was trickier than they thought and he had a mean right hand.

The December night was one of the worst Joe had ever known. Walcott knocked him down in the first with a right. Louis came steaming back but Walcott jigged away. He kept dancing, only stopping in the fourth to land another hefty right. Louis went down again. The first time he had jumped up before the count reached two. The second knockdown took more out of him. He rose when the referee reached seven.

Louis, dredging up his famed resilience, went after Walcott. He hurt the challenger in the ninth and pressed hard for the rest of the fight. Yet Louis could not nail a journeyman he would once have hammered. At the end of fifteen frustrating rounds, the ring announcer Harry Balogh read out the scores in a dramatic bark of a voice: 'Judge Frank Forbes scored the fight eight rounds to six, one round even . . . *Louis*!' The boos of surprise died away as Balogh moved on. 'Referee scored seven rounds to six, two rounds even . . . *Walcott*!' The Garden filled with cheering. Louis's left eye had been closed shut. The right side of his face was bloated. He waited for the final vote: 'And Judge Marty Monroe scored it nine rounds to six . . . *Louis*!'

Booing rumbled across the arena. Louis turned to Walcott. 'I'm sorry, Joe,' he said.

In his dressing-room, Louis insisted that his apology was for his own poor performance rather than the verdict. He thought he had won the fight – if only because he had remained the aggressor throughout. 'You gotta take the title away from the champion,' he argued, 'and Walcott was never going to do that on his bike, back-pedalling away all the time.'

'Smile, Joe,' a photographer said as he closed in on the fighter. 'You won.'

Joe's mouth flickered in response as he looked at the snapper between his puffy eye-slits.

'Wider,' the photographer urged, 'smile wider.'

'I can't open my mouth any wider,' Joe said thickly through his swollen lips.

He spent most of that night alone, drained and disconsolate as he sat in a darkened room. Joe had turned the lights out after he had seen his face. His head throbbed and his heart ached. He had won, but he had never felt less like a champion. Joe could still hear the booing from the Garden. The crowd told him what he already knew. He could no longer move and hit as he had once done so instinctively. His new manager, Marshall Miles, a good friend to both him and Roxy, wanted him to quit while he was still perched up top. Even his doctor had got all cross-eyed when they had a little old game of ping-pong a week before the fight. The doc thought Joe's reflexes on the left-hand side of his body had slowed noticeably. 'You can't take too many more punches to the head,' Dr Bennett said, 'no man can.' It wasn't that bad. Joe had never had much of a backhand on the ping-pong table. He was still OK. So what if a little drool sometimes oozed from the corner of his mouth.

The tax man soon sent him back to the ring. Joe went up to Pompton Lakes to resume training. And it was there, in the quiet of his camp, that his mind locked on Walcott. This fight would be about much more than paying another tax bill. This fight would be his salvation. The rematch would make everyone understand that he could whip the likes of Jersey Joe Walcott every night of his life.

Nothing less than a knockout would count. Joe had been a professional fighter for fourteen years. He had been through the fire of sixty pro fights. He was not about to succumb in number sixty-one – maybe his very last night in the ring. The contest had been delayed twenty-four hours after rain fell across New York on 24 June – the scheduled date of the contest. Joe had been down that rainy road too many times before to let it get to him.

He had learned from the first encounter with Walcott. This time he would not allow his emotions to take hold of him. He would fight methodically. Joe ignored the jeering as he stalked the flighty Walcott. He pressed ahead, diligently bearing down on the challenger. Walcott still danced away.

In Round Ten, as the struggle dragged on, the referee Frank Fulham said sharply, 'Hey, one of you get the lead out of your arse and let's have a fight.'

Joe closed in and, for once, Walcott traded with him. The punches from the champion made Walcott wilt. He backed away. His arms and legs looked suddenly heavy.

In Louis's corner his trainer, Mannie Seamon, said calmly: 'Go out and get him. Just get twelve inches away from him and when you catch him with that first punch give him everything you've got.'

The Bomber moved in for the eleventh round. He snapped out the jab. Walcott backed away again. More booing rolled down from the giant stands as Louis resumed the hunt. Walcott shimmied and shook as if daring Louis to come in even closer. Louis took up the invite. He stepped in fast and connected with a jarring right hand. Walcott veered towards the ropes. Louis closed the door on him. It was as if they were suddenly alone in a dark hole. Louis seemed to tower over Walcott as he banged him to the head and body, each blow shrinking the small black space between them.

Walcott swung wild and hard in desperation. He missed. Louis battered Walcott with two rights, a left, and one last right.

Walcott collapsed to the canvas. He lay on his back before, eventually, dragging himself on to his hands and knees. He shook his head urgently, as if he needed to stop an unbearable humming. Attempting his drunken rise, Walcott fell into the referee's arms.

Joe turned away. They were on their feet, screaming and cheering his name, as he walked to his corner. It was suddenly like one of the old nights. With his deadpan stare, he looked out into the arena. The darkness was lit by hundreds of flaring and popping flash-bulbs. Joe knew it was over. A minute later he walked to the heart of the ring. He reached for the microphone.

'This was for you, Mom,' he sighed. 'This was my last fight . . .'

Chapter Twelve

They Always Come Back

Chicago Stadium, 28 February 1949

Even before they burst through the huge paper hoop, emblazoned with the words *Harlem Globetrotters*, they had decided to leave the clowning to the expert. Ed Hamman, on his winter break from the Indianapolis Clowns, had arrived just in time. The Globetrotters and their latest recruit, Jesse Owens, could concentrate on their more serious tasks for the night. While Jesse would stand alone in front of a crowd of 22,000, and talk for ten minutes into a microphone before he drove his thirty-five-year-old body through yet another exhibition of speed, the Globetrotters would try to prove that they were the greatest basketball team on earth. They faced the Minneapolis Lakers – the 'world champions' who had won back-to-back NBA championships. The usually comical Globetrotters, including brilliant jokers like 'Goose' Tatum and 'Sweetwater' Clifton, were black; the Lakers, led by the imposing six foot ten inch George Mikan, were exclusively white.

The Globetrotters arrived on court first. Goose and Sweetwater exploded through the flimsy team banner, leaving the rest of the team to hop through an empty steel ring. As Jesse joined Ed the Clown on the sidelines, the Globetrotters formed a magic circle in the middle of the court. Their theme song, *Sweet Georgia Brown* performed by Brother Bones, the Globetrotters' musical entertainer, blared across the arena. The players flipped the ball from one set of hands to the next, making it dance with a dazzling zip.

Jesse reckoned it was just the clown's paint which made Ed look so sad as he watched the black players. Since they had toured the South together in 1939 with the Indianapolis crew, Ed had moved up a couple of stages in his clowning career. The *Chicago Defender* described him as 'the greatest clown in all sportsdom'. He had even provided the entertainment during baseball's 1948 World Series in Cleveland when he and his trained duck, Caledonia, took to the mound on a wave of raucous laughter.

Ed and Jesse knew that basketball was about to follow baseball across the colour line. Sweetwater, Goose, Ermer Robinson and the baby-faced dribbling ace Marques Haynes were just four Globetrotters who could claim to play basketball better than the more famous white stars of the NBA. At the same Chicago Stadium the previous February, their Jewish coach and owner, the five foot three inch Abe Saperstein, had pulled off the dream gig when he managed to get his team on the same court as the lily-white Lakers. They had matched each other shot for shot. With twenty seconds on the clock, the score was 59–59. The Globetrotters made their final surge for victory. With only seconds left, and twenty feet from the hoop, Ermer Robinson leapt and fired. The ball soared into the basket as the buzzer sounded.

A year on, they were ready for the rematch. The Globetrotters wore the collective and impassive game-face they had no need to use any other night on the road. They could thrash lumberjacks in the South and farmers in the Mid-west while mugging at the crowd and spinning the ball on their long fingers. The Lakers were different.

The tension snared Jesse as he watched his five friends step out of their spangled tracksuits and take to the floor. Apart from the fact that he had toured with them for almost two years, Jesse had always felt a kinship for the Globetrotters. He had told their fantastic story again and again at the microphone.

In 1926, in an attempt to boost attendances on their slowest dance nights, Chicago's Savoy Ballroom had introduced basketball as a way of kick-starting the evening. The house team – the Savoy Big Five – featured five black kids from the city's South Side. They had a great set of names. Jesse said each with relish: Toots Wright, Inman Jackson, Kid Oliver, Byron Long and Runt Pullens. Yet neither their names nor their trickery with the ball could save the Savoy Big Five. The Ballroom dropped their basketball nights in a matter of months. They turned to roller-skating as the next craze to woo the dancers of Chicago.

The Big Five were adrift. And then along came the chubby little hustler. Abe Saperstein persuaded his father, an immigrant tailor, to create some new uniforms for the team. As a way of lending glamour to a bunch of unknown Negroes from Chicago, he also hit upon the idea of stitching *New York* across the front of their shirts. 'Let them think we're some hot-shot team from the Big Apple,' Abe advised his dubious players.

The six of them took to the road in January 1927, driving through the freezing Mid-west in Abe's windowless Model T Ford. Jesse's memories of travelling with Dave Albritton and Mel Walker in the curtained Packard helped evoke the bone-chilling intensity of those journeys from game to game. They had faced the same troubles he remembered at roadside restaurants and cheap hotels across the sprawling states. There were even nights when, barred from every hotel or boarding-house in town, they asked to sleep in the local jail. To cash in on their novelty as black professional basketballers, while suggesting that their travel encompassed a more worldly itinerary, Abe made a name change in 1930. Saperstein's Big Five became the Harlem

Globetrotters. By 1934 they had racked up their thousandth win.

In the early 1940s they attracted a fresh crop of black players who could add clowning acrobatics to their winning ways. Goose Tatum, who played baseball for Ed Hamman's Indianapolis Clowns in the summer, transformed the Globetrotters with his freestyle improvisations. The players still had to wage a constant battle against Saperstein for a fairer deal. He claimed that Negroes needed less money than whites, as their 'living standards' were lower.

Saperstein, however, had never forgotten the 1936 Olympics and the blow Jesse Owens struck against the Nazis. He regarded Jesse, with his smooth oratory and smart dress, as an 'honorary' white man. Saperstein appointed him as the Globetrotters' marketing man and a half-time entertainer who added a little class to the antics of Ed the Clown and the ditties of Brother Bones.

That night, after the Globetrotters and the Lakers had slugged it out in another agonisingly close contest during the first half, Jesse mingled with the crowd, demonstrated his quick starts and spoke movingly about the history of Saperstein's outfit and his own Olympic triumphs. His attention was gripped in the final quarter as the Globetrotters scored their second successive victory over the world champions.

Jesse had been away from his family home, in Detroit, for seven long weeks. He felt a deep tiredness as one more face rushed towards him when the Globetrotters left the court. 'Jesse Owens,' the white man in the suit and thick glasses said as he stretched out his hand, 'I'm Leo Rose. I own the Leo Rose Clothing chain of stores here in Chicago.'

'Mr Rose!' Jesse replied with typical gusto. 'Thanks for coming over.'

'No,' Rose said, 'thank *you*, Jesse. That was a fine speech you made. Very impressive – but I think I can offer you something more. How do you like the idea of becoming the Executive

Director of Sports and Sales at Leo Rose Clothing? In fact, let me put it this way. How about moving to Chicago for good? How about Jesse Owens starting a brand new life?'

The next morning, on 1 March 1949, Joe Louis shut the door on his old life. He signed the letter, addressed to Abe Greene, the President of the National Boxing Association, which confirmed his retirement as world heavyweight champion. The eight months that had passed since his defeat of Jersey Joe Walcott had been filled with endless schemes. Truman Gibson, his closest ally in the American Army, had become his lawyer and chief adviser. While Joe had teased the press with hints about the possibility of returning to the ring for one last pay-day, Gibson set about finding the backers who would give them the capital to start their own promotional company. With Mike Jacobs no longer having either the zest or the health to run his Twentieth Century Sporting Club, Gibson saw a power vacuum in boxing.

Gibson and Louis eventually sold the idea of forming a promotional powerhouse called the International Boxing Club to two millionaires – Jim Norris and Art Wirtz. After Gibson had signed all the leading heavyweight contenders to the IBC, Norris and Wirtz would buy out Louis for $350,000 and pay him an annual consultancy fee of $20,000 and a small percentage of share profits.

The deal suited everyone. Louis picked up his final payout without taking a punch to the head, Gibson took his cut of ten per cent and Norris and Wirtz had the means to dominate boxing in the manner of Mike Jacobs, who received $150,000 for standing down in favour of the IBC as the main promoter at Madison Square Garden. The fighters also endorsed the change. They at last had a chance to win the title without having to face the Brown Bomber. The boxing commission accepted both Louis's retirement and the IBC's nomination of Jersey Joe

Walcott and Ezzard Charles as the top two heavyweights in the world. They would meet for the vacant title on 22 June 1949 in Chicago – exactly twelve years to the night that Louis had won the title as a twenty-three-year-old in the same city. He had been the youngest-ever heavyweight champion; and his record of twenty-five successful defences would almost certainly never be broken.

He took as much pride in the fact that the two men nominated to succeed him were both black. Even more significantly, the colour of their skin barely warranted a mention in the newspapers of 1949. Joe, and boxing, had finally shaken free from the ghost of Jack Johnson. Three years earlier, on his way to New York to watch Louis and Conn prepare for their second fight, Johnson's Lincoln Zephyr had veered off Highway 1 in North Carolina and smashed into a lamp post. On the evening of 10 June 1946, Johnson died from his internal injuries.

If they were liberated from the racial struggle which had scarred the careers of Johnson and Louis, Walcott and Charles could never fill the Bomber's position as a devastating knockout artist and, even more importantly, a cultural icon. They were doomed to a ceaselessly unflattering comparison.

To earn the last portion of his $350,000 payment, Joe promoted the fight. He was not much of a salesman. Dan Dunphy, the famous radio commentator, was charmed but bewildered by Joe's naivety. At a press conference Louis was asked, with less than a week left to the bout, how tickets were selling. 'The usual promoter's response,' said Dunphy, 'would be "oh, wonderful! I've got orders from Chicago, New York and so on." Joe, new to the promotion game and perpetually honest, said, "I don't know. We ain't sold none yet."'

In a tedious encounter, Charles out-pointed Walcott. The world groaned in dismay at the sight of their highly competent but uninspiring new champion.

Joe hung around as Charles's promoter for his first three

fights. He defended efficiently against the unheralded Gus Lesnevich, Pat Valentino and Freddie Beshore, but the combination of Charles as world champion and Louis as his promoter was disastrous. Charles was a hard-working and subtly-skilled former light-heavyweight who lacked a real knockout punch; Louis was a bored salesman. Only 6,298, the smallest crowd to watch a heavyweight championship contest, turned up to see Charles stop Beshore in fourteen rounds in Buffalo. Boxing, like Joe Louis, had fallen into a terrible depression.

When Joe visited Jesse in Chicago in the summer of 1950 their lives had taken contrasting paths. Jesse worked as a Sales Director for Leo Rose Clothing and acted as a public relations consultant for Leader Cleaners, who paid him a weekly retainer of $50 to market their laundry business. He had accepted a reduced role with the Harlem Globetrotters as their 'road representative' and, with Rose's encouragement, also taken on a managerial position at the South Side Boys Club – a youth recreation centre.

'Busy, busy, busy,' he grinned at Joe.

'Yeah?' Joe said. 'Jesse, you *always* been busy.'

The difference, however, was marked. After running for so long with the horses and clowns, Jesse had recovered his self-esteem. For years he seemed to lag behind Ralph Metcalfe and Dave Albritton. Ralph had moved from a position as track coach at Xavier University in New Orleans to work as the head of the Illinois State Sports Commission. Dave had coached at Alabama State College before returning to Ohio. He was being groomed for his first term in the state legislature. Unlike Jesse, both Dave and Ralph had also earned their university degrees – and each had gone on to complete his Masters.

Everything changed in Chicago. On 26 January 1950 Jesse was announced as the winner of an Associated Press poll to determine the greatest athlete of the past fifty years. He received

201 votes – almost double the combined tally of the two athletes who trailed him. Jim Thorpe, the 1912 Olympic pentathlon and decathlon champion, came second with 74 votes. Paavo Nurmi, who had won three golds at the 1924 Olympic Games, finished third with 31 votes.

The gushing Associated Press report, which appeared in every major newspaper across America, declared that, 'Jesse Owens, the greatest track athlete of the past half-century, today is a philosophical businessman with three daughters, one a freshman at his alma mater, Ohio State . . . Almost as sleek and lithe as when he shattered three world records and tied a fourth in a single afternoon and a year later dominated the 1936 Olympics at Berlin, Owens now makes it plain he can take fame or leave it alone. "My concern is my family and my respectability," he solemnly said. "I'm what you call a stable businessman now."'

Jesse would have gladly donated the money he picked up every Friday from Leader Cleaners to Joe's cause – but not even $50,000, let alone his paltry fifty bucks a week, could have rescued Joe. The IRS had just completed their trawl through Joe's chaotic accounts. Their initial assessment, that he owed $200,000 in back taxes from 1946, matched the figure that Truman Gibson had prepared him to hear. Gibson had tried to negotiate a 'conciliatory settlement', but the IRS, instead, went to work on the personal service corporation they had, in 1947, advised Gibson to establish. Joe Louis Enterprises Inc. was a dummy corporation which was meant to pay the fighter an annual income while it held on to the rest of his cash. If Joe had stuck to Truman's instruction, and lived off his salary, his debt would not have rocketed so dramatically. Yet Joe had rifled through everything in the company account. He was now subject to the highest rate of corporation tax. When the IRS added up all the numbers in red they rounded them up to $500,000.

'Half a million?' Jesse asked incredulously, remembering that he had declared himself bankrupt when he was $6,841 in debt.

'I can't believe it,' Joe said, 'but that's what they tell me.'

Jesse had always said that Joe was the world's softest touch. He remembered how, even at the height of his fame in 1940, after hammering Johnny Paychek in New York, Joe had turned to one of his handlers and shown him an empty wallet at 3.30 a.m. Joe asked for some 'meal money'. One of his posse slipped him $40.

Joe and Jesse then walked past an old fighter who had taken to the shoeshine box in an attempt to make a living on the streets.

'Shine, champ?' the old middleweight had asked Joe.

'Sure,' Joe said as he snapped out one of his Florsheims. 'How's life treating you, pal?'

'Oh, you know how it is, Joe,' the man said as he rubbed a rag across the champion's already shiny shoes. 'Sometimes good, sometimes not so good.'

'Well,' Joe said as he pushed the forty bucks he had just been given into those shoe-shining hands, 'you take care . . .'

They said Joe had earned over $4,000,000 in the ring. Jesse thought the figure could have been doubled and Joe would still have either spent it or given it away.

'Man,' Joe murmured to Jesse in Chicago, 'these tax guys keep showing up, day and night, sniffing around. This tax thing is eating into my brain.'

Jesse asked the obvious question: 'What you gonna do, Joe?'

'What else?' Joe sighed. 'I'm comin' back . . .'

In August 1950, at the age of thirty-six, Joe signed to fight Ezzard Charles. The contest was set for late September at his old fight playground of Yankee Stadium. 'I don't really want this fight,' the twenty-eight-year-old Charles said. 'Joe Louis was my boyhood idol. How can you fight someone you once wor-shipped? They tell me I got no choice.'

Ray Arcel, the sage and humane man in Charles's corner,

had accompanied more boxers into the ring against Louis than any other trainer. Although he was the best cornerman in America, Arcel had not inspired one of those eleven fighters to victory over Louis. Whenever they met in the middle of the ring before a bout, Louis would look at Arcel and say: '*You again?*' Charles presented Arcel with his first real chance of a win over the Bomber. Yet the diffident fighter was trapped by circumstance.

Arcel worried that Charles might let compassion blunt his own right to the championship. He spoke thoughtfully to the black fighter: 'Look, Ezzard, I know it's almost unbearable to go in against Joe. But you gotta do it. If you want them to call you "champion" you have to beat Joe Louis.'

'And if I beat him,' Charles said sadly, 'they'll surely hate me.'

'Yes,' Arcel agreed with a slight shift in emphasis, 'when you beat him they might hate you. But you'll still be champion. If you lose you'll have nothing.'

Louis was still the main man. He was guaranteed a thirty-five per cent cut while the champion stoically accepted the challenger's share of twenty per cent. With the details settled, the two men steeled themselves for a long and lonely night.

Joe had lost his taste, if not his heart, for battle. He wished he could be out on the golf course, or in bed with a girl, rather than in the ring. In the old days, when he was still young, he could set aside his thoughts of girls and golf and lose himself in the cruel delights of training. He had once loved every sparring session. When Jack Blackburn barked out his gruff instructions from the corner, Joe would thrill at the way the punches flew from him with a head-spinning beauty. He liked the way the sweat shimmered on his skin. A dozen years before, Joe could even see the point in running. No longer.

Joe had cut his dawn routine from ten miles to six. Another year on he found it even more difficult to get out of bed at five a.m. – especially when preparing for a fight which would only make money for the IRS. He halved his run to three miles and, in guilty compensation, added another day of sparring to the weekly ritual. It did not help much.

When they met for the weigh-in at Madison Square Garden just before noon on the day of the fight, an expressionless Louis scaled his heaviest fighting weight of 218 pounds. Charles came in at 184½. 'It was when they posed for the cameramen, with their dukes up,' Shirley Povich noted in the *Washington Post*, 'that you got the full significance of that thirty-three-and-a-half pound difference. Charles looked as if he didn't belong with Louis – he was too small – but there were items in his favour. He was lean and lithe, with washboard muscles lining his lower chest and abdomen. Louis suddenly looked fat and old. The bald spot on his pate was now bigger, and the hair thinning alarmingly. And he was flabby. Sleepy-eyed too, but then he always was.'

He turned those sleepy eyes on a shadowy man who stepped out of the curtained wings of the stage to press a court summons on him. Joe was still on the scales as the papers were thrust at him. The motionless fighter stared at the messenger. He refused to lift a hand to take the sheets shaking nervously in front of him. When the papers dropped to the floor, an official scooped them up and handed them to Truman Gibson.

'There was speculation,' Povich added, 'that it was in the suit of Louis's former manager, John Roxborough, who is seeking a part of Joe's purse tonight under an old contract. Joe, himself, was unbothered. He's been used before.'

Yankee Stadium, New York, 27 September 1950

They stood in the ring, Joe Louis and Ezzard Charles, each with his lowered head wrapped in a white towel. When he was introduced, Charles bowed to each side of the square ring. His half-cocked right hand pawed the air, as if he was already asking to be forgiven for fighting the idol. Louis danced in his corner, lost behind his towel and gown.

Five minutes later, naked from the waist up, his torso looked fleshy beneath the glaring lights. Although only 13,562 had made it to Yankee Stadium, a record television audience of 25,000,000 waited to see if the Bomber could become the first man in history to regain his heavyweight title. The old stone-face looked almost pensive. When the bell rang, Louis walked forward. He raised his arms in a little chest-expanding movement as if he had stepped out for a spot of exercise on a sunlit beach. The fighter they called the Cincinnati Cobra snaked towards him.

Ezzard Charles was a crafty technician. He used his slick hands and the angles of the ring to impose himself on his stalking opponent. Louis had the sombre air of a man who wanted to end the contest early with one big punch. The stadium was strangely quiet as two very different fighters searched for a decisive break. Although the impact of Louis's first heavy punch, a left hook to the head, was blunted by him missing with his following right, he began to box with a semblance of the old beauty in Round Two. Three fast jabs and a right to the jaw opened the way for another straight left. Charles blinked in hurt surprise. Louis could still punch. The Bomber forced the pace as the crowd, thick with sentiment, roared its support.

The fighters refused to clinch in either the third or the fourth as the referee, Mark Conn, circled them. As if drawn to the blazing toil, two moths flittered around their heads, spiralling away when a spray of sweat flew into the air as another hard punch landed. Spurred by memory, Louis threw a crisp left hook and a right. It was a stinging combination. Yet Louis, his co-ordination ravaged by time, then missed with three successive punches.

The left eye of each fighter had started to close as, in the fifth and sixth rounds, Charles took over. Whether fighting at a distance or moving up close on the inside, he dominated Louis. His punches were sharp and accurate. During the break before Round Seven, Louis winced as Mannie Seamon pressed an ice-pack against his face. Louis's only consolation was that his right hand had fattened the mouse under Charles's eye.

The middle rounds belonged to Charles. Louis looked dispirited as punches pounded into his sagging face and body. By the ninth they were both bleeding from the nose, but breath was being drawn in more jagged bursts by Louis. A slim chance opened up for weary Joe in Round Ten. A left jab and a jolting right rocked the champion. Charles backed against the ropes as Louis, the greatest finisher in boxing, moved in. But he missed with a right. He missed with a left. Charles had been spared. He outboxed Louis in the next two rounds – the rights raking Louis's head before, at the close of the thirteenth, Charles nailed him with four unanswered blows from both fists.

Louis bled profusely from the nose. His left eye was a grotesque mess of flesh. He rose slowly for the penultimate round. Louis needed a knockout. Midway through that three-minute stretch, a right uppercut staggered Louis. He clutched at the top rope to steady himself. His courage was undimmed. Louis fought back and, moments after the bell, he threw another right. Even then Charles retaliated with a piercing shot before the referee jumped between them.

Mannie Seamon and Marshall Miles had to lift Louis from the stool for the final round. In the centre of the ring the fighters touched gloves. For a moment they stared at each other. Neither could see out of his left eye but, while Louis kept missing, Charles kept landing. Two lefts and a right forced Louis to again rest his glove on the top rope in his own corner. After a fifteen-second flurry and clinch, they exchanged a few stray punches at the bell.

Louis was the first to congratulate the champion. Charles flashed a white gum-shield before he shook his head in wonder – both at the heart of his old hero and the brutal end of an era. Ray Arcel, a cotton-swab jammed in his mouth, wrapped an arm around both men.

The scorecards were a formality. Joe Agnello scored it twelve rounds to two, with one even, for Charles; Frank Forbes chose Charles by thirteen rounds to two. Ray Arcel turned to the loser. Even as the referee's own card of ten rounds to five was read out, Louis nodded to Arcel, reassuring his old rival that, somehow, he would survive the defeat.

Before the reporters piled into his dressing-room, he allowed the tears to mingle with the blood seeping from the cuts below both eyes. Joe Louis wept, not for the hurt etched into his face and his body, but for all that he had lost. It was only his second defeat in sixteen years in the ring; but he knew his fast hands and precise timing, his very youth and greatness, had gone for ever. Jackie Robinson and Sugar Ray Robinson crouched beside him. It was impossible to find words to console him.

The press-gang outside his door became impatient. They usually only wanted the winner; but, this night, they would not visit the champion until they had seen Joe themselves. He sat on the wooden rubbing table, his left hand dangling in a steel bucket of ice-water. Joe looked straight at them. 'I enjoyed the fight,' he said through split lips, 'and I want to thank you all. I done the best I can.'

'Is Ezzard Charles the best fighter you've faced?' a young reporter asked, as some of the aging hacks at the front scoffed in derision.

'No,' Louis said softly, 'I wouldn't say that. But he's a real good fighter. He's good in every department.'

'What about you, Joe?' someone asked. 'What were you thinking as the fight went on?'

'After the third or fourth round,' Louis said bleakly, 'I knew

I was washed up. And I knew from the seventh that I just could-
n't do it. I'd see the openings but I couldn't take them. It wasn't
a case of reflexes or anything. I just didn't have it. I'll never
fight again.'

When the last writer had lifted his gaze from a beaten Joe
Louis, and scurried down the passage in search of Ezzard
Charles, Joe's friends gathered around him. They looked down
in silence at the once unbeatable fighter. Joe resembled a blind
old man who was too sick or tired to even dress himself.
Eventually, Sugar Ray Robinson helped Joe step into his
trousers. Sugar Ray, who had lost only one of his own 117
fights, buttoned up Joe and gently tightened the belt around his
waist. He knelt down and tenderly worked Joe's big feet into his
shiny black shoes. Sugar picked up Joe's bags and, together, they
left the dressing-room. Sugar Ray Robinson led Joe Louis,
slowly and painfully, through a deserted ballpark and out into
the black and empty night.

Five days later, on Monday 2 October, Joe called a press conference. He wanted to retract his promise that he would never
fight again. 'My dressing-room statement was made in the heat
of excitement and without full consideration,' he said. His
bulging face twitched. He sounded less lucid as he pressed on.
'Now, however, I wouldn't say definitely I would fight again
and I wouldn't say definitely I wouldn't. I'm gonna take out
three or four weeks before I make up my mind.'

The decision had already been made. Joe would attempt a
second comeback. He needed the money, even though Truman
Gibson confirmed that, 'This morning, we have submitted a
compromise offer to the government to settle Joe Louis's delinquent income taxes. We are not in a position to discuss the
details until it has either been accepted or refused.'

Joe's face looked like a trampled hillside. Yet it was still possible, beneath the bruising and the swelling, to see his blank

resignation. The tax-man was the most uncompromising foe he had ever fought. Joe already knew the outcome. His offer would be rejected. He was in for another licking.

'Last night,' the *Chicago Daily Tribune* reported two weeks later, on 28 October, 'more than six hundred Chicagoans gathered in the grand ballroom of the Sheraton Hotel to honour Jesse Owens at a dinner for which Chicago has no precedent. Business and civic leaders, newspapermen and sportsmen joined with scores of other citizens to recall Owens's superlative performances. They came not only to praise Chicago's adopted son for his superiority in athletics but to pay tribute to his work with the youth of our community. Owens the humanitarian shared in the applause for Owens the athlete, America's brightest star of another era. Throughout the dinner there was a current of thought that Chicago, in honouring this young American, also praised a democracy that had produced him.'

As Jesse looked out at the audience, in their tuxedos and black ties, their pearls and evening gowns, he saw old friends and enemies. They had come to celebrate the Associated Press award he had won as the greatest athlete of the first half of the twentieth century. Avery Brundage and Dan Ferris nodded benignly at the resounding praise for Jesse. He smiled back while, on the inside, he remembered how they had hurt him. Through the applause he could still hear Ferris's snarl, in August 1936, that 'Jesse Owens is finished'; he could still hear Slavery Avery's insistence that his lifetime ban should never be lifted.

They were shameless. It seemed that whenever another camera pointed at Jesse and a guest, Brundage would jump between them so that his fat bespectacled face beamed in the middle of the frame. The President of the International Olympic Committee said nothing about the personal mark he had stamped on the evening. Apart from banishing Owens, Brundage had doggedly led the refusal to return the two Olympic gold medals won by Jim Thorpe – who finished second to Owens in the AP poll. The IOC had taken Thorpe's medals from him in the late 1920s, and wiped his name from the amateur record books, after it was learned that he had played baseball in the semi-professional bush-leagues in 1909 and 1910.

Despite competing against him in the 1912 Olympics, Brundage, who finished fifth in the decathlon behind Thorpe, resisted all attempts to restore the winner's name to the official history of the Games. Although Thorpe was a broken alcoholic, close to death, Brundage argued that 'forgiveness would tarnish the sanctity of our amateur sport'. Brundage would be linked for ever to the two greatest athletes of the first half of the century. One was black; the other was an American Indian. Slavery Avery had outlasted both of them.

Jesse also had his friends around him that night. Ralph Metcalfe presented him with a commemorative plaque while Dave Albritton and Mel Walker, his OSU team-mates, grinned and slapped him on the back. They had come a long way from the Packard. Larry Snyder, their old coach, had been one of the keynote speakers. 'In particular,' the *Tribune* noted, 'Snyder paid tribute to Mrs Owens who shared the evening of public attention.'

Ruth looked at Jesse smiling alongside her. She knew he'd loved her for twenty-two years; and for fifteen of those years she had been his wife. They had been good years, for the most part, and she had put up with his roaming more patiently than he could have hoped. Jesse was nowhere near as bad as Joe but, since they had moved to Chicago in 1949, Ruth had come to understand he was a sucker for attention. He was a man, and there were women out there who were none too shy about telling him how much they liked him.

When they were in Cleveland and Columbus and Detroit, Ruth lived a sheltered life. It was a world which revolved around home and looking after the three girls while Jesse was away with the Clowns or Globetrotters. She also occupied herself as the neighbourhood chairwoman of the Girl Scouts and as a leader of four troops of Marionettes and Brownies. It was a world Jesse knew nothing about – just as he told her little about his life on the road.

Ruth often said Jesse made her feel like he was a date rather than a husband. He took that as a compliment, although she would have far preferred him to be more of a husband. Ruth tried to seal the gap between them with a gloss. She said that the constant partings kept alive the excitement between them. Ruth felt it every time he returned from a long spell out of town with gifts for her and dolls for the kids. She, in turn, would make him his favourite meal and present the girls to him just the way he liked them to look.

Soon after they arrived in Chicago, Ruth had her first real jolt. She had been shielded by her immersion in what she called 'a nice and clean life'. Chicago taught her how little she knew. When they went out to functions the brazen Chicago women shocked and frightened her. They acted as if she did not even exist, as if they saw Jesse as just another guy to be hunted down. It was as if she was surrounded by a city full of Quincella Nickersons – the Hollywood deb with the dumb name who had tried to steal Jesse just before they married in the summer of 1935.

'You do what you want to do,' she told Jesse, 'but respect me and respect the girls. That's all I ask.'

Ruth felt closer to him and the girls than ever before on that wonderful night in Chicago. After all the heartache of him running against horses, the world had returned to its senses. Jesse would be cherished, rather than crushed. She had often said that when it came to other people, if not always his own family, Jesse, just like his friend Joe, was too much of a giver for his own good. 'He'll give you the shirt off his own back,' she said; and because she meant it she said it a little more coldly in Chicago.

Ruth was afraid that people would keep on taking things from Jesse as long as they lived.

That night the tide rolled back. With the girls around them, and eleven-year-old Marlene, the youngest, almost beside herself because her dad had been presented with their first television set, a glorious Zenith which seemed far more special than his Athlete of the Century bauble, it felt as if their new life had truly begun.

'His career may be over,' acknowledged Fay Young, the sports editor of the *Chicago Defender* in one of the final speeches of the evening, 'but Jesse Owens remains our most extraordinary athlete. Last month the greatest track man of the past fifty years ran the 100 yard dash in 9.7 seconds at a night game in Milwaukee. He was thirty-seven years old. But, as our ace reporter Russ Cowans wrote, "The slender Owens was out of his holes like a flash, floating over the terrain like a feather. He was breathing easy at the finish . . ."'

Chapter Thirteen

The Diplomat and the Fighter

The Olympic Stadium, Berlin, 22 August 1951

He flew over the city of ghosts. Berlin spread out silently beneath him. The bombed ruins could be seen from the air as the chattering Army helicopter arced towards the stadium. Only the gigantic arena remained exactly as Jesse had remembered it from fifteen years before. The Olympic Stadium had miraculously escaped the relentless aerial campaign which had driven the rest of Berlin to its bloody knees.

The city now lay at the heart of a new kind of global conflict: the Cold War. Even before the Nazis surrendered, the Allied leaders had reached an uneasy compromise. A defeated Germany would be controlled by four armies of occupation, with the Americans, British, French and Soviets each responsible for a quarter of the country.

Berlin was in the Soviet zone, eighty miles from the border adjoining the Western powers. Yet, as a supposed sign of unity among the Allies, the city itself, like the nation beyond, was divided symbolically into four sectors. The helicopter carrying Jesse Owens had flown from a military base in the American division. They crossed a fractured sprawl as they approached the stadium – which lay in the British zone of west Berlin.

Jesse could still hear the quiet voice of the German starter saying, 'Auf die Plätze . . . Fertig' just before the gun cracked in the Olympic finals. He could still imagine the chanting – 'Yess-say . . . Oh-vens, Yess-say . . . Oh-vens . . .' – and the blond, lanky German athlete grinning at him as they pushed each other in the long-jump final. Jesse, soaring over Berlin, thought of the two men who had tested him and Joe so hard in 1936: Lutz Long and Max Schmeling.

When Jesse returned home from the Games, he and Lutz exchanged letters. Lutz had been conscripted into the Army but they wrote to each other until late 1938. Jesse had heard nothing since then – apart from rumours that Lutz had died in combat in 1944. Three years earlier, on 28 May 1941, Reuters claimed that Schmeling, a paratrooper in the German Army, 'had fallen in the fighting on Crete'. Within a week Schmeling was being interviewed by an American reporter from his hospital bed in Athens, where he had been transferred after injuring himself while jumping over enemy lines into Crete. Schmeling cheerfully dismissed claims that German prisoners were being badly treated by their British captors. He so incensed Goebbels that he was charged with treason.

Jesse knew that Max had survived and had even boxed five times after the war – finally retiring in 1948 as a forty-three-year-old fighter. The fate of Lutz Long remained as cloudy as the sky covering Berlin that August afternoon. The American helicopter circled low over the stadium as Jesse stared at the scene below. From such a height it looked like a collection of matchsticks glued together, but he could see the portable court the Harlem Globetrotters had set up in the grassy oval. He knew that music would be blasting across the arena as the Globetrotters whisked through their routine of tricks. Jesse had been the Globetrotters' half-time support act throughout Europe – whether they laid their court over an ice-rink in Oslo or a bull-ring in Barcelona, at Wembley in London or the Palais des Sports in Paris.

His return to Berlin was the centrepiece of the tour. The US State Department, recognising the opportunity to entice Germany back to western concepts of democracy and freedom, had appealed to both Owens and Abe Saperstein, the Globetrotters' owner, for their support. The patriotic Negro and the hard-working Jewish immigrant needed no persuasion. While Jesse polished his most overtly political speech, Saperstein arranged for a US Army helicopter to deliver his star performer to the Olympic Stadium during the interval. Abe would then ensure that Jesse carried an American flag in each hand as he stepped from the chopper and ran towards the ecstatic German crowd.

As the helicopter landed, Jesse peeled off his tracksuit to reveal the same US team vest and shorts he had worn at the Olympic Games. Once the whirring drone of the rotors faded, the huge steel door opened. Jesse stood at the edge of the helicopter as he heard the announcement.

'*Achtung . . . Achtung!*' the amplified German voice boomed. '*Attention . . . Attention! Ladies and gentlemen, the greatest runner in the world returns to Berlin . . .*'

Jesse ran across the soft grass of the track's inner circle. He soon hit the red cinder. The crescendo sounded louder than the noise he carried in his head from 1936. Seventy-five thousand people were on their feet, grinning and stamping and clapping as he slowly passed them, sometimes lifting his hand in a shy gesture of recognition but more often just smiling to himself as he rounded the arena. The tumult escalated as he reached the home straight. He ran alongside the ribbon of cinder leading to the long-jump pit and his victory over Lutz Long. Jesse moved past the platform of champions where, on four separate occasions, he had stood to receive Olympic gold. High up on his right, the Chancellor's box, where Hitler and the Nazi leadership had watched him every day of that momentous week, remained empty.

Walter Schreiber, the Mayor of Berlin, sat in the front row of the crowd. Jesse veered off the track towards him. Schreiber reached over the wall and stretched out his hands. 'Jesse Owens,' Schreiber said, his voice cracking as the black runner looked up at him, 'fifteen years ago Hitler would not greet you or shake your hand. I will try to make up for it today by taking both of them . . .'

When they parted, Jesse held his hands in front of his face and smiled again, in recognition of both the gesture and an exultant cheer. The eyes of Abe Saperstein and his Globetrotters misted as Jesse climbed on the small podium that had been raised for his speech. None of them had been in Berlin in 1936; and the reaction of the German crowd seemed incredible.

Jesse spoke with the same ease he had shown when talking about Joe Louis to a gathering of 5,000 in South Bend, Indiana, or to a crowd half that size in some ballpark he passed through in the South with the Indianapolis Clowns. All the speeches he'd made in the past distilled into the conviction of that Berlin address.

Urging Germans and Americans to 'work together to stay free', Jesse whipped the crowd to a pitch of fevered delight as he neared his conclusion. 'Stand fast with us in the fight for freedom and democracy under the protection of Almighty God. That is what the United States of America stands for – and I know you are with us.'

Afterwards, he turned towards the dressing-rooms where he had spent so many hours preparing for the Olympics with Larry Snyder. Jesse covered his head in a white towel, as if he was Joe Louis leaving the ring. A young German boy, just into his teens, stood in front of him.

'Mr Owens, please, sir,' he said in accented English, 'will you sign your name here?'

Jesse scrawled his name. He barely looked down as he signed. It was only when he returned the fountain pen that his eye fell on the face of Lutz Long.

'Let me see that,' he said, as he reached for the scrapbook he had just signed. He stared at a faded photograph. 'That's Lutz Long . . .'

'My father, sir,' the kid said.

'Your father?' Jesse repeated. 'Where is he? Where is Lutz?'

'My dead father, sir,' the boy said.

'What happened?' Jesse asked. The boy looked away. Jesse tried again. 'We were friends, you know, me and your father.'

'Yes,' the boy nodded. 'He died in the war.'

'We should talk, son,' Jesse said as he led Karl Long down the tunnel. 'You and me should get to know each other.'

The Bomber was on a roll. His head was bald, his face was puffy and his legs were stiff; but, in his own Cold War against time, Joe Louis had won eight consecutive fights. His latest victory, a unanimous decision over Jimmy Bivins on 15 August 1951, came exactly a week before Jesse's Berlin run.

After the desolate loss to Ezzard Charles, his mother had begged him to retire, but he had no choice: the debts were still climbing. Joe began his third comeback. He had fought only five times in the four years following his post-war return to the ring in 1946. Joe now knew the only way he might shake the rust from his body would be through the kind of active campaign he had engaged in as a young fighter. He tried to rebuild himself by fighting the type of journeymen a new contender faces as he strives to compile an impressive record of wins without facing any undue risk. Joe boxed eight times in nine months.

The names on his hit-list were uninspiring: Cesar Brion, Freddie Beshore, Omelio Agramonte, Andy Walker, Lee Savold and Bivins. He fought both Brion and Agramonte twice, failing to secure a knockout in any one of those four bouts. It was only against Savold, the best-known of that humdrum collection, that he showed some of the old glitter. The combinations clicked and, in the sixth, Savold fell. Louis's dressing-room at Madison

Square Garden was filled with roistering celebrities ready to shout out that they were still his friends.

Joe believed that, with the right preparation, he would have a chance against Charles. He was sure he had one more big fight inside him. And he needed another big purse. Joe had made an average of $15,000 a bout since he resumed his career in November 1950. It was joke money. He was a million dollars in debt; and as long as that tax bill remained untouched he would need to cough up at least $50,000 a year just to pay the interest and the various penalties imposed on him by the IRS. It was hopeless. The more he worked, the less he had. Joe shrugged. He would try and take his mind off the tax nightmare on the golf course. Joe liked to play for $100 a hole. He paid up promptly when he lost, even if it meant taking out another small loan.

Before Joe could negotiate his challenge, Charles dropped the title to Jersey Joe Walcott. After being robbed on points and then knocked out by Louis in their two previous fights, Walcott was in no mood to offer him an early crack. The broke Bomber would have to look elsewhere for his six-figure cheque.

There was only one option. Rocky Marciano, a twenty-seven-year-old brawler from Brockton, Massachusetts, had emerged as the most dangerous white heavyweight in over a decade. The unbeaten Marciano had scored thirty-two knockouts in thirty-seven fights. The prospect of a remorseless, if crude, new star fighting a former champion was irresistible. Unlike his frustrating technical struggles against Walcott, a fight against Marciano would be raw and compelling. It would be war.

Joe could have done without such an unremitting opponent at that late stage of his boxing life but, once more, he felt as if the decision had already been made for him. He signed for the fight, the heavy drag across his heart eased only by the fact that he would receive forty-five per cent of a $300,000 gate in late October. Marciano, the son of a poor Italian immigrant who'd worked in a shoe factory in Brockton, accepted a pauper's cut of fifteen per cent. He was that hungry.

In his training camp up in Greenwood Lake, Orange County, an hour's drive from New York City, Rocky Marciano took to the lonely hillside roads. A chill ran through the dark early mornings. Marciano, however, burned inside. His dedication, dented in the bleak days following his knockout of Carmine Vingo, had returned with a vengeance. Back in December 1950, Vingo's bloodied face had taken one last hook from the Rock before he fell backwards in the sixth round of a wild fight. He was already slipping into unconsciousness when his head hit the canvas. At the hospital, Rocky watched Vingo slide silently between life and death as if his battered brain could no longer decide where it belonged. It was then, in fleeting moments, that Marciano wondered if he would ever fight again.

'You didn't hurt him,' his trainer Charley Goldman tried to reassure him. 'The kid hit his head. It could've happened no matter who hit him.'

'I know,' Marciano nodded. 'Don't worry, I'll be all right. Let's just think about Vingo.'

Carmine Vingo lay in a coma for five days. He was still in a critical condition on 7 January 1951 when, at last, he woke.

'I don't remember nothing about the fight, Rock,' Vingo whispered to his opponent.

'It was a helluva fight, Carmine,' Marciano said. 'It was my toughest fight. One punch you hit me so hard, I was just waiting for another one. If you had hit me then, I think that would have done it.'

'The best man won, Rock,' Vingo slurred. 'It was nobody's fault.'

'He could have done it to me,' Marciano told his friends later. 'I could have been in his shoes. Don't worry, I'm going for the title.'

now stood in his path. Marciano respected Louis –
part from his arduous running through the deserted
ains, he sparred over 110 rounds. It was hard to see his
brooding face, locked inside a head-guard which looked like a
gladiator's black helmet. The *New Yorker*'s great boxing writer,
A.J. Liebling, saw enough of the squat Marciano body to suggest
he was like 'the understander in the nine-man pyramid of
a troupe of Arab acrobats. He was bull-necked and wide-
shouldered, and even when he was merely walking around the
ring he kept rippling the muscles of his arms and back, as if
afraid that if he let them set they would tie up.'

Away from the ring, Marciano was a sight to behold. His
daily steak was prepared on the blue side of rare. The Rock
would chew each piece methodically over lunch, swallowing the
bloody juice with slow relish, before he spat out the masticated
pulp on his plate. After he had finished his training for the day
he would devour a steaming bowl of minestrone soup, a baked
potato as large as his fist and an enormous green salad. He then
drank a long glass of carrot and celery juice. The taste would
make his face sour as if he was ready to punish old Joe for forcing him to swallow such a vile concoction.

As the fight closed in, Marciano gave up laughing. He gave up
smiling. He became mean.

'Are you worried?' a visiting reporter asked him.

'No, I'm not worried,' the Rock glowered. 'It's just another
fight.'

'Do you think you'll win?'

'Win?' Marciano muttered. 'Yeah, I think I'll win.'

Later that night, Marciano snarled, 'That was a dumb fucking
question. If I didn't think I was gonna win, why the hell would
I be fighting?'

The Rock lived by an old Italian saying: *Fa i fatte e no
parole* – Do it. Don't talk about it.

*

The cold was less intense in Pompton Lakes but, surrounded by so many beautiful trees, it was impossible to miss the onset of fall. Joe noticed the slow turn as, with the passing weeks, the leaves changed colour. He felt his age as he ran five miles in the chilly mornings. Joe would head towards the Ramapos Mountains which had shadowed twenty-five of his fights since he'd first arrived at Pompton Lakes in May 1935, more than sixteen years before, to prepare for Primo Carnera – the Italian Man Mountain.

The new Italian kid, Rocco Marchegiano, or Rocky Marciano as everyone called him, had roots in Naples and Pescara but an accent straight out of blue-collar Brockton. Marciano and Carnera could hardly have been more different. When he fought the twenty-one-year-old Louis, Carnera was six foot seven inches tall and weighed 264 pounds. Marciano was five-ten and 187. This time Louis, three inches taller and twenty-five pounds heavier, would be the giant. Marciano was ten years younger with the greater depth of ambition and endurance. Yet Louis held an immeasurable edge in skill and experience.

Marciano came to boxing at an unnaturally late age for, as a kid, he had been more attuned to baseball than the ring. While he and his friend Izzy Gold had listened to Joe's demolition of Max Schmeling in 1938 as fourteen-year-old boys, agog at the crazy thought that Louis would make $350,000 for a couple of minutes' work, Marciano had never harboured any great boxing dream himself. His first pro fight had been in 1947, the year of Louis's scare against Walcott. Marciano next stepped into the ring sixteen months later, seventeen days after Louis knocked out Walcott in the rematch.

Marciano appeared to be a one-dimensional slugger. He could obviously hit, and had the face-forward intensity of a streetfighter, but he neither jabbed nor controlled the ring with the cool authority of the world's most renowned heavyweight. Joe felt ready.

Mannie Seamon and Marshall Miles, as much his friends as his trainer and his manager, were more fretful. They made Joe do most of his sparring at night, away from the press. There was something amiss with the right side of his body. They called in the doctors, but they could offer no remedy. The years of punches to his head had worn Joe down. He could no longer throw his right with any snap. And he struggled even more to move to that same side and away from an opponent's own right hand – the punch which had caused him so much trouble ever since Schmeling detonated it against the side of his face in 1936.

His occasional day-sessions of sparring were sparsely attended. One afternoon, only Liebling and Colonel John Stingo of the *New York Enquirer* represented the press in a tiny gathering of twenty-five. The days when a Louis training gig would draw thousands had disappeared. Even Joe had grown bored with his routine of shadow-boxing and sparring. 'It is hard,' Liebling agreed, 'to stay interested in your own shadow for twenty years.'

Instead of grinding on about the heavy threat of Marciano, Mannie Seamon lightened the atmosphere. 'Joe,' Mannie cracked as he wrapped his fighter's weathered hands in gauze and bandages, 'this is Colonel Stingo. He's seventy-eight years old and he wants to work a couple of rounds with you.'

'Glad to meet you,' a bemused Joe said to the Colonel.

Joe fell into an easy conversation with Liebling and the Colonel. They spoke of how they had all visited London in the war, of the taste of English apples and the exorbitant cost of black cabs. 'Louis also told about going up on a roof to watch an air raid his first night in London,' Liebling wrote. 'He said "The tracers was the most beautiful thing I ever saw."

'By the time Seamon had finished with his hands, Louis was in high good humour. "I'm sorry we got no boxing shoes to fit you, Colonel," he said to Stingo just before he went into the gymnasium. "So I guess I won't be able to work with you today."'

After a solid workout in which Louis showed a lean body, and a jab as sweet as ever, he strolled past the writers. 'He looked younger with his snap-brim hat on,' Liebling noted. 'It hid the bald spot. And in street clothes, after all, a superbly conditioned man of thirty-seven is still young. It's when he gets into a ring that age comes on him. Louis hovered over us for a while, but none of us could think of much to say. It was no use asking him how he felt, or whether he thought he could win this one, because clearly he was as good as anybody could get him now, and he never had a match in his life that he didn't think he was going to win, and sixty-nine times out of seventy-one he had been right. So why should he change his mind this time? Louis gave a small shiver and said, "Well I guess I better go in, or I might get a chill." We shook hands all around, and he went along to play cards with the sparring partners who belonged to a younger generation.'

Madison Square Garden, New York, 26 October 1951

On the morning of the fight, Jimmy Cannon suggested in the *New York Post* that, 'Nostalgia may govern my mood but it is impossible for me to be cynical about Joe Louis. The man transcends the fight racket . . . He is an honourable man of simple dignity who works at this dirtiest of all games with a crude nobility. As a pugilist this is a guy whose deportment matches his skills. Even now, at thirty-seven, slow and often clumsy, Louis is a reliable performer. The errors he makes are caused by a disobedient body. But his gameness is unimpaired and his intentions are pure.'

Cannon remembered how, after he had almost lost the first Walcott fight, Louis sat on a rubbing-table in his dressing-room. 'His face was swollen; he looked like a loser. "How is your cold?" he asked me. I had been laid up for a couple of days. It impressed me that a guy, bleary and angry, should be that considerate.'

A little less consideration had been paid to the gown Joe Louis wore to the ring that Friday night. The letters spelling out his name on the back had begun to curl away from the shiny material. Without his hat, or even a white towel, the top of Joe's bald head gleamed as he looked down into Marciano's pugnacious face.

The taller and heavier Louis wore dark satin trunks. Marciano, as fresh as he was fierce, was dressed in pristine white. A black slash ran down the sides as if each was linked to the furiously pumping pistons of his thick arms. At the bell, just as he had done before he faced Ezzard Charles, Louis lifted his own arms to chest level. He flexed them gently in mid-air. They were still working. He dropped them into a more familiar fighting pose, guarding his face and head, as Marciano swarmed towards him.

Marciano burrowed his head into Louis's chest and battered away at his body. Louis held him tightly. Marciano stuck close to him as they shuffled to the centre of the ring. His style unsettled Louis, who had always struggled against boxers fighting out of a low and awkward crouch. But as the round closed and Marciano pushed him towards the ropes, Louis let rip with a fast combination. A right and a left smacked home. The Rock did not budge. Instead, he threw a withering overarm right into Louis's face. It was the last blow of the round. Louis turned to his stool, his head hung low. He suddenly felt like he belonged on the other side of the hill.

Mannie Seamon pressed an ice pack against the back of Louis's head and spoke soothingly. They grinned and jabbered in Marciano's corner. Louis came out quietly for the second. He took a left to the head but fired a combination to settle the more excitable Rocky. Louis, needing to turn down the heat, began to box more confidently. As if his old joints had been oiled and warmed, he made his whirling rival miss with almost embarrassing regularity. Marciano, so compact at the start, looked ragged in the third. Louis ducked away from a right haymaker which scythed through the stale air of the Garden. Another right from Marciano flew wide as the old master stepped in and dished out a brief lesson in counter-punching.

Louis shaded the fourth and fifth rounds. His jab peppered Marciano's face. Sometimes, even his combinations flowed as he went to the body. Yet the discrepancy between this Louis and the Bomber who had ruined Carnera and Baer and Braddock and Schmeling was stark. The insatiable Marciano could absorb punishment all night long; he was being hit by blows which contained little of the timing and force that had once defined Louis's punching. Marciano pounded forward as if he knew that Louis would do no more than land a couple of mildly jarring hits at a time. The twin terrors that Louis had once unleashed on the ring – the stalker and the finisher – had both gone. Old Shuffling Joe had backed into his place. Still, even in reverse, he knew enough to have edged into a narrow lead at the end of Round Five. Charley Goldman was no longer smiling as, in Marciano's corner, he filled the small cuts that had opened over his fighter's eyes.

Marciano's ferocious intent was undimmed. He decided it was time to shake up the bald guy and jolted Louis in the sixth. Although Marciano missed again with two lefts, Louis was tired and wary as he backed away. Even when Marciano swung and lost his balance, Louis did not attempt to strike his lolling head. As the Rock rolled in again, Louis was forced to fight in suffocating close-up. He could no longer find the jab to keep Marciano off him. More tellingly, Louis had hardly thrown one of his trademark left hooks all night. He could not bear the thought of leaving himself open to another right hand.

A marauding Marciano dominated the seventh. He drove Louis around the ring as if he was a battered jalopy which could only be made to move by a crunching series of gear changes. Louis finally wheeled out the fast left hook. It was a sleek beauty; and it crashed into the Rock. Marciano took the punch on the chin as if Louis had just flicked him playfully with a soft cloth he might use later to polish the old boy's bonnet.

When Louis came out for the eighth, his cheeks were bloated. The swelling under his left eye had worsened. Marciano, puffy around both eyes, also bore the marks of a rough fight. Yet Marciano could see perfectly. He looked down at his weaker left hand as if wondering if the time had come. That look would soon become an omen. Marciano picked up the pace. Some of his punches missed; but more connected. It was turning into a slow beating. And then, in a devastating moment, the end came.

Barrelling forward in his low-slung way, Marciano made Louis back-pedal again. Then, rising fast, Marciano swung a left hook which, this time, was perfect in both its planning and its execution. The huge punch knocked Louis flat on his back. He hauled himself up on to one knee. As he listened to the dim count, his right glove held on to a rope. The rest of his swaying body leaned heavily on that same knee. Louis's lowered head almost touched the wooden corner post.

Rudy Goldstein, the referee, said later that, 'When a young boy goes down, he still has that hustle, that feeling inside like "I gotta get up". But Joe went down with a thud.' Goldstein had counted to eight when Louis clambered to his feet. The ref wiped the gloves of the stricken fighter on his cream shirt. He waved Marciano back in. Louis, trapped against the ropes, tried to weave and duck – but how do you duck a fighter who closes on you like a hammerhead shark with the taste of blood in its mouth? Marciano, in a cold frenzy, sank his jagged punches into Louis.

A tearing left made Louis's head drop. He was now wide open. Another left stiffened his body. After the numbing shock of that attack Louis sagged backwards. Marciano ripped another right hand into his collapsing face. Louis fell between the ropes. His head slumped over the edge of the canvas, dangling in front of a couple of startled photographers. His right leg was caught between the ropes. Louis was barely conscious, on his back, as the snappers tried to roll him under the bottom rope.

Sugar Ray Robinson, seated on the opposite side of the ring, had made his way around the perimeter as soon as Louis went down. Sugar's hand gripped the bottom rope as if to also stop himself from falling. He was only a few feet away from Louis as he shouted, *'Joe! Joe!'*

Rudy Goldstein reached him first. The referee, helped by Mannie Seamon and Marshall Miles, and a few stray hands pushing from the outside, dragged Joe back into the ring. 'Joe, Joe,' Sugar crooned as he held the fighter's head in his hands, 'you'll be all right, Joe. You'll be all right, man.'

Louis was helped to his feet. Shirley Povich, while lamenting the 'pathetic figure' of Louis the fighter, wrote in the *Washington Post* that, as a man, 'He was a champion to the last, breaking away from his handlers at the finish to shuffle unsteadily across the ring to shake the hand of the guy who had just licked him.'

In the passage outside his dressing-room, Josephine Baker, the singer and dancer celebrated across Europe and America, wept quietly for Joe. Her own name had been splashed across the newspapers two days before. Baker had been refused entry to the Stork Club in New York because she was black. 'Just to wait and shake his hand so he knows,' Baker said huskily to a reporter. 'You know, this is the kind of moment to show that to Joe Louis. Just to shake his hand – it's so important now.'

Inside the room, Sugar Ray cried openly. He was soon joined by Rocky Marciano who embraced his beaten opponent. 'I'm sorry, Joe,' Rocky said through his tears. Joe patted Rocky on the arm. He then called out a sad greeting to Ezzard Charles, who had hurt him far more than Marciano. The sight of such communal grief amongst so many extraordinary fighters was enough to choke the most jaded reporter. The Bomber was gone.

Only Joe looked out with a dry gaze. 'What's the use of crying?' he chided gently. 'The better man won, that's all. Marciano is a good puncher and he's hard to hit. I'm not too disappointed. I only hope everybody feels the same way I do about it. I'm not looking for sympathy from anybody. I guess everything happens for the best.'

When the press moved away, as if taking their leave at a wake, Joe stretched out on the hard rubbing-table. Dr Vincent Nardiello touched Joe's face and head in concern, and shone his small flashlight into each of Joe's bruised eyes. The fighter managed a wink.

The doctor murmured in his ear: 'Joe, you can't fight for at least three months.'

Joe turned his head. 'Doc,' he said, 'do you mind if I don't fight no more at all?'

They sat together in the Wedgwood Towers Hotel, Jesse and Joe, two middle-aged men who had heard enough of the old days to last them a lifetime. In the summer of 1952, on sweltering Saturday afternoons in Chicago, they met at the hotel Jesse had managed since he'd fallen out with Leo Rose, the entrepreneur who'd enticed him to the city three years before.

Jesse liked to think he was a tolerant guy, but the arguments between him and Rose had become increasingly bitter. Although the Leo Rose clothing empire was kept afloat by its Negro clientèle, Jesse was incensed by the policy which gave every white person who entered its State Street store a ten per cent discount. Rose described his strategy as 'broadening our market appeal'. Jesse walked out. He could live without the Sales Executive tag.

'I kinda like being called a hotel manager,' he cackled.

'Yeah,' Joe nodded. 'It's sorta classy.'

The Wedgwood was free and easy, opening its doors to both

black and white customers. It had broken away from the racial policies of hotels like the lily-white Drake which, even in 1952, were euphemistically called 'old-fashioned establishments'. The enduring problem had been highlighted in the *Chicago Defender*. 'A mixed dance troupe comes to Chicago after a successful Broadway engagement,' wrote Meredith Jones. 'The white members of the troupe stop at an exclusive Gold Coast hotel. Negro dancers in the same troupe must find lodging elsewhere. A widely-heralded play concludes its record-breaking run in New York City and the production, behind much fanfare, opens in Chicago's Loop. White members of the cast stop at a hotel near or adjacent to the theatre. Negro cast members, though the hotel does not refuse them, wearily board the subway and battle out to the Southside to seek rooms because "you get the feeling you are not wanted".'

'Hell,' Joe said, 'let them all come here. White dancing-girls, brown dancing-girls, black dancing-girls! It don't matter to us.'

'Sure!' Jesse beamed as if they were making a television commercial. 'Come on down to the Wedgwood . . . *everybody's* welcome!'

They loved to hang out together, kidding around, bouncing vague business ideas off each other in Jesse's smoky office. It was equally great when Jesse's daughters – Gloria, Beverly and Marlene – dropped by to say hello. Joe still tried to flirt with Gloria. She slapped him down. Gloria knew he was just a big old dog who thought he could get fresh with any girl he saw. He was wrong. She put him in his place. And Joe would laugh. When the girls left, Joe would sigh, 'You got swell kids, Jesse.'

'I know,' Jesse nodded. 'You too,' he said, thinking of Joe's nine-year-old daughter, Jacqueline, and five-year-old son, Punchy. They also lived in Chicago – with Marva and her new husband, Dr Albert Spaulding. It was complicated. Joe hated the idea of Marva marrying someone else and yet, soon after it happened, in 1950, he met the guy and liked him. Marva had made the right choice. Joe got used to the idea. He even liked the fact that Jesse played the odd round of golf with Al Spaulding.

Jesse felt more troubled. He might have been voted the world's greatest athlete, but he knew he was far from being the world's greatest father. The years slipped by and, before he even noticed, his little girls became young women. A couple of weeks before, on 8 August 1952, Gloria had turned twenty. Beverly was fifteen and even Marlene, aged twelve, had moved beyond the shiny-faced kid who'd been so excited to wear her black velvet dress with the pink bow and her new patent-leather shoes on the night he picked up his Associated Press award. While he had been out working with the Clowns and Globetrotters, their childhood had raced past him. Sometimes the thought made him unbearably sad. But then he would look at Ruth, and the girls, and he would think how lucky he had been. They had all turned out great. And they loved him. He was their dad and, even when he was away, he had never forgotten them. He just needed to stay home a little longer.

Joe's life was crazy. The tax business was worse than ever. He was drowning slowly in his debt. Joe was mixed up in so many worlds it sometimes seemed as if he hardly remembered he had kids of his own. Jesse worried when he heard how Marva had to do the damndest things to make the kids understand that Joe was still their father. She now knew that, wherever he found himself, Joe would probably still forget Jackie and Punchy. So, if it was their birthday, Marva would phone up a friend in that particular city and ask them to send a card. She asked the friend to sign it *love from Dad*.

But people still swarmed all over Joe. They all wanted to have a word with the old Bomber. They still wanted to touch him. Joe was always ready to do whatever they wanted. There was less time for either himself or his family. And then, just when they were about to despair of him, up Joe would pop to say a surprise hello to Marva, the Doc and the two kids he loved.

Joe had been shaped by everything that had happened to him both in and outside the ring. There was nothing he or Jesse needed to say. They knew what had happened. And so, in the Wedgwood, they would skim over the past. Jesse usually just lit another cigarette while Joe swung his feet up on the desk. They would kick back then, grinning at each other through the hazy cloud of smoke, wondering where life might take them next.

Chapter Fourteen

Under Scrutiny

'To visit Jesse Owens,' Norman Katkov revealed in April 1954, in a long and flattering profile of the man he still called *The Ebony Express*, 'you must go to the State Office Building at 160 North La Salle Street in Chicago. There, behind a door marked JESSE OWENS, SECRETARY – he's the Secretary of the Illinois State Athletic Commission now – you ask for him. The girl said he was supposed to be in, but that he hadn't arrived yet. "He's the busiest man I ever saw," the girl said.'

An hour and a half later, with no sign of the elusive Jesse, Katkov reacted wryly to her repeated efforts to reassure him. '"He'll be here" she said at 10.09 a.m. "He told you he'll be here," she said at 11.05 a.m. "If he told you he would, he will. He's the calmest man I ever knew," she said calmly. She was also the calmest woman you had ever seen. Also pretty. "Don't worry," said the girl. "Mr Owens will be here. He . . . *there*!" she said triumphantly as Jesse Owens came through the door.

'The same Jesse Owens, as straight as the side of a building, with the grin you remembered and the walk you had forgotten, moving only from the hips down, like those women you see in the travel movies, carrying a basket of something on their heads and walking like queens, every one of them. Jesse Owens walks like a king . . . now he came across the office with the big, warm, confident smile which either a champion or a politician and nobody else can give you, taking your hand, holding your elbow, moving you along with him into his office, asking how you want your coffee, ordering it for you as though specifying the color of the Cadillac you were getting, sitting back, lighting a cigarette and smiling all the time. "I didn't start smoking until eight years ago," he said. "Thirty-two years old before I took a drag," he continued, sharing this extraordinary tit-bit with you as though it were a court secret of indiscretion at Versailles a couple of centuries ago. What's more, he made you feel as though he *was* offering you highly classified information. "All the time I was running, why of course, as you will surely understand, I could not indulge in any of the vices." He made it sound as wicked as wicked could be.'

Jesse had the patter. He had the moves. And he still had the smile. That gleaming grin persuaded Katkov that, 'You would have granted him amnesty from murder, for with that smile Jesse Owens might just end up king of the world one day.'

He was working too damn hard to even feel like a prince; yet, in his prestigious $6,000 a year position, Jesse had begun to flourish. When he was still at the Wedgwood Hotel in 1952, Jesse had been approached by a friend of William Stratton, the Republican attempting to become the new Governor of Illinois. They had noticed his community work at the South Side Boys' Club where he'd made the right kind of headlines by inviting Joe Louis and Lionel Hampton, the jazz bandleader, to meet kids on that side of the city. Stratton offered him a deal. If Jesse campaigned for him, and helped broaden Stratton's appeal to a point where he became Governor, he would create the Illinois Youth Commission. The new State Department would be led by Jesse.

His past flirtations with both the Republicans and the Democrats had been driven by expedience. Although he had since dismissed his paid support for Alf Landon in the 1936

Presidential election as 'the poorest race I ever ran', Jesse recognised a real opportunity in Stratton's promise. He had the chance to finally dim the memory of all the clowns, dogs and horses he had raced in the wilderness.

When the Republicans swept the vote, with Stratton becoming Governor and Ike Eisenhower taking the White House, Jesse was rewarded with the head post at the State Athletic Commission. Stratton's delay in setting up the Youth Commission suited Jesse; for taking over an existing body in January 1953 meant he could slip into the prime seat and allow the men below him to maintain their established routine. With an active chairman, two commissioners and four inspectors all answerable to Jesse, he delegated the management of the department to them. He was also relieved to find that three women ran his office, arranged his meetings and luncheons, soothed his visitors when he was late and presented him with crisply-typed letters to skim and sign. That clerical efficiency, and the flexibility of the job, meant that Jesse could develop numerous other interests.

Apart from hosting a radio show, which featured a mix of jazz and chat on a Chicago station, he set up his own employment agency, Hub Personnel, and a public relations company, Jesse Owens and Associates. He still worked as a director of the Boys' Club in one of his many charity gigs. And five days a week, at variable times, he strode through the State office on La Salle Street.

He explained his working philosophy to Norman Katkov. 'All people like each other,' Jesse suggested breezily. 'It's just a matter of having them become acquainted. I'm not one of those tub-thumpers. I don't need a big car. I can drive a Chevrolet. A black one, too. Don't need those dig-me-Daddy colours. You don't get yourself ahead crying "Foul!" all your life. We all know what's wrong with this world. You know it. I know it. I can't change it with wild words. But I can bring two people, the other fellow and me, a little bit closer if I am a gentleman.'

America had become increasingly paranoid. Republican

politicians like Joseph McCarthy saw evidence of an insidious Communist plot to destroy America wherever they looked. While McCarthy and the Committee of Un-American Activities went on their witch-hunt, so State Department diplomats instigated a more subtle war to woo post-colonial Asian countries away from Moscow's influence.

Jesse's homespun patriotism chimed with the conservative times, and it was highlighted by repeated reports of his diligent allegiance. When he organised a boxing tournament at one of the poorest black schools on the South Side he was shocked by the absence of an American flag. He refused to allow the boxing to begin until one was found. Jesse then clawed his way to the top of the pole and hoisted the crumpled flag high. He was twenty-five feet above the ground when the Stars and Stripes finally flapped in Chicago's wintry wind.

Amid such flag-waving, and his belief that he could make any man he met his friend, the government came calling. In 1955, Jesse was asked to represent America on a two-month tour of 'friendship and goodwill' to India, Malaya and the Philippines. Each country represented a significant challenge. India, still in its first decade of independence, fell just outside the widening orbit of both the Soviet Union and China. While its colonial heritage reinforced its links to Britain, and therefore America, India's commitment to democracy had still to be examined in a sustained climate of Cold War. Both Malaya and the Philippines had already proved susceptible to 'Communist forces of insurgence', with dissident groups threatening revolt against their pro-American governments. Jesse would travel alone, under the benign banner of the International Educational Exchange Service, and attempt to spread a positive message about American democracy over the evils of Communism. His mission, it was stressed to him in Washington, was vital.

Rizal Memorial Stadium,
Manila, Philippines, 22 November 1955

Jesse Owens, dressed in his white shorts and Olympic vest, took in another gulp of breath. He felt old and tired. On the edge of the track, his hands cupped his throbbing knees. He tried to keep smiling as the Filipino kids surrounded him. It had been a long day at the end of a gruelling campaign which had seen him visit three countries and twenty cities in seven weeks.

Moments earlier, in his last athletic test of the tour, he had raced against the Filipino Olympic sprint squad. Jesse beat their five fastest runners over 100 yards in 9.7 seconds – which matched the time that had so astonished American journalists five years before. He had not felt so rough on that muggy night at a Milwaukee ballpark in 1950. Now his joints ached and his smoky lungs burned.

Even though he was sweating heavily, Jesse pulled on his frayed red Ohio State University track top. He wiped his face with a towel as he prepared to make his final speech of the junket, comforted by a sanguine truth. He might feel like hell but at least he had won the race – just as he'd won the diplomatic battle on every single day of his exhausting trip. By the time Jesse had reached Manila, the success of his assignment had been confirmed. *The New York Times* suggested that, 'as far as good-old fashioned propaganda goes, sending him here may turn out to have been a small inspiration'.

He'd held clinics every morning and afternoon, training 400 students at a time before he took the microphone to speak to curious gatherings which stretched from 500 people in the remote villages near Ipoh in Malaya to crowds in excess of 20,000 in Bombay, Kuala Lumpur and Manila. In the evenings, he would embrace local customs with relish. He'd devoured hot and spicy curries in New Delhi, while perspiring beneath his Sikh turban, and had helped prepare traditional Sakai meals in bamboo containers with native Malays. And still, every day, he had leapt over hurdles, done the long jump, taken on all-comers in a dash to the tape and, most important of all, talked the talk.

At the core of every speech he repeated the same themes. 'Some of you young athletes have great potential,' he said in Manila. 'Yet success is not easily achieved. Be prepared for sacrifice. Work hard. Take instruction. You have to travel a long and hard road. There is no short cut to the ultimate goal.'

In keeping with such well-meaning homilies, he imparted a more directly political message to both local and American reporters. 'This has been a beautiful journey through three remarkable countries. I have been struck most by the fact that some people have seemed reluctant to believe there are so many opportunities for the Negro in America. Yet I only need to look at my own life to see how much I owe to our American way of life. I have had a welcome chance to discourage the propaganda that the Negro is mistreated in the United States. For this reason alone my trip has been a success.'

Joe Louis had hit the skids. On 7 January 1956, he revealed the grisly truth in a ghosted article in the *Saturday Evening Post*. 'I owe the government well over $1,000,000 in back taxes. I don't actually know how much the total is, and I don't think the government does either. Almost every other week I seem to get a new bill. I know this, though: when you owe that kind of money you can't get out, because the more you make, the higher the percentage that's being taken out in current taxes. It's like doing roadwork on a treadmill. The faster you run, the faster they move that treadmill against you.'

That March, the IRS confirmed that Joe's tax bill had risen to $1,243,097. The *US News & World Report* calculated that the former champion would need to earn $310,000 a year for the next twenty years to clear both the existing debt and its ever-accumulating rate of interest. He had already lost an appeal against the thirteenth tax lien made against him, in September 1955, when the government claimed two trust funds which he'd established for his children in the late 1940s. The Federal Tax court ruled in favour of the government and emptied both trusts, containing a combined total of $65,688, on the basis that Marva Louis had set them up with money her husband already owed to the IRS.

Sympathy for the fighter, both from the public and individual US politicians, ran deep. While the Harlem Globetrotters and various youth organisations held benefits for the old Bomber, the Democrat representative for New Jersey, Alfred Sieminsky, lodged a bill in Congress to rescind Louis's tax debt. It was rejected.

Joe was desperate. Eighteen months previously, he had turned to the circus in an attempt to find an additional source of income. He toured small towns in the south-west in late 1954. Joe, billed as the 'Brave Brown Darling of America', entered the ring with a herd of elephants. He also held a whip while he stood warily at the edge of a cage in which a couple of sleepy lions sat on high wooden chairs. He felt like a clown, and so he soon ran away from the circus and into the sweaty arms of another garish form of entertainment. The money he made as a wrestling referee – at $2,000 a night – was far more than his ludicrous lion-taming gig. He spent four straight months on the road with the wrestlers, ruling over their groaning submissions and panting falls.

There were more glamorous offers. In May 1955 he was asked to host the opening of the Moulin Rouge Hotel in Las Vegas. In its quest to cash in on the influx of Negro gamblers to Vegas, the Moulin Rouge would open its rooms to 'all visitors'. Until then, even the richest black high-rollers had been forced to settle for downtown boarding-house accommodation. Although it was three miles from the Strip, on West Bonanza Road, the Moulin Rouge became the first integrated hotel in Vegas.

Joe had his mind set on more personal matters. He eyed the guest list and made special arrangements to be seated next to Rose Morgan – a black beautician who owned her own parlours in New York and Chicago. Joe liked the look of Rose. He also had an idea to pitch to her. Even if his previous products had failed – from the Joe Louis Milk Co. to Joe Louis Punch to Joe Louis Bourbon – he was still dreaming up new schemes. The latest was a cologne he hoped to market under the name of 'My Man'.

He soon concentrated on turning Rose into his woman. When she politely refused Joe's invitation to join him for 'a little night-cap' he looked at her like she was crazy. Maybe he had lost his touch, as well as his money. Joe forgot his financial woes and chased Rose. He followed her to New York and became even more addicted when she kept him at a distance.

Six months later, on Christmas Day 1955, Joe Louis married for the third time. After two weddings with Marva, Rose promised a fresh start.

Yet he was still broke, and catching more hell from the tax-man. The IRS began to monitor Rose's earnings. He had to ease the unbearable pressure. In February 1956, Joe met Ray Fabiani, a wrestling promoter in Philadelphia. Fabiani offered him a $100,000 deal, spread over a year, to become a feature attraction on the national 'grunt-and-grapple' circuit.

A month later, Joe Louis prepared for his wrestling debut in Washington DC. In an effort to drum up publicity, Fabiani arranged for his new star to visit the *Washington Post*. A picture of Joe wearing a pork-pie hat as he pretended to be a reporter, holding a telephone to his ear and sitting in front of a type-writer, was plastered across the front page of the *Post*'s sports section with the headline: LOUIS DOWN TO WRESTLING WEIGHT – *240*.

'Is this really the start of a new career?' Jack Walsh of the *Post* asked.

'I don't know,' Joe muttered ruefully. 'It may be a one-time only affair. It depends on how I do, how I like it and how the fans like it.'

He was asked about his first opponent – Don 'Cowboy Rocky' Lee. 'This boy Lee is pretty big,' Joe said, 'about 320 pounds, I hear. I've refereed him and I know he's a wild man. All I have to do is tame him, I guess.'

The Uline Arena, Washington DC, 16 March 1956

Snow fell over Washington that Friday. If the streets looked pretty in the morning, the pristine layers of white had turned to slush by early evening. A cold and soaking rain had moved across the city, dampening the urge of all but the most zealous grapple-nut to venture out into the night to witness the start of Joe Louis's wrestling adventure. The Uline announced a meagre crowd of 4,179.

Joe had been given a dressing-room to himself. The other groaners huddled together in the adjoining changing pit, wondering what he would make of their very different ring. Joe had expected to be swamped with painful memories of the past, of the far more meaningful nights he had shared with Jack Blackburn and Mannie Seamon as they wrapped his hands before he stepped out into an arena filled with anything from 30,000 to the record 95,000 who had watched him destroy Max Baer twenty years before. If he'd been forced to get to grips with Cowboy Rocky in New York, or even Chicago, the nostalgia might have been overwhelming. But of all his seventy-one fights as a professional boxer, he had only once fought in Washington – when he beat Max's brother, Buddy, in May 1941. That battle had resembled a wrestling match at the end. Baer's cornermen had stormed the ring in fury after their fighter was disqualified.

Joe struggled into a jockstrap. He pulled on his white socks and black wrestling boots before he turned to the navy-blue briefs they had picked out for him to wear. Joe hated the way his paunch hung over the elastic. He stared at his sagging and rolling flesh. His once flat chest had swollen into two soft brown baps, his nipples making them look even more like small breasts in the smeared mirror. He hitched up his wrestling briefs in an effort to hide at least some of his stomach. The bulge spilled out over both sides. Joe wondered if the big Cowboy would try to grab hold of those two squeezy handles he hated.

Buddy Rogers, who fancied himself as a blond Mr America, swung open the door without knocking. 'Hey champ,' he said, 'Jersey Joe's on his way.'

Jersey Joe Walcott, his bitter old rival, was also in the mire. He had been brought in to referee Louis's debut in an attempt to boost the gate. If briny tinges of jealousy came from Walcott, Louis felt some animosity of his own when Jersey Joe made disparaging remarks about the way black Americans revered the Bomber above any other fighter. Their two title clashes had been prickly affairs.

Yet Joe did not hate any man he had fought. Max Schmeling had come closest to resembling a personal enemy in 1938, and their bond was now stronger than any he shared with a former opponent. Early in 1954, after a day on the golf course in Chicago, Joe had returned home to find Max waiting for him in his lounge. Their embrace was as instantaneous as it was warm. When Max attempted to apologise for the ill-feeling generated by the Nazi press, Joe touched him on the arm. 'Max,' he said, 'forget all that stuff. I know it had nothing to do with you.' They had talked easily for the rest of that afternoon, and on into the evening, when they resolved to visit each other in both Germany and America.

He and Jersey would never enjoy that same affection, but there was a strange intimacy between them when Walcott visited him in the Uline dressing-room. 'I'm glad I got you in that ring with me tonight, Joe,' Louis said.

Walcott nodded. 'We better look out for each other.'

'Yeah,' Joe laughed grimly. 'I hear you also gotta take a few falls.'

'Joe,' Walcott said solemnly, 'I'm gonna be on the floor more times than you.'

'This is a crazy fucking business,' Louis said.

Walcott headed for the ring first, followed by Cowboy Rocky. Wearing an ill-fitting black cat-suit, the mammoth white wrestler played the part of the bad guy to the hilt. Joe heard the booing from his dressing-room.

'Remember, Joe,' Buddy urged, 'no punching.'

Louis ducked through the ropes to an ironic roar and, as instructed, did a clumsy jig of elation. He could not quite bring himself to break the stone-face habit. His dance was accompanied by a flicker of his lips rather than a cheesy smile. Cowboy Rocky glowered at him before he climbed on the top rope and threatened some loud-mouthed geek in the front row. The crowd howled.

When the bell rang the hardest task for Joe was to pretend he was either boiling with anger or writhing in agony. He was no actor. Exaggerated gestures of rapture and despair were beyond him. Whenever Louis dropped into a boxing pose, and the Uline thundered its approval, the Cowboy backed away in feigned terror, holding up his hands in surrender. Louis would pull his punch and the Cowboy would fall to the mat as if kicked in the face by a bucking stallion. As Louis tried to pin him to the floor, the Cowboy would jump up with surprising alacrity. The usual charade of grappling and moaning then resumed.

Walcott was involved in both the acting and the action. The ref was flipped across the ring twice before, after fourteen minutes, the prearranged end was completed. Walcott, having finally managed to break the 320-pound monster's grip on Louis's neck, tumbled to the floor. The Cowboy also stumbled dramatically. Louis's forearm brushed his face. The big old ham fell as if he had been hit by a real punch from the young Bomber.

Cowboy Rocky Lee crashed through the ropes. He clattered into a chair outside the ring. The Cowboy lay on his back as the count neared ten. Louis stood motionless in a corner. Walcott's arm made a flourish to signal the end of the performance. In a heartbreaking gesture of feigned delight, Joe Louis waved his arms in the air and rushed to the centre of the ring. His stomach and breasts quivered, as if in disgust at the sight of his scrawny act.

The Gable Armory, St Petersburg, Florida, 4 April 1956

Buddy Rogers, stark naked but for his white socks and ring boots, dominated their seedy dressing-room. The floor was stained and the paint on the damp walls had peeled away to leave patches of bare plaster. Buddy didn't care. He slapped his thighs and flexed his glistening torso whenever he impersonated rival wrestlers. Joe laughed with the others as Buddy entertained them with stories of a long gone grip-and-grapple tour through Texas. If Buddy was not quite as funny as he thought, snorting and tossing his dyed-blond mane in delight at his wit, Joe liked sharing changing facilities with the whole gang. His first night as a wrestler, in Washington, had felt far too lonely in his solitary dressing-room.

Joe understood why some people were outraged by the idea that he should try and earn a living as a wrestler. Although he would never say as much to Buddy and the boys, he was embarrassed by the notion himself. Yet there was no need to get steamed up about it. He needed the cash and where else, as an uneducated forty-two-year-old ex-prize fighter, could he make the sort of money they promised him on the wrestling circuit?

Ray Fabiani had assured him that eighty or ninety bouts a year could earn him an annual income of $150,000. They would need to hit some sold-out venues like Madison Square Garden for that to happen but, with Joe's legendary status in New York, Ray convinced him that nothing would stop them. Joe would get twenty-five per cent of every gate. If the start-up purses in Florida were disappointing, it was essential he learned his trade in modest venues. Once he could really wrestle they would start booking big-time dates for the Garden.

It all sounded logical to Joe, even though Rose thought he had gone nuts. After his first match in March, he paid $1,050 to the tax man and kept $150 for himself. When he got back to New York, he took Rose out for a celebratory dinner at Red Randolph's up on 124th Street and Seventh Avenue. Joe was in such a good mood he gave $100 to a pal at the bar – which still left fifty bucks to splash out on him and Rose.

When Joe told her about the Florida tour, Rose protested. 'Watching Joe Louis wrestle is just the same as watching the President of the United States wash dishes.'

'Well,' he answered, 'it ain't stealing.'

He still felt the same even though, before he stepped into the ring in St Petersburg, they had already counted the lean take for that Wednesday night. A crowd of 800 had been announced – which meant his cut would be $248. Joe tried not to be discouraged. After his Washington debut, it was only his third wrestling gig. With the money he had made on his two previous nights, in Tampa on Monday and Lake Worth on Tuesday, he had already cleared a grand for the week. And the next three nights – Fort Lauderdale on Thursday, Miami on Friday and Daytona Beach on Saturday – were certain to be more profitable.

Joe was still dressed in his suit trousers and a white vest. He had less than ten minutes left to change. As they had done in both Tampa and Lake Worth, Ray and Buddy had run adverts in St Petersburg which suggested that Joe would confront a well-known wrestler called Jim Mitchell – 'The Black Panther' from Toledo. It was a typical wrestling ruse. When the bell rang Joe faced, instead of Mitchell, a 'late replacement' – a clowning black grappler called Shag Thomas. Shag was happy to play the fall guy for $100 a night. He would do so again in St Petersburg when he stepped in for Mitchell who, despite the ads, had not been booked for a single night on tour.

A white man in a dark suit opened their dressing-room door. 'I'm looking for Joe Louis,' he said.

'And who might you be?' Buddy asked.

'Milton Gross – from the *New York Post*.'

Joe must have met a million hacks over the years. 'Hello,' he said. 'It's good to see you again.'

'You too, Joe,' Gross said as he held the fighter by the hand. 'It's been a while.'

'Sure has,' Joe agreed blindly.

'Am I interrupting anything?' Gross asked as his eyes flickered towards Buddy.

'No,' Joe grinned. 'Buddy's just talking about Texas.'

Gross drew Joe to one side. 'So how do you like the wrestling game?'

'I don't know if I like it yet,' Joe answered truthfully. 'I got to earn some money and I want to find out if I like it. I only got a few more dates on this tour and then I'll decide what sort of future I have in wrestling.' Joe suddenly felt ashamed. The guy looking up at him had probably seen him fight Braddock and Schmeling. What would he make of a pawing and slapping Shag Thomas?

'Joe,' Gross said, 'I see that the audience tonight excludes Negroes.'

'What do you mean?' Joe asked in surprise.

'I've been in town a few days and read all the adverts and pre-views,' Gross said. 'In each of them this one sentence kept hitting me in the eye.'

'What did it say?' Joe asked.

'"Negro spectators will not be allowed into the arena because of a lack of facilities."'

'I didn't know that,' Joe said, the hurt creasing across his face.

'It's been in all the papers in St Pete.'

'Monday I was in Tampa,' Joe explained. 'Last night I was in Lake Worth. I been travelling most of today. I didn't see any newspaper.' He turned angrily to Buddy Rogers. 'You know about this?'

'What's that, champ?'

'You know they don't allow coloured people in here tonight?'

'It's a small place, Joe,' Buddy reasoned. 'They don't have separate facilities.'

'What that's supposed to mean?'

'Well,' Buddy hesitated, 'down here, Joe, they don't like white and coloured folk to share the same bathroom.'

'I ain't going on,' Joe said bluntly. He walked out of the room. His mind switched back to that morning. When they flew into Tampa Airport he and Buddy were starving. Before they moved on to St Petersburg, they decided to grab a late breakfast. They were taken to a back room – a room for Negro diners. 'I lost my appetite,' Joe said. He felt even worse now.

Buddy came after him in St Petersburg. 'Joe,' he said, 'I swear I didn't know about any of this shit.'

Joe knew Buddy had a black wife. He wanted to believe him. 'I don't want to go out there,' he said.

'I guarantee this will never happen again,' Buddy said. 'Before I ask about the percentage of the next gate I'm gonna check if coloured people are allowed.'

'And if they say no?'

'Then we don't even step into that town,' Buddy vowed.

'I still don't think I should go on,' Joe repeated. He turned to Milton Gross. 'What do you think I should do?'

'You've got to make up your own mind,' Gross said.

After an agonising pause, Joe picked up his white towel. He stared at Buddy, his face cold and drawn. 'You guarantee it will never happen again,' he said softly. 'Remember.'

His spoof of a scrap against Shag Thomas began at 9.15 p.m. He allowed the villain to do most of the acting. Shag pretended to gouge out Joe's eyes. He feigned a gruesome bite of Joe's ear. Shag rolled his eyes in horror as Joe dropped into a boxing stance. He ran on to the apron of the ring and pleaded for help. At 9.29, bang on cue after fourteen minutes, Joe pinned Shag to the canvas to win the one-fall show. The white crowd barely cheered.

'Fourteen minutes is barely a watch-tick in the years Louis spent in the ring,' Milton Gross wrote. 'But watching Joe's role in the farce I had to wonder if those fourteen minutes weren't a lifetime. Each time the watch ticked it wore a little more off the legend that once was the Brown Bomber . . . the Joe Louis we knew is gone. He was a symbol of integrity. He was a man of unimpeachable pride and steadfast principle.'

Gross watched Louis leave the segregated building and move out into the darkness. 'He came down the stairs carrying his bag. It wasn't like the old days. He was Joe Louis but his shoulders sagged. He once was a champion and now he was a wrestler, but worse still he had done something he had never done before. The first was bad enough. The other could be unbearable when you're alone.'

That Saturday, having spent hours tracking him down, Joe handed over his St Petersburg check for $248 to Reverend Theodore Gibson – the president of the Miami branch of the NAACP (the National Association of American Coloured People). He had wrestled the previous two nights. In Fort Lauderdale, he had stood on the steps outside and waited until black men and women were allowed into the arena. And, as he had expected, there were black people at ringside in Miami.

Milton Gross had watched Joe grapple in Miami. 'Louis is not a wrestler,' Gross insisted. 'He never will be. He's in a phony business but, fundamentally, Louis cannot be a fake.' Gross's faith had been restored. 'The former champion will continue as a wrestler. He may fumble at his new trade. He does not fumble at being a man. His tax burden has made him do the first. It cannot change the second.'

Joe's groaning career came crashing down on 31 May in Columbus, Ohio, Jesse's old stomping ground. Cowboy Rocky Lee tossed him to the canvas. According to the script, the Cowboy was then meant to hold him in a headlock. Cowboy Rocky made a mistake. He jumped at Joe with both feet and, instead of just missing him, his hefty boots landed on the fighter. Three ribs cracked and, in the crush, Joe suffered a cardiac contusion.

'Oh shit,' Joe gasped through the excruciating pain. He had earned his last cheque as a wrestler.

An electrocardiogram revealed an abnormality in the damaged muscles of Joe's heart. The Illinois State Athletic Commission, as they had done in the boxing ring, denied him a wrestling licence.

Jesse Owens just escaped having to endorse that distressing decision. Six months before, on his return from Manila, Jesse had been invited by Governor Stratton to become the Executive Director of the newly established Illinois Youth Commission. Apart from fulfilling his original ambition, the promotion saved him from personally terminating Joe's last chance to make some money from the ring.

Jesse watched his friend turn next to the TV game-show circuit. Joe was invited on to *Masquerade Party* – where celebrities were disguised before being quizzed by a panel whose task it was to establish their true identities. He had more hope of hitting the jackpot when he and Rose appeared on *High Finance*, a Saturday-night quiz-show about current affairs. Dennis James, the beaming host, called him 'Champ' and made much of the fact that the legendary fighter was attempting to clear some of his $1.4 million debt. Joe had a sharp memory, and he and Rose studied the newspapers industriously in the build-up to each week's show. They lasted six weeks, before finally losing their champions' slot after winning $60,000. The IRS were waiting. As soon as Joe received the cheque they swooped. He and Rose fought back – and she was eventually able to hold on to her share of $30,000. Joe's thirty grand belonged to the tax-man.

A week later he and Jesse met up as usual in downtown Chicago. Jesse knew instantly that Joe was about to buckle. He drove them to his home on South University Street. They sat alone in the quiet of Jesse's study. The tears began to roll down the face of Joe Louis. He was inconsolable. His sobbing made a soft but terrible sound.

'Jesse,' Joe finally said when he lifted his head, 'you don't think they'll put me in jail, do you?'

Since his diplomatic foray into Asia, Jesse's speeches had become increasingly patriotic. Writing in the *Boston Traveler*, Arthur Siegel captured the impact of a typical public address from Jesse during the summer of 1956. 'Owens arose and, as he spoke, a hush fell across the Sheraton-Plaza in Boston. Owens said he'd take more than the five minutes they had given him – and he did. Yet his listeners never noticed time as they heard Owens tell about India and the five-year-old boy who begged for a rupee – "I had heard a child's voice plead, 'a rupee for food'. A thin little arm reached out. I kept walking toward the entrance, between rows of people. There was still that child's voice, begging, 'a rupee for food'. I couldn't stand it any more. I led the child into the hotel and up to my room. I bathed him because he was so dirty. I fed that poor little starved body. In that room were four newspapermen and one of them said, 'You shouldn't have done that. He's an untouchable.'"'

'In Boston, only the Owens voice rang out as he said, "In my country there are no untouchables. In my country nobody starves to death because he is an untouchable. That would never happen in my country – the country I love." So deep did his intense patriotism penetrate the emotions, there was a silence of maybe five seconds after that proud ending. Then there was an ovation.'

On 19 September 1956, J. Edgar Hoover, the Director of the FBI, ordered an urgent and widespread investigation into the private life and political convictions of Jesse Owens. He gave his instructions with personal relish in an FBI Memo numbered 77-72778-1. Special agents would go to work in fourteen cities across America – Baltimore, Birmingham, Buffalo, Chicago, Cincinnati, Cleveland, Dallas, Detroit, Los Angeles, New York, Philadelphia, Springfield, St Louis and Washington DC. Their task was outlined in the curiously jerky language of the Bureau:

Conduct thorough investigation as to character, loyalty, reputation, associates and ability of OWENS, *accounting for entire adult life including education, employment and any periods of unemployment. Ascertain and report identity and current addresses of all immediate relatives and make appropriate checks concerning each. Set out necessary leads by airtel except where use of teletype necessary to ensure deadline met. Assign case immediately. Afford continuous attention. To reach Bureau no later than 10/2/56.*

Hoover then wrote a formal reply to Scott McLeod, the Chief Administrator at the Bureau of Security and Consular Affairs:

Dear Mr McLeod:

   I wish to acknowledge receipt of your letter dated September 13, 1956, in which you requested an investigation of Mr Jesse Owens.

Please be advised that this investigation has been ordered and upon completion a summary of the results of the inquiries made will be forwarded to the Secretary of State through the State Department's Office of Security.

Sincerely yours,
John Edgar Hoover

Like Joseph McCarthy, Hoover was bent on smashing the Cold War commies, reds, pinkos, lefties and niggers who were plotting America's downfall.

His suspicions of Negro celebrities had been fuelled by Paul Robeson. A great black sportsman, singer, actor and intellectual, Robeson admired Joe Louis in particular, having sung the classic blues ballad *King Joe, Part 1*, with lyrics by Richard Wright and music by Count Basie, in 1941. Robeson, with Louis and Bojangles Robinson, had also been invited to counsel Jackie Robinson as he prepared to become the first Negro to play Major League baseball in 1947. He'd heard Jackie repeat his familiar line that, if it had not been for Joe and Jesse, he would never have made the breakthrough. Unlike Jackie Robinson's conservative heroes, Robeson remained a fierce critic of American racism.

The FBI had noted Robeson's campaign against the conscription of black soldiers in World War II. Robeson seemed even more dubious because, amongst the twenty languages he had studied, he could speak Russian. He had also sent his son to school in Moscow. The Committee of Un-American Activities blacklisted Robeson as a dangerous subversive.

Jesse Owens was no Paul Robeson. Yet Hoover suspected that the former Olympic athlete might be duped into supporting Communist causes. In 1953, Hoover instigated the first cursory FBI investigation into Owens. They uncovered little. On 15 October 1937, Jesse Owens had 'sent greetings to the Second

National Negro Congress'. On 23 October 1944, he was listed in the *Michigan Chronicle* as a member of the Committee to Seek Unity of Racial Groups. On 29 September 1952, his name had been mentioned in the *Daily Worker*, a Communist newspaper, in their report of a Youth Peace Crusade held in Chicago. Owens had been a guest of honour at the Crusade's sports festival.

The 1953 Owens file was tucked away in a cabinet marked *Foreign Inspired Agitation Among the American Negroes*. McLeod's letter gave the FBI the chance to dig deeper. In the wake of his success in Asia, McLeod informed Hoover that 'the President is considering the appointment of Mr Jesse Owens to a top-level position in the Department of State'. Yet the White House, gripped by Cold War paranoia, wanted FBI clearance before approaching Owens officially. Hoover just wanted to trash Owens.

The document contained 126 pages. On the FBI cover sheet, in bold capitals, a word and a name were printed:

SUBJECT: JESSE OWENS

A tick had been placed inside the boxed instruction *All References (Subversive & Nonsubversive)*. In the 'Type of Search Requested' section, *Vocations* and *Check for Alphabetical Loyalty Form* had also been ticked.

The reports came next, typed by Special Agents who checked his birth, school, university, marriage, tax and criminal records and delved into his work and credit ratings. The text centred around the interviews each agent had done with the friends, neighbours, teachers, lecturers, journalists and colleagues who had framed Owens's adult life from 1931, when he was eighteen, to 1956.

Names and events tumbled out. They were often stripped of any real context or authority – relying on the mix of memory, speculation and gossip that shaped the murky stream of interviews carried out by Federal Agents. Yet a picture soon cleared.

An official at the Illinois Youth Commission suggested that Owens was 'loyal and patriotic and of excellent character'. A tutor at Ohio State University, who had recently met Owens again, considered him 'an honest, trustworthy and moral individual . . . he related further that Owens is a "very interesting" public speaker'.

In the words of one agent, 'A teacher from his old school, East Tech in Cleveland, remembered that Owens, even as a high-school pupil, always exhibited good common sense. As an example she related that in the early 1930s the East Tech track team was returning from a trip to Chicago. During this period many restaurants would not serve Negroes and the East Tech team included some members of the Negro race. They stopped at a small town west of Cleveland to have lunch but, before the team entered a restaurant, Owens suggested she inquire of the management if they served meals to Negroes. Some of the other team-members were in favour of entering the restaurant and demanding that they all be served, but Owens told them that the Negroes could accomplish more for their race by peaceful means than by violence.'

Another female interviewee stated that 'the appointee has a "superb and overwhelming personality" . . . he is a very likeable person and has a good speaking voice. He is a clean-living individual who dresses extremely well, and in good taste . . . the appointee is a true American.'

A disgruntled employee at the Wedgwood Towers argued instead that 'he personally considered Owens to be a "ladies man" and that he had heard that the appointee, while manager of this hotel, had become involved with some women . . . he could furnish neither names nor dates and could not recall from whom he received this information'. A former reporter for the *Chicago Defender* said 'he had heard that Owens, in his younger days, was quite a "ladies' man"'.

Apart from the pair of 'ladies' man' labels, the only break in the pattern emerged with the revelation that 'the appointee' still had to clear a debt of $52.56 for a rotisserie he'd bought in Chicago on 9 March 1955. After he had read the last page, a leading FBI agent wrote his recommendation. The investigation into Jesse Owens should be discontinued with immediate effect.

A week later, the Department of State suggested to President Eisenhower that Jesse Owens should represent him at the 1956 Olympic Games in Melbourne. J. Edgar Hoover, however, had not been totally routed. While Jesse flew to Australia, oblivious to the furtive machinations of Cold War politics, the possibility of him being offered a position in the State Department was quietly withdrawn. The FBI retained his file for future scrutiny.

Chapter Fifteen

Strung Out

Comiskey Park, Chicago, 25 September 1962

Joe Louis, at the age of forty-eight, had begun to crumble inside. He was breaking apart, piece by tiny piece, and he knew only one way of making himself whole again. It never did last but, for a while, with a secret little hit of heroin or coke, he could sometimes feel like he'd felt twenty-five years before in this same stadium when he beat Jimmy Braddock to become the heavyweight champion of the world. Joe had never felt as certain of anything since; unless it was during the drug-rush which now took him to a hazy place he called Funnyland.

The woman he knew as Annie, a beautiful but dangerous girl with long black hair and a pretty Chinese face, had got him hooked. Joe remembered some dim Milwaukee afternoon in 1958 when, lost and hopeless, and divorced from Rose after barely eighteen months of marriage, he'd turned over in the lumpy hotel bed and, not quite understanding what she was doing, felt Annie stick the needle in him. 'Relax, baby,' she'd said when he tried to pull away, 'this is just what you need.' After a while he started to think she was right. Even a small shot of heroin was enough to have him floating inside his body, cut

326

loose and free from his headaches and taxes, back in that cool and happy space he had occupied with such conviction the last time he had fought at Comiskey Park.

Joe was trying to stay straight. Annie had disappeared and he was coming back to the life hardly anyone knew he had left. Everyone crowded round him at Comiskey Park to say how good he looked. Jimmy Braddock was as gentlemanly as ever. And so was the Rock. Rocky Marciano was smarter, or maybe just luckier, than any of them. He had retired, in 1956, as world champion, and had never come back. With his perfect 49–0 record, Rocky was the only one to get out in time. But Joe recognised the demons in the man who had ended his own career. Rocky was still driven by a compulsive fear that he would end up broke – even though he was in better shape than Louis and Braddock and Ezzard Charles, the fourth former champion on show. The year before, Charles had also turned to wrestling in an attempt to escape his debt. Even though they had all held the greatest title in sport, with its symbolic suggestion that the heavyweight champion of the world was the most powerful man on the planet, each man now carried a sign of doom over his head.

Jesse Owens sat across the ring from them. He and Joe were on opposite sides of the battle. They had picked different men to support in the most lucrative prize-fight in boxing history – a clash between fluttery Floyd Patterson and Sonny Liston, his cold-faced challenger.

Jesse backed Patterson, the tentative world heavyweight champion, whose diffidence offended the mobsters in Liston's corner. 'In their mind,' Norman Mailer wrote, 'Patterson was a freak, some sort of vegetarian.' The rest of America, like Jesse, thought differently. If their affection for Patterson was as modest as the boxer himself, their contempt for Liston was unbridled. 'This is a savage,' the press said of Liston. 'He should be hunted.' Liston was 'The King of Beasts'.

Joe had been boxing's cruel black animal in 1935. Few knew what he really thought or felt then. And Joe could tell that nobody really cared what Sonny Liston thought or felt in 1962. Nobody except Geraldine, Sonny's wife, and Joe himself.

Sonny Liston loved Joe Louis. He was one of the few men Sonny had ever respected. Joe liked Sonny because, away from the ring, the brooding heavyweight laughed, gambled and chased women. In a more public setting, Sonny was afraid of opening his mouth. He never knew what to say. His tongue lay still in his silent head as he stared blankly at everyone. Sonny looked murderous.

Joe knew that Charles 'Sonny' Liston was the twenty-fourth of twenty-five children sired by his violent father, Tobe Liston. Joe had seen the scarred map of Sonny's childhood in the old welts that covered his back and arms. Sonny told stories of how he had tried to make a buck in St Louis. 'I sold coal. I sold ice. I sold wood. I got fifteen bucks a week in a chicken-market cleaning chickens . . . On the good days I ate. On the bad ones I told my stomach to forget it. And me and trouble was never far apart. If a coloured kid's going to get by he's got to learn one thing fast – there ain't nobody going to look after him but him. I learned.'

Sonny Liston grew into a hulking kid. He knew it was better to scare people than to be scared yourself. 'I didn't have nothing going for me but my fists and my strength,' Sonny remembered. 'I'd be eating a day here, and a day there, but eating's a hard habit to get out of. Anyway these kids came along and they had the bright idea of knocking over this store. All I could see at the end of it was a great plate of food, and if we had to take a gun along to get it that was OK too.'

Sonny became a thief. They called him the Yellow Shirt Bandit because he wore the same yellow shirt, with the tiny black checks, to every robbery. In 1950 Sonny wound up in Missouri State Penitentiary in Jefferson City on a five-year stretch. He started boxing in jail. Sonny's prison stories reminded Joe of Chappie, his trainer, because it was in a stone jailhouse that Jack Blackburn began to teach men how to fight. Chappie was smart and steely. Sonny was clouded and vulnerable. They still used to chuck two or three prisoners in the ring to take him on as a gang. He knocked them all down.

Sonny had been traumatised. He was illiterate. On the outside he was soon in the control of gangsters who used him as an enforcer before they set him loose between the ropes to make them millions in professional boxing. That was the stark life of Sonny Liston. And they wondered why he did not smile more often. Joe knew. It was better to be a silent intimidator than some clown they could mock.

Sonny Liston was white America's worst nightmare. His unrelenting image as a 'bad nigger', controlled by mobsters like Frankie Carbo and Blinky Palermo, was also disowned by most black Americans. Jesse Owens had opened his *Sportstalk* column in the *Chicago Defender* on 24 June 1961 with a sigh: 'Well, Sonny Liston has done it again. This time he has been indicted for impersonating a policeman and, because of that, Sonny may have to impersonate the heavyweight champion of the world – because it's possible he'll never get a chance at the title himself now. When they tried to freeze Sonny out of a shot at Floyd Patterson's crown, I was one of the loudest dissenters, because I believed that this fellow who can't read or write, who had a background where he couldn't help but go wrong somewhere along the way, now had paid his debt to society.'

Jesse addressed Liston directly. 'What is a champion anyway? Sonny, you ought to think about that. He isn't just a guy who can go into the ring and knock anyone else down. He's someone who's excellent at what he does and tries to live up to it out of the ring as well as in . . . When you understand that, Sonny, you'll be ready to fight a man like Floyd.'

As much as he loved him, Joe thought Jesse knew shit about

boxing. Sonny was the man. He was the best fighter Joe had seen in years. Sonny had a left jab from hell, a punch even more telling than the Bomber's own beautiful jab. His hook could ruin any man. Sonny's right hand was a pretty mean cousin of that left. Unlike Floyd, Sonny made no fancy dance-steps. He was just like Joe in the way he stalked and hacked down his opponents.

On that freezing and misty night in Chicago, as Joe prepared to duck between the ropes to take a bow, it felt as if he was the only one rooting for Sonny. The President had even summoned the world champion to the White House. John F. Kennedy told Patterson: 'Well, you've *got* to beat this guy.'

Sonny was not the only fighter to be booed that night. Before the faded champions took their turn beneath the lights, the next wave of contenders were called up. Cassius Clay strutted around the ring when his name was announced. Rocky Marciano hated Clay. Joe was more tolerant. Cassius Clay was trying so desperately to get noticed that he reminded Joe of a demented puppy who kept pissing on the carpet when he could no longer contain his excitement. He would learn humility, Joe thought, once he had been smacked in the face a few times. Joe received the most resounding ovation of the night. Waving shyly to the crowd, he glowed inside. It felt good to hear that roar again.

The crowd jeered at Clay, but they rained down loathing on Liston. When the man with the microphone pointed, almost accusingly, at the challenger and shouted '*Sonny Liston!*' the booing rolled around Comiskey Park. Joe looked across at Sonny. His face was solid and still. In an attempt to make himself appear even more massive and menacing, he had stuffed a few towels around his neck and shoulders before he pulled on his white gown. His weight was announced at 214 pounds. From the stricken look on Patterson's face, they might as well have said that Sonny was a 300-pound monster.

The fight lasted two minutes and six seconds, two seconds

more than it had taken Louis to blast Schmeling. Liston moved with a solemn air of coercion. His clubbing blows destroyed the champion.

While the reporters sneered at Patterson's collapse, Liston found a rare note of grace. 'Patterson had fear in him,' he admitted, 'but he wasn't no coward.' Sonny promised to model himself on Joe Louis, 'who I think was the greatest champion of all and my idol. He did everything I want to do. I intend to follow the example he set and would like to go down as a great champion too.'

'Nobody's gonna beat Liston,' Louis said of his dark new disciple, "cept old age . . .'

Sonny knew black America had not been up all night celebrating his triumph as it had always done for Joe Louis. Still, the next day, Sonny hoped there would be a couple of dignitaries and maybe a thousand people to welcome him home to Philadelphia as the city's first-ever world heavyweight champion.

As he stepped from the plane, and looked out at the empty tarmac, Sonny's body slumped. Nobody in Philadelphia even cared enough to turn up.

Disdain for Liston was not just confined to Philadelphia. Arthur Daley, of *The New York Times*, thought his wit was withering: 'The public instantly dislikes Liston, and that's grossly unfair. The average fan doesn't even know the man. One really has to know Liston to dislike him with the proper intensity. He's arrogant, surly, mean, rude and altogether frightening. He's the last man anyone would want to meet in a dark alley.' Across the country, in the *Los Angeles Times*, Jim Murray was as damning. Accepting Liston as champion was akin to 'finding a live bat on a string under your Christmas tree'.

Three years before, in 1959, Joe had married Martha Jefferson, the first black woman to become an attorney in California. Gay

Talese, in an affectionate profile of Louis for *Esquire* in 1962, suggested that, 'Joe's third wife, while having none of the obvious sex appeal of his first two, has succeeded where they had failed because she is wiser than they, and because Joe was ripe for taming when he fell in love with Martha. She seems to be many things to him: a combination lawyer, cook, mistress, press agent, tax consultant, *valet de chambre*, and everything but caddie. "There's a soul about this man, and a quietness that I love," she said . . . Martha is aware of the number of women who still find Joe Louis sexually appealing, and would consider a night with him time well spent. "If those sort of women like living on the side streets of a man's life," Martha said, "I wish them well. But I am his wife, and when I come on the scene they got to get the hell out."'

The only two women Martha made an exception for were her predecessors – Marva and Rose. Joe's trio of wives had become friends. He laughed and said, 'I been married to three of the finest women in the world. My only mistake was getting divorced.'

There were twenty-five television sets in Martha's house. They had all been bought for Joe. Every morning he watched *Captain Kangaroo* with little Amber, one of two sisters that Martha had fostered. Amber called Joe her 'daddy'. She loved the way that, when they were alone in the house, Joe would sometimes cook meals that could have fed ten people. Amber was mad about both Joe and the Captain. Joe felt the same about her and that crazy kangaroo. Whole days vanished from his life, days when he did nothing but stare at the TV.

There were better days. Joe would drive out in the morning to the Hillcrest Country Club and play eighteen holes of golf and, if the mood stayed with him, he would move on in the afternoon to Fox Hills to play another eighteen. At the end of his best days he would rush home in the sun-streaked early evening and say to Martha, in a voice babbling with excitement, 'Well, sweetheart,

I finally got it today! After all these years playing golf I just realised what I been doing wrong.'

And then the next evening he would come home, throw his clubs in a corner, and mutter: 'I'm never gonna play that damn game again.'

'But, honey,' Martha said, 'you told me yesterday you *had* it.'

'I had it,' Joe agreed. 'I just couldn't *keep* it . . .'

Until she met Joe, Martha Jefferson had never even talked to a prize-fighter. She was soon looking out for two of the most famous heavyweights in boxing history – Joe Louis and Sonny Liston. Martha had previously described her first husband, a fellow lawyer, as 'a man exposed to books, not to life'. After her divorce, she vowed to meet men who were 'exposed to life, not books'. Martha could not have chosen two more definitive examples than Joe and Sonny.

Liston's image had soured further. Robert Boyle suggested in *Sports Illustrated* that, 'Liston has had the championship for almost a year now, and in that time he has become insufferable. He is giving back all the abuse he ever had to take. He looks upon good manners as a sign of weakness, if not cowardice, and he accepts gifts and favours with all the good humour of a sultan demanding tribute. Most of the time he is sullen. A contemptuous grunt passes for speech. He acts this way toward almost everyone.'

Except, of course, towards Joe and Martha. Sonny and his henchmen hired Martha to handle his fight contracts. He also accepted an offer to rent Martha's house in Denver. Sonny growled, in apparent delight, 'I'd rather be a lamp-post in Denver than the Mayor of Philadelphia.'

Sonny paid Joe to hang around his camp, just as Patterson had done, but this was different. Joe and Sonny knew each other's secrets. Unlike Jesse Owens and Joe's oldest friend, Freddie Guinyard, Sonny knew about the smack and coke. He was tempted himself, until Joe gave him a lecture about living clean as the world champion. They cracked up over that one. Joe knew all about the men who ran Sonny's life. They were both afraid of the Mafia – Sonny because he had felt their power and Joe because he had begun to imagine that Annie, the girl with the needle, wanted the Mob to kill him. They had their most fun when they hung out with Ash Resnick – which was almost all the time as Ash rarely left Sonny's side.

Ash, a big white guy from Brooklyn, had made it in Vegas while working as a front man at Mob-run hotels like the Thunderbird. He persuaded Liston to hold his compelling work-outs, in which he trained to a loop of James Brown's *Night Train*, at the Thunderbird – the hotel where Joe was given a free room and betting money in a ploy to drag in all those gamblers hungry to shake the hand of the Bomber.

Ash would sit between Sonny and Joe as they played craps. He was the fixer. Ash was the man who could get anything they wanted – whether it was drugs for Joe or a hooker for Sonny. They loved Ash, but Sonny and Joe feared the shadowy men behind him.

Most of the time, they felt like kings. Liston pulverised Patterson in the rematch. A week before that massacre Liston had confronted Cassius Clay. The kid had bawled across the casino floor – 'Look at that big ugly bear, he can't even shoot craps!' – when the champion was $400 down. Liston went after him. 'Listen, you nigger faggot,' Liston spat, 'if you don't get outta here in ten seconds, I'm gonna pull that big tongue outta your mouth and stick it up your ass.'

Later that night, when Liston again saw Clay, he went up to him and slapped him hard.

'Man,' Clay asked, his eyes opening wide in fright, 'what did you do that for?'

''Cause you too fuckin' fresh,' Liston said quietly.

Clay walked away in shock.

'I got that punk's heart,' Liston said.

*

When the contracts were signed for Liston's defence of his title against Clay in Miami on 25 February 1964, Jim Murray of the *Los Angeles Times* suggested that, 'It would be the most popular fight since Hitler and Stalin – 180,000,000 Americans rooting for a double knockout. The only thing at which Clay can beat Liston is reading the dictionary . . . his public utterances have all the modesty of a German ultimatum to Poland but his public performances run more to Mussolini's navy.'

Sonny and Joe were in a great mood when they landed in Miami in late January. Young Cassius was waiting as they stepped off the plane.

'Hello chump!' Clay hollered. 'Hey, you big ugly bear, I'm gonna whup you right now.'

Liston walked over to Clay. 'Listen,' he warned, 'this clowning's not cute.'

'I'm gonna whup you, chump!' Clay shouted again, his eyes almost as wide as his mouth.

An incredulous smile tugged at Joe's mouth. The kid was completely loopy. It had only just begun. Clay followed their car. The pretty challenger hung out of his window and yelled insults at the champion.

'Stop the car,' Liston instructed.

Clay's car pulled in behind the Bearmobile. 'Look, you little punk,' Liston seethed as he pushed his face right into Clay's. 'I'll punch you in the mouth if you don't shut up.'

Clay whipped off his sports-jacket. 'Come on, chump! Let's do it now!'

Joe stepped between the two fighters. Sonny was shaking with rage.

'I'm gonna show him, Joe,' Sonny promised. 'I'm gonna make him sorry.'

Billy Conn, Joe's former rival and friend, summed up the new public swing towards Sonny. 'Clay takes all the dignity away from the heavyweight title by acting like a big phony wrestler.'

Conn took solace from the certainty that, 'Clay can't fight now and he'll never be able to fight. He hasn't the experience. The only experience he'll get with Liston is how to be killed in a hurry.'

On the night of the fight, Conn's prediction was shared by most of the crowd of 8,297 who only half-filled the Miami Convention Hall. They were about to be shocked to the core.

For the opening two minutes, Clay showed off his dazzling reflexes as he made Liston miss with his normally deadly jab. Whenever Liston shot out his big brutal left arm, the brown glove at the end would land inches or sometimes even a foot short of Clay's disappearing face or elusive body. And even when Clay finally absorbed a shot to the stomach he slipped away so fast that Liston was made to look foolish. And then, with sixty seconds left, Clay's own jab flicked out as if he was snapping a stinging towel into Liston's fleshy face. He landed eight successive punches.

When he returned to his corner Liston refused to sit down, so deep was his frustration. At ringside, while earning a little money as an expert analyst for the closed-circuit broadcast, Joe Louis spoke with authority. He hated to say the words against Sonny, but Joe could not lie. 'I think we've just seen one of the greatest rounds from anybody in a long time,' Joe confirmed. 'I think Clay completely outclassed Sonny Liston.'

In the second, as Clay repeated his wizardry, he began to hurt Liston. A black welt rose up under the champion's left eye, becoming an irresistible target for Clay's fizzing punches. It soon turned into a cut. Clay began hitting even harder in the next round, taking time to set his feet and add weight to his punches rather than just delivering them through the midst of his dizzying dance-steps. Blood trickled from the gash which had opened up high on Liston's cheekbone.

Something more mysterious occurred in the break. Clay's eyes began to burn in the fourth, even though Liston only landed a few more punches than he had done before. By the end of the round it felt to Clay as if he had been blinded by some unknown substance on Liston's gloves.

'I can't see!' Clay yelled. 'Cut off the gloves!'

'Cut the bullshit!' his trainer Angelo Dundee shouted back as he sponged water into Clay's eyes. 'We ain't quitting now.'

Pushing Clay back into the ring, with the instruction that, 'You gotta go out there and run', Dundee watched his young fighter blinking and almost crying as Liston stepped forward. For the next two minutes Clay moved and clinched and moved again, taking punches but somehow preventing Liston from landing one of his big bombs. Slowly his eyes began to clear until he could once more focus on Liston and punch back rather than just run from the watery blur that had faced him at the start of the fifth.

He was almost home by the middle of Round Six as, with another virtuoso display, his jabs and crosses, hooks and upper-cuts, stunned Liston. Just before the bell, Clay sank two more hooks into Sonny's raw and gaping face.

Liston had had enough. 'That's it,' he said when he reached his corner.

After they had attended to his cuts and massaged his aching shoulders, Liston's cornermen tried to push the gum-shield back into his mouth.

Liston spat it out. 'I said,' he repeated bitterly, '*that's it*!'

The world's most ferocious fighter had quit.

Cassius Clay rushed to the ropes. His screaming, bug-eyed exhilaration replaced the deadpan silence Joe Louis had made famous when he won the same title in 1937. 'I am the King!' Clay yelped. 'I am the King! King of the world!' He pointed down at the white writers who had dismissed him. '*Eat your words!*' Clay shouted at them.

Joe did not know where to look – whether at the crushed figure of Liston, the shrieking sight of Clay or the overwhelmed reporters.

Steve Ellis, Joe's co-commentator, shoved a microphone into the winner's face. Cassius Clay roared on: 'I am the greatest! I shook up the world! I am the greatest thing that ever lived! I don't have a mark on my face, and I upset Sonny Liston, and I just turned twenty-two years old! I must be the greatest! I showed the world! I talk to God every day! I'm the King of the world! I'm pretty! I'm a bad man! I shook up the world! I'm the prettiest thing that ever lived! I shook up the world! I want justice!'

The following morning, the new champion confirmed his conversion to Islam. He then drove from Miami to New York and set up camp in Joe's favourite hotel in Harlem – the Theresa. Clay regaled reporters with stories of how his two-day road trip had been blighted by constant refusals from restaurants to serve him. He completed his account with a typical piece of poetic doggerel:

> *Man, it was really a let-down drag*
> *For all those miles I had to eat out of a bag*

On 6 March 1964, he announced to the world that he had changed his name. Cassius Clay had become Muhammad Ali.

In a rematch that was widely regarded as a struggle between the Black Muslims and the white Mob for control of the title, Ali met Liston again before a pitiful crowd of just over 4,000 in Lewiston, Maine in May 1965. Before even a minute had passed Liston went down from a short cuff of a right hand. Ali stood over Liston. His arm pumped in furious indignation as he screamed at Liston to get up.

Jersey Joe Walcott, the referee, looked as if he was still lost in that bizarre wrestling match he'd officiated between Louis and Cowboy Rocky Lee. Liston seemed to have collapsed in a display of appalling acting while Ali howled. Walcott managed to push Ali back to a neutral corner – by which point the time-keeper had reached the count of twelve.

'Twelve?' Walcott mouthed in disbelief.

'Twelve,' the counter nodded. 'The fight's over.'

The cry immediately rose up from the furiously suspicious crowd: *'Fix . . . fix . . . fix!'*

Joe Louis did not think it wise to ask too many questions. He just knew how much it hurt Sonny when they savaged him. Sonny was now reduced to 'the bum of bums, the nothing of all nothings'.

Joe tried to console Sonny in the only way he knew. He took him out in Vegas. They drank. He took him out in Denver. They took drugs. They were scared of the Mob and they were scared of the shadows. So they ran. They ran with the devil.

Jesse Owens, meanwhile, was hailed by *The New York Times* as a mid-'60s definition of 'a happy man'. As black protest spread across the country, Jesse offered white Americans a more hopeful picture of stability. The *Times* stressed that Owens 'is successful in business, he is a renowned speaker, he is a grandfather four times and he is a man at peace with himself . . . he remains one of the most magnetic of all sports heroes. People who have never met him idolise him. He has accepted this as part of his life, and he does not want to rock the boat.'

A reflective Jesse suggested that, 'More people have been kind to me than not, and they have looked upon my accomplishments more than the colour of my skin . . . [but] I came along at a time when the Negro in America needed an image. I got more than my share of adulation. Joe Louis was the other figure from that era. I think we fulfilled a need.'

The first half of the decade had been good for Jesse. In 1960, on television, *This Is Your Life* honoured his achievements and reunited him with his mentor – Charley Riley. There was a further mix of pride and nostalgia when, that autumn, he crowned his daughter, Marlene, as Ohio State University's Homecoming Queen before an adoring crowd of 83,000. That night, Jesse, Marlene and Jackie Robinson hit the campaign trail and supported his greatest friend, Dave Albritton, as he secured re-election to the Ohio State legislature.

There were still some notable losses. Ralph Boston, a twenty-one-year-old black American, broke Jesse's world long-jump record in 1960. Jesse's historic mark, set in Ann Arbor, had lasted for twenty-five years. The death of 'Pop' Riley followed a few days later. With the return of the Democrats to political power, Jesse also lost his position at the Illinois Youth Commission in January 1961. This last loss hurt Jesse the least, for he had already formed his latest public relations company, Owens-West & Associates.

Besides hosting weekly luncheons for black housewives at Chicago's Tiki Room, where Jesse peddled numerous kitchen products, he lent his smiling face to commercials for anything from grocery stores to real estate, from Lucky Strike cigarettes to Quaker Oats. To sell 'Tasty Tinned Beef Stew' he was marketed as 'The Man Who Ran Against A Horse'. He also received over 4,000 letters criticising his 'endorsement of alcohol' in a beer ad. Yet what was wrong with a mature fellow like himself flipping open a couple of beers after work? And, as Jesse beamingly proclaimed, Meister Brau was 'real honest-to-goodness draft beer – now in convenient cans and bottles!'

He was more amused by the slogan they used at the top of their Meister Brau sales pitch, where he was identified as JESSE OWENS, FAMOUS RADIO PERSONALITY. As the thirtieth anniversary of the 1936 Olympic Games approached, Jesse could finally believe he had moved beyond the giant shadow of his achievements in Berlin.

4800 South Beach Drive, Chicago, 20 November 1965

On the front page of that Saturday's *Chicago Tribune*, it was reported that 'Jesse Owens, 52, Olympic track star of the 1930s, was accused by the federal government yesterday of failing to file income tax returns from 1959 through 1962. The accusation was made in a four-count criminal information filed with the federal District court. The information also charged that Owens received gross income of $59,024 during the four-year period. State attorney Edward Hanrahan said that a summons would be issued, directing Owens to appear before the court and answer the charge. Bernard Kleinman, Owens's attorney, told the *Tribune* that Owens will be "vindicated of the charges by the court. We will certainly plead not guilty". Kleinman added that he would surrender Owens to federal marshals on Monday.'

When the newspaper called him the night before, Jesse had not been surprised. Owens-West & Associates had already suspended trading, such was the severity of the charge. He remained cool as the *Tribune* man quizzed him. Yet they included only one short quote from him in that shattering newsstory: 'I never tried anything that was dishonest.'

Jesse's eye was drawn to a line in the middle of the copy which stressed that, 'if convicted', he would be jailed and fined $40,000.

He was due to see Joe that afternoon. They had booked a golf foursome weeks earlier. The thought of walking the course with Joe, a man who had suffered more than most at the hands of the IRS, seemed strangely soothing. Jesse had just eaten a sandwich and was about to change into his golfing gear when the phone rang. 'I bet that's Joe,' Jesse said to Ruth, 'checking what time we're supposed to meet.'

Ruth returned to the bedroom a minute later. 'It wasn't Joe,' she said. 'It was Frank.' As Ruth murmured the name of Jesse's long-standing golf partner, a broken expression crossed her face.

'He said he couldn't make it. I asked him if he wanted to talk to you. He just said no. He said he was in a rush.'

'You don't think . . . ?' Jesse asked, his gaze dragging across the front page. Ruth nodded. 'That son of a bitch can go to hell,' Jesse said. 'There're a thousand people I can call and they'd be at the tee in forty minutes.'

Before he could pick up the phone, it rang again. The last member of their foursome claimed that a guest had turned up unexpectedly.

'That's OK,' Jesse said. 'Frank can't make it. Your pal can make up the four.'

'He's not a golfer,' the man said. 'Goodbye, Jesse.'

'Can you believe it?' Jesse said. 'I'd better call Joe . . .'

There was, of course, no problem with Joe. But neither of them were in the mood for golf.

'You sound like you need a drink, Jess,' Joe said.

'I reckon I do.'

'You stay right there,' Joe instructed. 'I'm on my way.'

Joe arrived with a bottle of J&B whisky. Jesse poured a couple of large ones. Joe looked closely at his pal. It was the first time, despite all their golf dates and get-togethers, he had studied him in years. Joe had been too numbed by his own problems to notice a change in Jesse. He now seemed old and tired.

Jesse had previously been disturbed by Joe's 'spaced-out' look, as he and Ruth described it, whenever they met. It was almost as if Joe had lost a part of his mind. He never seemed able to concentrate on anything he said or did. Jesse blamed stress, and maybe a few too many J&Bs, as the tax-machine turned the screw on Joe. Yet life was full of mystery. Just as Jesse fell into the same darkness so Joe had the look of a man who was moving back into the light.

'You're looking good, Joe,' Jesse said. 'You got out in the end.'

'Jesus,' Joe sighed, 'I been under the thumb of the IRS twenty

years. And if it hadn't been for Martha . . . well, I reckon they'd
still be asking for a million.'

Martha had finally struck a deal with the IRS. After they
had seized $3,500 of the $4,000 Joe made for appearing alongside Pearl Bailey at the Rivera in Vegas, Martha argued that
such tactics would drive her husband away from any future
work. She persuaded Dana Latham, the commissioner of the
IRS, to soften their stance. Although the IRS would not cancel
his debt, which was again in excess of $1,500,000, Latham
agreed that, from 1965 onwards, Joe would only be taxed on
his annual earnings.

'That's why I call her "Sergeant",' Joe quipped. 'She's giving
orders to the fucking IRS now! You want me to set the Sergeant
on 'em for you, Jess?'

'Let's hold her in reserve, Joe. If they send me to prison . . .'
Jesse paused for breath as the words tightened around him. 'I'm
gonna need all the help I can get.'

United States District Court, Chicago, 21 December 1965

Outside the courtroom, at five to ten on an otherwise ordinary
Tuesday morning, he stared at the sheet of paper pinned to the
wooden door.

UNITED STATES OF AMERICA

-vs-

JESSE OWENS

Ruth stood next to him, on his right, holding his hand. To the
left were his two lawyers, Bernard Kleinman and Frank Bellini.
The three state attorneys laughed quietly down the corridor.
Jesse wondered if they were chortling at the decision to change
his plea from 'Not Guilty' to *Nolo Contendere*. Kleinman and

Bellini had told him that, in plain English, he was now pleading 'No Contest'.

They were ushered into court and made to rise again when the Judge breezed in. At sixty-nine, Sam Perry was one of the oldest judges still working the courts in the Northern District of Illinois. Perry had a reputation for treating those brought before him as real people rather than legal appendages. Jesse, so his lawyers consoled him, had a chance with Perry. There were other judicial names who would have decided to put him away before anyone opened their mouth in court.

Yet it started badly for Jesse. The Judge looked straight at him as he spoke. 'If a witness wishes to come into this court and say, "I do not choose to contend the assertions that are set forth in the indictment", I invariably make a finding of guilty . . . while it is not a confession of guilt, it is a refusal to defend.' Judge Perry laid out the maximum penalty available to him. Four years in prison. A $40,000 fine.

'I have warned the defendant that on a plea of *nolo contendere* I always make a finding of guilty,' the Judge repeated. 'I now ask,' he said, 'what is the plea?'

Kleinman stood up. 'We plead *nolo contendere*, Your Honour.'

Jesse glanced up at Kleinman, as if he could hardly believe what they had done.

'And you,' Perry asked Jesse, 'you join in the plea of *nolo contendere* at this time?'

Jesse rose up in a hustle, like a young fighter trying to pretend he wasn't hurt. 'I do, sir.'

The first witness, Rose Chowanec of the IRS, suggested that he had not filed tax returns from 1954 to 1958 – the four years preceding the period for which he was on trial. Judge Perry upheld Kleinman's objection. 'We are not dealing with anything other than four years,' Perry insisted. 'You may go into those four – but not the others.'

'No return was filed for 1959,' Rose Chowanec stressed.

'How about 1960 for Jesse Owens?' the State Attorney, Thomas Curoe, asked.

'No return was filed,' Chowanec repeated.

'How about 1961?'

'No return was filed.'

'How about 1962?'

'No return was filed.'

'Thank you,' Curoe smiled. He turned to Kleinman: 'Your witness.'

'No questions,' Kleinman murmured.

Jesse looked away. That grim phrase, *no contest*, burned inside him.

The next witness, Francis Vallee, was the IRS special agent who had told Jesse they were ready to bring him down. Jesse knew his team were struggling. Even Kleinman's cross-examination of Vallee was interrupted. Judge Perry chipped in to emphasise that 'the man who does not file at all is doing more of a disservice than the one who files his return but chisels it somewhat. At least a man who makes a return, he puts it on the record, and he enables the government to start tracing his income.'

Jesse, a shambolic non-filer rather than a clever chiseller, straightened his tie anxiously. The next twenty minutes were excruciating as they pulled apart his chaotic financial life. When the State presentation closed, Perry said, 'I will have a final hearing and hear the defendant then.' Perry suggested the next appropriate date – a bleakly symbolic last day of the year.

'Your Honour,' Kleinman's assistant, Bellini, piped up. 'I think December thirty-first is a holiday.'

'I will be glad to back up a day,' Perry said.

After the worst Christmas they had ever known, Jesse and Ruth returned to that same courtroom on 30 December 1965. Kleinman had arranged for five witnesses to testify on Jesse's behalf – Judge Sidney Jones, Leo Fisher, the Sports Editor of the *Chicago American*, Jonathan James, the minister from Jesse's church, Kenneth 'Tug' Wilson, from the United States Olympic Committee and John Leonard, previously with *Sports Illustrated*. Joe Louis, with his own infamous tax record, was not considered.

The first three character witnesses proved loyal allies. Yet even their words, exemplified by Reverend James's assertion that Jesse is 'a very grand person to know', sounded vague when set against the prosecution's pithy line of defence.

'Reverend James,' Thomas Curoe began his typical cross-examination, 'do you consider it a moral obligation to pay taxes and file tax returns to the country of the United States?'

'I certainly do,' the Reverend James boomed.

'Thank you, Reverend,' Curoe nodded sagely. 'The witness is excused.'

But then, at last, in steamed Kenneth Wilson. The pugnacious 'Tug' reduced the courtroom to hushed awe as he spoke of Jesse Owens. He remembered that he had first seen Jesse run as a schoolboy at Soldiers Field in the summer of 1932. 'Jesse electrified the world with his performances,' Tug insisted with an exultant gesture. 'I wondered at the time how he could stand up under all this praise, but he did . . .

'As a matter of fact,' Tug argued, 'he was the symbol of American Olympics, because in 1932 he had won four gold medals in Berlin.'

Jesse had to stop himself shouting out a '1936' correction. He knew Tug was on his way.

'Hitler decreed there would be no Jews or Negroes competing,' Tug said with a sad shake of his head. 'That was the only time that the Olympic Committee or anybody ever backed Hitler down, except an army. Hitler had to change his view, but he walked out of the stadium when Jesse was presented with his fourth gold medal . . .

'He was very gracious and humble in winning,' Tug said of Jesse, 'and when he was licked I never saw him offer an alibi in the thirty years I have known him . . . he has always conducted himself with dignity. I have seen Negro groups that wanted to protest against the way the Olympic team was being run and handled. Jesse would quiet them down and tell them, "They are doing their best."'

Wilson was asked to describe Jesse's more recent diplomatic efforts. 'The State Department sent Mr Owens on many trips all over the world,' Tug explained, 'where even at his semi-advanced age Jesse would get out and show them. You might expect a small clinic. [But] there would be thousands of people there and he accepted the task of signing autographs and talking and everybody wanting to shake his hand with infinite patience. I am on a committee of the State Department that sends teams all over the world. Right now Jesse is at the top of the requests that come from Europe, Asia and all the world. They want to see him.'

As Wilson covered the tracks of Jesse's 'frantic career' he concluded that 'it would be hard for him to be businesslike. The demands on Jesse have been unbelievable.'

Kleinman read out a last citation from John Leonard. Kleinman lingered over the key words: 'No one has ever done a better job for the youth of America, for his race and for his country than Jesse Owens.'

Perry admitted, 'There is great difficulty in dealing with a defendant who is well known . . . [but] I am going to do exactly the same thing that I have done with every other defendant who has come before me, whether he was a bank robber or just somebody who lifted something from a post office . . . I will hear from the defendant on the day that I dispose of this matter. That day will be February the first .' He asked both counsels to sum up.

In his closing address, Kleinman argued that Jesse Owens 'did not file a return because, as Mr Wilson related, he was busy running from one event to the other, performing good works internationally . . . this man, in a world consumed with war and travail, has stood for friendship and peace . . . the defence's recommendation is that this Court grant probation to him on this technical charge.'

Thomas Curoe made a different recommendation. 'Here is a man who lives in one of the finest addresses in Chicago, lives one of the finest lives, has represented the United States in different functions, and has failed to meet the basic responsibility of filing an income tax return and paying his taxes. Mindful of the fact that Congress has set a maximum sentence of four years in prison and/or a $40,000 fine in this case, the United States Attorney for the Northern District of Illinois has directed me to urge the Court to sentence this defendant accordingly.'

United States District Court, Chicago, 1 February 1966

Three inches of snow were forecast to fall across Chicago that Tuesday afternoon when, just after one, Jesse Owens arrived at court. The bitter weather embodied the last ten weeks of his life. He and Ruth had packed for Judgement Day with gathering pessimism. It was hard to know what he might be expected to take to prison.

Jesse walked into court at 1.43 p.m. Two minutes later, Judge Sam Perry followed.

'Mr Owens,' Perry asked, 'is there anything else you wish to say?'

Jesse Owens stood up slowly. He wore a black suit and tie and a white shirt Ruth had ironed for him that morning. 'Thank you very much, Your Honour.' His voice was clear as he gestured to the exhibits table. 'These are returns which have been filed and stamped, if you care to look at them.'

The clerk handed the small pile of documents to Judge Perry. 'These are copies of the income tax returns which you have filed?' Perry asked.

'Yes, sir.'

'For the years 1959 through 1962, inclusive,' Perry read aloud. 'And the record showed you had already filed 1963 and 1964 income tax reports.'

'Yes, sir.'

Perry looked at the State Attorney. 'I am aware of them being filed, Your Honour,' Curoe nodded, 'and the amounts paid on them.'

'All right,' Perry said. 'Is there anything else, Mr Owens, that you have to say?'

'Well, sir, I certainly am regretful that this has to be brought up before you. There are many circumstances that perhaps caused this. I want you to know that this was not a wilful act to defraud the government. First of all, I might say that I only know one government. I have tried to serve it well during the time I have been on the face of this earth.'

Jesse's confidence grew as, after he compared himself to the captain of a track team who 'did not do the job that should have been done', he spoke directly to Sam Perry. 'For many years I have tried to build a reputation – and I do not know whether you know it or not, but I come from a family that were share-croppers of Alabama . . .'

'It is one of those little ironies of life,' Perry said, 'that you were born about sixty miles from where I was born in Alabama. I know the little town you come from, Danville. Some of my people come from Moulton, about fifteen miles from your town. I was raised there. I know your background. I know that what you say is true.'

'In trying to build an image in this country, and I have tried awfully hard to do it,' Jesse said, 'all I am asking is an opportunity to prove to my community, to my family and to my state and to my country, that I want to continue, as I have in the past, working with young people and working with people in general, trying to make this a better world and a better place for mankind to live. That is all I have to say in my defence.'

He sat down as slowly as he had risen. He waited for the verdict.

Judge Perry shuffled his papers and cleared his throat. 'I will not keep you in suspense,' Perry promised. Jesse's hands, on his lap, turned into fists.

'I do not propose to impose any extreme penalty upon you,' Perry said. 'I expect to fine you. I do have a few things to say first ... Taxes are the lifeblood of civilisation. Without them there would no law and order. Without law and order, there would be no protection for life, liberty and property ... now, because human nature is not as good as Rousseau said it was, Uncle Sam had to put some teeth in these tax laws. So they provided criminal statutes. One is for those who fail to file, and the other is for those who file false returns.'

The clock on the courtroom wall ticked on. Another five minutes of summary passed before the Judge finally said, 'Your tax delinquency must be treated, legally, as wilful for the reason that at all times you knew it was your duty to make such returns.'

Jesse hoped his face would not begin to twitch in the way he had once seen Joe Louis's cheek jump in distress.

'On the other hand,' Perry continued, 'you have been too generous. If I may say so, sometimes it appears to me that you should have had a manager. You have not been selfish enough, probably, to accumulate funds. I have looked at your return here and for the money that you have made, you are not a man of means. I can see where it has gone. It has not gone to riotous living.

'Your errors have been errors of omission rather than commission ... however, there must be punishment, for its deterrent effect upon others, not upon you. I am convinced that you will never need any more punishment, because you have suffered far more than John Doe, a man on the street, because you have cherished your reputation . . . now having looked at your record and finding that it is good, very good, I do not believe there is any reason why one error should prevent you going right ahead with your good work.

'It would be a travesty if I, under these circumstances, exercised my discretion improperly or excessively against a good citizen for one mistake . . . so I am going to fine you. You are hereby fined $750 for each of the four years, a total of $3,000. I am not going to place you on probation, because you do not need probation. You will pay your responsibility, without having to have a probation club over your head . . . I will give you six months within which to pay that fine. That is the judgement of this court.'

'Thank you, Your Honour,' Jesse said. He turned to his wife. Ruth was crying and smiling. He was free. He was still free.

Chapter Sixteen

Uncle Tom Blues

'More than twenty-five years ago, one of the southern states adopted a new method of capital punishment. Poison gas supplanted the gallows. In its earliest stages, a microphone was placed inside the sealed death chamber so that scientific observers might hear the words of the dying prisoner to judge how the human reacted in this novel situation. The first victim was a young Negro. As the pellet dropped into the container, and the gas curled upwards, through the microphone came these words: *"Save me, Joe Louis. Save me, Joe Louis. Save me, Joe Louis"'*

Martin Luther King, *Why We Can't Wait*, 1964

Muhammad Ali still remembered the tree. When he had been a small boy called Cassius his father had taken him to see it. 'Look at this tree,' Cassius Clay Sr instructed when they arrived at the appointed spot in their home town of Louisville, Kentucky. Little Cassius looked up at a tree which seemed no different to thousands he had seen before.

His father made him touch it. 'That's a very special tree.'

'Why?' Cassius wondered.

'Joe Louis leaned against that tree. He came down to Louisville for the day and we all followed him. And he stopped for a while to talk to some folk . . . and he leaned against that tree.'

Young Cassius shivered. Here was a fighter so great he made Cassius's daddy bow down to a tree. Here was a fighter so great it seemed as if they had named the whole town of Louisville after him. What would it be like to be a fighter as great as Joe Louis?

Muhammad Ali had not forgotten that memory. A few days before Judge Sam Perry made his sympathetic judgement of Jesse Owens, the twenty-four-year-old world heavyweight champion announced that he had appointed fifty-one-year-old Joe Louis as 'an adviser'. Ali was still so unpopular that, just to rile him, the overwhelming majority of writers persisted in calling him Cassius Clay. Wendell Smith of the black *Pittsburgh Courier* was typical in believing that, as he wrote on 29 January 1966, 'Clay's selection of Joe Louis as an adviser is an indication that Cassius now wants to improve his image.'

Ali's reasons were more complex. While he liked the idea of easing Joe's financial burden, Ali knew how much his father would love having the Brown Bomber on board as a cheerleader.

'We loved him in our house,' Cassius Clay Sr said. 'It doesn't get bigger than Joe Louis.'

Yet his son had another hero. Whenever he saw Sugar Ray Robinson, Ali would holler, 'The king, the master, my idol!' He persisted in his efforts to entice Sugar Ray to join his camp. However, like Jesse and Joe, Sugar regarded the Nation of Islam with suspicion. 'This slogan of yours,' he told Ali, 'this saying that "the white man is a devil", is just not right. You can't live without the white man – or the black man or the red man or the yellow man. People should be against hate, not with it.'

Jackie Robinson was another of the black generation linking Louis to Ali who rejected his brash rise. He lamented the way in which Ali had 'played and toyed' with Floyd Patterson in the ring on 22 November 1965, 'torturing him with an unforgivable cruelty and viciousness . . . people of all races and creeds deplored these tactics. I know I did. Such immature sadism makes Clay no bigger in the eyes of people ... I hope that Cassius will fool many of us who are disappointed in him. I hope that he will develop himself so that he will learn to wear the crown of the championship with the strength and wisdom and manhood that it should imply.'

Older Americans were made to feel most uncomfortable by Ali's prickly bursts of speech: 'Clay means dirt,' he insisted. 'It's the name slave-owners gave my people. My white blood comes from slave-masters, from raping. The white blood harms us; it hurts us. When we was darker, we was stronger. We were purer. When I was growing up, what did I see? Jesus is white. Superman is white. The President is white. The angels is white. Santa Claus is white. That's brainwashing, the biggest lie ever told children. Every year you buy toys and your children wind up thinking they came from some white man with rosy cheeks. They think everything good has to come from someone white.'

Having alienated both Sugar Ray and Jackie Robinson, Ali turned to Louis. Even if the older man seemed more likely to quietly take his pay-packet than engage Ali in ideological debate, Louis had already criticised him. When Ali's name-change was first announced, Louis told reporters that, 'I'm against Black Muslims, and I'm against Cassius Clay being a Black Muslim. I'll never go along with the idea that all white people are devils. I was born a Baptist and I'll die a Baptist. The way I see it, the Black Muslim wants to do just what we have been fighting against for a hundred years. They want to separate the races and that's a step back when we're going for integration.'

Three weeks later, on 18 February 1966, Louis left the Ali camp. The *New York Amsterdam News* reported that an irreparable rift had been caused by the fact that, 'Joe can't get along with the Muslim doctrine. "I have always believed that every man is my brother," Joe said.'

Yet the real confrontation between Louis and Ali centred around boxing, and the right of both men to call himself the greatest heavyweight in history. Although he had a deep respect for Louis as a fighter, Ali's unique style in the ring had been derided by the former champion. 'Can't throw a punch when he's movin' like that,' Louis snapped when he first saw Cassius Clay. 'Shouldn't pull his head back to get outta the way of a punch.'

While they tried for a few days to avoid the subject, Ali found the temptation irresistible. He began to tease Louis about his certainty that he was the better fighter. After Ali told Louis, in the midst of a joint television appearance, that he'd had a dream in which he knocked him out, the Bomber growled, 'Don't you even dream it.'

Ali's constant claim to be 'The Greatest' was answered with uncharacteristic venom by Louis. 'He can't punch,' he said of Ali. 'He can't hurt you and I don't think he takes a good punch. He's lucky there are no good fighters around. I'd rate him with Johnny Paychek, Abe Simon and Buddy Baer . . . I would have whipped him. He doesn't know a thing about fighting on the ropes, which is where he would be with me. I would go in to outpunch him rather than try to outbox him. I'd press him, bang him around, claw him, clobber him with all I got, cut down his speed, belt him around the ribs. I'd punish the body, where the pain comes real bad. Clay would have welts on his body. He would ache. His mouth would shut tight against the pain and there would be tears burning his eyes.'

Ali scoffed: 'Slow-moving, shuffling Joe Louis beat me? He may hit hard, but that don't mean nothing if you can find nothing to hit . . .'

Now that Louis was old and broke, and gone from his team, Ali lashed out. 'I ain't ever gonna end up like Joe Louis,' he promised. He saved the worst to last. He suggested that the great Bomber should change his own name. Joe Louis, so Ali said, had turned into Uncle Tom.

America had become a whirl of assassinations and riots and protests. Jesse and Joe were bemused by the shouted rhetoric. They were disturbed by the violent outbreaks of mass action and police reaction. John F. Kennedy had been shot dead. Malcolm X had been shot dead. America was at war with itself. America was at war in Vietnam.

As Muhammad Ali resisted calls for him to be drafted into the American Army, insisting that, 'I ain't got no quarrel with them Vietcong', older conservatives pointed to the contrasting example of Joe Louis in World War II. When Ali officially refused induction into the Army, Jesse Owens, who considered himself to be 'an American first and a black man second', said that, 'Clay has made a terrible mistake . . .'

Ali's courageous defiance, which would cost him his championship and lead to a three-year ban from boxing, was greeted with adulation and raised fists by his supporters. Jesse and Joe considered the gesture with disdain. 'The black fist is a meaningless symbol,' Jesse argued. 'When you open it, you have nothing but fingers – weak, empty fingers. The only time the black fist has significance is when there's money inside. There's where the power lies.'

In their early fifties, the battered figures of Jesse and Joe had already done enough, and endured too much. Having represented their race, the human race as Jimmy Cannon declared, for so long, they were now struggling for a more private form of survival. Joe continued to reel through life, regularly lacing his cocaine with heroin in the old Harlem drug mix, as he moved from wild nights in Vegas with Sonny Liston to a short stint as a casino greeter at the Pigalle Sporting Club in London's Soho. He staggered between stability with Martha in LA and trouble in the broken company of various New York hookers.

If Jesse's life was marked by a more prosaic recovery from his tax trauma, he was equally unwilling to demand sweeping political reform. 'Look,' he said, 'sometimes I'm so concerned just getting my *own* self together that I don't feel up to changing the whole damn world!'

It was hard for Jesse and Ruth to accept their daughters' involvement in Civil Rights marches and meetings. They were even dispirited by the style and modish gestures of the movement. While Jesse was aghast at the sight of his son-in-law, Malcolm 'Hemp' Hemphill, in a dashiki, Ruth pulled away in horror when, at one of their daughters' parties, she was greeted by a young man who offered her a 'black handshake'. 'I don't know anything about *that*,' she said witheringly.

'I am so sick of this race issue I could scream,' Ruth had told Barbara Moro in an interview in 1961. 'Battling here and battling there and battling the other place, I am just plain sick of it. But I'm one person and if I say it I'll be beat down to the ground.'

Like Jesse and Joe, Ruth found consolation in Martin Luther King. When she heard King talk for the first time at the 49th Street Church, near their apartment on Chicago's South Side, Ruth was overcome. 'He's like an angel,' she told Jesse.

Jesse regarded King in more human terms – for King's private life was not untainted by sexual wanderings. His numerous affairs made him more of a regular guy to Jesse and Joe. If Jesse disagreed with his stance on Vietnam, believing instead that it was every American's duty to 'answer the call', he found solace in King's conciliatory dream of justice and freedom for all.

Once, when he and King watched a television clip of Malcolm X, from his earliest Nation of Islam days, Jesse looked suddenly alarmed.

'What is it?' King asked.

'I thought I saw hate in your face,' Jesse said.

'You did,' King eventually answered. 'Whenever I hear

Malcolm and a couple of the others I begin to hate the white man too. But just for a while. It doesn't change anything when I get up and go out among them.'

Jesse trusted King enough to admit his own feelings of loss. He described himself as 'a fur-lined jockstrap' doomed never to transcend his achievements as a twenty-two-year-old.

'I never knew you that well, Jesse,' King said, 'but I always thought you might have to meet this problem someday. You were like a child prodigy who couldn't go on with what he'd done. And a man must have his work before anything else.'

'So what *do* I do?'

'All I can tell you,' King answered, 'is to build on what you know, what you love. You can't run any more, but isn't there something larger, something related to that part of your life, which you can use to anchor the new?'

At dusk, on a cool Thursday evening in New York on 4 April 1968, Jesse Owens walked back to his hotel. He strode past the small groups of people who gathered together against shop fronts and on street corners. There were usually only three or four in a huddle, talking in tones of soft and urgent distress. Jesse slowed as the clusters grew in size and frequency. It was then that he heard the name Martin Luther King and the word *shot*.

He stopped a woman to ask her what she knew.

'He's dead,' the woman said blankly. 'They killed him.'

Jesse said that, 'The words were like an actual physical blow to me, like running at top speed and suddenly hitting a thick wall of concrete that hadn't been there before . . . I think it was a French poet who said that a great man's dying is an imitation of the end of the world. Martin's death seemed that to me.'

Strangely, that morning had begun with the receipt of a letter from an old Nemesis. 'Slavery' Avery Brundage had written to Jesse to praise him for his half-hour television broadcast which rejected the proposed black American boycott of the 1968 Olympic Games in Mexico City. Jesse argued that the boycott should be abandoned because, 'We can bridge the gap of mis-understanding more in athletics than anywhere else'. Brundage, who had done so much to undermine Jesse after Berlin, acclaimed his 'enlightened remarks'.

Against the backdrop of assassination, a letter from Slavery Avery seemed devoid of meaning. Jesse spent that lonely night in his New York hotel room talking on the phone to Ruth, his three daughters and the countless other people who called him. After midnight, while Jesse prepared a eulogy he'd been asked to write, he was tugged back to Brundage's letter.

It was a harsh paradox to him that he and King should have lined up on opposite sides of the Olympic boycott. Where King backed the call for black athletes to withdraw from the US team, in protest against American racism, so Jesse continued to claim that 'there is no place in the athletic world for politics'. For a few hours that night, with Martin Luther King not yet in a coffin, Jesse wondered if he had been wrong all along. He then remem-bered King's suggestion to hold on to something he loved – and to try and build from it while it anchored him in the turbulent present. Jesse loved the Olympic Games. Martin Luther King, he told himself, would understand. Jesse would remain resolute, even if it meant being on the same side as old Slavery Avery, as he faced the seething young black athletes of America.

At the heart of the boycott stood the formidable Harry Edwards – a twenty-five-year-old black lecturer in Sociology at San Jose State College. Six foot eight inches tall and weighing 240 pounds, Edwards invariably wore a black beret, black sunglasses, a black jacket and jeans as he chomped on a cigar. A former college athlete, Edwards had become a fiery agitator whose diatribes were leavened by a mordant wit and some fashionably cutting soundbites. 'Humble is out now!' Edwards would bark. 'Action that is non-action is in!'

Edwards, who stored 'an arsenal of guns' in his apartment, insisted that 'a black man is a damn fool if he walks around with nothing to protect himself'. While stressing the need for black Americans to hit back – 'Violence is natural and desirable' – Edwards was a canny operator. A week after King's assassination, Edwards freighted the boycott with symbolic meaning by dedicating its actions as 'a solemn memorial to Dr King and his family'.

Edwards had argued previously that, 'I'm sure Jesse Owens grasps the whole Olympic picture, agrees deeply with us and would move to our support but for the bonds forged long ago.' Yet he despaired of the 'gullible and misinformed' Olympic icon once he watched Owens's televised appeal against the boycott. Edwards noted bitterly that 'Owens re-emphasised his ridiculously naive belief in the sanctity of athletics and spoke warmly about the friendships and understanding brought between blacks and whites through sports.'

Like Jesse, Joe Louis and Jackie Robinson also venerated 'the spirit' of the Olympic Games. 'Jesus Christ,' Joe complained after he had been quizzed hard about the boycott, 'all these people and reporters were coming to ask me what I thought. Here I was, doing my best to hold body and soul together. I gave them answers, but I don't think a lot of people were happy with what I said. Loud and clear, I said I didn't think blacks should boycott the Olympics. I mean, where the hell else can they prove what they can do in competition with the whole world?'

Edwards, who had always admired Louis, was particularly scathing towards the fighter's friends: 'Jesse Owens and Jackie Robinson belong to a controlled generation. We don't.'

The origin of the boycott stemmed from a smaller form of protest. In September 1967 Edwards and his tiny group of black supporters on the notoriously racist San Jose campus had presented a list of grievances to the college president – Robert D. Clark. The sombre catalogue highlighted the fact that the two hundred black students were still prevented from eating in white restaurants, finding accommodation in 'white houses' and gaining entry to any of the exclusively white fraternities. If the prejudice at San Jose was depressingly familiar, Edwards's tactics were strikingly innovative. He warned Clark that unless there was immediate change, he and his fellow demonstrators, rather than waving placards or marching in protest, would 'physically interfere' with the playing of the season's opening college football game at San Jose. It was the first time an American sporting event had been threatened in such a way.

Edwards also promised to 'burn down the stadium' if the college called in the police or the military to ensure that football was played. Clark cancelled the game. He also appointed America's first ombudsman to investigate racism on a college campus and agreed to black involvement in future athletic and academic decision-making processes. Harry Edwards had won his first battle against white authority. He accepted it as a further compliment when Ronald Reagan, the Governor of California, castigated San Jose's 'appeasement of law-breakers' and announced that 'this Edwards fellow is unfit to teach'.

'Reagan,' Edwards replied, 'is a petrified pig, unfit to govern.'

Two months later, on Thanksgiving Day, Edwards and fifty athletes met in the Sunday School room of the Second Baptist Church in Los Angeles. They decided it was time to take the San Jose protest to a far higher level. Edwards confirmed that they were ready to confront the might of white sporting power. Black athletes, led by San Jose's and America's star 200m sprinters, Tommie Smith and John Carlos, were intent on boycotting the Olympics.

'For years we have participated in the Olympic Games,' Edwards boomed, 'carrying the United States on our backs with our victories. Yet race relations are now worse than ever. Now they are even shooting people in the streets. We're not trying to lose the Olympics for the Americans. What happens to them is immaterial. It's time for black people to stand up and refuse to be utilised as performing animals for a little extra dog food.'

On 15 December 1967, Edwards and his Olympic Committee for Human Rights, supported by Martin Luther King, had held a press conference in New York. King's reasoned contribution was the most telling. He suggested a black boycott of the Games was one of the last routes left open for non-violent protest. Edwards then presented six demands which had to be fulfilled before the boycott would be lifted:

1. Restoration of Muhammad Ali's title and right to box in America.
2. Removal of the anti-Semitic and anti-black Avery Brundage as President of the IOC.
3. Banning all-white teams and individuals from South Africa and Rhodesia.
4. Addition of at least two black coaches to the US men's Olympic track-and-field staff.
5. Appointment of at least two black policy-makers on the US Olympic Committee.
6. The complete segregation of the bigot-dominated and racist New York Athletic Club.

Edwards added a rider to his fourth demand. 'Stanley V. Wright is a member of the coaching team but he is a devout Negro and therefore is unacceptable.'

As the weeks passed, the boycott gained momentum. On 15 February 1968, Brundage and the IOC pointedly readmitted South Africa to 'the Olympic family'. If apartheid had resulted in the banning of a white South African team from the 1964 Olympics in Tokyo, Brundage argued that they had taken 'sufficient positive steps' to return to international sport. He claimed that, for the first time in their history, South Africa would send a multi-racial team to the Olympics. Brundage neglected to mention that, to avoid the shame of forcing their white athletes to run or jump alongside blacks, the South African Olympic Committee would hold separate trials. White athletes would compete in 'Olympic auditions' in the country's finest stadiums. Their token black representatives would be selected from a few dusty try-outs in the townships.

If Brundage had been immovable in his refusal to lift life-bans from individual Olympians – whether they were Jim Thorpe, Eleanor Holm or Jesse Owens – he was oddly acquiescent towards countries like Nazi Germany and apartheid South Africa. The outrage was inevitable. African nations threatened to join black America in a mass withdrawal from the Olympics. Brundage asserted on 26 February that, 'The Olympic Games will continue no matter how many countries withdraw.'

The assassination of King added to the anger. 'I don't think any black athlete will go to the Olympics,' Harry Edwards thundered. 'If they do go, I don't think they'll come back. I am not threatening. I am not encouraging violence. I am assessing reality. I know the demeanour of the black people. They see a black man back from the Olympics and they'll say, "Look at the devil with the medal around his neck." Some of them are going to have accidents. You can't live with the crackers and come back to Harlem. The athlete who goes will face ostracism and harassment. People are fed up with those shufflin' niggers. Them days is long gone. The black athlete who goes will be a traitor to his race and will be treated as such.'

Harry Edwards had also decided on his latest catch-phrase. 'Jesse Owens,' he snorted, 'is a bootlicking Uncle Tom . . .'

Apart from a few thousand, who had either been in Berlin in 1936 or had attended a rare screening of Leni Riefenstahl's *Olympia*, Jesse Owens's gold-medal winning performances had not been seen by millions of Americans. Not one single clip of his legendary exploits had been shown on American television.

On 30 March 1968, five nights before the murder of King, Bud Greenspan's documentary, *Jesse Owens Returns to Berlin*, including some of Riefenstahl's achingly beautiful footage of the twenty-two-year-old black hero of the Nazi Olympics, was finally screened by an independent sports network on 180 television stations across America. Greenspan's poignant film had been made in 1964, yet the three national networks had refused to screen it. Narrated by Owens, the documentary featured a stirring mix of him performing in front of the sinister Nazis and an adoring German public. It also charted his return to the stadium alongside the Harlem Globetrotters in 1951 and interspersed the compelling archive footage with his and Karl Long's genial reunion. *Jesse Owens Returns to Berlin* was considered – by ABC, CBS and NBC – to be 'too black' for a mainstream audience.

'Why don't we show the negatives,' Owens quipped dryly to Greenspan, 'so that I'll be white and the Nazis will be black?'

The impact of the film in 1968 was instant. Jesse was back in the spotlight, once more answering questions about Hitler and the Nazis, as he tried awkwardly to equate the political situation in Germany in 1936 with the travails of America in 1968. He remarked that if the attempt to boycott the Berlin Games had been successful, he would never have had the opportunity to 'shock those Nazis'. He insisted that black runners like Jim Hines, Tommie Smith, John Carlos and Lee Evans, and a long jumper as extraordinary as Bob Beamon, deserved the chance to make their own mark on history in Mexico.

If those athletes were moved by the majestic sight on television of Owens in full flow in 1936, they were also aware of his ensuing suffering. 'John Carlos,' Harry Edwards wrote, 'could not understand how Owens could say that athletic competition brought blacks and whites closer when Owens himself, the great hero of the Berlin Olympics, was a victim of racism in his own country.'

Vince Matthews, a US Olympic 400m runner, remarked later that 'what you never hear Jesse talk about is what happened to him after he got back from the 1936 Olympics: how the AAU forced him to run in Europe, his businesses that failed, or when he ran against some horses as a publicity stunt.' Edwards added that, 'Jesse Owens is just another nigger – with four gold medals.'

A raw pain underpinned Tommie Smith's written commitment to the boycott in December 1967. 'It is true,' Smith's statement conceded, 'that I want to participate in the Olympics . . . but I also recognise the political and social implication of participating for a country in which the vast majority of black people suffer from unthinkable discrimination and racism. I therefore feel that it is my obligation as a black man to do whatever is necessary, by any means necessary, to aid my people in obtaining the freedom that we all seek. If I can open a single door that might lead in the direction of freedom for my people, then I feel I must open the door. I am not only willing to give up an opportunity to participate in the Olympics, but I am also willing to give up my life if there is even a chance that it will serve to dramatise, much less solve, the problems faced by my people.'

Jim Murray of the *Los Angeles Times* made the cheap jibe that Smith reminded him of 'a child that holds his breath to make his parents feel bad'. Yet Murray had not been with Smith on any one of the thirteen occasions when he and his pregnant wife, Denise, had been turned down in their bid to rent an apartment in San Jose that summer. Whenever the door opened, and their black faces were seen, a different white landlord repeated the familiar line – the property was 'no longer available'.

Jesse, who had been through the same experience in Columbus and Cleveland and Chicago, preferred to focus on the seemingly less prejudiced sporting arena. He was convinced that black Americans were approaching the promised land in sport.

In 1968, the ring and the track were dominated by black faces. More significantly, a quarter of all Major League baseball players were black, as were a third of American footballers and slightly more than half of all NBA basketball players. The majority of superstars in baseball and football were black while that year's NBA all-star team selected by *Sporting News* consisted of an all black lineup.

'Ain't that progress?' Jesse cracked.

Harry Edwards, Tommie Smith, John Carlos and their colleagues in the boycott pointed out more forcibly that discrimination in American sport, like society itself, was still rampant. The Los Angeles Lakers were the only NBA team not to insist that, when it came to sharing hotel rooms on the road, white and black players should be accommodated in separate quarters. Most National Football League organisations and baseball teams were also run on an unofficial quota system – limiting the number of black players they would sign. College sport, from San Jose to the University of Texas, was riddled with racism.

The force of the boycott, however, diminished with the IOC's reversal of their stance towards South Africa. With world opinion weighed against them, Brundage and his cronies reinstated the ban. African countries would now compete in Mexico. Edwards polled the twenty-six black individuals regarded as certainties for the American team. Thirteen were against the boycott, twelve were still in favour of withdrawing while one athlete was undecided. Edwards gave in reluctantly to the reality that 'those voting not to boycott could have easily replaced the boycotters, thereby rendering the sacrifices of these men useless'.

Athletes as ferociously competitive as Smith and Carlos were secretly relieved that they would have the chance to test themselves against the best runners in the world. It was decided that, as a form of dissent, no victorious black athlete would participate in any celebration or official presentation in Mexico. They instigated their own rehearsal at the Olympic trials in September by refusing to stand on the winning podiums erected by the American Olympic Committee.

Writing his enthusiastic preview of the Mexico City Games in the 12 October issue of *TV Guide*, Jesse poured a honeyed gloss over the 'Olympic heritage'. 'The Olympics is a place where people live, work and break bread together; it has brought about tremendous understanding and cooperation in racial matters. So I don't think the pride which our black athletes have in themselves and their country will allow them to do anything to embarrass the United States in so conspicuous a world arena. There were no more angry people than black Olympic competitors in Berlin in 1936. We had insults thrown at us by our host nation; Hitler didn't accord Negroes and Jews the same courtesies he did others who came to Berlin. That made us more determined to prove that, in the eyes of God, we were every bit as good as any man . . . I say to those boys today who are considering public protest against their own country that they would not only be hurting themselves, but they might aid in the end our strongest competition, Russia.'

The Olympic Stadium, Mexico City, 16 October 1968

'Maybe they're listening to their uncle,' Jesse Owens cackled into his microphone from the radio booth situated just below the highest metal rafters of the towering grandstand. 'I told John last night to go ahead and wear his black socks – but not to wear them above the calf. I suggested he cut them down so he wouldn't hinder his circulation.' On the brick-red track hundreds of feet below, as Jesse watched John Carlos walk towards the start of the first 200m semi-final heat, he admitted to listeners of his commentary for the Mutual Broadcasting System that he still felt uneasy about 'all this talk of boycotts and Uncle Toms. I'm old enough to be their uncle but I'm not their Tom. We don't need this kind of stuff. We should just let the boys go out and compete.'

Jesse had been relieved how the first few days of track competition had unfolded. On Monday 14 October, the black American sprinter Jim Hines had equalled the world record of 9.9 seconds in winning the 100m final. Hines was effusive in his praise for Jesse. 'He's the greatest track-and-field athlete in the history of America. I really respect him.' With his gaze fixed on a contract in pro football, as well as on the commercial opportunities now available to the 'World's Fastest Man', Hines had always distanced himself from the boycott movement. He had insisted all year that he would run in Mexico, 'Even if I'm the only black athlete there'.

Tommie Smith and John Carlos had, so far, restricted themselves to a muted protest. Smith was asked if his insistent refusal not to accept a medal from Brundage was 'because of the South Africa thing?' His reply was a simple, 'Yes.' Carlos wore his *Olympic Project for Human Rights* badge but said little that was controversial. Stan Wright, castigated by Harry Edwards as being a 'devout Negro' of a coach, just shrugged. 'If they can run 20.2 wearing badges, it's perfectly all right with me.'

In their opening 200m heats, they had both worn long black socks. Smith, in 20.2, was the first to break the Olympic record. He and Carlos, also timed later at 20.2, looked ready to run much quicker.

As Carlos dropped down on to his haunches in the opening semi-final, Jesse predicted the pain the sprinters would endure over 200m at an altitude of 8,000 feet. 'They'll look down that track and around the curve,' he whispered dramatically into his radio mike, 'and they'll think their legs can't carry the weight of their body. Their mouths will be spitting cotton. They'll be reminded of all the months and years of races and all they've learned – and that it's all going to go within twenty seconds or so.'

Carlos and Smith each won their semi-final in another new Olympic record of 20.1 seconds. It had been easier for Carlos. Smith, in stretching away from seven other fading sprinters, felt a slight tear in his groin. He was carried to the dressing-room on a stretcher, his mind swirling with what he considered to be 'an eighty per cent certainty' that he would miss the final. The team doctor massaged and taped the upper thigh as Smith realised again how much he had always wanted to run in the final. The pain began to ease.

Only Peter Norman, the Australian who'd finished second to Carlos in 20.2, looked likely to threaten their assault on the final – as long as Smith did not break down.

In the final, Smith was in lane three; Carlos alongside him in four. The man with the gun wore a black hat. He spoke quietly to the runners.

The gun cracked. Carlos was fastest from the blocks. He held the lead as they approached the bend. They took the curve and hit the home straight. The two runners in the blue vests and black socks were flying. Tommie Smith burst into the lead, his long legs streaking beneath him. His eyes locked on the finish. John Carlos looked across the track at him. His calf muscles were tightening as they neared the end. Tommie had him.

Tommie Smith grinned helplessly and raised both his arms high and wide as his chest broke the white tape. It was close to perfect. Smith first, in a world record of 19.8, Norman second, Carlos third, both in a flat twenty seconds. Tommie and John. The two boys from San Jose. The two black men who had led the boycott.

Only Smith and Lee Evans, the 400m star, had discussed what they might do if Slavery Avery tried to shake their hands. Evans came up with a plan for them to wear a black glove. 'That'll really trip him out,' Evans laughed. 'We'll keep our hands under our sweats, so they won't know about the gloves. Then, when he goes to do the hand-shake, we pull out the black glove. He might have a heart attack and die from seeing that.'

Linda Evans and Denise Smith, the two runners' wives, went shopping for black gloves in Mexico City. Tommie Smith held his pair in the tunnel as he, John Carlos and Peter Norman waited for the celebratory call to the podium.

Tommie Smith was the first on the rostrum. A stifled ripple of surprise washed across the stadium as he rose. In his left hand he held his shoes. His feet were covered in black socks. He bent down carefully to place his shoes next to his feet. Norman applauded while Carlos looked straight ahead. When it was his turn, Carlos climbed up in his black socks. They each wore a small black scarf.

Their necks were soon draped with medals – gold for Smith and bronze for Carlos.

The first notes of *The Star Spangled Banner*, of *Old Glory*, sounded. Tommie Smith reacted instantly. His head dropped. His right arm pointed to the sky as stiff and straight as he could hold it. Sheathed in a black glove, his hand had curled into a fist. To his left, a foot below him, John Carlos also hung his head low. His left arm was raised. He wore the second black glove on his clenched left fist. Peter Norman, out of respect, had pinned John Carlos's *Olympic Project for Human Rights* badge on to his tracksuit.

The American anthem resounded. Tommie Smith and John Carlos, their black gloves shimmering, stood like statues. There was the merest twitch of Smith's lips as he looked down. His eyes were closed as he silently said the Lord's Prayer.

'My raised right hand stood for the power in black America,' he told Howard Cosell of ABC later that night. 'Carlos's raised left hand stood for the unity of black America. Together they formed an arch of unity and power. The black scarf around my neck stood for black pride. The black socks with no shoes stood for black poverty in racist America. The totality of our effort was the regaining of black dignity.'

Their bowed heads were for two men who had died in the struggle. 'We put our heads down low,' the two runners said before they walked out into history, 'for Malcolm and for Martin . . .'

Jesse Owens, urged on by Avery Brundage and other irate members of the US Olympic Committee, met with the track team the following night. Having been through the hoop of expulsion himself, Jesse knew what was coming. Smith and Carlos were about to be banned for life and sent home 'in shame'. There, they would be met by white insults and death threats. Their lives would never be the same again.

Jesse's slim hope was that he could reach some sort of unlikely compromise between the black athletes and the white administrators. 'I want to talk to Tommie Smith and John Carlos,' he told reporters. 'I believe a man has a right to express his opinion and I don't think anybody should get mad.'

Jesse believed that if the Committee refrained from sending the two men back to America, attention would switch to the track and the field where Bob Beamon, another black American, had just set a new world record in the long jump with a leap, astounding even at altitude, of 29 feet 2½ inches: almost two-and-a-half feet past Jesse's own supposedly miraculous leap in Ann Arbor in 1935. They just needed to escape the politics to revel in such beauty.

Jesse thought Tommie Smith was 'a high-class boy'. He praised him generously for his 'monolithic concentration' both before and during his 200m final. If he could swing Tommie round to his way of thinking, they might be able to concoct some sort of diplomatic argument to persuade Brundage and the rest to draw back.

At the start of the meeting, Jesse Owens's deep voice echoed with gravity. 'I'd like the white athletes in the room to leave. It's nothing against you other fellers personally, but these are my black brothers. I want to talk to them. I think you can understand.'

Black athletes like Carlos, Lee Evans and Vincent Matthews looked up at Jesse, snickering in disbelief. They had never heard him talk about 'black brothers' before.

'Why should we ask them to leave?' Matthews jibed. 'These guys supported us all along.' Hal Connolly, the white hammer-thrower who was a close friend of Carlos, nodded his approval.

'Hal's staying,' Carlos insisted. 'But what's the point of this meeting anyway? It ain't gonna change nothing.'

'It might,' Jesse said, 'if we act reasonably.'

'Reasonably?' Carlos sneered. 'Listen, it don't make no difference what I say or do. I'm black.'

'You tell him, John,' Connolly said.

'You know, Carlos,' Owens erupted, 'you talk about Whitey this and Whitey that. Everything's "get Whitey out of my hair". But now, in the most private and important meeting of all, here you are with good old Whitey!'

The young men either laughed or stared blankly back at him. Jesse Owens was fifty-five years old. He was past it. Jesse knew it was time to leave.

'It don't make no difference what I say or do,' John Carlos repeated as the old runner stood up slowly. His voice was thick with sarcasm. 'I'm lower than dirt, man. I'm black. *I'm black.*'

Chapter Seventeen

The Desert

They went home together. In Birmingham, Jesse Owens and Joe Louis were almost halfway between the two Alabama share-cropping shacks where they had been born. Oakville, the desolate patch of black farmland which was Jesse's first home, lay eighty-five miles to the north. In the south-eastern corner of the state, ninety miles from Birmingham, Joe had uttered his first cry in a wooden shanty still found on Bell Chapel Road, a dirt track off Route 50, just outside LaFayette, at the red clay base of the Buckalew Mountains.

Jesse was fifty-six; Joe was less than four months from his own fifty-sixth birthday. They repeated the same journey they had made a year before. Then, Joe had been the first man to be inducted into the Alabama Sports Hall of Fame. This year would mark Jesse's turn. Three hours later, in Birmingham's Municipal Auditorium Exhibition Hall, he would receive his bronze plaque. The ornate message proclaimed Jesse and Joe as:

Champions of History
Through Their Athletic Exploits

They Achieved Lasting Fame
For Alabama
And for Themselves

Birmingham itself was marked by a different kind of fame. Seven years earlier it had been described by Martin Luther King as 'the most segregated city in America'. It was a city where Negroes were still lynched and castrated, where a visiting US Senator was arrested because he walked through a doorway marked *Coloureds*, where parks and schools and hospitals were demarcated as *Whites Only*. It was the city of Eugene 'Bull' Connor and George Wallace. Connor, the virulent Commissioner of Public Safety, had been most proud of his ability to 'handle the Negro and keep him in his place'. Wallace, on his inauguration as the Governor of Alabama in January 1963, had made a state pledge of 'segregation now, segregation tomorrow, segregation forever . . .'

Three months later, King led the Civil Rights campaign of non-violent direct action which changed America for ever. He and the black people of Birmingham targeted all those stores in the city centre which refused to sell food at their luncheon counters to 'coloureds'. They held sit-ins and marches, prayer-sessions and mass meetings where King called on Joe Louis to galvanise people by his sheer presence. By 23 May 1963, after fire-hoses and police dogs had been turned on King and thousands of peaceful protesters, all of whom had been equally undeterred by arrest and imprisonment, the stoical battle of Birmingham had been won. The Alabama Supreme Court forced Bull Connor and his fellow commissioners out of office as *We Shall Overcome* rang across the city.

Yet in 1970, in a Birmingham hotel room, Alabama's most famous fighter mumbled to himself. 'I ain't scared,' Joe Louis said as, the sweat streaking his crumpled face, he began to dismantle the huge air-conditioning vent. 'I'm Joe Louis, heavyweight champion of the world . . . I ain't scared.'

Jesse walked across the room to his friend, saying his name softly in an attempt to soothe him. Joe looked up at Jesse. It was OK, Joe said, they were going to be fine. He had just found the hiding place. Joe pointed at the vent. He was sure the poison gas had been stored somewhere deep inside.

Jesse glanced at Martha Louis. It looked like her heart had cracked. Jesse did not know who he should try and comfort first – the agitated figure of Joe or his suffering wife. Martha made the move. She hurried over to Joe. He had managed to remove the iron grille covering the vent.

'C'mon, honey,' she said.

Joe turned towards her angrily. 'Are *you* working for them now?'

Jesse crouched down next to Joe. He listened in bewilderment as his old friend told him about the Mob and the prostitute called Annie. She had put out a contract on him. The Mob had been after him for years. They would not rest until they had killed him.

When Jesse tried to reason with him, Joe shrugged impatiently. He had work to do. He knew there was not much time left before they started shooting gas into his room.

Joe rubbed his face anxiously. Smears of dirt from the grille lined his cheeks and brow. He peered into the darkened vent. The room was already cast in shadow for Joe had closed the curtains. He had also torn the pink shades from both bedside lamps. Joe had unscrewed each, removing the naked bulbs and throwing them into the waste basket. He always checked the lamps first to make sure they were not secretly recording him. He then turned his attention to the bed, tearing it apart to ensure that it contained nothing dangerous. Jesse saw that its base had been separated into two sections and, with the raised mattress leaning against them, turned upright. Joe had draped a sheet over them in such a way that, with two little flaps pulled back at the bottom, it looked as if he had constructed a tent in the middle of his hotel room. He was now tackling the vents. Joe always searched a room in that order. Lamps, bed, vents. It helped calm him. He knew that if he completed each task methodically he had a chance of staying alive.

As Joe squeezed through the open vent, he used a long paper cylinder in his left hand to tilt one of the ceiling lights so that it shone directly into the black outlet. He pushed his large head into the cramped opening. Joe grunted in relief. He could see the line of nozzles. Drawing his head carefully out of the vent, he smiled sadly at Jesse and Martha. He told them the shocking truth. Each nozzle, he explained, was filled with poison gas. The Mob were just waiting for him to fall asleep before they flicked a switch and filled the room with gas. His eyes widened. He would not have stood a chance.

Joe chuckled as he saw the expression on Jesse's face. There was no need to look so worried. He would seal them up nice and tight. Martha's eyes filled with tears as her husband hummed quietly while he worked. He wedged the iron grille back into place. Joe then reached out for a reel of thick insulation tape. His hands moved with some of their old speed as he covered the vent with black tape. Nothing, not even a tiny sniff of gas, could escape now.

Joe walked wearily towards his tent. He ducked down and sat quietly beneath the canopy of his sheet. Martha knew he would need to rest. She led Jesse into the adjoining suite. Martha could no longer stop herself. She began to cry as she told Jesse the truth. Joe was losing his mind.

Martha told him about Annie, the mysterious woman from Milwaukee who had first introduced Joe to heroin. He was convinced that Annie, who he said was making porn flicks for the Mafia, wanted him dead because he had left her. He told Martha that the FBI had even warned him to stay away from Annie because she was linked to the murderous Mob. Joe's paranoid delusions had become increasingly tortured. He imagined that the Mafia had let loose their most lethal killer, a hitman called 'The Texan', to track him down.

Wherever he went, Joe was certain that he was being followed by either a gang of mobsters or the solitary Texan. Whether he was at home or in the alien world of another hotel, he would always take the necessary steps to protect himself. Joe was terrified of being gassed to death; and traumatised by the menacing sound of an elevator rising from one floor to another before it released the imaginary Texan.

The fear did not end there. The Brown Bomber thought the Mob might have planted dynamite in the walls and gone to extraordinarily complicated lengths to poison him. Joe would not eat unless Martha tasted his food first. When he was in his worst stages of the crack-up he would silently watch people at his table. Once they had finished eating, his hand would stretch out and take the scraps from their plate. At least that way he knew he would not be putting poisoned food into his mouth.

Martha told Jesse about their trip to pay homage to Rocky Marciano, who had been killed in a plane crash on 31 August 1969. Joe had bent down over the open casket and kissed Rocky. While that gesture had been spontaneous and heart-felt, the rest of the trip had been distressing. During lunch at a hotel, soon after the funeral, Joe asked the waiter to wrap his dessert in paper. When Martha asked innocently if he was saving his cheesecake for later, Joe laughed bitterly. Was she stupid? He was taking his poisoned cheesecake straight to the police.

If it had not been so tragic, Martha told Jesse, she might have laughed. It had been going on for more than a year. One day Joe just gave up playing golf and started shuffling round the house in the same old clothes. Jesse, knowing how much Joe loved both golf and clothes, almost smiled at those unmistakable signs of trouble.

Martha, however, did not reveal everything. She could not bear to tell Jesse about the baby Joe had fathered in 1967 with a New York cocktail waitress and part-time prostitute – Marie Johnson. Martha and Joe had taken the baby into their home in 1968. Joe seemed bewildered by the arrival of another life into his darkening world. It was left to Martha to care for the little boy.

Joe had been briefly hospitalised in June 1969 when he collapsed on a New York Street. Fears that he had suffered a heart attack were soon replaced by a diagnosis of a mental breakdown. While Joe told reporters that his illness was caused by 'the humidity and too much activity', Martha and the doctors knew the real truth.

Jesse stared at the husk of a man he had admired more than anyone. He had forgotten how many hundreds of times he had used the example of his friend whenever he brushed up against another despairing man or an angry kid who told him, 'I can't take it no more. I've had it with this country.' Jesse would churn out the same line he had used over and over again. 'You *can* take it, just for a little longer. Look at Joe Louis. Joe's been taking it longer than anyone and he's still the greatest man you'll ever meet. Joe ain't about to quit. Why should you?'

Joe had never quit. He had not given up even on those terrible nights when the blows rained down on his unprotected head, as Ezzard Charles and Rocky Marciano doled out their gruesome beatings. Those punches had done some awful damage. So had the drugs. But Jesse thought of all the other painful moments he had witnessed – the days when Joe was compared to an animal or the nights when some lug came up to him in a bar and punched him in the face just because he was the most famous nigger in America. He remembered the frightened tears the old boxer had shed when he thought the IRS were about to jail him.

Jesse watched Joe murmur and sway, and then sway and murmur again. He recalled the stories of Joe's father. They had taken Munroe Barrow away when Joe was just two years old.

He was institutionalised in the Searcy Hospital for the Criminally Insane in Mount Vernon, Alabama in 1916. The following year, Joe's mother, Lillie Barrow, was told that her husband had died in the asylum. Jesse had never found out what Joe really felt when, twenty years later, in 1937, just eight days after he had won the title, it was discovered that his father was still alive – in that same Alabama institution. Munroe Barrow did not know that his son was world champion. Although his sisters went to visit him, Joe chose not to see his father. A year later, in 1938, his dad did finally die.

Joe loved his step-father, Pat Brooks. It had been Pat who had taken them to a new life in Detroit in 1926, not long after he and Lillie had been jolted one night in Alabama. They were driving home near midnight in Pat's Model T-Ford when they were surrounded by Klan horsemen. The ominous call went up to lynch them. And then, beneath one of the white hoods, came the words which saved them.

'That's Pat Brooks,' one of the invisible Klansmen said. 'Let him go. He's a good nigger.'

They left Alabama for the North soon afterward. They made it to Detroit where Joe found boxing and set out on the road to the championship and the incredible life which followed.

'Come,' Martha eventually said to Jesse. 'Help me dress him . . .'

And so they washed and dressed the big man. They calmed him. Martha knew that Joe would be all right once he was outside again and around people. She also knew that Joe would never forgive her if he missed Jesse's big night in Alabama. Slowly, as they talked gently to him, the light came back into Joe. He smiled as they adjusted his bow-tie and brushed down his tux. He cocked an eye at Jesse. The runner looked as fit and smart as ever. Jesse was gonna knock 'em dead. They walked out of the hotel room together and stepped out into the Alabama night in their glad rags.

They swept downtown and, once they reached the Exhibition Hall, Joe kept it up. He was at least a version of his old self. He shook hands and nodded. He mumbled and nodded some more. He managed to feed himself without anyone noticing anything unduly strange about him. And then, once the dinner gave way to the speeches, Deadpan Joe watched Jesse rise up and accept his place in the Alabama Hall of Fame. Joe's face split open in a smile. He brought his hands together and clapped until they hurt.

They left together. Martha knew they did not have long before Joe collapsed again. Jesse felt as if he was being torn apart as the fighter clung to him. Joe began to mumble. He told Jesse they had been friends longer than he could remember. Jesse had been good to him. As his own voice grew husky, Jesse said the words back. Joe had been good to him for thirty-five years.

A tremor ran through Joe as he looked back. He had seen something. Jesse looked over his shoulder. No one was following them. 'It's OK,' he said. 'Joe, listen to me. Nobody wants to hurt you. Everybody loves you, Joe, they *love* you.'

'I can feel him,' Joe whimpered as he huddled into the thick overcoat of the great runner. 'It's The Texan. Run, Jesse, *run* . . .'

The first day of May 1970. Joe was eating an apple and watching television when the four men walked quietly up the driveway. Martha's friend, the Reverend Carl Walker, stood alone in the kitchen. He swung open the back door. The trio of deputy sheriffs stepped into the house. They were followed by Mose Trujillo, a liaison officer from the Probate Court.

Trujillo carried the court order, signed by Judge David Brofman, which directed 'the Sheriff of the City and County of Denver to pick up the respondent at 2675 Monaco Parkway, or wherever he may be found in the City and County of Denver, and deliver respondent to Colorado Psychiatric Hospital, FORTH-WITH'.

'He's in the front of the house,' Walker said. 'I'll go tell him you're here.'

The policemen nodded silently. They knew the distressed heavyweight was not expecting their arrival.

Trujillo had seen the medical letters from Louis's doctor, Robert Bennett, as well as the report of Dr John H. Macdonald, the chief of forensic psychiatry at the Colorado General Hospital. After an informal forty-five-minute house call, which did not raise Joe's suspicions, Macdonald confirmed Martha's assessment. Her husband was seriously ill.

Although Martha had virtually given up her legal practice to look after Joe, she had found the time to study Colorado law. She knew that, with official medical support, she could obtain a court order to hospitalise her husband for three months. Once she had Macdonald's backing, Martha moved quickly. The court agreed that Joe should be committed for 'observation, diagnosis and treatment for mental illness'.

Martha had consulted regularly with Joe's two children from his first marriage – Jacqueline and Joe Jr. Although he was still only twenty-two, Joe Jr resolved that he would sign the consent forms. His father would hate him for doing so, at least for a while, but Joe Jr insisted that, 'My dad needs help. I'm going to sign.'

After Carl Walker had led him into the kitchen, the old Bomber was distraught. 'You can't do this to me,' he said.

No one attempted to stop the legendary fighter as he picked up the telephone and asked the operator to connect him to the White House. The five men in the kitchen fidgeted as they waited.

'This is Joe Louis,' he said into the receiver. 'I want to speak to President Nixon . . .'

'Forget it,' Joe finally muttered. 'I'm calling the newspapers.'

Wary of using force to drag Joe Louis to hospital, the men responsible for his committal tried to humour him instead. As the situation spiralled out of their control, they allowed Joe to call both the *Denver Post* and the *Rocky Mountain News*. Within twenty minutes, reporters and cameramen crammed his lounge. 'I asked you here,' Joe said, 'because I can't figure out why my family thinks I'm nuts.'

Joe's attorney in Denver, Irving Andrews, had also been summoned by Reverend Walker. 'Look, Joe,' Andrews said, 'we can't fight a court order. I think you should go.'

The old fighter went into his room and packed a small leather bag. Joe pulled a brown overcoat over his fawn trousers and white sports-shirt. He opened the fridge and picked out a crisp apple for the ride. Joe took a bite and then he nodded. 'OK,' he said. 'Take me away . . .'

Newspapers across America ran a restrained UP Agency report on 2 May 1970 which confirmed that 'Joe Louis underwent initial treatment today at Colorado Psychiatric Hospital. Louis, the former world heavyweight boxing champion, was admitted to the hospital yesterday on a "hold for treatment" court order requested by his son. The fifty-six-year-old champ was taken from his summer home in Denver by three uniformed sheriff's deputies. Louis appeared tired and distressed, but went quietly. "He was surprised and depressed that he was being committed," said a family friend. "His sickness has shown itself in different ways. Sometimes he's real low, feeling like he's in the bottom of a pit. And then he feels like he could still lick the world."'

'Doc' Young of Chicago's *Daily Defender* noted that 'no one held a testimonial for Joe on the thirtieth anniversary of his ascension to the world's heavyweight throne. No one honoured him last year on his fifty-fifth birthday. Yet Joe was one of the greatest men this nation ever produced. Tallulah Bankhead rated him as one of the three greatest Americans. She ranked him with Presidents. And she was right. Joe Louis was much, much more than a championship fighter. He was an incomparable human being.'

*

In the late summer of 1970, Jesse travelled to Denver to visit Joe. Once he arrived in the city he took a taxi to 1055 Claremont Street. There, on the seventh floor of the Veterans' Administration Hospital, he found his friend. At his own request, Joe had been transferred after five days in the Colorado Psychiatric Hospital. 'I'm a veteran, ain't I?' he asked. They arranged a private room for him on the Veterans' psychiatric ward.

The transfer did not start well. Joe hated the sound of the hospital elevator, which he imagined would bring The Texan to his bedside. He was also convinced that the Mob were about to gas the building. Joe had to be tranquillised four times a day with Thorazine. Gradually, his acute paranoia came under control. By the time Jesse saw him it had faded completely. With reduced medication, Joe was no longer sedated or complaining of wooziness. His anger towards Martha and Joe Jr had dissipated. If he was not quite the old Joe, he seemed tranquil and wry to Jesse.

'We got a guy in here,' he told Jesse, 'who keeps saying he wants to shoot all the Germans. He tells us he sleeps with a Luger under his pillow. Just as well he ain't got any ammo left.'

Joe liked the people on his ward. Every day he shared the $5 worth of fruit Martha brought him with everyone on their floor. He was described as the wisest listener in their sessions of group therapy. Joe even talked a couple of patients out of trying suicide, giving them hope they would get back with their families one day.

Jesse laughed when he heard how Joe had just won $2 as the ward's champion in a putting contest. There was not much competition, Joe admitted, but it was great to win again. He was also intent on keeping the peace. A girl on his ward wanted a newspaper, so Joe bought one and placed it on her chair. Another patient came by and took it away. The girl hit the man, and Joe made sure they talked about the incident in their group. He told her it was wrong to hit anybody. She knew he was right.

They chuckled when, over a couple of cigarettes while sitting out in the garden, Joe told Jesse about the day another patient had pointed at him. 'See that guy?' the patient said to his wife and son, 'he's famous. He knocked out Schmeling in Berlin and Hitler walked straight out of the stadium. He was that mad.'

Joe set the man straight. He told him it was Jesse who had annoyed Hitler in Berlin.

'Only one thing matters now,' Jesse grinned. 'You're getting better.'

'That's why I like you, Jess,' Joe nodded. 'You always see the bright side.'

While his doctors advised that the court order should be extended for a further three months, Joe had shown sufficient improvement to be granted a weekend at home in early September. After two successful breaks in Denver, Joe and Martha were allowed to travel to Las Vegas on 18 September for a three-day trip. Vegas, they all knew, would be the big test. The temptations of his old life would be at their strongest. There was also an additional danger. Once he was in Nevada, Joe could not be compelled to return to hospital in Denver. He would be outside the jurisdiction of Colorado law.

'We have to start trusting him again,' Martha argued.

The visit to Vegas went better than they had dared hope. Joe was relaxed and relieved to be back among ordinary people. He gambled a little and played a round of golf. Joe saw some of his old buddies, like Ash Resnick, now the front man at Caesars Palace. Resnick had organised a luxury suite for Joe and Martha at Caesars. Even in his hotel room Joe was cool. He ignored the air-conditioning vents and the light-bulbs. In the casino he did not once wheel round in search of The Texan. And, most import-ant of all, he cheerfully boarded the plane back to Denver. On Monday morning he returned to hospital.

The next step in his rehabilitation occurred on 16 October when, as *The New York Times* reported, 'Joe Louis left the Veterans Administration Hospital today after a five month stay for treatment of an emotional disorder. Wearing a cap from the city park golf course and a bright orange sweater, Louis smiled quietly and waved to reporters as he departed from the hospital with his wife, Martha. Louis was expected to spend the weekend in Las Vegas and return to Denver for continued outpatient treatment.'

For the next two months, Joe took his medication and faithfully attended the day sessions of therapy in Denver. The lure of Vegas, however, was irresistible. He loved the desert air and the glittering neon. During his weekend jaunts to Caesars, Ash Resnick filled his head with a plan. Ash wanted Joe to do 'some meeting and greeting'. He wanted Joe to shake hands and sign autographs and to be seen at the tables. It was the kind of thing Joe was already doing most weekends. The only difference was that Ash would pay him a steady wage.

Joe saw his chance when Dr Martin, his therapist in Denver, revealed that there would be a two-week break in their programme. Louis decided that he'd had it with doctors. He was never going back to that nuthouse in Denver. Joe was staying out in the desert. He and Martha and their adopted and fostered kids would move permanently to Vegas – where the former world champion would work for Caesars Palace as a greeter.

Joe saw Sonny Liston a few times after his return to Vegas in mid-December. Same old Sonny. Dark and heavy. Sonny. What a name. What a life.

Three weeks later, on 5 January 1971, Geraldine Liston returned from spending Christmas with her mother in St Louis. She found Sonny dead in his underwear at the foot of their bed. His body bulged like a grey balloon. Crusted streaks of blood ran from his nose to his open mouth. The police took away the body. They said that Sonny had probably died six days before. A gun and a glass of vodka lay on the table next to his bed. Detectives also found a small amount of marijuana and heroin in a cupboard. There were needle marks on his arms. Anyone who knew Sonny knew that he had a pathological fear of needles. The autopsy listed the cause of death as lung congestion and heart failure.

Everyone in Vegas had a theory. Sonny had been killed by the Mob. Ash Resnick had hired a hitman to give Sonny a 'hot shot' to pay him back for not taking a fall in one of his last fights. Sonny had kicked his fear of needles and overdosed. Even in death, Sonny Liston personified Joe's most paranoid delusions. Sonny, unlike Joe, had been hounded by the Mob. He did die a mysterious and perhaps terrifying death.

'Sonny always had it the worst,' Joe said.

Joe was a pallbearer at Sonny's funeral. He turned up late. He had been playing craps at Caesars. 'Sonny would understand,' Joe said as he threw the dice one last time in honour of his friend.

At the funeral, alongside Joe, sat Ella Fitzgerald and Doris Day. Sonny and Doris, Joe pondered, who would have thought it? They sang *A Closer Walk With Thee*. The Inkspots warbled through *Sunny*.

Four hundred people marched away from the Palm Memorial. They swung down the Strip. All the gangsters and hookers and gamblers came out to gawp at the last Sonny Liston show. Joe was sweating by the time they reached the cemetery at Paradise Memorial Gardens.

They lowered the coffin into the ground. The simple plaque above the grave was enough to break Joe's heart:

Charles 'Sonny' Liston
1932–1970
A Man

After his own life almost slipped from him in a Chicago hospital, when he was stricken by severe pneumonia in 1971, Jesse was persuaded to follow Joe into the desert. Ruth chose Arizona over Nevada. Scottsdale, after all, was a more refined refuge than Vegas. Ruth had never felt any lasting affection for Chicago and, with Jesse's health now vulnerable, she overcame her natural reticence and made the decision for both of them. If Jesse was initially reluctant to swap the rush of big city life for the simpler pleasures of breathing clean air beneath the sunlit Camelback Mountains, he soon came to relish both the golf courses and their more affluent lifestyle in Arizona.

If he also replaced his restless habit of smoking a pack of cigarettes a day with a more sedentary puffing of his pipe, Jesse resisted any other notable transformations. His 1972 book *I Have Changed* was more a misnomer than the apology he claimed it to be for his previous literary effort – *Blackthink*. Published two years earlier, *Blackthink* had won glowing reviews from the white media while becoming notorious amongst his African-American critics. Although he tried, in the limited company of his white ghostwriter Paul Neimark, to address Harry Edwards's accusation that he was a 'bootlicking Uncle Tom' and to pinpoint failings in black consciousness, *Blackthink* was remembered most for its glib political philosophy. One sentence in particular came to haunt Jesse. 'If the Negro doesn't succeed in today's America,' he claimed, 'it is because he has chosen to fail.'

In *I Have Changed*, he stepped back from that problematic statement. 'Deep down,' he conceded, 'I knew better. There aren't near as many exceptions if your skin is white.' Jesse tried hard to understand 'the militant' by stressing the enduring inequities which characterised America. He acknowledged the absence of black faces in big business and conventional politics but admitted that 'uncompromising' African-American activists like Eldridge Clever and Angela Davis frightened him 'a little'.

Jesse was more comfortable with his usual routine which involved him churning out his favourite homilies week after week. He was still away from home for almost ten months every year, visiting three or four different cities a month, as he clocked up an annual tally of 200,000 air miles. His appetite for work, as a motivational speaker and publicist for his long list of corporate clients, was insatiable.

While his income climbed towards the $100,000 mark, his polished patter was not universally revered. If most people who met him were swept away by the force of his personality, *Sports Illustrated*'s William O. Johnson was one of the few to cast a jaundiced eye over Jesse's showmanship. Johnson decided that he was a combination of a 'nineteenth century spellbinder and twentieth-century plastic PR man, a full-time banquet guest, eternal glad-hander and evangelical small talker. Muted, tasteful, inspirational bombast is his stock-in-trade. Jesse Owens is what you might call a professional good example.'

To give his readers a sample of a standard Owens rap, Johnson transcribed Jesse in full conversational flow: '"Mostly, I'd say the substance of my speeches is sheerly inspirational. I work for my payday like anyone else, and things fall into a routine. I have a speech on motivation and values, one on religion, one on patriotism. Some parts are interchangeable, but I'm talking to kids most of the time. I tell them things like this . . ." His voice made a slight adjustment, and suddenly it was deeper, and it became a kind of dignified holler that bounded about the restaurant of Schrafft's Motor Inn. "Awards become tarnished and diplomas fade," said Jesse Owens in full cry. "Gold turns green, and ink turns grey and you cannot *read* what is upon that diploma or upon that badge. Championships are mythical things. They have no permanence. What is a gold medal? It is but a trinket, a bauble. What counts, my friends, are the *realities* of life: the fact of competition and, yes, the great and good *friends* you make . . ."'

'His voice readjusted to show he was no longer orating. But an intrinsic consciousness of the sound of his voice remained. "Grown men," he said softly, "stop me on the street now and say, 'Mr Owens, I heard you talk fifteen years ago in Minneapolis. I'll never forget that speech.' And I think to myself, that man probably has children of his own now. And maybe, *maybe*, he remembers a specific point I made, or perhaps two points I made. And maybe he is passing those points on to his own son just as I said them. And then I think" – Jesse's voice drops close to a whisper – "then I think, that's immortality."'

Jesse and Joe always met, near the end, in Las Vegas, when the old runner would cruise through town to address a corporate function at one of the hotels on the Strip. Joe would be greeting at Caesars, smiling softly amongst the tuxedoed dudes manning the gaming tables and the Valley girls sashaying across the casino floor as fake Cleopatras.

Jesse would amble through the sliding glass-and-gold doors. His gaze would inevitably be drawn to a crowd around a blackjack table near the entrance. They came from near and far to talk to Joe Louis, from Boulder City and New York City, from LA and Kalamazoo. They were grandmothers with blue-rinse hair and superfly soulmen in purple cat-suits. They were young girls with autograph books who were not quite sure what he had done in the ring and they were paunchy men with ciné-cameras who had listened to him fight when they were still little boys hiding their radios beneath the darkness of the sheets. They shouted out phrases like, 'Hey, champ!' as if they were expressions of such minted freshness that they had never passed any lips but their own. They punched him lightly on the arm or held their own dukes high as if they almost hoped that Joe Louis might take a pop at them.

There were some who said it was degrading, that it tarnished a noble legend to have the great Joe Louis hanging around Caesars Palace as a paid greeter. There were some, mostly those who did not know him, who compared his role to that of a glorified doorman. The way they told it, Joe Louis was a pathetic figure who scraped at the feet of gamblers who barely knew his name. Yet everyone, whether it was a grinning Frank Sinatra or an open-mouthed family from Idaho, came to him. He was still Joe Louis.

Throughout the mid-1970s, Jesse saw a shadow of the man he had once known. Jesse himself was a bloated impression of the supple and graceful young runner Joe had first met in 1935. They were men in their sixties. And Jesse still knew that pain and terror was buried deep in old Joe, for fear of the poisoned gas and The Texan had not been wholly consigned to a psychiatric ward in Denver. There were random outbreaks of paranoia – but they could be controlled and concealed. They were also tempered by Joe's own pleasure in the confined world he had settled into in Vegas.

He and Martha and four children of varied parentage lived in a large ranch-house at 3333 Seminole Circle, a mile from the Strip. Most days, after a stint on the golf course, Joe would amble over in the late afternoon to Caesars to sit around and lose the daily allowance the casino gave him to play the tables. Joe would have a few drinks and something to eat before he'd be called up by Resnick or Sinatra, by Sammy Davis Jr or Billy Eckstein, or by someone else less famous from the fight days, and he'd wander off for a few hours of entertainment before he returned to complete his stint around 2 a.m.

It was not the role Jesse would have chosen for him, but it was impossible to miss the warmth that lit up the work of the Strip's most famous handshaker. Joe opened himself up to the most mundane people. It gave him pleasure to make people feel happy. Even when they made the rare mistake of thinking he was someone else, Joe got a kick out of that Vegas schtick.

'Don Newcombe!' an old dear exclaimed when she saw Joe. 'You're my favourite baseball player! How're you doing?'

'Well,' Joe drawled amiably, 'I'm doin' fine, thank you, ma'am.'

'Won't you sign this for me, Don?' she asked as she pushed her Keno card towards him.

'Sure,' Joe said. He wrote down *Don* and then he turned and whispered to his pal, 'how do you spell "Newcombe"?'

Jesse could not let go of the hustle. He maintained a voracious schedule of work. It was impossible for him to give up travelling and talking – perhaps because his career as an athlete had been curtailed so cruelly. Even at the age of sixty-six, he could not bear the thought of stopping again in mid-flight as he had been made to do when he was just twenty-two.

He used his pocket diaries so scrupulously that there was rarely an empty page to signify a day free from people. They were embossed in gold on the outside with words like *Pocket Secretary* or *Personal Day Planner*. His last diary, a slim *Pocket Dater*, stretched from October 1979 to December 1980. The black leather cover was dimpled with raised little nodules. Jesse liked to run his fingers across that bumpy surface when he was in the middle of a tedious meeting.

He began filling the pages in early October. A string of appointments culminated in a trip to New York to make a television commercial for American Express during the last two days of the month. It was one of the credit card company's standard celebrity endorsements and they booked him into the Plaza Hotel. The shoot exhausted Jesse. He spent hour after hour being filmed as he repeated the same words over and over again.

As he stepped off a New York sidewalk he smiled that famous smile, and spoke in his deep and rolling voice: 'Hello . . . Do you know me?' He began walking, while still looking straight into the camera. 'My name is Jesse Owens . . .'

On and on it went as they searched for the perfect take. 'Hello,' he would boom. 'Do you know me? My name is Jesse Owens ... Hello ... Do you know me? My name is Jesse Owens ...'

Even the patience of an old publicity wizard and diplomat could eventually stand the parroting no longer. 'That's it,' Jesse grunted to the young director. 'No more. I'm tired now.'

The next two months were even harder. In November he shuttled back and forth between Phoenix, where he now lived, and Chicago, Dallas and New York. A December spiral was meant to take him from Dayton, Ohio on Tuesday 4 to St Louis on Thursday 6 to Wooster, Ohio on Friday 7 and New Jersey on Saturday 8 before he reached Chicago for a three-day slot from the Sunday to the Tuesday. On Wednesday 12 December he was booked to address the Columbus Merrymakers at a dinner at the Sheraton. He would then travel to another function to be held in Orlando the next day, Thursday 13.

He could not complete even half that timetable. In the middle of his speech to a religious group in Dayton he began coughing uncontrollably. He made it to St Louis, only to almost faint on the podium. Jesse finished his speech this time, but he cancelled the rest of his appointments and flew to Chicago where Ruth was visiting their three daughters.

On the day he was meant to be with the Merrymakers in Columbus, Jesse Owens received the shattering news. Doctors at the Michael Reese Hospital confirmed that he was suffering from adenocarcinoma – a form of lung cancer associated with heavy smokers. The cancer was spreading fast and wide. They gave him three months to live.

Jesse and Ruth flew back to Arizona in the middle of January. They wanted to feel the sun on their faces during their last days together.

Jesse still carried his little diary. Where he had once always filled out the bare facts of his life on the first page, marked

'Personal Details', they now remained blank. In the past he had always stipulated 'No Penicillin' next to the Blood Type box. He left the entire space open this time. Jesse also left empty the boxes for 'Allergies', 'Medical Information' and the plain-speaking 'I'm Taking Medication For . . .' slot. He could not see the point of writing out *Chemotherapy*. There were more little boxes to tick if you suffered from diabetes, epilepsy or a heart condition. But there was no box for cancer.

On 25 January 1980, Jesse was admitted to the University of Arizona Hospital in Tucson. A hospital spokesman revealed that 'Jesse Owens said today, "This is the biggest battle of my life and with the help of Dr Stephen E. Jones, I'll win this race."' After it was agreed that he should be treated as an outpatient, Jesse and Ruth took a side exit to avoid the waiting photographers. They drove home, through the unrelenting rain, to Phoenix.

Jesse tried to recover some of his old verve. As President Jimmy Carter discussed the possibility of an American boycott of the Moscow Olympics, Jesse told the *Columbus Dispatch* on 7 February that, 'Politics and world events should be kept out of the Games'. He returned to another familiar argument to insist that, 'A person's race has nothing to do with success. In this country, thank God, you get what you want. You can achieve any goals you set for yourself.' Ruth preferred to focus on the fact that Jesse had gained five pounds since his return from hospital. 'My husband,' she said, 'is quite a man.'

His remission did not last long. On 21 March Jesse was flown by helicopter from the Good Samaritan Hospital in Phoenix to the specialist cancer ward at Tucson's University Hospital. A week later, on 28 March, Harold L. Enarson, the President of Ohio State University, wrote to him:

Dear Jesse,
    It is with the greatest pleasure that I write to tell you of my intention to present two recommendations to the

Board of Trustees of the University on April 4. I am
confident the Board will approve both enthusiastically –
the first is to name the Ohio State track in your honour –
as the Jesse Owens Stadium. The second will be to name
in your honour the three new recreation centres ... as
long as the Ohio State University endures, your name will
remain a visible reminder of excellence and opportunity,
for these are the foundation blocks on which this
university has been built.

Congratulations. Our thoughts are with you as we
extend our warm best wishes to you and your family.

Six years before, Jesse had told the *Arizona Republic* that, 'If I were to change anything in this world it would be the business of eulogies. A man should hear his own accolades and praises while he's alive to enjoy being a living legend. It's no good naming a school after him once he's gone. Besides, he'd do a lot more to justify his name on a building if he was still alive.'

The OSU letter arrived too late. On Saturday 29 March, the Tuscon hospital revealed that Jesse's condition had 'taken a turn for the worse'. Dr Stephen Jones confirmed that, 'He is now in a critical condition and is quite weak. There's evidence of lung infection. His general condition has deteriorated in the last twenty-four hours.' Jesse Owens had slid into a coma.

When they told Joe Louis the news, he could not stop shaking. He had already been rocked by the strange story he had been following in the newspapers and on television. The voice of the evangelical radio preacher from Irving, Texas had echoed across his screen a few hours before the phone rang. 'I'm making the midnight cry,' the preacher wailed. 'This is the midnight hour. The rapture is very, very near.'

The 'rapture' supposedly occurs when millions of Christian believers suddenly vanish from the face of the earth. According to the Texan preacher they are 'swept up to join Jesus in heaven'. He predicted that the rapture would take place in two days' time, on Tuesday 1 April, when 'about half of the present-day population of America who know Jesus personally as their saviour will be taken'. President Carter and the Republican presidential contender, Ronald Reagan, would share in the rapture. It all sounded pretty spooky to Joe – especially as it was being foretold by a man the newspapers called 'The Texan Preacher'. 'Things are coming to an end,' The Texan yelped.

At 5.40 on Monday morning, 31 March 1980, Jesse Owens took his last breath. Ruth was at his bedside. Later that day, across the Atlantic, in Vienna, Simon Wiesenthal, the man who had devoted his life to hunting down Nazi war criminals, repeated his suggestion that the famous avenue leading to the Olympic Stadium in Berlin should be named after Jesse Owens. He had made the appeal before, only to be told by the authorities in West Berlin that streets could not be named after living persons. 'It is shameful we have had to wait for his death,' Wiesenthal said, 'but now it will happen. Everyone who travels through Berlin will always hear the name of Jesse Owens.'

Among the tributes which flooded America, the *Chicago Sun* struck a cautionary tone. 'It is an ironic footnote that, on the day following Mr Owens's death in Arizona, William B. Shockley, the physicist and Nobel Prize winner, appeared on a national television programme expounding his views on why restriction of the birth rate would be a good thing for poor rural blacks in the South . . . if the Shockley remedies had been mandatory in 1913, when Mr Owens's parents were poor rural workers in Alabama, his birth would have been forbidden.'

That same day, on 1 April, the *Detroit Free Press* reprinted a quote from Jesse. 'After the Olympic Games in Berlin, I came back to my native country and I couldn't ride in the front of the bus. I had to go to the back door. I couldn't live where I wanted . . . and of course Joe Louis and I were the first modern national sports figures who were black. So neither of us could do any national advertising because the South wouldn't buy it. That was the social stigma we lived under . . . when Joe and I came along, blacks in America had no image. Jack Johnson, the fighter, could have helped, but he tarnished his own image. Joe Louis and I sat down together and talked. We agreed the only way to help our people was by deeds. We bled on both cheeks. But we lived in that vein. We didn't make waves. There was no scandal. We were called Uncle Toms later. But the 1960s were something else. Back then, our way was the only way. Sometimes, it's hard for people to remember that.'

'God only knows why,' Dave Kinred wrote in the *Washington Post* exactly six months later, on 1 October 1980, 'but they rolled in Joe Louis in a wheelchair right in the middle of Muhammad Ali's press conference. The old champ had his heart repaired three or four years ago and he has suffered three strokes since. The Brown Bomber's skin is yellow grey, the colour of old newspaper clippings. He can't see or speak much.'

Ali, aged thirty-eight and about to endure a grotesque beating from the reigning champion and his former sparring-partner, Larry Holmes, rushed over to the wheelchair. Joe, wearing a cowboy hat and boots, hardly seemed to notice Ali. 'Joe,' Ali crooned sadly, 'I'm gonna put a whuppin' on him. You gonna be there, Joe? I watched films of you the other night, Joe, you and Schmeling. Your combinations were something else. That one-two you hit Schmeling with, that's what I'm gonna hit Holmes with. I might do it in one round. So don't be late, Joe, you might miss it.'

Joe Louis sat blankly in his chair, barely able to move a muscle in either his face or body. Ali hunched down, away from the cameras, and he softly said, 'You feelin' any pain, Joe?'

The old fighter managed to grunt and nod.

'You eatin' good, Joe?' Ali asked anxiously.

Dave Kinred heard 'another chilling grunt. This one meant no. To the cameras, Ali said, "Thanks for comin' by, Joe, it's gonna be a great fight," and then Ali bent low to this warrior once mighty, saying in a whisper, "I'll try to come see you, Joe, before I leave, I'll come to your house."'

On 11 April 1981, Don King wheeled out Joe Louis for Larry Holmes's next defence of his title against Trevor Berbick. King hollered and hailed the old Bomber as, a pace-maker still ticking in his chest, Joe managed to lift his hand in a gentle wave.

Fourteen hours later, at 9.45 a.m., Joe Louis collapsed at home. A siren-screaming ambulance rushed him to the Desert Springs Hospital. He was already dead. At 10.05, a doctor's confirmation of 'death as a result of cardiac arrest' was formally recorded.

Max Schmeling, speaking from Hamburg in Germany, said that Louis 'was the type of fighter every pro wanted to be. He was a boxing genius. We became very good friends. I am shocked and grieved by his death, although I cannot say it was unexpected.'

President Ronald Reagan made an official statement. 'Outside the ring he was a considerate and soft-spoken man. Inside the ring, his courage, strength and consummate skill wrote a unique and unforgettable chapter in sports history. But Joe Louis was more than a sports legend. His career was an indictment of racial bigotry and a source of pride and inspiration to millions of white and black people around the world.'

Dismissing reminders that he had called Joe Louis an Uncle Tom, Muhammad Ali insisted, 'I never said that – not that way, anyhow. That's demeaning. Look at Joe's life. Everybody loved Joe . . . from black folks to red-neck Mississippi crackers, they loved him. They're all crying. That shows you. Howard Hughes dies, with all his billions, not a tear. Joe Louis dies, everybody cries.'

Joe Louis, like Jesse Owens, died at the age of sixty-six. At the request of Martha, his wife for the last twenty-two of those years, his body 'lay in state' in a boxing ring at Caesars Palace before his funeral was held in the hotel's Sports Pavilion on Friday 17 April 1981. Frank Sinatra introduced the spoken praise while Sammy Davis Jr sang *For The Winners* before a crowd of 3,000. The eulogy was delivered by the Reverend Jesse Jackson who had also stood with a bowed head at the funeral of Jesse Owens in Chicago.

In Las Vegas, Jackson's voice rang out in celebration: 'With Joe Louis we made it from the guttermost to the uttermost; from slave-ship to championship. Usually the champion rides on the shoulders of the nation and its people but, in this case, the nation rode on the shoulders of the hero, Joe . . . when Joe fought Max Schmeling what was at stake was the confidence of a nation with a battered ego and in search of resurrection, and the esteem of a race of people . . . God sent Joe from the black race to represent the human race. He was the answer to the sincere prayers of the disinherited and the dispossessed. Joe made everybody somebody . . .

'We all feel bigger today because Joe Louis came this way. He was in the slum, but the slum was not in him. Ghetto boy to man, Alabama sharecropper to champion. Let's give Joe a big hand-clap. This is a celebration. Let's hear it for the champ!'

The applause rolled around the arena as Jackson began to cry out as if he was testifying from a pulpit: 'Let's hear it for the champ! Express yourselves! Wave to Joe now, give the champion a wave!'

Three thousand people rose to their feet and, with a muted roar, lifted their arms.

'Wave to Joe,' Jackson exhorted, 'wave to the champ!'

The mourners waved to the blue desert sky outside.

'Joe,' the Reverend whooped, 'we love your name! We love your name!'

Jesse Jackson, preparing to become the first African-American to stand for President, felt his eyes glitter as he cried again, *'We love your name!'* He remembered how his own name was entwined with those of Jesse Owens and Joe Louis. Soon after his birth, in 1941, his parents had made a small tribute to two men they revered. They called their son Jesse Louis Jackson.

Epilogue

Memento

As we walked down South Oakley Avenue, in the black Hilltop region of Columbus, Ohio, Earl Potts told me some of his favourite stories about Jesse Owens and Joe Louis. 'They're like mementos,' he said of his stories, 'and I figure if I keep talking about them they'll stay alive just a little longer. I used to worry that the names of Jesse Owens and Joe Louis might disappear with time. It seemed inevitable. And yet, somehow, these two guys keep rising up. Every four years, at the Olympics, Jesse Owens pops straight outta the box as if he's still that twenty-two-year-old kid in Berlin. And the legend of Joe Louis keeps rolling along, nice and steady. Joe Louis is a mighty hard name to forget.'

Earl was big on mementos and memorials, on erecting plaques and organising commemorative runs through Jesse Owens's old university town. Yet he did so with a light and humorous touch. 'Hell,' he said within ten minutes of our first meeting, 'forget all this "Earl" stuff. Everyone who really knows me calls me Wimpy.'

I liked listening to Wimpy's stories about the nights Joe Louis used to fight. He had only been five years old in 1938 when Louis knocked out Max Schmeling. 'That night was my first real vivid memory. We were a pretty ordinary black family living in this poor part of Columbus. But, that night, we felt kinda extraordinary. We were humming. We were flying. The whole street crammed into our house. No one owned a radio so all the families in this street pooled together to hire a radio for the night.

'A hush settled over our house just before the fight. I was perched on a knee right close to the radio. All around me these big faces were quiet and sombre. I could tell, even as a little kid, that we needed Joe to win. Two minutes later everyone went crazy. Joe had won! Joe had won! We kept up the habit. Every time there was a Joe Louis fight we would do the exact same thing. Hire a radio and get together with the whole street.

'They were some of the most special nights of my life. I guess they mattered so much because the rest of the time we felt anything but special in Columbus. It was against the law for blacks to live in white neighbourhoods. There were streets we were not allowed to walk along. We were not allowed to eat in white restaurants. We were not allowed to watch movies downtown. We were second-class citizens. Joe Louis made us feel first-class.'

Although he had lived in Columbus all his life, Wimpy's loyalty to the town was restrained. 'Well,' he said slowly, 'this is my home and it's all I know. But it still makes me angry to think how Columbus treated Jesse Owens. Jesse always spoke beautifully about Columbus. But Columbus never embraced him back. After the Olympics, Jesse got those huge ticker-tape receptions in New York and Cleveland. But back here Jesse just caught the street-car to Hilltop and travelled home alone. He'd been all the way to Berlin, messed up Hitler in the Olympic Stadium, and yet he was still just another local Negro who had to step to the back of the streetcar in Columbus.'

Wimpy and his family had been neighbours of the runner on South Oakley. In the 1940s, when Jesse returned to Columbus, 'he was always ready to play at the ballfield just up the street.

That's how we got to see Jesse and Joe together. Joe would bring his softball team out to Columbus. It was like a dream. Joe Louis in *our* neighbourhood! And he was friends with our buddy, Jesse Owens, who lived on the very same street as us.'

Fifty years later, in 1994, when Wimpy was sixty-one, he started his campaign 'to set up a monument outside Jesse's home on South Oakley. Oh man, it was difficult . . . but, in the end, we got there.'

As we looked down at the simple plaque which now stands outside Jesse's old house at 292 South Oakley Avenue, Wimpy and I swapped memorial stories. I told him how, in the summer of 1983, an attempt to erect a monument in honour of Owens outside the courthouse in Moulton, Alabama, seven miles from his birthplace in Oakville, had been blocked by local white politicians. Sixty-four residents of the black Oakville farming community submitted a petition to have the memorial transferred to their land. Yet the night after the four-foot marker was set in place at a remote crossroads, five white men backed their pick-up truck towards the slab, slung a chain around its base, and tried to haul it out of the ground. After a few minutes of strain the chain broke.

Early the next morning, the black people of Oakville gathered around the memorial to inspect the damage. The granite had chipped around the edges where the chain had bit into it. It was otherwise unscathed. The message of tribute still stood out in gold letters:

Jesse Owens
1914–1980
He inspired a world enslaved in tyranny
And brought hope to his fellow man.
From the cotton fields of Oakville
To the acclaim of the whole world
He made us proud to be Lawrence Countians.

There was one other flaw in the granite. A year had been mistakenly taken from his life. Jesse Owens had been born in 1913.

There was less confusion or controversy elsewhere. Simon Wiesenthal's wish for the boulevard leading to the Olympic Stadium in Berlin to bear the name of Jesse Owens was fulfilled. Ruth Owens and her daughters also set up the Jesse Owens Foundation which, under the directorship of Marlene Owens Rankin, continues to thrive in Chicago. 'When Jesse died,' Marlene said, 'people from all over America sent us money. These were just ordinary people who had been touched by him. This was their way of showing their love and respect for him. We opened a fund which soon reached $6,000. We set up the Jesse Owens Foundation. Every year we offer scholarships to around thirty-eight students across America. Apart from giving money to help them complete their education we remind them of everything Jesse had to overcome.'

Joe Louis has his own share of monuments. A $34 million riverfront stadium in Detroit was commemorated as the Joe Louis Arena while a $350,000 two-ton, twenty-four-foot-long sculpture of an arm and a fist was raised in tribute to the old Bomber on the intersection of Jefferson and Windsor in 1985. It has since been moved to the more sedate setting of the Detroit Institute of Arts. Caesars Palace has its own statue of its most remembered greeter. It stands seven-and-a-half feet tall and weighs 4,500 pounds, having been carved from the same marble quarries in Italy which supplied the pure white stone for most of Michelangelo's sculptures. The inscription reads *The Immortal Joe Louis* but, guarding the entrance to the casino's Olympiad Sports Book betting centre, it's surrounded by constantly jangling slot machines.

Joe Louis is buried at Arlington Cemetery on the edge of Washington DC, in a military graveyard. His old friend, Jesse, is buried on the black South Side of Chicago. I once travelled to his graveside with his eldest daughter, Gloria Hemphill. 'On the day we buried him,' she said as we drove to the cemetery, 'the snow fell across these streets. I thought of the last time I had seen my father. He always called me "Sis". As I sat at his bedside Jesse took my hand and said, "Hey, Sis, I've had a good life. If I had to do it again I'd have everything stay exactly the same. So don't cry."'

The grave lies next to a small lake in the shady heart of Oak Woods Cemetery. It is a pretty and secluded patch of ground. A tiny American flag is planted in the half-moon of flowers which circle the front of the grave. Two small marble podiums, inscribed with the five Olympic rings, stand on either side of the main tombstone which reads:

Jesse Owens
Olympic Champion
1936

Wimpy became increasingly wistful as we passed through the darkening streets of Columbus. 'In the 1930s and '40s,' he said, 'the doors to all these houses would be left wide open on a Saturday night. People would move in and out of each other's homes and they would never think about closing a door behind them. There was no need. And as kids, after we had seen Jesse or Joe play some ball we would sit out on the diamond and just shoot the breeze about them until one or two in the morning. Those were beautiful nights.'

As we completed the circle and reached the corner of South Oakley again, Wimpy pointed out a few stray prostitutes hitting the Saturday-night streets earlier than usual. He also stopped outside a derelict red-bricked apartment block on Oakley. We were two houses away from Wimpy's own home. 'They turned this into a crack house a while ago. I had to fight like crazy to get them out of here.'

Wimpy and I walked another block until we reached 292

South Oakley – Jesse's old house. 'I've got one more story to tell you about this house,' Wimpy said. 'It was 1996, the year of the Atlanta Olympics and I'd been heavily involved in getting the route of the Olympic torch run diverted past Jesse's place on Oakley. It was one big hassle but we pulled it off. The torch came down here, on a Friday evening in September, around seven o'clock. It had been raining all day long but, round about six in the evening, it started to clear. The sun came out at 6.45. And it was flooding across the Hilltop as the torch passed the house of Jesse Owens.

'The house now belonged to this couple called Morris and Tina Shelton. And Tina told me this heartbreaking story. She had been married to Morris for over twenty years and they had three sons. But Tina's mother and father had never met her husband. Morris was black. Tina was white. And her folks could not bear the thought of their daughter having married a black man. But they were crazy about the kids. Tina used to take the kids over to the grandparents' house on the other side of Columbus and they would have a great time. But, always, it ate into Tina. Her mom and dad had never been to her house. They refused every invitation to meet her husband. After twenty years, I guess, you give up hope of those kind of people ever changing.'

Wimpy pushed back his baseball cap and wiped his brow. It was a warm evening and he seemed bemused again by the story. 'To tell you the truth,' he said, 'I didn't know whether to laugh or cry whenever I thought about the Sheltons. It always hurt me a little that it should happen in Jesse's old house. Anyway, one day, out of the blue, Tina's mother phones up. She and the father have heard all about the Olympic torch run being re-routed past the Jesse Owens house – which, of course, is now their daughter's house. They want to come over and watch the passing of the torch.

'So Tina says, "Well, Mom, that would be great. But, you know, I'm only going to let you and Dad come to my house if you agree to meet Morris – my husband." And, incredibly, the mother says, "OK, we'll do that." After twenty years, *twenty years* in which they have insisted they will never meet their black son-in-law, the mother and the father come over on the Friday afternoon. And Morris and the father shake hands and they go over and sit on the couch in the lounge and they start talking as if they've known each other for twenty years. They acted like they were the oldest buddies in the world. And soon the mother's insisting that they stay overnight. So Tina yields because she's overwhelmed. Her mother and her father even invite Morris to their place – "You can come over anytime," they say. It's as if those twenty years had never happened.

'And that evening they all stood together outside Jesse's old house as the Olympic torch came down South Oakley Avenue. It was a magical end to a sad story. That was some day. I looked up at the sky and I said, "Hey, Jesse Owens, you may not know it, but you just brought about the integration of a divided family. Good work, old man, good work."

'And then I thought of all those nights when we used to listen to Joe Louis fight on our rented radio. It hit me again. Everything's different now. We ain't ever going back to the old days. And you know what? I was glad. I was glad.'

Postscript

A Different Race

Washington DC, 5 November 2008

On a cold and grey afternoon in Washington DC the jubilation that swept through the streets all night had gone. The screaming crowds and honking cars which engulfed the capital city until dawn, confirming Barack Obama's election as the new President of the United States of America, had been replaced by a low drone of traffic and the throaty hum of Joe Frazier singing to himself in an anonymous hotel room.

'I ever told you I was a great singer?' the old fighter asked. Three rings glittered on his gnarled fingers as Smokin' Joe, a heavyweight crooner with the blues in his bones, whooped: 'I'm still smokin', man!'

It might also have been said on bleaker days, when Frazier was alone at home in Philadelphia with only his haunted memories for company, that a mere wisp of smoke still rose from the ashes of his legacy. Frazier's immense achievement as a great black world heavyweight champion in the 1970s, at a time when boxing carried such sporting and political resonance, was torched by Muhammad Ali's taunts.

As easy as it was to love Ali, and especially his enduring image as the bravest, funniest and most significant sportsman since Joe Louis and Jesse Owens, he was cruel to his bitterest rival. Demeaning Frazier as 'flat-nosed' and 'backward', as a gorilla and an Uncle Tom, Ali's banter was soured with malevolence. Having been so scorched in the past, it was little wonder that Frazier's name did not appear among the black pioneers exalted that week alongside Obama.

Ali himself, meanwhile, had been celebrated again as the black American who, after Martin Luther King, did most to confront racial prejudice in a once seething country.

'That ain't nothing,' Frazier shrugged at his neglect, 'because I lived with it for years. And I ain't the only one. Where are the tributes to Joe Louis this week? Where are the tributes to Jesse Owens? I don't see 'em either. But we know how this story started way back when down in the South. It started with Joe and Jesse and all they did. I just followed the same path as 'em. I did my fighting and stayed quiet.'

Frazier looked weary when I pointed to the morning newspapers spread out on the bed. The front pages told the same story, even though each headline was shorter and more exultant than the last. The *Washington Post* attempted something sober and magisterial – **Obama Makes History** – in big, black, bold typeface. There was almost surprise in the two words – **President Obama** – which the *Washington Times* used to convey the magnitude of the election of a first black American to the White House. The *Examiner*, meanwhile, relied on the exclamation of a single name – **Obama!** – to capture an historic day.

'Yeah,' Frazier said, pushing the papers to one side, 'but it's also important we remember. I know my destiny. I was born into animosity, bigotry and hatred. We had water for white folks, and water for coloured folks. White lines, black lines. I came from Beaufort in South Carolina and it was tougher than Georgia, Mississippi and even Alabama, where Jesse and Joe were born before me. I guess they had it harder than me, but my parents

were also sharecroppers. They had no money. I was one of fourteen [children] and had to work on the land from when I was
seven. My parents suffered back in them days.'

Frazier eventually took the Greyhound bus, 'the dog', from
the South to Harlem. He ended up working in a Philadelphia
slaughterhouse. 'I was the drain man. My job was to make sure
the blood went down the drain. But sometimes, early in the
morning, I'd go down that long rail of meat and work on my
punching. That's how [Sylvester] Stallone got the same idea for
Rocky – just like he used the story about me training by running
up the steps of the museum in Philly. But he never paid me for
none of my past. I only got paid for a walk-on part. *Rocky* is a
sad story for me.'

The old champion gestured to the turgid skyline. 'They want
to make Obama like a *Rocky* story, with big headlines running
like a rainbow for one man. I like Obama. I think they picked a
fine guy in him. Hearing him speak, it sounds like he's going to
be fair and clearcut. So I'm happy we got a black man at the
head of the table. It's about time. But this ain't about one man.
It's about a whole long line of black folk. Most of us might be
forgotten today, but I remember Joe Louis. I remember Jesse
Owens. Let's sing a song about 'em today. Let's give 'em some
light too.'

The bad blood between Frazier and Ali was darker and more
tangled. But in Washington, at the start of an apparent new era
for America, Frazier offered a reminder of how he and Ali were
once friends – and of his own political link with a very different
American president. 'I helped him out,' Frazier said of Ali. 'We
were black men, following on from Joe Louis, both champions,
and I felt sorry for him in a way.'

In 1967, having embraced Islam and changed his name from
Cassius Clay, Muhammad Ali refused to fight in the Vietnam
war. 'I will face machine-gun fire before denouncing Elijah
Muhammad and the religion of Islam,' he insisted. 'I'm ready to

die.' As the heavyweight champion of the world, and at the height of his dazzling powers, Ali was stripped of his title and his licence to box.

Broke and vilified and in exile from the ring for three years, Ali started calling Frazier, his eventual replacement as world champion. 'He'd be phoning every other day,' Frazier recalled. 'He'd say, "You got my title, man! The title Joe Louis and me both won! You got to let me fight you!"'

As he repeated that plea, Frazier slipped into an impersonation which sounded less like Ali in his fast-talking pomp than his old foe after Parkinson's disease had made his speech slurred and halting.

Frazier lets slip a strange smile. 'I said, "OK, I'll see what I can do." So I went to see President Nixon at the White House. It wasn't difficult to get a meeting because I was heavyweight champion of the world. That showed you the power of boxing back then. No heavyweight champion today could do that. But Joe Louis could. And I could. I came to Washington and walked around the garden with Nixon, his wife and daughter. I said: "I want you to give Ali his licence back. I want to beat him up for you." Nixon said, "Sure, I'd like that." He knew what he was doing and so Ali got his licence back.'

Frazier had also given Ali money, but that did not stop the animosity which welled up in the returning hero. Ali was initially amusing. 'Joe Frazier is too ugly to be champ. He can't talk. He can't box. He can't dance. He can't do no shuffle and he writes no poems.'

But the joking soon stopped. 'Joe Frazier is an Uncle Tom,' Ali ranted, echoing a jibe directed at both Owens and Louis in the late 1960s. 'He works for the enemy.'

Frazier's son, Marvis, winced on the sofa opposite his father and me. 'I used to get beat up every day at school by guys who would say, "Your dad's a Tom." It was terrible.'

In later years Frazier's resentment was such that, when asked his opinion about Ali lighting the Olympic torch at the 1996 Atlanta Games, Smokin' Joe said: 'I think he should be pushed into the flames.' He also wrote in his autobiography that, 'I'd like to rumble with that sucker again, beat him up piece by piece and mail him back to Jesus.'

Ali and Frazier shared a trilogy of hurt in an unforgettable series of fights. The third and deciding contest, in Manila in 1975, was somehow won by Ali who called his victory 'the closest thing to dying'.

Considering the brutality of that bout, which may have contributed to the onset of Parkinson's Disease in Ali, Frazier said: 'I still believe I won. The proof is in the pudding. I'm here talking, walking. I'm sixty-four and, yeah, I'm still having fun. I hope the Lord will forgive him. I don't care who you are – whatever you done as a young man it bites you in the butt. Trust me. Sometimes God comes down and puts his hand on you if you're too big in your thoughts.'

He paused and rearranged the morning papers in a neat pile as if, in so doing, he could drag himself back into a more hopeful present. 'Look,' Frazier said of Ali, 'he hollered a lot but, hey dog, it's more than thirty years. I don't hate anyone. Let him try and put his life back together. We done with fighting. We been through enough wars. Today is a good day. We got a black president. I don't see it changing the lives of too many people but, still, it's something. It makes me think that what we did, starting with Jesse and Joe, meant something. We did our bit.'

The old black-and-white wounds of the past had not healed entirely. And Frazier, whose joy in Obama was so muted, remained less susceptible than most to romantic dreams of sudden transformation in America. 'What can he really do?' Frazier asked, with piercing clarity. 'Obama can do a little – but I know not a whole lot is gonna change just because he's in the big house. It's another step, that's all. It's bigger than most, but don't go crazy. Jesse and Joe would know. We come from that different time. Water for white folks, water for coloured folks. White lines, black lines. We now drink the same water, I guess, but you know what? I still see the same black and white lines. They just gone a little grey – like that sky.'

Frazier pointed out of the window of a hotel which, back in the 1930s, would have been reserved for whites only. America, and much of the world beyond this vast country, had changed since the first breakthrough of Owens and Louis. But it still felt as if a grainy and necessary dose of realism had been instilled by Smokin' Joe after such a fevered night of celebration.

'We been through too much, dog, to get carried away,' he said. 'I'm happy. But I ain't forgetting ...'

Two months before I met Joe Frazier, I sat in another hotel room, on a September day of gentle sunshine in London, and spoke to a very different African American sportsman. Reggie Bush, then an imposing twenty-three-year-old running back for the New Orleans Saints, carried a contrasting nickname to Smokin' Joe. Bush liked to be called 'The President'. His wealth and self-belief was evident when he considered the rise of Barack Obama and his own possible political future.

'Obama helps us believe anything is possible,' Bush said, his gold tie and waistcoat looking as shiny as the diamond stud in his ear. This sporting president already recognised his own considerable clout in America. Apart from being a former runaway winner of the prestigious Heisman Trophy, for the outstanding performer in college football, he had become the second-most endorsed player in the NFL in his first season – trailing only the feted quarterback Peyton Manning in 2006. Such glittering status encouraged Bush to speak his mind.

'Every election you hope you're going to take a step forward with the next president, but with Obama you have the feeling that this is someone who will not be just a good president but a great president. I met him at a private event he held in LA and, yeah, I definitely hope he wins – not because he's black but because he's the right guy for the job.'

Having also met the outgoing president 'quite a few times', he grimaced at sharing a surname with George W. Bush. 'I just try to be the better Bush,' young Reggie said with a wry grin. The better Bush, the multimillionaire sports star who looked and spoke as if he had the whole world spread out before him, did not miss a beat when asked if he would like to follow Obama into politics and perhaps, one day, even into the White House. 'I would definitely love to do something like that. Maybe even when I'm in football there might be time for some political stuff.'

I looked at Bush, as polished as he was smart, and asked him a question I doubt had ever been put to Jesse Owens, Joe Louis or Joe Frazier. Did he truly believe that, one day, he might eventually stand for president? Bush nodded. 'I definitely feel that, if I work hard enough, it could be a possibility. But it's not like I sit down and think, "I would like to be president of the United States!" As a kid you might say that kind of thing, but as you grow up you realise that to become president is a tough achievement. So I don't know how realistic it is for me. But I believe that if I set my sights on it I can achieve it.'

It was still hard to believe the better Bush would end up in the White House – but his sporting renown and work in New Orleans, devastated by Hurricane Katrina three years before, in 2005, had led to him being lauded. 'Reggie Bush is, for want of a better word, a god,' Rob Callahan, a police chief in Louisiana had gushed. 'Everyone here knows what he's doing for hurricane victims.'

Bush moved on to talk about how he and some of his New Orleans Saints team-mates had spent part of the pre-season in 2008. 'You really don't need a hurricane to knock some common sense into you. So a few months ago, back in June, we went to Holly Grove, a local neighbourhood, and rebuilt five homes that had been lost in Hurricane Katrina in 2005. We dug holes, we painted, we re-landscaped the lawn. I painted a whole house and it was no easy task. But it was humbling. After three years in a trailer, this family went back to a place I'd helped make nice again. That was my reward. Anybody in their right mind, if they had their head screwed on tight, would want to do it.'

Bush and his American counterparts in the National Football League were as lavishly paid, and often just as self-centred, but it was hard to imagine many Premier League footballers agreeing to rebuild some ruined homes for ordinary families. Yet it seemed as if a week on a building site might not be a bad way to inject a little humility and reality into the lives of footballers like Cristiano Ronaldo and Ashley Cole who had previously been compared to 'slaves' when their wages were under £100,000 a week.

Yet the much more damaging fallout from Hurricane Katrina continued – and encouraged Bush to show some political muscle to match his rippling power as a running back. Reflecting on the failure of his presidential namesake, George Bush, to respond to the impoverished and mostly black victims of Katrina, Bush pointed out that, 'even now, three years on, people are living in trailers. So whatever the government did is not enough. The sad thing about New Orleans is that there's corruption in the political arena. I don't know how most politicians feel, but I feel ashamed that people in this city have not only to worry if their child is going to be alive the next day – they also have to worry about their own government stealing money from them.'

Bush had studied political science at the University of Southern California and he stressed his belief that 'sport is heavily involved in politics. I think they go hand-in-hand. I feel that athletes have a political voice, and it's a powerful voice.'

In his first full season in the NFL, he raised spirits in demoralised New Orleans while leading a team that shocked America by reaching the NFC Championship game in January 2007. If he had struggled initially to adapt from college football, Bush unleashed his explosive and elusive running in the second half of that debut season. Facing the Chicago Bears for the right to play in the 2007 Super Bowl, a 78-yard downfield rush by Bush resulted in a touchdown that brought the Saints within two points of the home team. Bush wagged his finger at the Chicago linebacker Brian Urlacher before somersaulting in joy – a slice of showboating that saw him fined $5,000 by the NFL.

Chicago claimed that Bush's antics inspired their subsequent victory. 'Whatever,' Bush snorted. 'Maybe it did. But it was a fantastic play and I got caught up in the moment. The bottom line is they made it to the Super Bowl ahead of us.'

It was hard to know how much Bush might achieve on the football field, or in the political arena, but his ambition was obvious. He also illustrated the contrast between a twenty-first century star in American sport, where outrageous affluence and opportunity was obvious, and the black pioneers who had preceded him.

Jesse Owens and Joe Louis would have been astonished by the sense of entitlement that distinguished another modern African American sporting superstar, LeBron James, whom I interviewed on numerous occasions. I first met James during the same trip to America as my visit to Washington to see Joe Frazier. The NBA basketball giant, who had swapped his previous alias of 'The Chosen One' for an equally immodest tag of 'King James', ambled down an echoing corridor in the basement of the United Center in Chicago late on a Saturday night in November 2008. Sweat rolled from his face and his tattooed arms as, without any shoes, he stepped out in his long black socks.

The rest of his team, the Cleveland Cavaliers, recovered behind a closed locker-room door after another win on the road. But, as if he could hardly bear to leave the scene of his latest triumph, King James had lingered on the court which Michael Jordan once dominated in Chicago.

James intentionally wore the same number for Cleveland, 23, that Jordan made his own for the Chicago Bulls and it was hard to shake the comparison in a pulsating fourth quarter. With the score tied at 77–77, James buried another massive three-pointer from the edge of the court as he set about transforming a tight NBA game against a Chicago team desperate to overturn their loss in Cleveland a few days earlier – when James scored 41 points. But the next great face of basketball rolled over the home side in a display of individual brilliance. Another perfectly executed three-pointer from deep within a crowded court finally broke the Bulls and the Cavaliers eased away to win 106–97. James had again scored 41 points.

The 6ft 8in, 250lb king was whooping by the time he completed his shoeless shuffle to the locker room. Two ice-buckets were waiting for him in the far left-hand corner of a room steaming with basketball players in various states of undress. 'I'm real happy,' James said as he stripped off his sodden socks and dunked his feet in the deep freeze. 'Once I get in the zone they can put as many men on me as they like and it just don't matter. They brought the double-team on me and I still got those three-pointers off. They brought the triple-team on me and you see the three-pointer I still sank? Damn near broke their hearts.'

James ripped off his vest and used it to wipe his face. 'They played me just like every team in the NBA is gonna play me. I accepted their challenge. I'm not going to do that every night. I'm not going to be perfect every fourth quarter, but each time I'm gonna try my heart out to put my team in a position to win – and tonight I did that. I feel real good.'

It was always meant to end up like this for a young basketball player who had been called The Chosen One since he was a teenager in Akron, Ohio. James went straight from school to the NBA as the No1 draft pick in 2003 – when he signed a $90 million (£61 million) shoe contract with Nike even before he had made his debut for Cleveland. He had driven the unfashionable

Cavaliers to the preceding three play-offs – making their first-ever appearance in the NBA final in 2006 against San Antonio Spurs. And in 2008, after picking up Olympic gold as part of the US team in Beijing, James had become only the third man, after Richard Gere and George Clooney, to make the cover of *Vogue* in the magazine's 116-year history.

A month on from Chicago, in a hotel room in Denver, the big man spoke intently. 'Since you saw me in Chicago, I've been playing the same high level because the next step is to win the NBA championship. All the guys on the team understand that's my goal.'

Three years before, when he was still only twenty, James shocked American sport by walking away from his agent and setting up his own company, LRMR Branding & Marketing, with a trio of friends from Ohio. This was not a 'brand' which young black men, barely into their twenties, were meant to control and own. 'The NBA were definitely nervous because they had never seen anything like this before,' James said. 'They were used to the traditional concept of a guy coming into the NBA with an agent who handles his day-to-day business. But I wanted to run my own thing and be totally hands-on.

'I can't think of anyone else taking care of their own brand at such a young age. I just had confidence in myself and the guys around me. We knew it was going to be a big challenge. We were going into new territory and we'd get a lot of heat from people determined to downplay us. They thought we were too young and inexperienced but that motivated us even more.'

Few sportsmen would be confident enough to discuss business strategies with a seventy-eight-year-old billionaire like Warren Buffett – but James was animated when explaining his unlikely friendship with the American investor rated as the world's richest man in 2008 by *Forbes* magazine. Buffet had suggested that James was more 'financially mature' at twenty-three than he had been at fifty.

'Warren is definitely a great guy,' James crooned. 'He taught me to follow my gut. Whatever decision you make, it's almost always best to go with your initial instinct.'

James was then the market-leader in generating NBA advertising revenue – earning over $25 million a year in endorsements, $10 million more than Kobe Bryant, the next-highest earner – but he and his schoolboy friends had been even more commercially savvy. Rather than just accepting straight sponsorship deals from Coke, Microsoft and Nike, James had pursued contracts in which he received an equity stake in companies which use his image to sell their products.

None of this would matter if James did not play outstanding basketball – and in November 2008 he became the youngest player to score 11,000 NBA points, being almost a year quicker than Bryant in reaching that milestone. He was chasing three goals: to win a first NBA championship and to become a global sporting phenomenon as well as a billionaire. 'I'm getting close,' he told me coolly. 'You know one of my favourite lines in *The Godfather* is to "move while you have the muscle". Right now I've got a lot of muscle and I'm moving real fast. I'm heading in the right direction on and off the court.'

Eighteen months later even Reggie Bush, with his presidential talk, was surprised that, in the summer of 2010, James should showcase his new choice of team as a television extravaganza he called 'The Decision'. After seven years as their star player, James phoned Cleveland just minutes before announcing Miami as his next destination live on television. A career move was supposedly being repackaged as glossy entertainment. Such unvarnished ego was swamped by embarrassing hubris as disappointed rivals and indignant fans unleashed their condemnation.

We met again in London in December 2011 and the aspiring billionaire still seemed to be recovering from a different kind of abuse to that suffered by Louis and Owens. 'It's definitely tough when you read a lot of negative things that say you're selfish or you don't play the right way,' James said. 'But, for me, I've only played one way: for the team.'

That new team, the Miami Heat, had lost the World Series that previous summer when they were defeated 4-2 in a potential seven-game final by the less glitzy Dallas Mavericks. James was dismissed by many for his corporate sensibility but defeat had hurt him badly. 'I only got over it a couple of days ago,' he said wryly after six months of pain. 'It was definitely heartbreaking. But it's made me a better player. I'm a better person as well for it – just in terms of focusing harder, zeroing in even more. It's made me critique my game and work out who I am as a person.'

I asked James if he was taken aback by the ferocious criticism of his screening of 'The Decision'? 'Um, yeah. I was surprised by it because I was making a decision for myself. I was doing something that I believed was going to make me happy and freshen me up. But looking back I can understand why a lot of people were upset. That definitely wasn't my intention: to upset people. I can't say I would change anything – because it would change so much that is leading to the future. But, yeah, there is definitely a better way I could have handled it. A lot of people were hurt by it – and I apologise to them. At the same time, you should never be afraid to do what you believe in.'

James insisted that, in choosing to show 'The Decision' on television, he was motivated by a desire to plough back the money he earned into African-American communities. 'My thinking was built around those kids who would benefit from me making this decision, all these underprivileged kids that would get the millions and millions of dollars I'd receive. That was my whole motivation. It's definitely been projected that I'm greedy and egotistical. You can get angry but, you know, I'm satisfied when I go to those kids' clubs all over the United States that they don't forget the moment when their gymnasium was refurbished, or their library or media centre, and they went from big old computers to laptops. As a professional athlete a lot is going to be said about you – but I just try to move forward and achieve my goals. You've got to go through the tornado to get to the clear weather. I feel we went through it and now we're headed on the right path.'

So much had changed for black sportsmen in America. When I began working on this book in a new century, I travelled to Chicago to meet Ruth Owens, Jesse's wife, in July 2000. At eighty-five, she made a telling comparison between the lives of Jesse and Joe and their sporting counterparts in the twenty-first century. 'I switch on my television now,' she said, 'and whenever a game comes on I see black fellers in starring roles. Black men look like they rule sport in this country now. It's the only area where they are right on top. It was nothing like that in the 1930s. America was white and that was that. I can't say it bothered me much. Like everyone, I just knew it didn't do you no good to dream of making it to the big time. It was impossible. And then, y'know, along came Jesse and along came Joe . . .'

Rather than worrying about whether or not he would be allowed into a white hotel or served food at a roadside diner, as Louis and Owens had done in the mid-1930s, LeBron James decided to expand his 'global portfolio' by securing a minority stake in Liverpool FC after he cut a deal with the club's American owner, Fenway Sports Group. Fenway reached agreement with James's company, LRMR, to represent him around the world. In return James would also become a minority owner in Liverpool. On signing the deal, King James said he was 'excited to be affiliated with this incredible organisation' and looked forward to donning a red shirt and visiting Anfield.

'The first time I stepped on an NBA court I became a businessman,' James said. 'This is a great opportunity for me.'

Liverpool apparently regarded the partnership as a way of expanding their own brand. 'Very few athletes can match

LeBron James's global reach, appeal and iconic status,' they said in a press release. 'The business opportunities for both of us being identified together in emerging international markets will result in unforeseen opportunities that neither would have been able to realise alone.'

All of this explained why, before our third interview, the long wait for King James unfolded in a luxury hotel suite large enough to fit a stylish apartment. It seemed a very big space for small talk with a quartet of people I had just met. But they were 'the people' assigned to a basketball superstar visiting London. They, in turn, were expected to liaise with the separate group of 'LeBron's people', who were with him a floor above us in this swish Soho establishment.

There had been much discussion between the different sets of people and my latest interview with James had been arranged, cancelled, rearranged and then delayed. I had called it off two days previously when LeBron's people were not prepared for him to discuss the smouldering controversy surrounding his move from Cleveland to Miami. But it was my turn to be surprised. The interview had been salvaged when James's team backtracked and agreed he would answer questions about 'The Decision'.

When James arrived, his entourage of eight disappeared behind the divide of our massive suite. James and I settled down alone on a plush sofa. As an easy prelude, I asked him about his first visit to Anfield, when Liverpool drew 1-1 with Manchester United. He had hailed it on Twitter as an 'unbelievable experience'.

James polished the memory: 'That came from the simple fact of how passionate and loyal those fans are. But to walk through the facility the day before – to see all the history and achievements was very powerful. Liverpool have won nineteen league championships [they had actually won only eighteen] and it meant a lot to read about King Kenny and Steven Gerrard – a hometown kid who now captains the team. And then to be at

Anfield and see forty thousand fans screaming at the top of their lungs, the whole game, was an unbelievable experience.'

I noted the smooth King Kenny reference. When he met Liverpool's manager, did James find it easy to tune into Kenny Dalglish's Glaswegian accent? 'King Kenny is something else! His accent is very strong. So it was very difficult to understand what he was saying – but it was great being around him and [Luis] Suárez and Gerrard and those guys. I was very humbled that they knew me. And you just know this is a club that will widen their global appeal. Any time you have so much history and so much power behind their story, there is great potential to continue that expansion. Liverpool are definitely one of those clubs like Man U – and the Dallas Cowboys and the New York Yankees. There are some teams and logos you see, no matter where you are in the world, and you know exactly who they are and what they mean.'

It was interesting, in a way, to hear the epitome of a twenty-first-century sporting sensation talk so smoothly about 'branding' and 'global appeal'. But it also felt distinctly odd that racism should be sidestepped so markedly in James's eulogies of Liverpool's commercial potential. The previous month, in October 2011, Luis Suárez had racially abused Manchester United's Patrice Evra in a verbal altercation which had damaging repercussions for English football – most of whose supporters believed it had moved beyond the grim days when black players were subjected to monkey chants and bananas were thrown at them.

The Suárez–Evra controversy would rumble on for almost a year, with Liverpool handling the issue poorly while their striker was banned for eight matches and fined £40,000. It echoed the calamitous fashion in which Chelsea's John Terry, then England's captain, mouthed the phrase 'fucking black cunt' at Anton Ferdinand of Queens Park Rangers. Terry's words were said on 23 October 2011, eight days after Suárez ridiculed Evra's skin colour, and it seemed telling that less than a month later we were apparently compelled to sidestep the controversies in an interview with an African-American superstar – and shareholder in one of the implicated English clubs.

James did not feel qualified to discuss either case, which were then subjected to heated legal and media scrutiny, but amid the opulence of his London hotel suite I wondered how far we had moved on from the bigotry that had framed the lives of Owens and Louis. He was a multi-millionaire but James seemed neutered by his corporate interests. I thought instead of Smokin' Joe Frazier who, even in the heady wake of Barack Obama's election, had remembered a time when there was segregation.

Ambivalence also shrouded an encounter with one of Jesse Owens' successors as the world's fastest man. Justin Gatlin had won 100m Olympic gold in 2004, sixty-eight years after Owens did the same in Berlin. Yet Gatlin no longer belonged with Owens in the list of celebrated sprinters because, in July 2006, he had failed a routine drugs test and been banned for four years. He had not been on the comeback trail for long when I went to see him training at a track inside Disney World, Orlando, in August 2011.

Gatlin professed his innocence, and insisted that he had been framed, but I was more interested in two contrasting segments of our interview. He explained how he had fallen for sprinting in Brooklyn where, as a boy, he suffered from Attention Deficit Disorder and had felt truly happy only when hurdling over every fire hydrant as he ran to a small woodland area near Sheepshead Bay. 'Hurdling those hydrants told me I was athletic,' he said, 'and it made me feel calm and happy. But I was most interested in finding bugs and grasshoppers. That's why I liked losing myself in the woods. If I hadn't have become a runner I would definitely be a zoologist now. It's hard academically for an ADD sufferer – but, doing something they love, they can be the most focused person of all.'

The little black boy from Brooklyn who wished he could have become a zoologist ended up being derided as a drugs cheat. But Gatlin had a sense of sprinting history and he hailed Jesse Owens as the ideal to which he had once aspired. 'I would've liked to have been a force for good like him,' Gatlin said of Owens. 'I know there was worse racism back then but, maybe, life became more complicated in the modern world. Maybe they were happier as athletes, even if they had less opportunity as men.'

In an empty locker room adjoining the heart of Disney World, where Gatlin dealt less in cartoon fantasy than the reality of his controversial comeback from a doping suspension, he cut a more sombre figure than Owens ever did as a former Olympic champion. He might have had a point when comparing the tangled mess of sprinting today with the purer glory of Owens at the Nazi Olympics. But Owens had been allowed to run in only one more competitive race, an insignificant relay, after he won his fourth gold medal. Unlike Gatlin, preparing himself for a tilt at Usain Bolt in the 100m final of the London Olympics, Owens had been reduced to racing horses and cars. It was wrong to believe that Owens had had a much easier life as a sprinter in the 1930s – even if it was simpler to understand because everything in the past seemed to be cast in such stark black and white.

Gatlin soon re-emerged as one of Usain Bolt's most muscular challenges. On the eve of the 2012 Olympics, I sat alone with Bolt as he reacted to the fact that Gatlin had regained some of his old speed and ferocious commitment. At a meeting in Zagreb, the American had even appeared to spit into Bolt's lane.

'He's an old-school athlete,' Bolt said of Gatlin. 'Back in the day it was all about intimidation. But I'm not intimidated by Justin Gatlin. It won't work with me.'

Bolt, instead, relied on both his staggering reputation and a renewed appetite for hard work to send a shiver down his rivals. 'This will be the moment, and this will be the year, when I set myself apart from other athletes in the world,' Bolt told me in a quiet but dramatic statement of intent on the brink of London 2012. The world's fastest man spoke with unusually serious concentration as he stressed his belief that he would seal his legacy in London.

'A lot of legends, like Jesse Owens, have come before me,' Bolt said. 'But this is my time.'

Bolt duly beat Gatlin in London and repeated the hat-trick of gold medals which he had also won four years before – at the Beijing Olympics. But when I think of my three interviews with Bolt – one on Hellshire Beach in Jamaica and two in England – the same memory returns. At each of those encounters the name of Jesse Owens echoed aloud.

'If I could be anyone before me, I'd want to be Jesse Owens,' Bolt had said in 2013, when Jamaican sprinting was beset by a doping scandal and he insisted on his own clean approach by winning the 100m and 200m at the world championships in Moscow. He said much the same in 2012 and 2010 when I asked whom he most admired as a sprinter and who still surpassed Bolt's achievements on the track. On both occasions he said, 'Jesse Owens.'

Years later, Mike Tyson would look down at an old edition of this book in his office in Henderson, just outside Las Vegas, and sigh at both the beautiful and the tragic in the lives of Owens and Louis. He lamented the fact that, in December 1936, less than six months after Berlin, Owens had raced a horse in Havana. 'Can you believe that shit? How could they do it to Jesse Owens?' And gazing at photographs of his great predecessor he said, with aching simplicity: 'Oh, Joe Louis ...'

Tyson reflected on his bleak and violent childhood in Brownsville, Brooklyn, when his mother had offered him little love. Tyson said: 'When I told my mom I was going to make something of my life, that people believed I'd become the best fighter on the planet, she just shook her head. She said, "Son, ain't you ever heard of Joe Louis? There's always someone better than you." With Joe Louis she was right.'

New York, 11 January 2014

Brownsville and Sheepshead Bay felt a long way away when I walked through Brooklyn on the second Saturday morning of a new year. Jesse Owens and Joe Louis transfixed me again – even before I took the subway from Brooklyn to the Bronx. I started at Avenue H, on the Q train, and the black man in the ticket booth cackled mournfully when I asked how long it might take to reach the outer fringes of the Bronx.

'You crazy?' he asked. 'You goin' all that way up into the Bronx? You sure, mister?'

I nodded, without telling him I was on my way to visit Billy Johnson, surely one of the last men alive who had seen Owens run competitively and Louis fight in a world title bout. Johnson was in his late-eighties and I had stumbled across him by chance – while researching a new book.

'You got to talk to Billy Johnson,' I was told because he had seen most of the great champions who had fought in New York from the 1930s to the 1980s. Johnson had hung out at Gleason's Gym and, later, at the Times Square gym which another compelling old fight character I knew, Jimmy Glenn, managed for years.

Yet it was only when I discovered that Johnson had also seen Owens in New York in 1935 that it became imperative to travel across the sprawling breadth of the city. Where else would I meet someone still alive and able to talk about his memories of Owens and Louis?

When I told Johnson that I was based in Brooklyn for the week, he laughed. 'You got a journey ahead of you,' he promised me down the phone. 'You won't get no taxi to take you up here.'

I was happy riding the subway and, working on this latest book, I had travelled from Brooklyn to Manhattan to Harlem and Long Island. 'For the Bronx,' Johnson said, 'You just go into the city and take the 5 train all the way.'

Johnson told me that once I moved out of Manhattan and headed up into the Bronx it would seem as if 'the 5 train turns into a black train'.

In Harlem I'd interviewed Bobby Miles, a cousin of Ezzard Charles, the former world heavyweight champion who had beaten his idol, Joe Louis, at Yankee Stadium in the Bronx. Harlem had been Louis's playground but the south Bronx had been his battlefield – from the night he knocked out Max Schmeling in 1938 to the more crushing defeat he had suffered twelve years later against Charles. Miles lived in a beautiful house in Harlem and he made me feel as if I was back in the days of the Brown Bomber.

But only Johnson, I was told, could talk about Owens and Louis with equal conviction. And so on that crisp yet icy Saturday I clattered along the Q track. Further back in Brooklyn, near Avenue Z, the Q train went all the way to Sheepshead Bay, home to Justin Gatlin. But as we rumbled forward in the opposite direction we reached Atlantic Avenue – a clear sign that we had left Brooklyn behind for Manhattan.

At 14th Street Union Square I switched to Billy Johnson's favourite 5 train. The further along the line we went, moving from one station to another, the more apt his description became as the 5 train turned into a black train. Eventually, deep in the Bronx, I was the only white face in a quietly swaying carriage.

It took an hour and three quarters to get to Johnson's apartment in the Bronx – but the long trip from Brooklyn was worth every stop on the subway for, inside the spry old man's home, I found a small treasure-box of an archive. Johnson, who lived alone but was looked after by his daughter from across the street, had transformed each of the three rooms into a sporting shrine. As he took me from one to another, pointing proudly to the photographs and posters of black icons of the past, from Owens and Louis and Jackie Robinson to Muhammad Ali, from Kareem Abdul-Jabbar to Michael Jordan, he gave me a detailed history lesson with a light touch. He made me feel as if his stories brought back each event to life – especially when he reached for his files of cuttings.

He showed me some old newspaper articles, some of which I remembered from my own trawl through the *New York Times* and the *Amsterdam News*, which recorded Owens's achievement in breaking three world records and equalling another in the space of forty-five minutes in Ann Arbor on 25 May 1935.

'That was the greatest act of sporting excellence the world has ever seen,' Johnson said, before grinning shyly at the grand statement he had just made. 'Well ... at least in my humble opinion.'

Johnson then told me how, in celebration of his tenth birthday, his parents had taken him to see Jesse Owens run just six weeks later. 'It was right here, in the Bronx, on the ninth of July 1935,' Johnson said, the lucid, almost poetic words rising excitedly in his old voice. 'I remember it was a rainy Tuesday night. But it could have snowed for all I noticed of the wet. To be allowed to go out at night, on my birthday, and see the great Jesse Owens run was the best present a ten-year-old boy could have ever had.'

I thought Johnson might start to cry amid the painful sweetness of his memory and so I asked him where Owens had run in the Bronx. 'Ohio Field,' he said softly, and I briefly wondered if he had become confused, as Jesse ran for Ohio State in 1935. Johnson repeated the name. 'Ohio Field, on the banks of the Harlem River, right here in the Bronx. It was University Heights, and NYU played college football there. That night Jesse came to town and he took on a sprinter you may have heard of – Eulace Peacock.'

Johnson said Eulace Peacock's name with such delicacy that

the story I'd written all those years ago lit up inside my head again. I remembered how Peacock had beaten Owens repeatedly in the summer of 1935.

'Five times in six days,' Johnson said. 'He had Jesse's number all right.'

What happened on the night of Johnson's tenth birthday when Peacock and Owens raced at Ohio Field? 'I remember one thing more than anything else,' Johnson said. 'I damn near burst with excitement.'

He chuckled and dug deep into his collection to find the cuttings which described that race. 'Look here,' he said. 'They all talk about the rain. It rained and rained. I don't think Jesse minded because, about just a week before, he'd married Ruth ...'

Did Johnson believe that the distraction of being newly married might have been a reason for Owens losing so often to Peacock? 'Now that's a colourful question,' he chortled. 'Peacock was just quicker than him for a while. You got a story that you could write right there. The Eulace Peacock Story. That kid might have done what Jesse did in Berlin ... and won at least three golds on the track. But fate worked another way. The running gods wanted Jesse Owens to beat the Nazis.

'Even though he lost to Peacock that night, by less than a step over a hundred yards, I still loved Jesse. He had that stardust. You couldn't take your eyes off him. He might have lost a few races to Peacock but, damn, he was unstoppable every other time. He lifted us right up. He gave us hope we'd never had before.'

I asked Johnson about Joe Louis. Had he seen Louis knock out Schmeling three years later at Yankee Stadium, again in the Bronx? 'No I didn't,' he said sadly. 'My parents loved boxing, like we all did, but they were worried about the huge crowd that night. I was only thirteen and so I stayed home with my mother and my younger brothers. But my daddy went. We listened to the fight on the radio and I was convinced I could hear my daddy's voice hollering after it was all over. I know it's crazy but that was the kind of belief we had in Joe. He made us think everything was possible.'

The fight that Johnson remembered most was Louis's comprehensive points defeat to Ezzard Charles. 'I was twenty-five in 1950 and so I was a man. But I still cried that night Joe lost to Charles . . . even though I admired Charles. He was a fine heavyweight and a good man. But he sure wasn't Joe Louis. So isn't that strange? The strongest memories I have of Jesse and Joe in the Bronx were both from nights they lost. But that matters about as much as the rain that fell on my tenth birthday. You'll have heard this before, but it's true. It's the truest thing I know. Every one of these men [Johnson waved to the black sportsmen on his wall], and all these kids today making their millions, owe it to Jesse and Joe.'

I asked Johnson what he thought of African-American sportsmen today, mentioning my encounters with Reggie Bush and LeBron James – who had since won successive NBA titles with the Miami Heat. The little old black man shrugged. 'I ain't got nothing against them. They're making money and living this incredible life. Eighty years ago they would have turned to boxing or the track. But now they have much more opportunity. I just hope they don't forget who made it possible for them. I just hope they don't forget that the rest of black America is not a football field or a basketball court. The rest of black America is still struggling.'

Johnson looked up and nodded shyly again. 'Well, that's just in my humble opinion . . .'

I made Johnson laugh when I said, after a couple of hours, it was time for me to catch the 'black train' out of the Bronx. 'Yeah . . . it'll turn back into a black-and-white 5 train once you hit Manhattan again.'

He was right. For fifteen minutes we rattled through the Bronx on a subway filled with black faces. It was Saturday

lunchtime and the mood was quiet and almost sleepy as the
train swung from side to side. I knew Jesse and Joe would have
recognised the familiar old American divide – as would have Joe
Frazier, who had died on 7 November 2011, three years and a
couple of days after we'd met in Washington DC.

In 2014 Barack Obama was already deep in his second term.
He looked a much older and wearier president with all the sheer
joy of his reaching the White House having been drained by the
harsher and more disappointing realities of politics and real life.
'I don't see it changing the lives of too many people,' Frazier had
said in his gruff but sage way when he anticipated Obama's
presidency. 'But, still, it's something,' he had murmured in his
downbeat celebration of America's first black president.

Two particular sentences from that interview still rang out.
'We had water for white folks, water for coloured folks. White
lines, black lines,' Frazier had said. Those words evoked my
own past in South Africa, under apartheid. And they seemed res-
onant again on a wintry day in the Bronx on the black train.
There were just black faces on one part of the 5 train, up in the
Bronx, and many more white faces further down, near
Manhattan. It was the same old black-and-white wound of
America, South Africa and other countries, too.

Sport had always been a playground, and so it was easier in
American football and basketball to turn a fantasy of equality
into the reality of riches earned by Reggie Bush and LeBron
James. If some black men had become coaches, rather than just
players, it was still clear that almost all the owners of clubs were
resolutely white. In time that might change – even if there won't
be a romantic new rainbow nation as once imagined for post-
apartheid South Africa or an Obama-led America.

The 5 train moved on slowly towards Manhattan and, with
every stop along the way, the faces around me began to merge
into different colours. Accents changed and tourists drifted into
our carriage. The black and white lines were no longer so clearly

demarcated. I plugged in my earphones and started to listen to the gravelly old voice of Bobby Johnson on a battered and tiny recorder.

'You want me to talk about Jesse Owens and Joe Louis?' he said at the start of our recorded interview. 'Nothing could make me happier. Life might not be perfect but, without them, it would have been unthinkable. That's why I never get tired talking about them. Jesse and Joe started a whole new story. It's not over and who knows where it will end. But they give us the start. It always comes back to them ...'

Notes on Sources & Acknowledgements

This book stems from a curious combination of the mundane and the mysterious. I would not like even to guess the number of hours, weeks and months I have spent these last few years hunched over microfilm reading-machines in buildings across America and at the British Library's Newspaper Archive in Colindale, where I began my increasingly obsessive search to verify a one-line claim I had stumbled across – that Jesse Owens had once raced against Joe Louis.

More significantly, I was reminded constantly that no amount of laborious newspaper research could produce the same density of emotion and knowledge that sprung from actual interviews with people who knew Jesse and Joe when they were still alive. The time I spent with Ruth Owens in Chicago, less than a year before her death at the age of eighty-six, was especially illuminating and poignant. Whether it was listening to Ruth describe the way she used to watch Jesse running down a church alley-way when he was her schoolboy sweetheart, or the pain of their post-Olympic years, or his friendship with Joe, the pathos of those memories was sharpened by the lucidity of her story-telling.

Even the racy and humorous prose of the 1930s could never quite equal the wit and insight I heard while interviewing Ruth Owens or Eddie Futch, the legendary boxing trainer and Joe Louis' old friend from Detroit, nor could it re-create the startling immediacy of an eye-witness account supplied by Jim Cruter. It took a long time but, slowly, the winding stories began to link and hold together and, almost by accident, I had uncovered my own chosen method of research – moving between the hushed Smithsonian Institute and Library of Congress in Washington DC, the great Jesse Owens archive at Ohio State University in Columbus and the newspaper library in Colindale while, simultaneously, setting up my own interviews.

Sometimes I tried to kid myself that I was a low-grade detective, for a clue dropped in a conversation could often be confirmed and clarified by a newspaper article. A vague allusion in an ancient report, meanwhile, could be transformed into a miraculously vivid and deeply personal recollection by someone who had been at the described scene or had copies of Jesse or Joe talking into a hissing tape about how they had felt during that particular moment in their shared history. And so cassettes and films and videos and books were added to my ever-expanding mountain of cuttings and interviews.

The way in which I came to listen to the voice of Eulace Peacock, Jesse's great rival, offers one example of this strange process. It also depicts the essential luck entailed in tracking down the more obscure incidents or lost characters who re-emerge in this book. Duncan Mackay, the athletics correspondent for both the *Guardian* and the *Observer*, kindly steered me in the direction of Mel Watman, who seems to know more about track-and-field history than anyone in Britain. Mel had supplied me with numerous contacts in America, not least the venerable sprint historian Donald Potts, and gave me a pile of clippings and books – one of which was Neil Duncanson's *The Fastest Men On Earth*. I discovered that Duncanson's book had accompanied an ITV television series which coincided with the build-up to the 1988 Olympic Games. Mel Watman promptly sent me the entire documentary season on tape.

I was obviously most intrigued by the short film Duncanson had made about Jesse Owens – and especially by the interviews he had secured with Eulace Peacock who had died in December 1996 at the age of eighty-two. Peacock, talking softly and nervously in his checked jacket, only appears on *The Fastest Men On Earth* in a thirty-second clip – but my interest was such that I wrote to Neil Duncanson at Chrysalis Television. I was struck again by the sheer generosity of some people. Besides loaning me all his taped interviews with Peacock, he offered additional cassettes featuring interviews with the late Marty Glickman, the Jewish runner who had been dropped unexpectedly from the US Olympic team in 1936, as well as Harrison Dillard and Lindy Remigino (Olympic 100m Champions in 1948 and 1952).

Eulace Peacock had never been interviewed before on television. He literally froze in front of the cameras. Yet I now could hear the sweet grace and heartbreaking pain of stories he told alone in conversation with Neil Duncanson in front of a small cassette recorder. And so, in Chapter Four of this book, as Eulace tells Jesse about travelling across America by train, his voice drives my narrative.

The difficulties of researching and writing this book were, in the end, overcome by the many people who were willing to help me. The people listed below are just the most important of those who either spent time with me in detailed conversation about specific scenes or characters in this book, or helped set up those interviews by introducing me to previously elusive figures. In different ways, I owe something to each of the following and would like to acknowledge their contributions:

Claude Abrams, Byrd Archer, Susan Bachrach, Bill Baker, Joe Louis Barrow Jr, Dominic Calder-Smith, Bill Cayton, Rodney Charnock, Tamar Chute, Gil Clancy, Rosemary Cooper, Jim Cruter, Trish Dulko, Neil Duncanson, Angelo Dundee, Lou

Duva, Ed Dyer, Bouie Fisher, Martin Fletcher, Eddie Futch, Russ Galen, Joe Gilbert, Alberto Gomez, Kathryn Harris, Pete Hedge, Gina Hemphill, Gloria Hemphill, Reuben Jackson, Mercy Jalandoni, Hank Kaplan, Dave Kelly, Jack Lindsay, Steve Lott, Duncan Mackay, Larry Merchant, Bill Miller, Al 'Blue' Mitchell, Tim Musgrave, John Nolan, Ron Olver, Ruth Owens, Marlene Owens Rankin, Joe Porter, Donald Potts, Earl 'Wimpy' Potts, Beverly Prather, Mike Simms, Tommie Smith, Walter Smith, Emmanuel Steward, Art Stubbs, Chris Sykes, Hilton Tanchum, Paul Tilzey, Jack Tree, Don Turner, George von der Lippe, Mitchell Wake, Gene Walker, Ray Ward, Mel Watman, John Woodruff, Amber Young, Limmie Young and George Zeleny.

In particular, I would like to thank Ruth's and Jesse's youngest daughter, Marlene Owens Rankin, who heads the Jesse Owens Foundation, for her time and patience. The interviews and exchanges I shared with Marlene and her sister, Gloria Hemphill, in Chicago and at the graveside of Jesse were among the most stimulating of all the conversations which shaped this book. Gina Hemphill, Gloria's daughter, as adept in discussing her grandfather, Jesse, or her friend, the former 400m great, Michael Johnson, bridged the cinder tracks of the 1930s with the big-time world of professional athletics today.

Joe Louis' son, Joe Louis Barrow Jr, proved to be consistently helpful and brilliantly eloquent in addressing the lives of both his father and Jesse Owens. His support was invaluable as I approached the last months of writing.

Humane insights into Louis and his trainer, Jack Blackburn, were given to me by magnificent cornermen like the late Eddie Futch, Walter Smith, Gil Clancy, Bouie Fisher and Jack Lindsay. My ten-year-old interview with Lou Duva about Joe and Rocky Marciano proved beneficial when I came to write about the final decline of Louis as a fighter in 1951.

Mitchell Wake's transcripts of interviews with the late Freddie

Guinyard, Joe's best friend, were more than useful – as were Barbara Moro's lengthy interviews with Jesse and Ruth Owens in 1961 for the Illinois Historical Society. The FBI sent me copies of their 1956 file on Jesse Owens, while the North Illinois District Court supplied me with the complete transcripts of court proceedings during Jesse's tax trial in 1965-66. Similarly, access to transcripts or tapes of old interviews with Dave Albritton, Mel Walker, Charlie Beetham, Carl Lewis, Jimmy Braddock, Billy Conn, Ezzard Charles, Rocky Marciano and Ash Resnick from a variety of sources, stretching from the ARCO Archives to private collectors like John Nolan, helped fill in many of the missing gaps.

When it came to film material of Jesse and Joe, the tireless and informed contributions of Rodney Charnock and George Zeleny cannot be understated. Rodney, of the Athletics Archive Consultancy, was as enthusiastic as he was encyclopaedic in his knowledge of track-and-field, while George sent me tapes of almost all Joe Louis' fights – in between emerging as a constant and amusing source of information about the Brown Bomber, Crystal Palace and Fullers' Ale.

I also came to count Bill Baker as a humorous friend in cyberspace. In his more official capacity, Professor William J. Baker of the University of Maine is the author of the most incisive book yet written about Jesse Owens. He sent me numerous articles and videos which deepened my understanding of Owens and the period in which he and Louis were at their pinnacle.

Similarly, George von der Lippe, the translator of Max Schmeling's autobiography, moved from being an expert I interviewed to an enlightened source of information about the old German fighter. He generously sent me his own translated versions of Schemling's most recent interviews.

Beyond the Julian Black Scrapbooks, covering Louis' career until World War II, the newspapers and magazines I relied on most, from 1935 to 1980, include the following: *Cleveland Call and Post, Cleveland Gazette, Cleveland News, Cleveland Plain Defender, Chicago Defender, Chicago Tribune, Columbus Dispatch, Detroit Free Press, Esquire, Jet, Liberty, Life, Look, Los Angeles Times, Manchester Guardian, New York Amsterdam Post, New York Daily Mirror, New York Daily News, New York Evening Journal, New York Herald Tribune, New York Post, New York Sun, New York Times, New York World Telegram, Newsweek, Pittsburgh Courier, The Ring, Sport, Sports Illustrated, St Louis Post-Dispatch, Time, The Times* and the *Washington Post*.

Of the hundred-odd books I read while preparing to write my own, I would like to highlight some of the most instructive. Joe Louis has been well-served by biographies – and I found Chris Mead's *Champion Joe Louis* a cogent account of Louis' relationship with the white American press, and Richard Bak's underrated but detailed *Joe Louis: The Great Black Hope* to be particularly interesting. The descent of Louis into psychiatric care was handled sensitively by Barney Nagler's *Brown Bomber: The Pilgrimage Of Joe Louis*. I also found the following to be useful: Joe Louis' autobiography, *My Life*, written by Edna and Art Rust, Joe Louis Jr's *The Brown Bomber*, Gerald Astor's *And A Credit To His Race*, and Lenwood G. Davis's biography, *Joe Louis*.

Apart from William Baker's *Jesse Owens: An American Life*, I read with great interest Jesse's moving, if occasionally strange, collaborations with his ghost-writer Paul Neimark – *Jesse: The Man Who Outran Hitler, Blackthink* and *I Have Changed*.

The 1936 Olympic Games have been studied in detail by Richard Mandell's *The Nazi Olympics*, while Susan Bachrach's book of the same name provided a timely update.

George von der Lippe's excellent translation of Max Schmeling's autobiography was essential to my research – especially for Chapter Six of this book where Schmeling's early years and his meetings with Hitler rely heavily on that autobiography. As for further background on Nazi Germany, I was glad to have an excuse to read Ian Kershaw's masterly twin-volume biography of Hitler.

The chapters on Joe Louis and Sonny Liston were inspired by a quartet of great but very different books – Thomas Hauser's *Muhammad Ali*, David Remnick's *King Of The World*, Rob Steen's *Sonny Boy* and Nick Tosches' *Night Train*.

A full account of the Negro baseball circuit – covered in Chapter Ten – is provided by Bill Heyward's and Dimitri V.Gat's entertaining *Some Are Called Clowns*.

I also spent much productive time reading Dave Anderson's and Sugar Ray Robinson's *Sugar Ray*, Maya Angelou's *I Know Why The Caged Bird Sings*, Arthur Ashe's *A Hard Road To Glory*, James Baldwin's *The Fire Next Time* and *Nobody Knows My Name*, Ralph Ellison's *Invisible Man*, Harry Edwards's *The Struggle That Must Be* and *The Revolt Of The Black Athlete*, Jon Entine's *Taboo*, Marty Glickman's *The Fastest Kid On The Block*, Allen Guttman's *The Games Must Go On*, Jim Haskins's and N.R. Mitgang's *Mr. Bojangles*, Lena Horne's and Richard Schickel's *Lena*, William O. Johnson's *All That Glitters Is Not Gold*, Martin Luther King's *Why We Can't Wait*, A.J. Liebling's *The Sweet Science*, Vincent Matthews' *My Race Be Won*, Frederic Mullally's *Primo*, Randy Roberts's *Papa Jack,* Jack Olsen's *The Black Athlete,* Evert M Skehan's *Rocky Marciano*, Jules Tygiel's *Baseball's Great Experiment*, David Wiggins's *Glory Bound* and Sunnie Wilson's *Toast Of The Town*.

I would like to thank both Matt Tench and Brian Oliver, of *Observer Sport Monthly*, for commissioning a feature from me on Jesse Owens which, following my first trip to Chicago, they ran in September 2000. That article and trip, which they sponsored, provided this book with additional impetus.

My former agent, Jane Bradish-Ellames of Curtis Brown, first encouraged me to consider going back into history and even suggested the name of Jesse Owens years earlier. I owe her a great deal – not least for putting me together with Jonny Geller who saw this book through to its completion.

I was fortunate to have the input of three accomplished editors – Tim Binding and Rochelle Venables at Scribner in London and David Hirshey at HarperCollins in New York. Tim, as always, was great in providing a generous overview while subtly pointing out the many ways in which I could patently improve the book. And, whether she was providing a close reading of the text or doing any one of a hundred other tasks on my behalf, Rochelle had the gift of making me think that she was working on nothing else but this book.

David Hirshey, apart from sharing my phobias during Arsenal's double-winning season, while proving himself the most zealous and informed Gunner in American history, saved me from my worst excesses while remaining unstinting in his support. He would have already received his Ray Parlour replica shirt but for the fact that he's New York's answer to Patrick Vieira.

For this new edition, I owe a particular debt to Ian Marshall for his decision to re-reissue the book with an updated version. Thanks to Ian and everyone at Simon & Schuster who worked on the 2014 update – and for the help given to me by Usain Bolt, Reggie Bush, Luol Deng, John Dower, Justin Gatlin, LeBron James, Billy Johnson and Bobby Miles.

My parents, Ian and Jess, were great as usual – and my gratitude for all they have done continues to grow rather than diminish. This is also the first book I've written since the arrival of Isabella and Jack, and one day I hope to write a book for them as compelling as *Angelina Ballerina* or *Hairy Maclary*. All of which, naturally and most importantly of all, leads me back to Alison, my wife, who has shared everything in these pages with me – from the moment I first read about the race between

Jesse and Joe to our joint impersonations of Jesse running across a track of hot coals to her reading and refining each new chapter months before anyone else saw it. She knew instinctively when I had to be boosted or cajoled or just listened to while I rambled on and on about two guys called Jesse and Joe. The best moments in this book belong to her – the rest is pretty much mine.